The Diaries of Absalom Watkin

A Manchester Man 1787–1861

Dedicated to the memory of my father
Edward Ingram Watkin

The Diaries of Absalom Watkin

A Manchester Man 1787–1861

Edited

by

Magdalen Goffin

ALAN SUTTON

First published in the United Kingdom in 1993 by
Alan Sutton Publishing Limited
Phoenix Mill · Far Thrupp · Stroud · Gloucestershire

Published in the United States of America in 1993 by
Alan Sutton Publishing Inc · 83 Washington Street · Dover · NH 03820

British Library Cataloguing in Publication Data

A catalogue record for this book is available from the British Library

ISBN 0-7509-0417-8

Library of Congress Cataloging in Publication Data applied for

Typeset in 10/11 Bembo.
Typesetting and origination by
Alan Sutton Publishing Limited.
Printed and bound in Great Britain by
The Bath Press Ltd, Bath, Avon.

Contents

Contents

Illustrations

Introduction

Absalom Watkin was born in London in 1787, the son of an innkeeper who died when the boy was young, leaving him poor and with little hope of advancement. In 1801, when he was fourteen, Absalom accepted an offer to work for his uncle, who had a small cotton business in Manchester. Eventually he came to own the firm and was rich enough to buy a country house, Rose Hill, in Northenden. How he did so he records in the diaries he kept from 1811 to 1856.

His family came originally from Wales. Absalom was very proud of his Welsh blood but his father had been one of the many sons of a yeoman farmer of Audlem, a village a few miles from Nantwich in Cheshire. The land was not sufficient to support a large family and his children had to make their living away from home as best they could.

When Absalom first set foot in Manchester it was a small manufacturing town, the embryo of what it was to become. He lived with his uncle and aunt in a house surrounded by meadows and cherry trees not far from the River Irwell. A windmill stood on high ground close to the present Town Hall; Every Street, near Piccadilly, was a country lane; children slid on the pond at Strangeways. As time goes on one sees with Absalom the transformation of the small town into a great city.

The price of this transformation was heavy. Absalom was in daily contact with poverty and from the beginning involved with the many movements to assist the victims of too rapid and haphazard industrialization. After his death the *Manchester Guardian* put him among 'the fast fading list of people connected with our city who fought the battle of reform when its cause was unpopular and its advocacy dangerous'. He helped to write the famous Protest against the Conduct of the Yeomanry at Peterloo, drew up the Petition in favour of the Parliamentary Reform Bill of 1832, was closely concerned with the movement for undenominational state education, and was from the first a member of the Council of the Anti-Corn Law League.

Yet Watkin's diaries are very much more than a conventional account of the progress of a self-made man who happened to live in an important place at a critical time in the history of this country.

Absalom's was a complex character. Part of him wished to be valued and acclaimed by his contemporaries, another part wanted to contemplate the beauties of nature and live a cloistered life of reading and study. Business was not congenial

to him. 'I had to work or starve,' he said bleakly on one occasion. 'So I worked.'
He disliked his warehouse and it is remarkable how little he refers to what he
actually did there. His heart was elsewhere, in his library and beloved garden. His
son, Sir Edward Watkin, the Liberal Member of Parliament and friend of W.E.
Gladstone, became one of the greatest railway promoters of the age. He is
remembered as the man who built nearly two miles of the first Channel Tunnel.
Another son, Alfred, became Mayor of Manchester. If Absalom had been as
ruthless and as single-minded in the pursuit of worldly success as Edward he would
undoubtedly have accomplished more than he did. But he was not, and the
conflict within his nature is revealed in the diaries.

He used them to express the sometimes violent emotions he had to keep under
control in his daily intercourse with his family and business colleagues. The diaries
show the intensity of his reactions not only to people but to ideas. He could not
confide in his wife because she was the cause of so much of his unhappiness. It
may be that many of the vituperative comments about her were unjust,
unreasonable and exaggerated. It is not surprising that she retained the narrower
values and manners her husband had the opportunities to transcend.

When the diary starts Absalom is only twenty-three. He is set on improvement,
sometimes comically eager to do the right thing, occasionally facetious, always
earnest and even priggish. He has all the pedantry of the self-taught. Yet a probing
intellectual curiosity mingles with this, an almost morbid sensitivity, and an acute
awareness both of physical beauty and the spiritual reality at the heart of things. He
delighted in poetry, had a keen eye for women, loved visual scenery and showed
an immense and highly informed interest in flowers and trees. His mental and
physical energy was remarkable, yet it was mixed with periods of sudden and
complete prostration.

Factually Absalom was an honest, observant and careful recorder. A
contemporary once remarked upon his love of truth. However, we must
remember that we are separated from his birth by more than the number of years
his birth was separated from the defeat of the Spanish Armada. Because he lived in
the machine age and speaks like us, it needs an effort to realize how different in
some respects his life really was. Moreover, if the inner being of those we live with
in the flesh day after day remains elusive, how much more is this true of someone
we meet mainly through the distorting medium of his own pen.

In 1920 extracts from the diaries were edited by one of Absalom's great-
grandsons and published by Fisher Unwin. The work was well done and accurate
but, as the editor stated in his introduction, the entries selected included none of
those passages 'originally intended for the eyes of the writer alone'. In other words,
only Absalom's respectable, public face was revealed, the actual human being
hidden.

If matters had ended there, this book could never have been written. However,
it happened that my father, E.I. Watkin, another of Absalom's great-grandsons,
who as a child had lived with Sir Edward at Rose Hill and had a particular interest

in the diaries, read the manuscript while he was an undergraduate at Oxford. Realizing how much the printed version had left out and fearing for the safety of the originals, he asked to borrow them and laboriously copied out by hand all that had been omitted. It was fortunate he did so. In 1947, probably for snobbish reasons, the diaries were taken into the garden of Absalom's grandson, a former High Sheriff of Cheshire, and there were burnt.

The printed diary contained about 80,000 words. My father copied out approximately a further 206,000. His copy of the unprinted text is the only one in existence. This book is intended to be a picture of a man and his times, not a complete edition of the diary. In order to keep within a reasonable length only a portion of the entire text can be given here. To avoid constant interruption, no indication of diary entries left out has been given.

The frequent references to the price of food, travel, rent, etc. and to wage levels, are among the most interesting features of the diary. Yet these amounts are drained of their meaning unless we have some idea of their present-day value. To state the exact purchasing power of the pound in Absalom's lifetime would be foolhardy. However, figures compiled by the Central Statistical Office would suggest that, as a rough rule of thumb, Absalom's pound was worth £50 at 1990 prices. To put it another way, the purchasing power of his pound has been reduced to a little over twopence. More is said about this in Appendix Two.

Lord Briggs, the former Provost of Worcester College, Oxford, was good enough to read through the original draft of this book and I should like to thank him for his advice and encouragement. Mr Bernard Adams, formerly Chief Reference Librarian of the British Council, kindly undertook research on my behalf. Mr Rowley Atterbury has given me valuable assistance. Mr John Dillon most unselfishly allowed me to make use of his collection of books about the early history of Manchester. I am indebted to Mr A.G. Rose for his account of the Plug Riots given in the *Transactions of the Lancashire and Cheshire Antiquarian Society*, 1958. Mr and Mrs Nicholas Reed Herbert took the trouble to find some of the pictures included here and I am grateful to them. The Public Libraries of Manchester and Tunbridge Wells have given me unfailing assistance. My old friend, Judge Monique Viner, QC, has given me constant encouragement and help. So has my sister Perpetua, who married our cousin Hugh Ingram, the last editor of the *Illustrated London News* to bear the name of the family who founded it. Above all, I am grateful to my husband, Richard, for many years of patient advice and for sharing my interest in Absalom.

Magdalen Goffin
Silcocks, 1993

CHAPTER ONE
'This motley life'

In London, on 24 February 1806, Betty Watkin wrote a long letter to her son, Absalom. The news of Trafalgar was but three months old, the battle of Austerlitz had been fought in December, William Pitt the Younger had been dead for only a few weeks. She did not refer to these matters. There would always be wars and rumours of wars. Absalom was nineteen, living in Manchester and working for a cotton merchant.

The original letter shows that Betty Watkin spelt badly and punctuated hardly at all, but that was not unusual for someone with little formal education. She was a widow and she was poor. We know from her grandson that she let lodgings and got up linen and fine lace. The entire letter shows deep and sincere piety. Anxious but not agitated, she answered her son's letter the same day as she received it. The punctuation has been added: 'Pray my dear son, what little strange extrordanery uneasynes has found the way to your breast? What plagues or crosses has rendered this motly lif of yours unhappy to make you think it's not worth having?'

Why did he say that no one alive was happy and that he had been miserably cheated? She was three times his age and could surely be a judge of youthful follies. He wanted so ardently to learn music, he was writing poetry about the beauties of the countryside. He was evidently in love.

If we are disrespected by the object we love, thank God for his goodness in preventing us from obtaining our desire . . . If God makes you rich, thank him this goodness that he has blessed and chose you as his stuard. If poor and obleged to work hard and live hard, thank God for it, for if we was rich we mite be wicked and be in everlasting torment hereafter.

Whatever the future held, if he had led a Godly life nothing in the entire world could hurt him. Let him be happy, religion was never designed to make our pleasures less. He should drink coffee or camomile tea in the morning to cure his headaches, and if he ever plucked roses make sure he wore gloves to protect his feelings. He must drive all nonsense from his mind and dispel his gloomy sighs unless he wished to be laughed at as a fool in love.

The red seal has been carelessly torn. The paper has a hole in it both there and in another place where the pen had dipped into too much ink and a word scratched out. Perhaps the letter was written by candlelight in the dark of a winter's evening. Betty Watkin ended it on the other side of the first sheet. Let him not be ashamed to let her know the meaning of his letter. 'I remain your loving mother and pray God for your happiness here and hereafter.' She added a postscript on the fresh page. She was replying by the twopenny post but was sorry to put him to the expense of paying for it. He must let her know how he got on with his aunt. She hoped that he would never neglect his master's business and always be just and honest.

We never hear Betty Watkin's authentic voice again. In the future it reaches us indirectly, mediated by her son, her daughter-in-law and her rich and famous grandson who tried to immortalize her in the church window of her native Devon when all the time her body lay in the graveyard up Cheetham Hill in Manchester. She had ink on her fingers when she folded her letter and smudged the paper both back and front, but the address was written carefully: Mr Absalom Watkin, At Mr Smiths, Marchant, Back Square, Manchester. Singal.

Betty Watkin was the daughter of a West Country farmer, a member of the old Devonshire family of Sayer. In the summer of 1786 she had married Thomas Watkin in Bath, at Walcot church where Jane Austen's parents had been married a generation before. Where she met Thomas or what she was doing in Bath, we do not know. He was then twenty-seven and a private in the First Regiment of Guards, commanded by the Duke of Gloucester, and enrolled in Captain Playdell's Company. On his marriage he made up his mind to leave the army and obtained a certificate signed by John Wilkes entitling him to exercise any trade within the Kingdoms of Great Britain and Ireland. He decided to become an innkeeper.

Betty had been strongly influenced by the Protestant revival and was a Methodist. Although the extreme horror of intoxicating drinks had not yet taken hold of the Evangelical movement, she may not have relished her husband's trade or the company it attracted. She conceived a child within a month of her marriage and the baby was a boy, born within the sound of Bow bells, on 27 June 1787. He was called Absalom and christened at Bromley, Kent, where his mother had relations and where he was later to go to school.

Thomas may not have been a very satisfactory husband. He was certainly restless. For a time he kept the Falcon at Stoke Newington, the backcloth for some of Absalom's earliest memories. Then he took the White Bear in Newport Street, near Leicester Square, before moving yet again, this time to the Hope in Banner Street. He died of consumption, aged forty, as landlord of the Fortune of War, near St Benet's church by Paul's Wharf.

St Benet's is a Wren church which miraculously survived the fire bombs of the Second World War. It is the official church of the College of Arms and the Welsh church in London. The Fortune of War stood at the corner of Benet's Hill and Thames Street, a stone's throw from the church and with a clear, close view of St Paul's Cathedral. Absalom was just twelve when Thomas died. In after years he spoke with pain of his gradual realization that his father was ill. Thomas became bent, his voice low and husky; towards the end of his life the man who once proudly marched erect with his regiment, crawled with crooked legs up Holborn Hill.

Betty Watkin had another son, who died when he was very young. Absalom was everything to her. He went first to the village school at Bromley, then to one in Old Fish Street and finally to a small school behind St Nicholas, Coldharbour. While he was there he took French lessons from an émigré abbé forced in his old age to leave his country because of the Revolution. He was poor and ill and needed the few pence Absalom's mother gave him for his lessons. He spent most of the day alone with his rosary and his breviary, and taught from his bed. This must have been to some purpose because he introduced Absalom to Racine and Corneille. When he was himself old, Absalom's eyes used to fill with tears when he remembered the abbé and how he used to say, 'Ah, you are von lazy bones' when his pupil failed to prepare the lesson.

Absalom was a voracious reader and remained so to the end. He once remarked that reading had been 'the great, enduring and uncloying pleasure' of his life. He read at meals, while walking, in a coach, and at night often until the early hours of the morning – Shakespeare, Ben Jonson, Milton, Pope, Dryden, Gray and Collins; then the prose of Swift, Defoe, Johnson and the works of Addison to improve his own style. He loved particularly travellers' tales, to live in strange realms where fact and imagination could mingle freely. No one taught him Greek and he picked up only a smattering of Latin.

Had he lived in another age or belonged to a different social class undoubtedly he would have gone to the university. Even then poverty was no absolute bar to higher education, but Absalom did not go to a grammar school, he had no patron and would have had no means of keeping himself at Oxford or Cambridge even had his nonconformity not prevented his attendance.

His father's brother, John, came to his help. Thomas and John Watkin were two of the eleven children of a farmer at Audlem, a village in Cheshire. The children had all to make their own way in the world and John was precisely one of the 'hearty husbandmen sucked into the gulph of sickly traffic' whose fate John Byng, the future Lord Torrington, so rightly lamented. He decided to go to Manchester and to take his chance in the developing cotton business. This he did with a fair measure of success, founding the firm of Lees and Watkin. He had one son himself, and when he learnt of his brother's death in London and the narrow plight of his widow, suggested that in time Absalom should join him in Manchester to learn the business.

It is almost impossible for us to imagine Manchester as it was in 1801 when Absalom stumbled out of the London coach after thirty hours on the road. Unrecognizable perhaps, yet already containing in its smoky depth the germ of all it was to be; among its people even then a broad thrust for improvement, a compound of financial acumen and high-mindedness which in time was to make it one of the most remarkable monuments to self-regulated capitalism the world has ever seen.

It had been a manufacturing town for centuries but only comparatively recently, as a contemporary put it, 'enriched beyond the power of calculation' by the manufacturing of cotton, the making of velvets, fustians, checks, prints and muslins of a kind as numerous as the sands of the sea. Its success, another contemporary remarked, had hitherto been unknown in the history of commerce.

With the cotton came the machinery necessary to sustain it: iron wheels, cylinders, pipes and boilers, tinplate, leather, reams of paper, dyes and bleaches. Yet the town Absalom first saw was still a small place. In 1745 it had a population of about 17,000. Its population now, excluding Salford, was just over 70,000. Fifty years later this was to rise to over 303,000. Fifteen years before Absalom's arrival there was one large steam-powered spinning mill, that of Richard Arkwright. Fifteen years after his arrival there were eighty-two. Naturally Byng thought Manchester a 'dog hole'. He was shocked by its ugliness because he was a product of pre-industrial England. The countryside through which he travelled was then largely unspoilt and as lovely as the architecture of its towns, villages and great houses.

So far have we allowed our vision to be corrupted, surrendered to the savagery of the concrete block, so ruthlessly have we destroyed our past, that we would be amazed, not by the ugliness, but the beauty of Manchester as it was when Absalom first saw it. Of course the town was already sooty and shabby, the streets were narrow, for the most part unpaved and soon to be clogged with enormous horse-drawn wagons laden with raw cotton or bales of cloth. Cellar dwellings were increasing together with the newly built, densely crowded tenements of the poor which were served by a common pump and frequently had no drains, so that garbage and excrement had to be thrown out of windows and doors.

Nor, since its growth and function had been different, was Manchester laid out with the spacious squares of a county town. Yet for all that, Absalom would have seen the Assembly Rooms, the Infirmary, the Collegiate Church, St John's church, St Ann's, St Peter's, Trinity chapel, St Stephen's Salford, the Theatre Royal, the Grammar School, Chetham's Hospital and Library and, within a few years of his arrival, the second Exchange, the Portico Library, and the rooms of the Literary and Philosophical Society. The middle classes had not yet fled to the suburbs. The seventeenth- and eighteenth-century houses of doctors, merchants, manufacturers and tradesmen were still intact, together with a host of half-timbered houses belonging to an earlier age.

Beauty of another order had not yet been totally devoured. Within a short distance of what today is the centre of Manchester were country lanes, cottages and gardens, and merchants' houses with extensive lawns and orchards. Ancoats Old Hall, with its park and trees, stood at the end of Ancoats Street. Love Lane, now Every Street, not far from Piccadilly, was a small country road with green hedgerows and ivy-covered cottages. Strangeways was to remain rural for another twenty years, with children sliding on the ponds and playing in the grounds of the hall. A windmill stood on the high ground a stone's throw from the present Town

Hall. Ten years after Absalom's coming to Manchester it was advertised for sale as a 'strong and well-accustomed windmill, with dwelling-house, and extensive garden with a pond in the centre'.

Hulme was not yet built, nor much of Ancoats. Leases had been granted only recently for the building of houses in the country at Chorlton-on-Medlock. Ardwick and Rusholme were outlying villages. The houses across the river Irwell in Manchester's twin town of Salford, although dense compared with the open spaces of Broughton, were interspersed with trees, hedgerows and copses. Beyond Salford and separated from it by yet another bend in the river, the farms and meadows of Broughton extended to Kersal Moor. Prestwich was reached by a footpath or through leafy lanes and separated from Broughton and Cheetham by a small brook. To the south-west, Eccles was a village four miles in the country.

Absalom was just fourteen when he arrived. Few people could have been more unsuited to the life which lay in front of him. The cast of his mind was both academic and creative, his temperament artistic. His uncle used to say that to survive in Manchester he needed his face rubbing with a brick, and to the day he died he was the victim of the 'little, strange, extraordinary uneasiness' to which his mother referred. Like her, he was deeply religious and, as she had perceived, very susceptible to feminine charms.

His Uncle John, together with his second wife and his son Thomas, lived near Agecroft Bridge in Whit Lane by the side of the River Irwell, where today the earth sweats under the weight of concrete and plate glass and the never-ending procession of traffic grinds over the tarmac into the city. In Absalom's time that part of the Irwell was clear and alive with fish, his uncle's house surrounded by meadows, its garden full of flowers, grassy walks and cherry trees. Not far from its gate, women still drew water from the well.

The surviving diaries for Absalom's early years in Manchester are sparse; a great deal of what he thought and felt at this time can be gathered only indirectly from what he wrote later. At first he was intensely lonely, he knew no one and probably could not readily understand the dialect of those he worked among. It seems that neither his Uncle John nor his Cousin Thomas were interested in books or ideas, and that they thought his ravenous reading as odd as his solitary rambles round the countryside. Every morning he walked to his uncle's warehouse.

Manchester was full of warehouses. They formed a dense undergrowth of small and medium-sized firms set beneath the chimneys, and their business could be very diverse indeed. The part they played in the production and distribution of cotton was crucial, for they were the vital link between the factory and the non-factory system of production. The factories spun the cotton into yarn; the owners or managers of the warehouses decided the amount, quality, type and price of the yarn they wished to buy and made arrangements to put out the yarn to be woven into cloth by the hand-loom weavers. The power loom, although already invented, did not come into general use until Absalom had been in the trade for over twenty years. Although a number of businessmen were both merchants and manufacturers, John Watkin's firm was a small one. It seems likely that he dealt only in yarn and undyed calico for other merchant manufacturers to weave and process.

In his uncle's warehouse Absalom learnt accounting, business methods, and the complexities and pitfalls of the cotton trade. He taught himself Dr Byrom's system of shorthand, which he used for literary, not commercial, purposes – for historical and botanical notes and the intimate passages in his diary. It is significant that, even when he owned his own business, he says very little about what actually went on in his warehouse. We do not know how many people he employed or what he thought of them. He mentions the Cotton Exchange only once or twice. Evidently he found neither the work nor his companions congenial. However, as he was later to remark, he had to work or starve, so he worked.

With sufficient application intelligent people can make a success of almost anything. The details are obscure; apparently John Watkin sold all or part of his business to a Mr Thomas Smith who carried on at Back Square and appointed Absalom as his manager. It is not clear what arrangements were made for John's son, Thomas Watkin. He was nothing like so able as Absalom, for although he remained in the cotton trade, he never made much money.

In April 1807, when he was nearly twenty, probably with his mother's help, Absalom bought Mr Smith out. He gave the business his own name and moved to new premises in Cannon Street. At last he was his own master.

CHAPTER TWO

'The street was crowded with people mostly wearing the blue and white cockade'

The home in Whit Lane was broken up. Thomas Watkin married a girl named Mary and his father, John Watkin, decided to retire from business to enjoy what was left of his life on a property he had either bought or inherited in his native village of Audlem. Absalom invited his mother to come up from London and keep house for him. With her bit of capital and his savings they were able to buy a small house in Ravald Street, Salford.

It was not altogether a propitious moment to set up business on one's own. The French were masters of Europe and for a time it looked as if economic encirclement might complete military triumph. Cotton imports fell, operatives were put on short time, bread was dear and Manchester disturbed by strikes. But Absalom was young and full of energy. His life was in front of him; the French had not landed. Napoleon Bonaparte might strut as he pleased but the ports were not paralysed, neither was trade dead. Absalom went on steadily with his business. Profit meant release, freedom to do what he wanted.

Nevertheless the dreamer in him planned to escape. When he declared so passionately to his mother that he had been miserably cheated, he meant it. His expectations were so high, his feelings so keen, life must have more to offer than the warehouse and the state of the market.

In the early summer of 1810, perhaps in his warehouse where he was constantly tempted to read or to write poetry, perhaps in the home he shared with his mother among the clump of houses in Ravald Street, he drew up a lengthy paper. He called it 'A Plan for the Proper Employment of My Time From This Day, May 18th, 1810, to the Day of My Death.'

He was nearly twenty-three years old. For the next twelve years he would attend strictly to his business but, by self-denial and avoidance of all trifling pursuits devote at least three hours daily to a rigorous course of study. This would include divinity, history, natural and experimental philosophy, geography and the laws of his country. However, since this life was but a preparation for another, the pursuit of knowledge and the accumulation of wealth must never be allowed to stand between him and the welfare of his fellow men.

By the time he was thirty-five he would have acquired sufficient capital and learning to leave his business and go on his travels. He would visit Paris, Rome, Constantinople, Athens, Egypt, the Holy Land, India, South America and lastly the United States, where he would make a special pilgrimage to see the statue, the house and the library of Benjamin Franklin.

> Suppose my travels occupy seven years, I shall at my return be forty-two. Having published my travels, I will consider how I may do most good. I will employ the knowledge I have acquired in promoting, to the utmost of my power, the spread of religion and the happiness of my fellow creatures.

The surface serenity of Absalom's 'Plan of Life' was misleading. He lived, and would always live, on a knife-edge between hope and despair. A temperamental melancholy, a sense that defeat was certain, that all attempts to make a splendid, happy, holy life for himself would come to nothing, wrestled with the conviction that a man of his talents could and would achieve his purpose. Moreover, at that time he was frequently in love and troubled by sexual desire. Nor was that all. He did not doubt the truth of Christianity, but began to feel the need of a firmer intellectual foundation for belief than that provided either by his own feelings or the assumptions of his mother and those of the evangelical circles within which he moved.

Absalom worshipped mainly in one of the many Methodist chapels which were springing up so rapidly in Manchester and Salford. His character, however, would not allow him to conform easily to any one organization. He belonged to a branch of Methodism which had broken away from the main body after John Wesley's death because it wanted complete separation from the Church of England and a more democratic form of government than what it considered to be the dictatorship of the Annual Conference. This group called itself the Methodist New Connexion, and in 1814 had over 800 members and 207 places of worship. William Booth, the founder of the Salvation Army, was once one of its ministers and it was not reunited to the parent body until 1907.

To what, Absalom now asked himself, was it connected? He set himself a course of rigorous theological reading both in the Fathers of the Church and later writers on Christian evidences. He had been a lay preacher for some time; he now read at home every morning a portion of the New Testament and again when he was at his warehouse. He must be strict with himself. God had promised that all who sincerely seek the truth should find it.

September 17th, 1811. I resolve to avoid as much as possible all unprofitable and useless reading. I will give all my studious hours to the best authors, and these I will read again and again, seeking only Truth and yielding only to Reason.

His business prospered and the number of his friends grew. Most of them were

Methodists of the New Connexion, some lay preachers like himself. All were ardent in the pursuit of knowledge.

One summer evening in the year of the great comet, 1811, Richard Watson, a leading Methodist preacher, together with a young business friend of Absalom called William Makinson, had coffee at Absalom's house. Makinson had got it into his head that he had discovered an 'incipient' formation of red sandstone on Kersal Moor, or Karsay Moor as the local people called it. Fired with scientific zeal, all three set out for the moor. The evening was lovely, after sunset their path illuminated by the unusually brilliant stars and the radiance of the comet. They spoke about nature and the appearance of comets and in the strange light felt with their hands the corrugations of the bank where Makinson had led them, probing the red sand with the tips of their fingers. While walking home they decided to form the Literary and Scientific Club, which was to survive for nearly fifty years and to give Absalom more 'unalloyed happiness' than anything else in his life.

The Club, as it was called, met once a week in one of its members' houses, had tea and supper, debated, joked and read papers on literature, botany and chemistry. Its proceedings were secret, and when they were young its members were joyful. Later it widened its scope and, if it lost a little of its *élan*, its meetings remained for Absalom 'so many streams of light' which spread their cheering influence over the length of his life.

He determined to give up all romantic projects for the moment and to avoid reading fiction. Instead he studied botany, medicine and anatomy. That February he attended a lecture on the spleen, kidneys and female organs of generation.

February 23rd, 1812. It was illustrated by the body of a female and that of a girl – the sight (from the putrescency of the bodies) was horribly disgusting.

Distress in Manchester was widespread. There had been a series of bad harvests and the trade war had closed many export markets for cloth. Food prices were high while wages had been reduced. A large, hungry, restless body of labourers existed, most of whom worked in appalling conditions and were denied even a minimum of domestic decency.

That April a meeting called in the dining-room of the Manchester Exchange to congratulate the Prince Regent on his retention of the Tory ministers was invaded by a mob who smashed the chandeliers, broke the furniture and, mistaking it for that of the Regent, slashed the portrait of Colonel Stanley, one of the county MPs. The crowd was dispersed by the military under the command of Colonel Clay and a camp established on Kersal Moor to keep the peace. Those owning even a small bit of property are always fearful of the mob and vivid memories of what had happened in France intensified alarm. Further disorders and resolutions for parliamentary reform stimulated the more conservative inhabitants of Manchester to form a local branch of a 'Pitt Club' for the purpose of 'celebrating the birthday of that great patriotic and illustrious statesman, the Right Honourable William

Pitt'. Each member was to wear a medal suspended from a blue ribbon and costing two guineas.

Absalom saved his two guineas. He had not yet come to revere the memory of Pitt. On the contrary, he read a provocative paper to the Club on the needless prolongation of the war. Napoleon's assumption of supreme power in France, he argued, was none of our business and his personal character irrelevant. Were his intentions towards England and her neighbours so aggressive that we had to fight an interminable war, plunge ourselves into ruinous debt and, by trade restrictions, so impoverish the working class that the government faced revolution?

In the middle of May he heard the news that his Uncle John had died suddenly at Audlem and set out for Cheshire immediately. He travelled by coach to Nantwich and walked the remaining six miles to Audlem. He stayed with his aunt, attended the funeral and learnt that his uncle had left him £400, approximately £20,000 in today's (1990) money values. The legacy therefore was quite substantial, yet there is no mention of it in the diary. We know of it only from reading John Watkin's will. In the same way as sexual references went into shorthand, reticence of another kind made Absalom omit many of his financial transactions.

In June, a month before the Duke of Wellington won the battle of Salamanca, Napoleon's army crossed the Niemen and plunged into the depth of Russia. By December that army had ceased to exist and a war that had begun when Absalom was only six years old entered into its final stages.

In the new year, 1813, seventeen Luddites were hanged at York but Absalom does not refer to it. Sometimes on horseback, sometimes on foot, he went miles to preach in chapels at Stockport and Colne, and as far as Bury, Macclesfield and Bolton. He remained perplexed about the evidences for the truth of Christianity. He could believe nothing against reason and would seek theological knowledge from the Scriptures alone. In April he heard a preacher of great reputation in Manchester whose name was Gatliffe. He was shocked.

April 16th, 1813. He is a good speaker but to see him affecting piety was to me an aweful sight. May I never forget it.

But he was not satisfied with his own performance.

May 30th, 1813. I talked too fast, with emphasis, hurried myself out of breath, used too many epithets, substituted sound for sense, used hard words, made too many confident assertions, had too little feeling, suffered myself to be fluttered.

He read some pages of Emillius that made him very sceptical and uneasy. His great friend and fellow preacher, Mr Grime, had accused him of using tricks in argument to gain his point. He resolved to cultivate personal piety, to seek truth and truth only, and to guard very carefully indeed against overstating an argument either in speaking or writing.

November 18th, 1813. Mr Medcalf spoke to me of leading a class. I resolve not to do so till my opinions are more settled and my piety greater.

He felt gloomy. How silly were his pursuits, how foolish the effort to please others when the only certainty in this life was pain and death.

That spring Wellington's army slowly advanced through France, and on 12 March 1814, the very day Absalom wrote a poem against war, the inhabitants of Bordeaux proclaimed the restoration of the Bourbons. Soon the Allied leaders were drinking the health of King Louis XVIII, and at the end of the month Paris capitulated. The rejoicing for the success of English arms and the restoration of the French monarchy lasted three days in Manchester. On the morning of 18 April, Absalom watched the triumphal procession and in the afternoon walked with his schoolmaster friend, John Andrew, to see the preparations for the evening celebrations.

April 18th, 1814. All the windows cleaned, and the women with busy hands and serious faces fixing their candles and ornamenting their windows. The carpenters and the lamp men fixing transparencies, lamps etc. The street crowded with people, mostly wearing the blue and white cockade. Business, except the selling of cockades, transparencies etc. at a stand.

At nine in the evening he joined his friends the Makinsons. The Makinsons lived in Oldham Street. They seem to have been of Irish origin. In the bitter, later years, Absalom would refer to his wife as an 'Irish fool'. They may have been plantation Irish, taking their Protestantism to Ireland and back again, or like so many of their immigrant countrymen, embraced Protestantism through carelessness or convenience and then came sincerely to believe in it. Absalom's friend William Makinson was a Methodist of the New Connexion and, like him, a lay preacher attached to Mount Zion, their chapel in Oldham Street.

The family was a large one, extending from the lower to the middle of the social spectrum, and was typical of the fluidity of the British class structure. Some of the family were tradesmen or ran one of the many small businesses dependent upon the explosion of Manchester's mercantile activity; others shaded into the professional classes as attorneys or schoolmasters. Mr Makinson senior was the proprietor of what was later to be called an 'adventure school', meaning a day school kept by a man who made his living from it. No qualifications were required to open one and they were numerous. Mr Makinson specialized in mathematics and commercial subjects. He may have kept an excellent establishment, but on the whole the reputation of these schools was not very high.

His son William was a married man. That evening he took Absalom to the house where his sister Elizabeth lived with her parents. Probably he hoped for a match. Elizabeth, however, did not join Absalom, William and two other friends for their sightseeing.

> We went down Oldham Street and into Market Street. Here, particularly at the bottom, the crowd was great and the press extreme. We got through and went along Exchange Street and St Ann's Square and up King Street. At Mr Greg's, in King Street, was a fine illumination of about a thousand lamps in the form of a rainbow. Proceeding to Mosley Street, we were much pleased with the Portico, the pillars of which were wreathed with lamps, and the Assembly Rooms. Mr O. Hulme had some fine transparencies. We went into Portland Street, down Piccadilly and along Oldham Street to the Makinsons. I got home, much tired, about one in the morning.

His mental distress continued unabated. Difficulties about the truth of Christianity continued to torment him and his anguish expressed itself in prayer.

> Remove the doubts which perplex my mind. Enable me to love what is just and right and to do whatever I discover to be commanded by Thee. Save me from weakness and instability. Bless me with firmness, perseverence and uprightness in all my pursuits; with calmness and peace of mind. May I desire nothing inordinately. Suffer me not to despair, though all things are against me.

He preached a charity sermon at Bolton.

April 24th, 1814. A little fluttered at first, but towards the end better.

The widespread addiction to sermons was not motivated by piety alone. They were a species of entertainment in an age that had so little to divert it. Some people discussed sermons in much the same way as a later generation would discuss a television programme.

The 'old church' in Manchester, now the cathedral, was the medieval Collegiate Church of St Mary, St George and St Denys, administered by a Warden and Fellows. It was referred to as the 'old church' to distinguish it from St Ann's church, built in the reign of that queen among the corn fields in what is now St Ann's Square. One Sunday later that year Absalom first went to hear Mr Robberds preach at the famous and fashionable Unitarian chapel in Cross Street before going on to the cathedral. In 1828 Robberds was to have the Revd William Gaskell, the husband of the writer Elizabeth Gaskell, as his assistant. The sermon, Absalom considered, was 'a good discourse'.

August 14th, 1814. Having stayed the conclusion of the service, Mr Andrew and I went to the Old Church and heard part of a sermon by Dr

Gaskin. The thoughts were trite, the language mean, and part of the pronunciation vulgar.

In early June he went on an excursion with John Andrew and other friends.

June 3rd, 1814. Met the singers of our chapel – went to Bowden, sung two hymns on the steeple. The day was spent pleasantly and innocently.

He was in love with Elizabeth Makinson.

Only one likeness of Elizabeth is known to have survived, a pencil portrait drawn by an artist named Minasi seven years later. By then Elizabeth was expecting her third child. On the surface the match was a very suitable one. Absalom had his own business and if his mother's presence in the house was a disadvantage in some respects, it could be useful in others. Absalom was a Methodist of the New Connexion, a preacher like Elizabeth's brother, sober, God-fearing and fond of study. She could not have known then what a complex, nervous, and at times tortured human being she intended to take as a husband. It is not likely that she understood either his ambition to make a name, his passionate commitment to ideas or his desire to create a space about himself within which, hermit-like, his spirit could live.

For his part, not only was he in love, he had been that many times, but he was in love sensibly and it was returned. Elizabeth came from the same background, her brothers William and Joseph were both in a moderately prosperous way of business, both met Absalom every week at the Mount Zion chapel and at the Club. No one could accuse him of being unwise in his choice of a wife.

At the end of June Absalom celebrated his twenty-seventh birthday. After breakfast he, Elizabeth and another friend walked the seven miles through fields and woods from Manchester to the village of Radcliffe by the side of the Irwell. Radcliffe was distinguished by its connection with a particularly grisly legend. It was here, the tale ran, that out of jealousy Sir William de Radcliffe's second wife caused her beautiful stepdaughter, the fair Ellen, to be killed, cut up, cooked in a pie and served to her father. As a punishment for this terrible deed, Ellen's stepmother was burnt and the cook condemned to stand in a cauldron of boiling lead.

June 27th, 1814. We walked slowly and talked pleasantly. We called on Mrs Fielden and family, friends of Miss Makinson. We dined. Miss Makinson played some tunes on the organ. We had the key of the church. Looked at the tombstone of 'Fair Ellen' who is said to have been killed by a cruel stepdame. We read the epitaphs in the churchyard and were surprised at the number of women buried there of the name Betty. We returned to Mrs Fielden's and as the whole family are singers and my friends too, they began to sing. They continued playing and singing until nearly eight o'clock. We came home through Prestwich and talked of friendship, happiness, etc., pleasantly. At half-past ten we parted and thus ended one of the happiest days of my life.

Absalom and Elizabeth were married in her parish church, St John's, Deansgate, on 3 November 1814.

CHAPTER THREE

'Giving himself more to literature than to politics'

Ravald Street lay between Broughton Road and King Street, not far from that part of the River Irwell that separates Manchester from Salford. We do not know with what feelings Absalom's mother welcomed Elizabeth to her new home. Absalom was her only child and she had now been mistress of his house for nearly seven years. Elizabeth Makinson, however, was the kind of person Betty Watkin understood. In many ways she had more in common with her than she had with her own son. Sometimes in the evening Absalom read aloud to his wife and mother but more often read silently. William Wordsworth's *Excursion* and the three volumes of *Waverley* were not long out and he was eager to finish them.

The Club met at his house for the first time since his marriage. After they had gone home and his wife and mother retired to bed, Absalom settled down to read Middleton's *Free Inquiry into the Miraculous Powers Ascribed to the First Ages of the Christian Church*. The book served to increase his natural scepticism. He was convinced from what he read that 'they who are called the Fathers of the Christian Church were generally credulous and weak men and sometimes great liars'. But the matter did not bother him in the same way it would once have done. He was coming to realize that truth had its own validity, independent of the folly of those who maintained it.

Folly of a different kind was soon to claim the attention of a world not particularly concerned with Christian evidences. Early in March 1815 news reached Manchester that Napoleon had escaped from Elba and landed near Antibes. On 19 March he was back again in Paris. The spectacle of a man so recently reviled by his fellow countrymen now acclaimed as a saviour, and the person who only the previous year had been welcomed as their legitimate sovereign now departing in haste, amused Absalom greatly.

March 29th, 1815. Loyalty to the Bourbons! The shouts with which the National Guard welcomed the King and the <u>nonchalance</u> with which, in a few days, they went over to Napoleon! The opinion is held that there is now in France a vast number of men, fit only for war, who must be <u>exterminated</u> before Europe can be at peace.

They would have to fight yet again the man *The Times* described as that 'viper of Corsica'. But Absalom's real attention was elsewhere. At that moment he was preoccupied with his own affairs.

The details can never now be known, but sometime in the spring of 1815 Absalom allowed his ambition to overcome his intense caution. He risked his capital in a business venture that failed, found himself deeply in debt – in fact ruined and in danger of prison, in those days a very likely eventuality. The business he had put his capital into was the Yorkshire firm of Brook and Lister. In an attempt to recover his money Absalom obtained a Warrant of Attorney in Manchester and with a heavy cold and the headache which so often afflicted him in times of stress, crossed the Pennines to Bradford with the writ in his pocket. He walked the six miles from Bradford to Baildon where Brook lived, served the writ and seized the firm's business assets. That covered his debts, but not his ventured capital. But it meant that Elizabeth would not have to start her married life with a husband languishing in jail as an undischarged debtor, nor would his mother be deprived of a home.

The matter was complicated, negotiations long drawn out and the frequent journeys tedious. In April he set out for Baildon again. Leaving Manchester by coach at six in the morning, he reached Bradford at one o'clock and walked to Brook's house. He had the ability to distance himself from any immediate anxiety provided that he had a book in his hand, and he read a translation of Plato's *Phaedo* far into the night. He awoke next morning with an appalling headache which he ascribed, not to reading by candlelight, but to a damp bed.

While the Austrian and Russian armies were making their slow way towards the French frontier in the campaign that was to end in the battle of Waterloo, Absalom went on fighting to save what he could from the crash of his own making. He travelled backwards and forwards between Manchester, Bradford and Halifax in his efforts to get his money; anxious, uneasy, self-accusing and at times utterly exhausted. It was a hot May and from Baildon he walked to Otley and Guiseley and back again.

May 5th, 1815. In ascending the hill from Otley, I was frequently obliged to stop by the steepness of the hill and the heat of the day. In doing so I had at every halt a more extensive and more beautiful view of Wharfdale. After tea, sick with over-exertion, having walked twenty miles in this hilly country, in boots and on a very hot day. Fell asleep on Lister's sofa and woke in about an hour, much refreshed.

He rescued a poor drowning crow from the water which ran through Bradford and recovered his spirits sufficiently to be amused by one of his travelling companions. An old hale-looking man who got into the coach at New Inn, Blackstone Edge, and rode a few miles with them, boasted of his feats in hunting. He declared that he had hunted from his sixth year and was then in his sixtieth, and that he loved it as well as ever. He had gone to bed, he said, as drunk as a pig and got up next morning and run forty miles before breakfast. 'Aye,' and 'he could do it still.'

Back in Manchester, Absalom picked up the threads of his life, but his capital was considerably reduced. He heard his brother-in-law, William Makinson, preach 'a poor, confused sermon' on repentance, went to Grime's house for a meeting of the Club where he read a paper on the treatment of animals, and in the September after the battle of Waterloo went for a few days' holiday near Runcorn with Elizabeth. He travelled by coach to Altrincham where he had breakfast, by boat to Walton, and then walked to Mrs Byrom's house at Moore.

September 8th, 1815. A very pleasant situation; dined, read part of The Velvet Cushion. Walked through the village; admired the garden of a Mrs Gleave; there was a fine rose the height of the door, full of flowers and several geraniums put down in the borders. Tea at Mrs Byrom's with Mr and Mrs Peter Byrom and Miss Cheshire. Sat for some time after tea talking and singing. Looked at the cows. Walked to Daresbury church about sunset, the evening was delightful, the sky a most beautiful red and the moon just rising. The churchyard is thickly set with tombstones, we went round it and sat down for some time in the church porch.

They were up early.

September 9th, 1815. From the window we had a prospect of the country, the canal, pretty in itself, but set off by all the glories of a lovely morning. Breakfasted, and after prayer went to our friends at Mrs Byrom's. The dew yet glittered on the grass and heightened the fragrance of the honeysuckle on the gates. I sat down alone in Mrs Byrom's parlour, read the fine description of the good pastor in The Velvet Cushion and then looked at the beauty of the morning and thought of my own numerous blessings and raised my heart to Him 'who crowneth the year with His goodness' and felt truly happy.

That year John Thelwall came to lecture in Manchester.

When Absalom was sixteen and feeling very lonely living with his Uncle John and Cousin Thomas in Whit Lane, he had come across Thelwall's memoir of his life. This had encouraged him to continue his own studies in an atmosphere by no means favourable to intellectual pursuits. That was not the only effect Thelwall's writings produced. His days as a revolutionary were now over but there had been a time when Thelwall belonged to The Society of the Friends of the People and together with Horne Tooke had been sent to the Tower on a charge of High Treason. His radical views probably had a far greater influence on Absalom than he cared to admit.

Although Thelwall now devoted his time to the theory and practice of elocution, Absalom thought his manner too laboured and vehement, and that he moved his arms about needlessly. He was lecturing on the English poets, and Absalom went to each talk, relentlessly taking excerpts and subjecting Thelwall's conclusions to analysis. The lectures ended with Thelwall's own rendering of Mark Anthony's speech over Caesar's body, which, he said, had given rise to the making of modern Europe and therefore affected each one of his hearers. It was an impressive performance and excited Absalom's imagination. He started to plan an epic poem on the life of King Alfred.

In November he composed, not the opening stanzas of the epic, but verses to Elizabeth on the occasion of their first wedding anniversary. The celebration was not long over when he heard that his friend Mr Grime was unwell. He hurried over to Grime's house and read him William Paley's *Reasons for Contentment* for an hour. The attempt to encourage the sick man failed. At midnight one of Grime's servants set up a loud knocking on the Ravald Street door. Mr Watkin must come at once. His master was very ill indeed.

November 21st, 1815. I went. He was up, dressed and at prayer in the bedroom. He declared that he felt himself dying; requested me to lose no time in making his will. He sent the servant for his mother; his wife was extremely agitated and alarmed. I did not think him dying but thought it best to comply with his request. I sat down to write his will. As he dictated he drank freely of brandy and water; to 'keep him up' as he said. By degrees I ventured to tell him that I thought he was not dying. He persisted he was. His mother came. He took leave of her. During this time he drank, as I learnt afterwards, nearly half a bottle of brandy, mixed with warm water. This and his talking made him sweat most profusely, yet he persisted that he was cold and dying. I at length prevailed on him to get into bed. I sat by his side and made memorandums of what he wished me to do as one of his executors. At length he felt himself warm and began to think he should still live.

He was to do so for another twenty-four years.

Nothing could for long banish Absalom's anxiety about his financial position. So much had been lost so quickly and the getting of it had been burdensome. It was not altogether his reduced means that worried him. In eighteen months' time he would remark after reading Edward Gibbon's *Memoirs* that he was able to enjoy life and support a family on much less than the income of between £300 and £400 a year the historian complained about. What frightened Absalom was fear of total loss, bankruptcy and the starvation of his dependants. Nor were his fears groundless. The cotton market was uncertain and business failure common. For the small businessman profits were slim anyway, the price of raw cotton fluctuated and the merchants and manufacturers were at the mercy of other forces over which they had no control.

One afternoon towards Christmas William Makinson came round to the warehouse. He had in his pocket a letter from a former member of the Club called Hallworth. Hallworth had left Manchester to keep a school at Wavertree, near Liverpool. He was now giving it up to become an ironmonger.

December 15th, 1815. He spoke of the situation he was leaving in such terms as made me think it a very good opportunity for any person qualified to teach. The question of my own fitness came strongly to my mind at the time and occupied my thoughts after I got home.

December 16th, 1815. Rose thinking about the school. At breakfast it became the subject of conversation and my wife expressed her desire that I should undertake it. I concluded to speak to Makinson about it. I got tea with him, we considered the matter and it appeared to us that it would be advantageous; but we determined, before concluding upon it, to write to Hallworth for particulars. We did so. And thus at a time when I thought my situation fixed for life, I am very probably on the eve of moving more than thirty miles and commencing a business which is entirely new. I feel acutely even at the thought of leaving my friends and the advantages (of a literary and religious nature), which I enjoy here.

Instead of writing, Hallworth came himself to Manchester and offered Absalom his home as well as his school. Absalom decided to go at once to inspect it. Wavertree was then a village of a few thousand inhabitants to the east of Liverpool, full of old houses, elm trees and the sound of rooks.

December 22nd, 1815. Set out for Liverpool at half past five in the morning. Got to Hallworth's house about noon. After dinner looked round Wavertree. The house is smoky but delightfully situated.

December 23rd, 1815. Left for Manchester at two and got home about eight. Concluded to have nothing to do with the school.

On Christmas Day he wrote to Hallworth declining the offer. We do not know his reasons but he was safe. He would not have to leave Manchester.

Now the threat was lifted he settled back thankfully into the routine of the warehouse, the Club, preaching, discussions with Grime about future punishment and cataloguing his books. He tried not to take the book he was reading at home with him to Cannon Street. If he were to repair his losses the business would need all his attention. Instead, he stayed up reading far into the night.

April 3rd, 1816. A fine but rather cold day. Continued Robertson's America. I see, from the narrative of Robertson, to what care, labour and difficulty all persons who will do some great thing are exposed. I see too the

value of decision, but I begin to discover the necessity of adding address and
courtesy to resolution and perseverance. What detestable cruelty, what
causeless aggression, attended the Spanish conquests in America! What a
malevolent being, too frequently, is man!

Absalom loved his garden, and that spring worked in it for hours at a time
sowing mignonette, stocks, sunflowers, china asters and columbines, parsley,
lettuce and onions. In the middle of June 1816, Grime called for him at five in the
morning and together they walked to the remains of the Roman Post in
Broughton.

June 15th, 1816. Our walk was delightful; we spoke of the corruption of
morals on the Continent, particularly among the French, and agreed that war
with such people, accompanied by heavy taxes and some distress, was better
than intercourse and probably introduction of their vices; we thought better
of the late Mr Pitt, from considering that he had perhaps saved us from such a
contamination. We then spoke of the war and were somewhat reconciled to
its horrors by reflecting that it had carried off a number of wretches who
could hardly live with safety to Europe.

This was not what Absalom had been saying a short time before. His
conversation with Grime represented but one crude segment of his considered
opinion, but there can be no doubt that he had shifted to the right. This was partly
because he now belonged in a modest manner to the capitalist class, partly because
age and experience had tempered the reforming zeal of his early years in
Manchester. Neither his social class nor his intelligence would have allowed him
to join the Church and Tory party in Manchester. Nor could he have been happy
with the radical reformers. His was the cautious liberalism of one who has his roots
in the parliamentary opposition to Charles I, who owed more to John Locke and
the Declaration of Rights than he did to Tom Paine.

Nevertheless, Absalom was far more deeply involved in the moderate reform
movement in Manchester than the diary entries of the time suggest. He was a
friend of J.E. Taylor, in a few years to be part owner and first editor of the
Manchester Guardian, and also of Archibald Prentice, the tireless reformer and free
trader shortly to edit the *Manchester Gazette*. Prentice was a Scottish presbyterian
who had come to Manchester to open a muslin warehouse. Both he and Taylor
had met Absalom the year before on the occasion of Absalom's first silent venture
into active politics.

In February 1815 he had attended a meeting called in the Dining Room of the
Exchange to oppose the protectionist Corn Bill, which kept the price of bread
artificially high in order to safeguard the landowning interest. The importation of
foreign corn was prohibited until the home price reached eighty shillings a quarter.
During the war farmers had been encouraged to cultivate marginal land in order to

grow cereal crops. With peace and the lifting of the blockade they were faced with a glut of cheap imports from abroad which might flood the market, undercut their own prices and mean that they were growing a crop no one would wish to buy. That was the reasoning behind the Corn Laws, but it was not one accepted by many in Manchester.

Among those at the meeting besides Absalom, Taylor and Prentice were Kershaw, Baxter, Brotherton, John Shuttleworth, and the two Potter brothers, Thomas and Richard. Richard Potter was later to refer to this group as 'a small and determined band', and Prentice himself called them 'a little circle of men, faithful among the faithless, to liberal principles, who subsequently threw the shield of their protection over the intended victims of government oppression'. Prentice must have thought this description a little too emphatic as far as Absalom was concerned. 'Mr Absalom Watkin,' he added, 'giving himself more to literature than to politics, was nevertheless on the way to useful action.'

This group, whose names appear over and over again in the diary, did not by any means always agree among themselves about principles or methods, but they persistently worked to ameliorate the effects of that industrial capitalism from which, to a greater or lesser extent, they themselves profited. If in his youth he had ever done so, Absalom had long ceased to look to France for political inspiration. Now he read the four volumes of Marmontel's 'most interesting Memoirs'.

June 25th, 1816. He gives a clear account of the rise of the Revolution in France. The weakness of the king, the inability and frequent change of the ministers, the progress of infidel and republican principles, and the ambition of the worthless villains who conspired to produce it. When I closed the volume and reflected England had probably been preserved from similar atrocities in some measure by the counsels and firmness of Mr Pitt, I felt a degree of veneration for a man of whom formerly I thought but meanly.

He set lupins between his strawberry rows and everlasting sweet peas among the willows, started to teach himself Italian and read Burke.

July 22nd, 1816. He saw, with the eye of a prophet, the evils that would fall upon France from the mad, destructive schemes and the outrageous folly and wickedness of the National Assembly. I have no doubt that his work contributed to save this country from the contagion of infidel and levelling principles. May his memory be honoured!

His own affairs remained unsettled. Brook and Lister were still struggling to repay more of their debt, and in the summer Absalom paid another visit to Yorkshire.

August 1st, 1816. After tea walked to Baildon Moor, thence to a wood called the Spring. After leaving the Spring we proceeded to a high hill about a mile off and from its summit had a very extensive view. I could perceive two of the churches in Leeds and part of the ruins of Kirkstall Abbey. The variety of prospect is remarkable. On one side Leeds with an intervening woody country, on another cultivated vales with little wood, and Shipley and Bradford breaking the uniformity of the scene. On the third, huge dark mountains, clothed with heath and uncultivated rise towards heaven.

That night he began to write a poem in blank verse which he called 'Absence from Home'. He was still in love with his wife. On his return he went to Liverpool.

September 5th, 1816. Spent the evening at Hallworth's. Slept in the house of an old Welsh woman in a little bed in a small room the walls of which were by no means free from bugs; did not rest well.

Absalom had brought his Whit Lane cat to Ravald Street and that October she fell ill.

October 8th, 1816. This evening our poor cat, whom we have had since 1809, died – she has been ill about a fortnight and has died more sincerely lamented by us and much more missed, than many a man of substance is by his friends.

She had left a little kitten.

October 9th, 1816. Today our little kitten (old puss's son) died. The poor little thing only began to be ill yesterday. The death of our two cats has filled our house with mourning. My mother and Elizabeth weep, and our fireside seems to have lost its usual delight, now the cats do not enliven it.

October 10th, 1816. Buried little Kit with its mother under the elder tree in the yard.

Three weeks later they were no longer alone.

November 3rd, 1816. We now have another cat. It is a fine black tom which came crying to the back door last Monday night and being admitted and kindly treated was immediately familiar and soon quite domesticated. After mature deliberation we have agreed to call it Muff.

Alas, Muff caught the same infection and died after barely a month, but two weeks before Christmas yet another cat arrived.

December 6th, 1816. We have today got another cat in the same manner as the last. It came crying to the door and fled and will not leave us. The poor animal appears by its extreme fearfulness to have been badly used.

It lived and that autumn, about the time the little kitten died, Elizabeth conceived.

She was seven months pregnant when Absalom, Grime and their schoolmaster friend, John Andrew, left Manchester on a May morning for a week's tour of Derbyshire. They left in the coach for Buxton at six in the morning and arrived at ten o'clock, Absalom reading Voltaire's *History of Charles XII* for most of the four hours on the road. After an excellent breakfast at the Shakespeare Inn they walked out to see Poole's Hole, which they had been told was the first wonder of the Peak.

May 26th, 1817. Went into it, conducted by two old women and a girl. The entrance is low and narrow and the interior dark, damp and slippery. In a rugged part Grime fell, cut his ankle and scratched his hands. When we were about half way, Andrew let off some crackers which he had brought with him, which made a noise like thunder in the caves which surrounded us. He was, however, mortified to find that they went off indifferently.

They were overcharged by the old woman and Grime felt sorry for himself. He examined his wound and 'called out lustily for old lant or red bottle, or some remedy for the cut in his leg'. Grime may have been using the Lancashire word for stale urine, supposedly efficacious for injuries, while 'red bottle' was a popular, all-purpose liniment then put up by a Salford doctor.

The following day Dovedale came up to expectations. It was covered with cowslips, orchises and wild garlic, the water of the Dove so clear that they drank from it eagerly. At the entrance to a cave called Reynard's Hall they met a group of people they had noticed when they were far below. They explored the cave, inside which Andrew let off the remainder of his fireworks and then ate the provisions they had taken with them. Andrew had brought a 'spying glass' and through it perceived that the group they had met at the entrance to Reynard's Hall were now walking towards them. They introduced themselves as a Mr Hardy, his daughter, her friend and another young man who had come from Derby. It turned out that all of them except Mr Hardy intended to make an attempt on a famous beauty spot called Thorpe Cloud. Still wearing their greatcoats and carrying their umbrellas, Absalom's party prepared to make the climb.

But before we reached the foot of the Cloud, it began to rain heavily. None of our new companions had umbrellas but as we each of us had one, we were able to afford them shelter. I happened to give up mine to the two ladies, a piece of civility for which Andrew and Grime rewarded me by a profusion of jokes on my gallantry which as they were told in French and understood only by ourselves, gave no offence to our new acquaintances.

The jokes and the French continued on the road back to Ashbourne, where old Mr Hardy lived. After a walk of three or four miles they parted from their new acquaintances in the market place there, then drank wine at the Bell where they were spending the night. As the evening was fine, they took another walk into the churchyard. Here they were both gratified and puzzled to hear their French translated by some passers-by. On inquiry, they were told that Ashbourne had been a depot for French prisoners of war, who had taught the townspeople a smattering of their language.

Wearing their greatcoats and carrying their umbrellas they set out the next morning to walk the twelve miles to Matlock Bath. Here they climbed the Heights of Abraham to the summit now reached by cable car and, not content with that, explored the vast caverns of the old lead mines beneath, where the sides and even the roof glittered with different coloured minerals.

Next day they climbed to the top of Matlock High Tor, a great rock that rises perpendicularly from the River Derwent, and while the trout they had ordered for dinner was cooking, went over Sir Richard Arkwright's home, Willersley Castle, then occupied by his son. Arkwright's cotton mill by the side of the river interested Absalom less than a large gooseberry bush he had noticed fastened to the wall of the castle garden. He measured a branch and found it was over thirty-three feet long, but the gardener told him it was done for curiosity, they had little fruit from it.

One of the objects of the jaunt had been to see Chatsworth and Haddon Hall, and by means of hiring a carriage they succeeded in visiting them on the same day. Absalom appreciated Chatsworth from an aesthetic distance. But the rooms were so large and lofty that he could not help thinking that they must 'be cold in winter and I almost pitied the owner of this magnificent house for wanting a snug warm room like mine'. He saw the gardens as they were before they had been transformed by Joseph Paxton's genius.

May 30th, 1817. Leaving the house we went to look at the water- works. There is a duck which spouts water, a tree which spouts water, horses and lions which spout water, river gods and monsters who spout water, a large artificial cascade and numerous concealed pipes to spout water on the unwary. The reservoir which supplies these things with water covers, I think the man said, fourteen acres of ground, and yet they have only water enough to throw about now and then for a short space of time at once. It would, he said, require a river to keep them constantly spouting and foaming. Of all these water wonders, it was only the cascade which appeared to me worth the trouble of making, and to cover fourteen acres of land with water only to play tricks with it, did not please me.

Haddon, however, seized Absalom's imagination. It had not been lived in for a long time and was almost empty of furniture.

> At Chatsworth the magnificent rooms and costly furniture were shown to us by a stately housekeeper elegantly dressed. At Haddon, our conductress was a respectable-looking woman well stricken in years whose grey hair, old-fashioned print gown, precise clean appearance and rather mumbling speech were perfectly in unison with the objects she pointed out to us.

The 'stately housekeeper elegantly dressed' was undoubtedly Mrs Gregory, whose niece Paxton fell in love with on his first morning at Chatsworth and whom he was later to marry. The Haddon housekeeper had neither Mrs Gregory's presence nor her authority.

When she showed them the green velvet bed cover embroidered by Lady Katherine Manners, to her utter terror Grime leapt over the wooden rail which protected it and lay on top of the fragile cloth. Fortunately no damage seemed to have been done, nor were they turned out. On the contrary, whether the old lady was frightened of her three visitors it is hard to say, but she allowed them, one by one, to rock each other in the wooden cradle of the Dukes of Rutland, to wander freely in and out of the empty, interconnecting rooms and up the towers, where Absalom pocketed a plant, not because it was rare, but because he wished so much to grow something from Haddon in Ravald Street. Haddon Hall touched a chord of pleasing melancholy.

> The deserted rooms through which we passed had for ages been the scene of pomp and mirth and hospitality. All the passions, whether good or bad, which actuate the human breast, had here been called into exercise. The first cry of new-born life and the last groans of feeble age had echoed within these walls repeatedly during the centuries. The towers of Haddon glitter in the sun or are shaken by the blast, but their eyes behold them no more.

The day was not ended yet. From Haddon they drove to Bakewell and first looked at the Bath, a pretty building over a poor spring, before walking to the church.

> We found the church door open and went in. The clerk was in the reading-desk putting the strings into the proper places for Sunday and humming a psalm tune which he perhaps intended to set.

They left Derbyshire at the end of May, travelling to Buxton in an overloaded coach along precipitous and narrow roads. The scenery was beautiful, but Absalom was too afraid of the coach overturning to look out of the window. Two months later, at ten in the morning, his wife was safely delivered of a fine girl.

CHAPTER FOUR

'Left Manchester on the coach for London'

The baby was named Elizabeth after her mother and grandmother. She was christened at St Stephen's, Salford, by the author of *A Word For My Country*, the strongly conservative clergyman Melville Horne, and soon afterwards innoculated with 'cow pock matter'. Absalom took time from his warehouse to attend drawing classes three mornings a week, picked wild flowers in Broughton and blackberries on Kersal Moor, and in the autumn walked to his former home in Whit Lane.

October 9th, 1817. When I got into the meadows between Agecroft Bridge and Whit Lane, I observed that the beauty of the scenery had been spoiled by levelling some hedges and most of the trees they contained; but especially by clearing the ascents of the brushwood and bushes which when I lived in Whit Lane, gave them so much beauty. The two lofty trees, too, which stood in the middle of the field next to Whit Lane and broke so agreeably the uniformity of the meadows, have been felled and no trace of them remains. Where the well was on the declivity above them, a sizing house has been built and the eye is no more to be gratified with that pleasing appearance of pastoral life, a young woman drawing water at the well. Great alterations and not for the better have been made about the house my uncle inhabited and that of Mr Douglas. As I passed alone through places so familiar to me, the remembrance of the past came strongly to my mind. The pleasures, the follies and the sorrows of that period of my life are gone, but the impression they have made upon me will remain till I can no longer either think or feel.

That month Napoleon's carriage and the objects captured with it were put on show in Manchester. The carriage found its way eventually to Madame Tussaud's but unfortunately was burnt in the fire there in 1925.

October 27th, 1817. The plates and instruments taken with the carriage are very rich, being mostly in gold. Among the pictures, I was most struck with one representing Bonaparte on the morning of the battle of Moskva, exclaiming, as the sun rose, 'It is the sun of Austerlitz!'

National triumph soon turned to grief.

November 8th, 1817. The papers this morning informed us that Princess Charlotte, after being delivered of a stillborn child, died in a few hours. This was an event quite unexpected. Youth and health appeared to promise her a numerous offspring and length of days. Everyone expected it and the blow is so sudden that everyone is sorry. I am not apt to sympathize with the great, but to die suddenly at little more than twenty-one, with such prospects as she had, appears so hard a fate that I have been sorry for her all day. She died about two in the morning of November 6th.

One Sunday in the spring of the following year, 1818, Absalom went out of curiosity to hear High Mass celebrated in the Catholic chapel at Mulberry Street.

It had not proved easy to impose an alternative version of Christianity on a country that had been Catholic for nearly a thousand years. When Queen Elizabeth's archbishop, Edmund Grindal, started an inquiry into the state of the Collegiate Church in Manchester, he discovered to his horror that not all the pictures in the church had been defaced or the old shrines removed. He would have been even more horrified had he realized that Laurence Vaux, warden at the beginning of the Queen's reign, had successfully put most of the vestments and plate out of the commissioners' reach. In his will Vaux had directed that the church's treasures should be held 'until such time as the College should be restored to the Catholic Faith or until Catholics should live in it'.

That time never came. The old faith was kept alive by some of the Lancashire gentry, but by the middle of the eighteenth century a handful of Catholics only remained in Manchester and Mass was celebrated by the banks of the Irwell on a temporary altar set up in a building used as a dye-house during the week. However, the same reasons that drew Absalom to Manchester applied to others. The industrial expansion of the town offered work and opportunities, and Catholic recusant families from other parts of Lancashire moved in together with the Irish and Italians. St Chad's was built in 1774 and by 1794, the year in which St Mary's, Mulberry Street was built, the number of Catholics had risen to about 2,000. By the turn of the century they had increased to almost 20,000, and fifty years later to 100,000.

Probably Absalom had never been to a Mass before and one would have expected him to have been horrified. By that time Protestants had become so alienated from the roots which fed them that Catholicism generally was looked upon as a totally different religion. He was not horrified; what he saw was to him an interesting survival, one that in no way either involved or challenged his own belief or practice.

April 19th, 1818. Heard High Mass at the Catholic chapel in Mulberry Street, and a sermon from Mr Briggs, one of their priests. I was pleased with the chanting of the Latin service, and thought their pomp and ceremonies, though numerous and some of them trifling, yet likely to produce a powerful effect, especially on the ignorant.

He was restless. He had visited Whit Lane and now he wanted to go back still further into his past, to return to London and see the places he had known as a child. The Dovedale expedition had been a success. He made arrangements to visit London with Grime and Andrew in early May.

Two coaches besides the Mail left Manchester daily for London. The Mail carried only a few passengers. The others took eleven people outside and six inside, besides the coachman and the guard. Absalom and his party booked outside seats, probably because they were cheaper.

May 7th, 1818. Left Manchester, on the coach for London, at half-past three in the afternoon, in company with Grime and Andrew. We had scarcely any rain and passed the evening and night very cheerfully. Grime and Andrew even ventured to sleep on the coach.

May 8th, 1818. Pursued our journey on the coach. At daybreak we found ourselves near Tamworth. We passed Coleshill, the place at which Falstaff and his gang robbed the carriers, and got to Coventry about six in the morning. There we saw the effigy of Peeping Tom fixed in a niche in the corner house. We were very hungry but were not permitted to breakfast before we got to Dun Church, which we reached about eight o'clock. Here we got a good breakfast and then set off again in high spirits. The road for some miles was bordered on each side by fine large trees and presented the appearance of a noble avenue. We dined at Brickhill and fared sumptuously. This circumstance made us all very cheerful and gave Andrew an exuberant flow of spirits.

When we got to St Albans, twenty miles from London, there was a very great appearance of rain. It soon began to fall and kept increasing. The rain fell more and more heavily. Our umbrellas formed a number of spouts, and instead of sheltering us from the rain, collected it, and poured it upon us from their different points. At one time a stream came directly upon my nose, another in the back of my neck, a third in my bosom and one or two in my breeches. We were all thus situated and had scarcely patience to bear with temper what we could not avoid.

They arrived at the Axe in Aldermanbury at eight in the evening. It was over twenty-eight hours since they left Manchester. Their trials were by no means over. They could not afford an inn and had taken the precaution to procure two letters addressed to people in the City who kept lodging houses. The rain was still coming down in torrents and they waited in vain for a hackney coach by the courtyard where they had been set down. At last they abandoned the idea of a coach and getting a porter to carry their baggage, waded despondently after him to a lodging house they had an introduction to in the Old Change. To their great disappointment the servant told them that all the rooms were taken. Their second letter was addressed to a house in Paternoster Row. To get there they had to walk close to Absalom's beloved and revered St Paul's Cathedral, to see which was one of the main reasons he had returned to London.

Thither we bent our steps. We had to pass St Paul's and as there was still light enough to distinguish its majestic dome rising towards heaven, I pointed it out to Andrew and inquired what he thought of it. I got such an answer as to be expected from a man who finds himself houseless, in a strange place, in the midst of a dismal night and who is tired, unwell, wet and hungry. 'I am disappointed. It does not answer my expectations.'

The lodging house in Paternoster Row was full up too, but the landlady took pity on them and allowed them to leave their luggage there while they went to a house of a friend of hers in Aldersgate. That also was full. They returned in despair to Paternoster Row. The kind landlady sent them to inquire at Dolly's and the Chapter Coffee House. The Coffee House offered beds but no fire and where then could they change their clothes? They stood arguing acrimoniously outside in the pouring rain and decided in the end to go to the Castle and Falcon. It was well they did so, for the rain continued all night. There they got a fire, changed their clothes and, too exhausted to eat, drank a cup of hot coffee and got into bed. They were up at seven next morning and breakfasted on coffee and warm new bread before hurrying off to see St Paul's.

Absalom was fascinated by St Paul's. He never came to London without spending hours there. Such a vast building so close to his old home, the Fortune of War, may have acquired a significance in his imagination that transcended its physical being. Surprisingly, it does not seem that as a boy he ever ventured inside. He writes as if its interior were an entirely new spectacle. He was shocked by the multitude of civic monuments it contained.

May 9th, 1818. The design, too, of almost all the monuments was perfectly heathenish; Fame and Victory, Neptune, Britannia, and several river gods, to say nothing of sphinxes, crocodiles, etc. seemed rather out of place in a Christian temple.

Later they went to Doctor's Commons and the Herald's Office.

Then walking down Benet's Hill, we passed St Benet's churchyard, where my father is buried, and the Fortune of War, the house in which he died. The house is altered, many of the windows stopped up and the bar placed on the side of Paul's Wharf. We went to the riverside, the scene of my boyish adventures. I beheld all these objects with interest and am much struck with one circumstance respecting them. They all appeared less, and the distances shorter, than from my recollection of them. Yet so strong are early impressions unless corrected by frequent re-examination of the object, that now I am returned, I have a clear recollection of those scenes as they appeared to me seventeen years ago but I cannot recall the appearance they exhibited this day fortnight.

The three of them were tireless. From Paul's Wharf they went to the Mansion House, the Royal Exchange, and crossed the street to the Bank of England.

We entered and sauntered from office to office through this immense building, in which I was told nearly six hundred clerks are employed. A great deal of business was going on, and apparently with great regularity and dispatch. When we had satisfied our curiosity we left the Bank and proceeded to Leadenhall Street. We now felt inclined to eat and going into the London Eating-house, we regaled ourselves on beef and broccoli and porter, and made an excellent dinner for about a shilling apiece.

On Sunday they found Piccadilly filled with carriages.

May 10th, 1818. The rattle and bustle and the number of carriages, persons on horseback and foot passengers, increased as we got nearer to Hyde Park. We entered Hyde Park and proceeded much more than a mile along that part appropriated to pedestrians and which is parallel to the carriage-way. No hackney coaches are admitted, but the road was thronged all the way with carriages and horsemen, as close together as was consistent with moving along. Many of the carriages were filled with ladies, some of whom appeared to have no desire to conceal their charms. Many thousand persons thronged the footway. It was only possible to move very slowly and in some places there were frequent temporary stoppages. There was plenty of room on the grass, but most people chose the crowded gravel way, that they might observe the carriages and be seen themselves. Everybody was smartly dressed – the majority expensively so. Almost everybody seemed to be well and appeared to be pleased. We looked at the carriages, the ladies, the liveries and the dresses till our eyes were tired.

We went slowly through the Green Park to Buckingham House, the residence of the King. It is a plain building. Then we entered St James's Park, and enjoyed the cool shade of the trees. The Chinese bridge over the canal in this park attracted our notice and we went to it. This is one of the paltry follies of the Court. It is built of wood and was erected at no small expense to exhibit fireworks in honour of our victories in France. The hooks for the fireworks yet remain in the wood, and a sentinel is stationed on the bridge, I suppose to prevent people stealing the boards or setting it on fire. We passed over it with some degree of contempt for those who threw away public money in erecting it and went to look at the 'Regent's Bomb'. This is a huge mortar left by the French when they abandoned the siege of Cadiz and presented by the Spaniards to the Regent. It has been fantastically mounted on the back of a large bronze dragon and placed opposite the centre of the Horse Guards.

On the way back to the inn they examined the new structures of Waterloo Bridge and looked at Somerset House. But they had not travelled all that way for nothing. After a short rest they set out again, this time towards the City and the Monument, where on the way Absalom contrived that they should pass his old school in Fish Street. Back once more at the Castle and Falcon, Absalom reflected on the day.

> I felt very strongly the superiority of quiet, regular domestic enjoyments to all the glare and shout and bustle which I had witnessed. It was well enough to see it once, but to think of living in it would have been not a little unpleasant to me.

The immediate worry was financial. The inn was too expensive for any of them. Next morning Absalom called on his brother-in-law, Joseph Makinson, William's brother. It seems that at that time Joseph had business connections with London, where he lived and rented a warehouse. Joseph suggested that two of the party lodged with him and one with a neighbour. They celebrated the move by going that night to the theatre at Covent Garden.

> **May 11th, 1818.** We obtained good seats without difficulty. The house is splendidly decorated and lighted with gas. There is a beautiful chandelier over the centre of the pit, from which the mild yet brilliant light produced by a great number of jets of gas diffuses an agreeable lustre over the whole interior of the building. The theatre is very well ventilated. The rabble in the galleries, immediately upon their entrance, began to throw orange peel, etc. into the pit and continued their sport the whole of the evening.

The tragedy was *Bellamira*, which Absalom thought a foolish piece. It was followed by the burlesque *Bombastes Furioso* and the evening ended with a pantomime called *Harlequin Gulliver*. Nothing could better illustrate Absalom's essentially innocent nature than his reaction to the pantomime. He was absolutely enchanted and described it in his diary with minute detail. The Lilliputians were all children, the scenery in proportion to their size.

The boy who represented the Emperor of Lilliput performed his part to admiration. He trod the stage with an air of dignity and ease, saluted the ladies of his court, flourished his handkerchief, took snuff and gave his hand to the Empress in a most imperial manner. The Brobdingnagians were so accoutred as to be from ten to twelve feet high. The children were of a proportionate size. The scenery consisting of a corn field and a farmyard and house was in proportion to the size of the people. There was an apple tree, which being shaken by the clown, discharged upon his head a quantity of apples, larger than pumpkins. A girl came upon the stage pushing before her a child in a go-cart and taking a fancy to the clown as a plaything, she tucked him under one arm and with the other whirled her go-cart and baby across the stage.

This led Absalom to consider the nature of size. The deception showed that our judgement of it was arrived at by nothing more than comparison with what we expected to see. The evening ended badly.

We had eaten nothing since dinner and left the theatre tired, heated and faint from want of food. When we got into the street we sought for an eating house but finding none we liked, went into a fishmongers. Grime and I regaled upon oysters and pickled salmon, the remembrance of which makes my mouth water, and quenched our thirst in a quart of porter. Andrew, who dislikes fish, became sick with seeing us eat and went out to seek a beef shop. We stayed and made an excellent supper and to our surprise found Andrew at the door, he having found no place at which he liked to eat. It was now between twelve and one, and tired as we were, we had a long walk to our beds. To crown all, we found no house at which Andrew could sup and he was compelled to proceed with an empty stomach and little patience. We did not reach Joseph Makinson's till two in the morning and were tired in the extreme. I never saw Andrew look so ill.

A day later Absalom visited his old London home.

May 13th, 1818. I left my companions and went past the White Bear in Newport Street, the first house in which I lived in London. It is much altered though still a public house. The cobbler's stall in the front is removed and the sign taken down. I left it and went down Ryder's Court and through Cranbourne Alley, both of which were familiar to me at seven and eight years of age, to Leicester Square where I met Grime and Andrew.

The three of them spent hours looking at Westminster Abbey where a guide showed them not only the ancient monuments but the place where the bodies of William Pitt and Charles James Fox, covered with a plain flag, lay a few yards from each other. After viewing Miss Linwood's Exhibition of Pictures in Needlework, they visited the Mechanical Theatre and watched sunrise over the Rhine, Napoleon's landing on St Helena and a scene of storm and shipwreck.

We then went to an eating house in Whitehall and dined on a la mode beef. This is beef stewed to rags, very highly seasoned and with a good deal of gravy. We did not much like it. After dinner we determined, as none of us had ever eaten any ice, to cool our throats with a glass apiece. We got it at a pastrycooks near Westminster Hall, but our teeth ached so confoundedly and our <u>insides</u>, as my mother would say, felt so queer with the struggle between ice and pepper, that we shall I am sure, never envy the rich their ice creams or be inclined to give sixpence any more for a pain in the stomach.

They then met Joseph Makinson as arranged, who took them through Westminster Hall into the lobby of the House of Commons to see the place where Mr Perceval had been so recently assassinated.

One of the great objects of Absalom's visit south was to visit the village of Bromley in Kent, where he boarded for some years when he was young. Why he had done so is a mystery. Perhaps he was a delicate child and was sent there for the sake of his health, for Bromley was then absolutely in the country. His mother may have been unable to look after him for reasons connected with the birth and death of his brother. The early separation from his parents could have intensified the tendency to neurotic anxiety with which he was born. He breakfasted at Charing Cross before taking the coach. His companion was an 'intelligent gentleman' who had spent some years in India.

May 15th, 1818. He had no doubt but that the native Princes would, in time, successfully expel the Europeans from India. Every soldier sent from this country costs the East India Company £20 to carry him over; £15 being the contract price of the passage and £5 more being required for necessaries. Our loss in our Indian warfare was more from disease than the sword. The intense heat quite enervates Europeans and exposure to the sun generally produces fever.

The man from India got out at Lewisham. Absalom had no need to talk. This journey was a quest into his past more intense than anything he had yet undertaken.

As the coach passed along through a fine country, I noticed with pleasure the hawthorn in blossom in the hedges, the meadows filled with rising grass nearly ready for the scythe and the apple trees in full blossom. As we drew near to Bromley these agreeable appearances increased.

They were there by eleven. Absalom recognized the white weatherboard houses and the square Market House. After a meal at the inn he made his way to Wigmore Green where he had lodged with people named Pocock, and passed the white gate leading to a house he thought belonged to the Archbishop of Canterbury. It was more likely the entrance to the country house of the Bishops of Rochester, that quiet retreat where Bishop Francis Atterbury plotted to overthrow the House of Hanover in favour of the Stuarts. Absalom remembered the gate vividly. He was walking along the same road he had travelled when he had left Bromley as a child of seven. The distance was less than he had imagined, 'but there is a great difference between the length of the legs at seven and at thirty years of age'. He soon found the turning to the Green

> and passed under the shade of the horse chestnut trees, the fruit of which I had collected as a boy. An opening in these trees, the spreading boughs of which completely overarched the road, presented me with the little Green and the cottage at the end of it in which I used to live.

The garden with its walnut trees remained much as it had been when he left it. He picked a bunch of wild flowers in the lane, then walked up towards the wood where he remembered the sweet violets grew, listening all the time to the cuckoo calling. To his great mortification he found that the violets were all out of flower. He learnt that Mrs Pocock had died some years ago and Mr Pocock had moved nearer to the Green.

> I found the old man, he is seventy, at work in the garden and still hale and good looking. He is fleshy and has a plump, round, deep brown-red face. After some explanation he recollected my having lived with him and we went together to a neighbouring public house, the Bird in Hand, the only one at the Green and talked to him of old times over some porter. When this was done we parted with great cordiality, he went to his work and I walked towards Bromley. I have travelled a good deal and seen many agreeable spots, but none which I should prefer to Wigmore Green. Sometimes I have supposed that as I saw it when a child, the strong impressions which objects make upon children may have deceived me, and that when I returned to it I should be disappointed. I have now seen it again and the impressions of my childhood are confirmed. Entering Bromley and being too soon for the coach, I went into the churchyard. I saw the yew trees from which I and my playfellows were accustomed to gather small red berries, very sweet, which from their slimy nature, the children called, with more propriety than elegance, 'snot' berries.

He had one final pilgrimage to make before he left London and that was to Stoke Newington, the village where his father had had the Falcon inn when Absalom was four years old. He had left this expedition to the very day of his departure for Manchester. John Makinson, Joseph's brother, agreed to go with him. Absalom was up soon after five o'clock.

May 16th, 1818. It was a lovely morning and our walk was very pleasant. We went through the fields to Islington and along the highway to Newington Green. Crossing the Green, we proceeded along some fine meadows, in which we heard the cuckoo, to Stoke Newington and entered the village just at one end, by the church.

Bromley was the place of Absalom's most treasured recollections, Stoke Newington among his earliest.

I suppose I was at the time between four and five years of age. I recollect comparing my old shoes with my new ones, riding on a horse with my father, biting my brother's lip until it bled, stealing some mint and radishes out of Mr Smith's garden, wondering at the hoarfrost on the tiles of the opposite houses, and above all, I recollect a kind old lady who lived near us, Mrs Guinand, I think, who had most excellent stewed pears, the red colour and rich spicy taste of which I remember to this day.

They drank some porter in the Falcon before walking back to London where they found Grime and Andrew still in bed.

Grime, who was a carrier's agent, wished to remain in London for the present, so that afternoon Absalom and Andrew left in the *Telegraph* for Manchester without him. This time Absalom had taken a seat inside and Andrew travelled separately on top. Absalom was suffering a reaction from the exertion, the excitement, the relentless sightseeing and the sharp impressions made upon him. He felt feverish and utterly drained of energy. His head ached violently until they reached Woburn, where it was relieved by a cup of tea. After that he slept.

CHAPTER FIVE

'A reform meeting held in open ground near St Peter's church'

For all Absalom's praise of quiet domestic enjoyment, his homecoming was a disappointment. Soon after his return an ominous sentence appears in the diary: 'Discontented with the state of things at home and rough, too rough, with Elizabeth.' It was the first rumble of the storm whose violence was to wreck their marriage.

The Makinson family were unfortunate that summer. Elizabeth's brother, Alexander, who had broken his thigh the previous winter, returned to Manchester in the last stages of consumption and Absalom spent part of his thirty-first birthday witnessing a post-mortem on his brother-in-law's hip. Hardly had Alexander died when his brother William's wife, who had been ill for some time, began finally to fail.

> **August 2nd, 1818.** Saw Mrs Makinson after dinner. She is a great deal altered since I last saw her and looks worse; but she is still cheerful, suffers little pain but at times feels great weariness. Having no doubt of being happy after death, she appears desirous to depart.

She died three days later. William needed a change and it was decided that he, his brother Joseph, and Grime and Absalom would spend a holiday at Chester. They left Manchester at six in the morning. In the coach Absalom read some pages of William Paley and when they were driving through the De la Mer Forest got into conversation with a young man who was employed planting it.

Chester was a place Absalom knew well and loved. They stayed at the Red Lion and William's grief was diverted by going round the cathedral, now cleaner than it used to be, looking at the castle and walking along the city walls. One day they made an expedition to Absalom's ancestral Wales, going by steam packet to Flint. The journey took two hours and they paid one shilling and sixpence each for the use of the best cabin. It was wainscotted with mahogany and made Absalom consider how fine it would be to have a study like that. He imagined his library so arranged that the books were placed behind hinged panels. Already he was moving away from Salford in his mind, moving away indeed from the cotton business and the necessity of earning his living at all. In his 'Plan of Life' he had given himself twelve years to buy his freedom. Eight of them had passed.

When the autumn came he went with Joseph and Grime for another short expedition, this time to High Legh, a hamlet near Altrincham which was an excellent place for nutting and the gathering of mushrooms and blackberries. Absalom calculated that when he was walking easily he went at the rate of seventeen or eighteen minutes a mile. They set out for their walk at five in the afternoon and arrived at High Legh when it was already dark. The only public house within a mile was the Bear's Paw, but the people there were in bed 'and determined not to hear us'. Luckily Joseph Makinson had some relations in the neighbourhood and at this house they got a good supper.

September 10th, 1818. With some scheming on the part of our hostess, Grime and I were accommodated with a very hard bed upon which the fatigue of our walk enabled us to sleep soundly. Joseph Makinson slept with a lodger and by his account fared better. Grime, who sleeps at home in a bed as soft as down, was much more incommoded than I was.

Absalom rose early next morning.

September 11th, 1818. The house in which we had slept is a neat cottage in the midst of a garden at a little distance from the highroad between Liverpool and London and in fine country. The swallows were skimming about and everything looked fresh with dew and glittering in the sun. A pair of swallows had built in the porch of the house and were now almost ready to leave the nest. These rural objects revived all my love of the country and made me desirous to live in such a place as this. Imagination was ready to tell me that <u>here</u> with my books and my garden every day would pass in peace and enjoyment.

They spent five hours nutting and gathering mushrooms before walking home to Manchester. Absalom spent part of the time daydreaming. He had learnt that a six-roomed cottage with a large garden could be rented for £6 a year. The tax would be £2 more.

On Boxing Day 1818 'our little girl began to go alone'. She was taking her first stumbling steps towards a future to be very different from the one destined for the child Absalom's wife had just conceived.

Hallworth despaired of finding employment in England and was preparing to go to America, leaving his wife and children to follow later. Absalom had no wish to imitate him.

February 3rd, 1819. Several pages the Eclectic Review. The critique on Fearon's Sketches of America most interesting. The latter gives such a picture of the dirt and vices of the Americans as is sufficient to deter me from all thoughts of crossing the Atlantic. One fact is remarkable. The women are all pale and all, even the young Quakers, use rouge!

One evening he remembered with satisfaction as he drank his tea that it was four years exactly since he had set out across the Yorkshire hills to serve the Warrant of Attorney against Brook and Lister.

March 21st, 1819. <u>Then</u> I was heavily in debt, ruined and in danger of prison. <u>Now</u> I have no legal debts which I cannot readily pay. I have a small capital and a business which if properly attended to, will in all probability, be sufficient for the comfortable support of myself and my family.

Not many people in Manchester and its neighbourhood had reason to be so thankful.

The two main groups of the cotton operatives were the spinners and the weavers. Since the introduction of steam-driven machinery the cotton thread had been produced in factories, which meant the herding together of men, women and children under regular discipline in one large building. Those were the spinners. The life of the weavers was different.

The power loom had been patented by Edmund Cartwright in the year of Absalom's birth only a little while after Samuel Crompton's mule, but its use had spread very slowly indeed. The expansion of factory spinning meant an enormous increase in the volume of yarn and the consequent lowering of its price, yet the extra production was not met with the rapid introduction of the power loom as one would have expected, but a greatly increased number of hand-loom weavers.

There were reasons for this. At first power looms were costly to produce and they might need expensive modifications. They were labour-intensive and not so adaptable to the vagaries of transient fashion as the hand loom; besides, to turn over to factory production meant dismantling the established system of putting out twist from the warehouse to be made up by hand.

People like to own their own tools, to be their own masters, to think of themselves as independent. The hand loom was comparatively cheap, the skill could be acquired by immigrant workers, it could be carried out at home, even if the 'home' was a rented room, damp enough for the cotton and just large enough to hold the loom.

The spinners had the more regimented life but they received a regular wage, low as it was, and the fair number of those employed to look after the machines were paid more. To keep their independence and their livelihood the weavers were prepared to accept lower wages and often squalid working conditions. They outnumbered the spinners by about two to one. It has been calculated that in Manchester at this time there were roughly 40,000 hand-loom weavers to 20,000 spinners. Both groups were exploited as the poor had always been.

The hours of the agricultural labourer were long, he was miserably paid, his occupation was tedious and his domestic comfort slight. The lot of skilled or semi-skilled spinners or weavers working at home or in the embryonic factories in their masters' attics was not much better. Their hours, too, were excessively long, the work monotonous and badly paid, the rooms noisy, crowded and hot. Moreover, the operatives were as much at the mercy of their employers as were farm labourers.

Harsh conditions for others were a matter of course. The reformer Jeremy Bentham held the most brutal ideas about the management of paupers and even the enlightened James Kay-Shuttleworth approved of transporting indigent families from the country to the industrial districts where the children would 'gradually become more equal to standing twelve hours a day'.

In Manchester thousands of human beings lived in cellars or tenements built back-to-back with no room for an outside privy; men, women and children worked from six in the morning until eight at night, hundreds under the same roof, in such conditions that they sweated and itched and smelt. Their diet would be considered intolerable today. Yet Absalom lived by the manufacture of cotton, by selling twist and pieces of grey cloth and calico from his warehouse. Without it there would have been no house, no garden and no books.

The spring of 1819 was a fine one and Absalom spent as much time as he could out of doors. Although he wanted to move farther away from the town, he was fond of his part of Salford. It was so leafy, and close to the wide stretches of Kersal Moor with the country beyond. Christmas he disliked; it meant endless cold days and entertaining relations. Good Friday, however, was a day for relaxation, if possible to be enjoyed in the open.

Drinkwater's Grounds were towards Prestwich.

April 9th, 1819. Spent the afternoon in gardening. Walked after dinner with Grime, Andrew, Davies and Joseph Makinson to the aquaduct on the Bolton canal. We returned through Drinkwater's Grounds, after regaling at a farmhouse on new milk and oat cakes. The country has a most beautiful appearance – the trees just coming into leaf, the ground covered with a profusion of primroses, anemones, and daisies. Our walk was one of the most pleasant I have ever taken.

A week or two later the primroses were followed by bluebells. Grime, Elizabeth, Joseph and Andrew together with all their children went to fetch fresh milk from the farm, and the children were drawn home by the grown-ups in a miniature coach belonging to Andrew's family.

The Club had expanded. Dr Carbutt, Mr Davies and Mr Jervis had been added to its members. Davies was later to become librarian of the Literary and Philosophical Society. Carbutt was a clever, sarcastic man of great ability but contemptuous of the opinions and conduct of others. Absalom once heard him speak with emotion of his unhappy childhood and had no doubt that many of the mistakes that led to his failure in life could be attributed to this source. The discussions at Club meetings became more scientific in character. Lengthy papers on electricity, hydrostatics, mathematics, geology, chemistry and Absalom's special interest, botany, were read by each in turn. Grime prided himself on his knowledge of chemistry and spent hours in front of his study fire trying to calcinate oyster shells to produce phosphorescent light.

Someone else was playing with fire. On 1 January of that year, the radical Henry Hunt had addressed a meeting of 8,000 operatives at St Peter's Field, an open space by St Peter's church near the centre of Manchester. Hunt was then forty-six. His sincerity and his ability have been called into question both by former allies and his opponents. However that may be, he was indisputably a demagogue, an incendiary who breathed his verbal warmth on dangerously dry tinder.

Laissez-faire was never an inflexible system, but it was widely thought that it would be a short-sighted policy for the rich considerably to diminish their income to help the poor. If they did so, it was believed, they would not be in a position to employ the labouring classes in such large numbers.

Moreover, even had the economic and psychological barriers to intervention been overcome, the state had not developed the administrative tools to deal with social problems on such a large scale. The first Sir Robert Peel's reforming factory legislation had proved very difficult to implement and he himself now concluded that the present distress was 'entirely beyond the control of parliament'.

A species of economic Calvinism prevailed. In Manchester, Mr Gatliffe, the Fellow of the Collegiate Church, whose affected piety had so shocked Absalom, accepted that no efforts made by the poor or anyone else could save them from destitution. Taxation was 'ponderous', he wrote to one of the magistrates, and the middle classes were likely to fall into the state of the lower

> and the lower into a state of starvation. But what can Reform, or any other nostrum of political agitation do here? We are suffering from the effects of the late war and bad harvests and must wait patiently until the tide turns.

Many at the sharp end, however, were not prepared to accept such economic determinism. No one expected the central government to cure poverty, that was a fact of life. But they did expect the government at least to try to do something about it. The Radicals maintained that since the government refused to act, distress was political in origin and required a political remedy. They proposed a fundamental reform of parliamentary representation so that the people's grievances could be heard, discussed and redressed.

Open-air meetings attended by thousands of workers demanding reform were not uncommon, and alarmed those who were for ever on the alert after the excesses of the French. The Revd Melville Horne, who had christened Absalom's daughter, spoke for a generation of Englishmen of a certain school when he equated Catholics, Radicals, and Atheists.

Absalom had an acquaintance with a man named Joseph Johnson, a brushmaker in a small way of business. Johnson was far more to the political left than Absalom. That summer, as Secretary of the Manchester Patriotic Union Society, he had invited Hunt to visit the town again and to stay with him. 'Trade,' Johnson wrote, 'is almost at a standstill, nothing but ruin and starvation stare one in the face. The state of the district is truly dreadful and I believe that nothing but the greatest exertions can prevent insurrection.'

Much of what really happened on 16 August 1819 in St Peter's Field, Manchester, will never be known. Few events taking place within such a short compass of space and time, in front of so many eye-witnesses, have left the historian quite so perplexed. Prejudice, political propaganda, faulty observation, bad memory, constant repetition of inaccurate reporting – all have combined to produce conflicting accounts of what was indeed a tragedy, small in loss of life yet so symbolically significant. But what is thought to have happened is in its way as important for history as what actually happened. The propaganda value of Peterloo was incalculable and transcended by far the exact number of dead and injured or the precise blame to be attached to magistrate or agitator.

An estimated 60,000 people were gathered on the open ground by the church; it would be an alarming sight even today with all our sophisticated devices for crowd control. It may or may not have been true that the language of the Radicals outran their actual intentions. In any case, they presented a threatening appearance, with constant drilling, marching and banners. A week before Peterloo a mob had attacked the police at New Cross, a poor district in Manchester. Moreover, for all his display of moderation, that July Orator Hunt had presided over a popular meeting which had carried a motion repudiating the authority of Parliament on the ground that it did not represent the people.

Yet the distress was obvious, a meeting to demand fundamental political rights appeared reasonable to the liberal-minded, to others undesirable but difficult to prevent. Through it all ran the element, not precisely of class-consciousness, but the perennial fear respectable people have of the mob. Whatever the surface gaiety of the crowd, the atmosphere was tense. With hindsight we can see the folly of allowing such numbers to gather in a confined space with only mounted soldiers to implement the wishes of authority. In these circumstances, however good their intentions or controlled their demeanour, once the cavalry had entered the crowd, death was certain. But an error of judgement is not the same thing as criminal irresponsibility.

Manchester had its roots deep in the past, which was why at the time of Peterloo it was run as if it were still a village. Subject to the jurisdiction of county magistrates and administered by a confusing number of authorities whose functions often overlapped or were duplicated, its governance was dominated by a closely knit business elite consisting for the most part of Church of England Tories, although the Dissenters by then probably outnumbered the Anglicans by two to one.

Its chief officer was the borough-reeve, who was elected by the Manor Court to serve for a year. He was assisted by a paid permanent deputy constable, who had thirty men under him; two unpaid constables elected by the court; churchwardens from the Collegiate Church, who paid the day police out of the poor rate; and finally the police and improvement commissioners, who were responsible for such public services as lighting and cleaning the streets and for the maintenance of fifty-three night watchmen. There were four uniformed beadles and special constables from fourteen police districts could be called upon in case of need.

The majority of the borough-reeves were active cotton traders of some kind or another, as were members of the Manor Court. They knew that civic peace was essential if the business community were to thrive but also knew that without military help the constables and beadles were as helpless as dormice.

Absalom was not present at Peterloo. We can only guess who his informants were.

August 16th, 1819. Today there has been a reform meeting held in the open ground near St Peter's church. Hunt, Johnson and others were the leaders. Very great numbers of people attended from the neighbouring towns with flags, music and caps of liberty. Many women attended and took part in the meeting. Soon after the arrival of the leaders the magistrates and soldiery interfered. The flags and caps of liberty were cut down, the leaders apprehended, both male and female; and some resistance being made, some were killed and many wounded. The town is still in a great ferment. I have since learnt that there have been further disturbances during the night. The conduct of the magistrates and soldiers is much blamed. There was no appearance of riot till the Manchester Cavalry (Yeomanry) charged upon the people. In their fury they rode over the special constables, one of whom, if not more, was killed and many wounded.

It has been stated that Absalom drew up the famous Declaration and Protest signed by 5,000 people, which expressed the 'utter disapprobation of the unexpected and unnecessary violence by which the assembly was dispersed'. That he drew it up alone is most improbable, but it is likely that he had a hand in it, together with J.E. Taylor and Archibald Prentice. Since neither Absalom nor Prentice were present at Peterloo, and Taylor for only part of the proceedings, they had to rely upon 'the undoubted information' they claimed to have received. This information almost certainly came from another reforming friend of Absalom, the Unitarian cotton dealer John Shuttleworth, brother of William Shuttleworth, a Methodist minister. John was actually present and was later to give sworn testimony against the Yeomanry.

From the moment the shrieking fugitives fled the field, leaving eleven people dead or dying and an unknown number injured, tension in Manchester mounted. Next morning Absalom heard that there had been more disturbances at New Cross but he went to work as usual.

August 17th, 1819. At about half-past ten o'clock this morning information was received by the magistrates that the people from Oldham and Middleton were approaching to the number of from thirty to fifty thousand (some said a hundred and fifty thousand) armed with pikes etc. Immediately orders were given to close all shops and warehouses and to clear the streets of carts and all obstructions. The military were all assembled, infantry, cavalry and cannon. A state of confusion and hurry and dismay, truly ridiculous, took place. People ran about as if the pikes had been close behind them and most people left their warehouses and went home. Some few remained and lo! in about an hour, the pikemen not appearing and the magistrates being informed that there never had been the least foundation for the report, their former orders were countermanded and business in some measure recommenced.

For all that, things in Manchester were never quite the same again.

Strange threads bind human beings to one another. We do not know who ordered the Yeomanry to enter the crowd at Peterloo but it was the Tory squire and magistrate William Hulton who told the mounted Hussars to disperse the meeting. Hulton had a son who in after years saved his schoolfriend William Gladstone from death when a sandbank on which they were playing at Southport collapsed.

Towards the end of September, Absalom met Grime between five and six in the morning and together they picked blackberries in the dingle below Prestwich church. Absalom took them back to his wife, who was expecting her second child. A week later she gave birth to a son. The baby was christened Edward William by Mr Melville Horne, soon to be exceedingly alarmed by the report that William Cobbett had arrived from America bearing with him a box containing the bones of Tom Paine, which he planned to bear in triumph through Manchester.

As Christmas 1819 approached, William Makinson tired out Absalom by keeping him up late describing his courtship of his new wife. The birth of another child had made Absalom more nervous of financial collapse than ever. So many apparently flourishing firms had failed. He felt acutely the precariousness of life and the extent of his domestic responsibilities. It was cold, the children were unwell and kept him from sleeping at night. He felt so low that he copied out Dr Abernethy's prescription for nervous debility, depression of spirits and mental imbecility: three drachms compounded spirit of ammonia; four drachms compounded ditto of lavender; four drachms tincture of castor oil; seven ounces camphorated julip. Mix. Three tablespoons to be taken four times a day.

It must have been effective. The old king died in February 1820, and Absalom found sufficient energy to walk round the town to hear George IV proclaimed.

February 5th, 1820. I went to hear the first proclaiming which was in St Ann's Square. A discharge of cannon from the New Bailey preceded the ceremony. Then the proclamation was read by, I think, the Borough-reeve and at the conclusion the women waved their handkerchiefs, the military their swords, the <u>part</u> of the people shouted 'huzza' but in a very feeble manner for it was a wet, uncomfortable day and George IV is not very popular. When the sounds ceased, the bands played 'God Save the King' and after that the magistrates, soldiery and such of the inhabitants as chose to walk in procession proceeded to the next place of proclamation. The Manchester Yeomanry, who have not been assembled since the sixteenth of August, were present on the occasion and received from the people hisses and revilings in abundance. The regular troops were cheered.

Hallworth had succeeded in finding employment in the United States and summoned his wife and children to join him. Absalom bid her a sad farewell, that was another link severed, he would surely never see her again. The parting disturbed him. Times were so bad that Hallworth had to leave England. Suppose he himself could not keep his head above water? He played with some schemes for increasing his capital but resolved to take no risks, to attend to his business punctually and not to read at the warehouse or indulge in any unnecessary expenses.

The spring was slow that year. In late March the grass on Kersal Moor was still withered and the trees black and bare. Perhaps it was the lowness of the time, perhaps like many better critics than he, Absalom could not adjust easily to different imaginative forms, but he read Wordsworth's poems in *Lyrical Ballads* and considered them one of the 'silliest things for the use of grown men that I have read for many years'.

Annoyances mounted. Grime suddenly moved house to Prestwich, to get there and back meant a ten-mile walk. Then William Makinson invited him round to be introduced to his new wife, 'having been particularly requested to do so by him'.

May 31st, 1820. He did not speak to me nor remained in the room many minutes. They did not even give us time to drink their healths. The bride is a plain looking, homely, reserved woman, said to be twenty-seven but apparently older and giving no signs of education, grace or good breeding.

It was another black mark against the Makinsons. That, together with the anxieties of the time, caused Absalom's skin to itch and tingle at night. He was shocked to hear of the bankruptcy of the firm of Askew and Dewhurst.

June 17th, 1820. I have always thought they were doing better than from the event, they appear to have done. I have often wished I could be as successful as they were and now I find that I was at the time more successful.

I will endeavour to learn from this discovery to be grateful for my own success and not to rate too high the apparent success of others. But the principle use I would make of this misfortune and my own former imprudences is to assist me in making and keeping proper resolutions.

The accession of George IV raised the question of Queen Caroline, the mother of the unfortunate Princess Charlotte. While remaining within the letter of the law as it applied to the royal children, George IV, while Prince of Wales, had in effect bigamously married Caroline for the sake of money and an heir. He could not bear the sight of her. He was prepared to risk any public scandal to get rid of his wife; she was as determined to be awarded the honour due to a Queen of England and that June arrived to claim it. A wave of synthetic emotion swept the country, swelled partly by dislike of the King and his ministers, partly by pity for one many considered to be a wronged and courageous woman. A Bill of Pains and Penalties depriving the Queen of her titles and dissolving her marriage on the grounds of her adultery went before Parliament.

Opinion in Manchester was divided. The borough-reeve refused Mr Baxter's request to call a public meeting to protest against the proceedings against the Queen so he presided over an indignant assembly in the Manor Court Room instead, whereupon the High Church party held a counter-demonstration at the Police Office.

In high summer Absalom walked through the fields and lanes to have tea with Grime at Prestwich.

July 9th, 1820. I noticed the dog rose, scabious, tufted purple vetch, honeysuckle, bell flowered heath, purple vetch, yellow vetch and the large yellow horse-shoe vetch, wild sage, bell flower, two sorts of cranesbill, elder, small and larger speedwell, St John's wort, ragwort, foxglove, ragged robin, and two or three flowers the names of which I do not know.

In November, the Bill of Pains and Penalties failed and Absalom marked the illuminations in Manchester. Yet in August, while Orator Hunt still languished in gaol, not many had bothered to attend a gathering to celebrate the first anniversary of Peterloo. It seemed that for the moment people were more interested in the gossip of foreign chambermaids than the cause of reform.

CHAPTER SIX

'Four hundred and one barrels of ale, more than twenty oxen and sixty sheep were distributed'

Reading was Absalom's abiding joy; walking came close to it. Cold weather did not deter him and in January 1821 he walked to Prestwich and back after work for a meeting of the Club at Grime's house.

> **January 20th, 1821.** A pleasant evening, but on my part too much sarcasm. The walk thither was very pleasant. Prestwich bells were ringing just as we got to the further side of the moor and the sound recalled to my mind many recollections of days that are fled for ever. Our return by moonlight with a little frost crisping the grass and hardening the paths; the sheets of vapour giving the low ground the appearance of a sea.

Increased membership of the Club meant some reorganization.

> **January 27th, 1821.** We made the following resolutions. One: the object of this meeting is the improvement of the members in Science and Literature. Two: no papers on politics or religion shall be received by this meeting. Three: no member shall be allowed to disclose anything which passes in the meetings of this Club on pain of immediate expulsion.

Two weeks later Absalom set out for a walk with John Andrew. They had intended to go to Didsbury but by some fortunate mistake found themselves at Northenden, a village about eight miles distant on the Cheshire side of the Mersey, in those days called and spelt 'Northen'. They examined the old church of St Wilfred, with its Tatton and Egerton monuments, then walked round the churchyard where Absalom himself, his wife, his daughter and his son Edward were one day to lie.

> **February 11th, 1821.** The evening was beautifully fine. We heard the robins and throstles mingling their notes with those of the singers who were practising in the church. We went to the Tatton Arms, (the Boathouse).

Andrew ate a large quantity of bread and butter and cheese and sat before the fire, swallowing luncheon after luncheon, and talking <u>at intervals</u> to a very pretty servant girl, with a look of supreme satisfaction. I suppose we walked more than thirteen miles.

Absalom's spirits rose with the coming of spring.

March 16th, 1821. I was struck when I went to the warehouse with the soft and beautiful light of the sun, the dryness of the streets, the increased vivacity and playfulness of the children and the general air of alacrity which the fine weather appeared to produce. Sowed mignonette, parsley, lettuces and pansies and set nasturtiums.

He walked to Prestwich again to see Grime, who appeared in his nightcap nursing a toothache and was with difficulty persuaded to go to Manchester to have it pulled out.

Absalom himself was planning another visit to London. He wished particularly to see the frieze from the Parthenon that Lord Elgin had bought from the Turks and then sold to the nation. Joseph Makinson now lived permanently in Manchester and they decided to go together. Absalom thought Joseph a typical Makinson. His home was untidy, his crumpets dirty and his teacups always smeared. Yet he was fond of him.

At the end of April he got up at three o'clock in the morning, met Joseph and both of them left for London in the *Regulator* coach at a quarter to five. It was Good Friday.

April 27th, 1821. Joseph Makinson took an outside place. When we left Manchester my companions were two rather young women, sufficiently dull. At Stockport old F. the spinner got into the coach and he and I got into conversation. I found him as I expected, shrewd, confident, vain of his wealth, but not deficient in that sort of information which a man acquires by conversation and journeyings. In the pauses of conversation I noticed the country through which we were passing: the verdure and freshness of the trees and fields, the blossom of the fruit trees and the appearance of many common flowers make travelling very agreeable at this season of the year.

After Buxton the country grew more barren and cheerless.

Few trees, no hedges, a bare turf in the place of grass rising thickly, no <u>hedge</u> birds, no flowers, no cattle but some dirty ragged sheep and diminutive lambs and this cheerless prospect rendered dismal by thick heavy rain.

Things did not improve until they dropped down towards Dovedale and

Ashbourne, where the country once more became green, the birds sang and Absalom's spirits rose as they approached Derby and their dinner. He found it tedious and painful to sit in one position hour after hour and when the horses were changed or the hill steep, took the opportunity to get out and stretch his legs. He gazed out of the window with satisfaction at the neat, rich, cultivated Midlands.

> The fields of regular figures surrounded by tall thorn hedges kept with much care and usually mingled with thriving young trees; the herbage luxuriant, the pastures filled with fine cattle and fat sheep. The country is not dead level but gently undulating; fine seats frequent on the knolls shaded by well-grown trees and commanding extensive views; white spires and steeples rising above and contrasting with the trees and red tiled houses of the hamlets which are numerous. Such is Leicestershire. I have nowhere else seen such appearances of skilful and successful husbandry.

They had tea at Leicester and from then until daybreak he attempted to sleep. They reached London at ten o'clock next morning and went to their lodgings at the bottom of Friday Street near St Nicholas Coldharbour, a district Absalom had known as a child.

Leaving home released his energy like a spring. Despite the long and tedious journey and the snatched sleep, almost at once he set out sightseeing in the city, stopping on the way to attend a book auction where he bought some bargains to take home with him. In the evening they went to hear Madame Camporese sing in the 'Serious Opera of Tancred'. Walking to the Opera House they visited Dr Johnson's old home at Bolt Court. The Coffee House there had a bust of Johnson as its sign.

> **April 28th, 1821.** The Opera House is large and brilliant, illuminated by a huge chandelier pendant at the top of the house and pouring out streams of gas-light. The drops scene or curtain, representing a temple or palace filled with statues of heathen deities, is very well executed. The Orchestra was full. The boxes, after some time, were pretty well filled and the gallery much better than the nature of the entertainment would have led me to expect.

He was up in good spirits at seven next morning, which was Easter Day, determined to visit as many churches as he could.

He went first with Joseph to Whitehall Chapel. They had the bad luck to arrive just at the same time as the officers and men from the Regiment of Guards, so were kept standing outside until the military had paraded in. Above the soldiers' heads were flown flags and standards captured from various countries; the *Invincible* flag, taken in Egypt, near the chapel entrance; beneath the organ the Eagles from Waterloo flanked by two immense flags of crimson silk taken in Canada. The flamboyant absurdity of the Rubens ceiling delighted Absalom. The apotheosis of James I looked down so incongruously on the sober Communion Table and grave countenances of the Guards.

After Whitehall it was St Margaret's, Westminster, and then St George's, Hanover Square, which was so crowded that they could get standing room only in the gallery. On coming out they saw George IV's cousin, the Duke of Gloucester, and his wife.

> **April 29th, 1821.** The Duke, a handsome man but less so than fifteen years ago when he was in Manchester, had on a blue French coat, buff waistcoat and black silk handkerchief. The Duchess, a lusty woman, looking like a landlady, had a green figured sarsnet dress and a bonnet of straw with few ornaments.

She was a daughter of George III.

Without any apparent consciousness that their behaviour was in any way singular, they had dinner and then went on to St Paul's where they heard the organ and the choir, then to St Stephen's Walbrook, to find the clergyman there preaching to six people only. They hurried on to Salter's Hall, where they heard Mr Collier preach to a large congregation; a good sermon spoilt for Absalom by grammatical lapses. The day was nicely rounded by a visit to the chapel of the Magdalen Asylum, the refuge for prostitutes.

> Here the prayers were well read, a tolerably argumentative sermon on the Resurrection of Jesus was preached and some hymns were sung very well by the Magdalens. The preacher stated that about fifty young women are annually restored to their friends by this institution. Most of those who are recovered from vice are under twenty years of age!

Absalom had much of beauty and interest to cram into a single week. It was not his nature to allow the hours to slip through his fingers. He visited the Guildhall, St Paul's (where he caught a man in the act of writing his name on a monument), the Law Courts and the Custom House, and saw the Crown Jewels at the Tower of London. He wondered about their real value and imagined what fine and productive estates a mere fraction of them could purchase.

He paid a shilling for an inside seat in a coach to go to Hackney to see some of his mother's relations. It did not take long to leave the crowded streets behind and reach the country and the snug retreats in the midst of gardens he loved so much. But the warning signs were already there. Later in the day, wandering by his old haunts down Thames Street to Blackfriars Bridge and along St George's Road, he realized that he was on unfamiliar ground. He was walking on streets which were fields when he left London twenty years earlier.

He spent hours before the Elgin Marbles in the British Museum but was disappointed. They fell below the picture his imagination had formed of them. Perhaps it was his own ignorance of sculpture. He expected little from the House of Commons and was proved right. Orator Hunt was in Ilchester Gaol.

May 2nd, 1821. Arrived at the House of Commons and giving my half-crown to the Cerberus at the door, I was readily admitted. I stayed between two and three hours. I heard first a debate on the Petition of Mr Turner of Glasgow complaining of false imprisonment. Then some remarks on Ilchester Gaol and finally a debate on the Army Estimates which produced two divisions, at the second of which I quitted the House. I heard in the course of the evening Mr Bennet, Colonel Davis, Sir R. Wilson, Lord Palmerston, Lord A. Hamilton, Mr Hume, the Lord Advocate of Scotland, Mr Monteith, Alderman Wood etc. Not one of them could justly be called a good speaker. The Opposition had always the advantage in argument and Lord Palmerston was clearly convicted of making a false statement, to which he replied by four or five lines of Latin poetry not at all to the purpose. I left the House of Commons with a very contemptuous opinion of all those whom I had heard.

Only one day was left and he spent part of it visiting the new Roman Catholic chapel at Moorfields. Although he was cut off from any real knowledge of Catholicism, he remained curious about it and the previous autumn had again heard High Mass, this time celebrated in the new Catholic chapel at Granby Row in Manchester. The chapel at Moorfields, restrained on the outside, was glorious within. Its architect, John Newman, had assisted Sir Robert Smirke in drawing up the plans for the new Covent Garden theatre and his work there evidently influenced his design for Moorfields. The drama of our Redemption was enacted at the high altar before fluted pillars, behind which stretched a grand panorama of the crucifixion so painted and lit as to give the illusion of infinite space. The chapel was later destroyed, like the magnificent liturgy for which it was designed. Absalom and Joseph left London the next day at half-past two in the afternoon.

May 4th, 1821. About midnight, being asleep in the coach, it stopped and I was awakened by Joseph Makinson who was on the outside, that I might hear the nightingale. It was one of the most beautiful nights I ever beheld. When the coach had stopped no sound was heard but the note of the nightingale breaking with sweet but powerful melody on the stillness of the night.

On this night Napoleon died at St Helena and in the north of England the presses were making up the very first number of the *Manchester Guardian.*

There was a good deal of opposition in Manchester to any celebration to mark the Coronation of George IV. His message of thanks to those who had dispersed the crowd at Peterloo had not been forgotten. Some went so far as to suggest that in the event of a procession the Manchester Yeomanry should ride in it with their heads turned to their horses' tails. This opinion did not prevail. On the evening of 18 July, Absalom walked to the Market Cross at Salford to watch an ox and a sheep being roasted whole. On the day itself, the firing of cannon and ringing of bells began at dawn.

July 19th, 1821. At half-past seven in the morning a procession was formed of the Sunday School children amounting to twenty-four thousand. In the forenoon the officers of the town, the clergy, military and different trades formed another procession. Several bands of music, a great number of flags and the insignia and the implements, in some cases the productions, of the different trades made this procession, though fatiguing enough to the actors, very pleasing to the spectators. The whole procession was an hour and twenty minutes in passing the place where I stood with Elizabeth and the children.

His wife must have been exhausted. Their daughter was only four, Edward not yet two and she herself six months pregnant. All was orderly and good-humoured then, but the evening presented a very different scene.

Four hundred and one barrels of ale, more than twenty oxen and sixty sheep with a proportionate quantity of bread were distributed, not with the greatest order, to the people. Drunkenness and quarrelling ensued. Men, women and children lay dead drunk in the streets and many of those who could still use their limbs were fighting in the most brutal manner. Several accidents occurred and three persons were killed and fourteen taken badly hurt to the infirmary.

The *Manchester Guardian* came out with a forthright denunciation of the degrading scenes. It blamed much of them on the improvident, dissolute and filthy Irish, whose extensive immigration had inflicted a deadly blow on the health and comfort of the working classes in Manchester.

Dislike of the Irish is a disturbing and constant feature of the time. Many in Manchester thought of them in much the same way as numbers of Western Europeans today think of immigrant workers from Africa, India or the Near East. Manchester was swamped by the Irish. It was cheaper for them to reach the north-west of England than it was to get to London and there were more opportunities for employment.

They came from the lowest strata of society and often from homes which in England would be thought scarcely fit for pigs. The peasant Patrick Prunty, who changed his name to Brontë, came from just such a home into the comparative affluence of Haworth Parsonage, but that route could be taken by few only. The Irish were freely abused both in speech and in print. Newspapers were not then fettered by any race-relations legislation nor inhibited by those restraints that a later society, for the most part, feels appropriate in dealing with the problem.

For some people trade had taken a turn for the better. Absalom felt encouraged and, despite the urgent exhortations he gave himself not to spend a penny more than necessary, he employed an artist called Minasi to draw pencil portraits of himself, his wife and his mother. Underneath his own picture he wrote in a very small hand '*pas à pas òu va bien loin*'.

Almost at once he became prey to acute fear and uncertainty, triggered off by his wife who imprudently had lent Andrew some money. Andrew visited them less frequently now. There had been some unpleasantness at the Club that summer between him and Joseph Makinson which led to his resignation. Absalom was sorry. Andrew was a lively, cheerful man whose income was too small for the support of his family. The Club provided relaxation at little expense. Absalom feared he would be tempted now to spend too much on drink. His own wife, however, must learn not to lend money to people just because they asked for it. His fears too were increased by a chance conversation he had had with a once-prosperous cotton merchant who confessed that things had gone so badly with him that he could now hardly get a living. Andrew came round at night.

September 23rd, 1821. It was about his affairs. He is in difficulties. How many are while I am prosperous. I determine to be, if possible, more industrious than ever. To spend nothing, <u>no, not a farthing</u>, unnecessarily. To be, in the greatest degree of which I am capable, <u>cautious</u> whom I trust.

This caution took the form of property investment.

Manchester and Salford were growing at a tremendous rate. The population of both towns was a little over 84,000 when Absalom first arrived. It now reached over 130,000. Local government was exercised by the Improvement Commissioners who had rudimentary powers to regulate speculative builders, but these powers were inadequate to meet the challenge of a greatly increased population working in intensively industrial conditions.

In the country it was different. Absalom did not intend to build slums. He was interested in residential development farther out. Another loop of the River Irwell, which separated Manchester from Salford, divided Salford from Broughton. Broughton was a separate township, a country place where only 900 people lived in an area the size of Manchester. There it was real country, scattered cottages and farmsteads, grazing cattle, meadows, ponds, streams and hawthorn hedges. If it occurred to Absalom that he was destroying the very thing he loved, tearing up the ground for the sake of people he was always trying to avoid, he does not say so. Modest suburban development was necessary to house the Manchester middle class. He intended to make a decent profit out of social need.

Country landlords were powerful and could be particular about the disposal of their property. Most of the land at Broughton was owned by the Clowes family of Broughton Old Hall. Mr John Clowes strictly controlled the sale of land within his estates, allowing no small properties to be built, only superior residences with gardens, and in places of his own choosing. Mr Clowes was a clergyman, a Fellow of the Collegiate Church in Manchester, and liked to preach wearing pale, lavender-coloured gloves. He reserved to himself the ground rents after sale, and in consequence became not merely very rich, but as a tribute to his calling, benefited the community at the same time.

The land Absalom had his eye on was close to Broughton Lane, towards the land of Lord Ducie at Strangeways and the village of Cheetham Hill. The plot grew potatoes and was known as Frog Place. Early in September he bought 'one thousand, two hundred and ninety-six yards at twopence a yard'. Grime came in on the deal and bought the same amount. The surveyors measured it and a square of forty yards was agreed on. The same afternoon, Grime and Absalom watched the foot of his wife's brother or cousin, John Makinson, being cut off above the ankle. That, or more probably the calculation of the number of bricks he would need, set Absalom off into another spasm of doubt and fear.

He got up early in the morning and arriving at Frog Place at seven found to his dismay that Lord Ducie's steward from the Strangeway's Estate had put a locked gate across the road and the men employed to dig up the potatoes were unable to get in. Eventually the gate was removed and an agreement made between Lord Ducie and Mr Clowes's tenants about the upkeep of the road.

Absalom decided to build three terraced houses on his plot, and when they were completed to live in one of them himself. He employed no architect or contractor. He agreed with the builder on the plans and himself ordered 1,200 stock bricks. Everything happened very quickly. Hardly had the potatoes been dug up before a saw-pit was made, the timber delivered and the cellars excavated. Absalom's mother put her money into the enterprise and Joseph decided that he too wanted to have a share. The name Frog Place was ugly. Absalom called it Woodlands instead and when in early October his wife gave birth to their second son he was called John Woodlands Watkin.

It was all proving too much for Absalom. He could not be at the warehouse and Woodlands Terrace at the same time. The bricklayers were not sufficiently active and then said they would not come again unless the road were mended. No sooner had this been attended to than the stonemason said he would not work either because he had no mortar; a pile of sand was stolen, the kitchen walls were badly built, there was a delay in getting sufficient bricks. Absalom was overwhelmed with anxiety, particularly at night. The day they built the fronts of the houses the baby was fretful in the evening and Absalom's wife asked him to nurse the child on his lap. This he did while Joseph read aloud passages from *The Canterbury Tales*. On the last day of November the roofs were put on, but the following night Absalom was awoken between two and three in the morning by the wind.

December 1st, 1821. The house shook, the wind roared and the bricks from our neighbour's chimney came rolling over our roof to the ground. I

lay in bed and thought of our buildings which I hardly expected to stand
against such a hurricane. When it was fully light however I could see them
from my window, still standing.

A gardener he wished to employ estimated £11 for putting the garden of one
house in order for planting. This was excessive, and Absalom employed another
who asked for less. Hardly had the second man been employed than his wife came
round to Ravald Street and told Absalom that her husband had been apprehended
for assaulting the bailiffs sent to make a distress for the Poor Law. On Christmas
Eve 1821, Absalom succeeded in getting the man out of prison but at a cost to his
nerves. He found his bed damp at night and nothing caused him more anxiety. He
rose unwell on Christmas Day, grieved and angry at the 'unkind negligence' of his
wife and half-fearful spent the evening on his accounts.

Spring 1822 brought with it an increase of building activity with further
vexations, intensified by a dream his wife had of falling from a great height. She
and his mother agreed that this meant Absalom would lose his money. The
plasterers complained about the bricklayers and the bricklayers complained about
the plasterers, Lord Ducie closed the road again and Absalom had toothache. The
houses were too fine for him. It would be imprudent for them to live there. His
business failure might be repeated. He would do better to let them all and profit
from the rents. Yet he greatly enjoyed planting out the gardens, designing their
shape, deciding where the flowerbeds were to be and where the orchard, ordering
the trees and imagining them as they would be in five or six years' time.

They moved to Broughton at the end of April. Absalom had written three
papers for the Club; he had attended to his cotton business; he had supervised
carpenters, bricklayers, plasterers, painters, gardeners and nurserymen; he had
moved with two adults, three small children and all his possessions from a house he
had lived in for many years. That was a wrench and the whole thing had been a
strain. On his thirty-fifth birthday he looked back upon the past year as almost the
unhappiest he had ever experienced.

> **June 27th, 1822.** I have increased instead of lessening my expenses. I must
> continue to expend more than I did a year ago. More money ought to be
> gained, yet business, from the great competition, is less productive.

If he no longer wrote his wife poems, he still loved her and still hoped for
domestic tranquillity, and as he walked with her and the children along the shady
lanes of Broughton that August, he felt that he could yet be happy.

Absalom was on the committee of the Commercial Clerk's Society, a
benevolent institution founded in 1802 to help tradesmen and clerks who had
fallen on bad times. The entrance fee was high, from three to five guineas
according to age, and the annual subscription was one guinea. From this and
voluntary contributions, provision was made for sickness, destitution and old age,

as well as for wives and children. Once a year the Society held a fund-raising dinner to which Absalom had been invited. It was the first public dinner he had ever attended.

October 4th, 1822. We had a great variety of meats, but when so large a number dine together it is impossible to be so comfortable as with a few friends. I observed some persons who ate prodigiously. After dinner Brierley, the borough-reeve, gave the toasts. The first was King George IV. It was drunk in a bumper standing and with what is termed 'four times four', that is to say, as soon as all present have emptied their glasses the president cries 'Hip-hip-hip-Hurra!' in unison, sixteen times, waving at the same time the empty glasses round their heads. There was something so ridiculous in seeing about a hundred and twenty men, several advanced in life, shouting like children, that I could not refrain from laughter. After the shouting 'God Save the King' was sung, the company still standing and joining in the chorus. I was much struck with the effect which was gradually produced upon the company by the wine. When we sat down to dinner there were many grave and moody countenances, but after the wine had been drunk for some time, every face appeared gay and there was no doubt almost everyone felt pleased. The toasts were delivered with very little intermission and very early in the evening a most grossly obscene one was given by the chairman and received with applause!! Some obscene songs were volunteered and received with gross satisfaction! After about an hour and a half the bad effects of drinking and shouting began to appear. More noise, less order and louder shouts. At this dinner for the first time in my life I tasted a piece of pineapple. It is a delicious fruit having a rich perfumed taste and almost appearing to melt in the mouth from its extreme juiciness. I left about eleven o'clock having drunk more wine than I ought to have done though I was by no means intoxicated. My head ached violently all night.

He had not really enjoyed himself. He was rather shocked at what he had witnessed; a certain priggishness struggled with other elements in his character. For him the most important thing was to lead a regular life, free from anxiety.

He picked blackberries with the children, his wife began to read Gibbon's *Decline and Fall* aloud in the evening, and he wrote papers on Metaphysics and the Vital Principle of Plants for the Club. Gibbon had not got very far nor was the blackberry pie long digested before his mother had a dream which both she and his wife yet again interpreted as meaning heavy financial loss. That was the second time. He did not believe in the truth of dreams. However, he would write the fact down and so put the matter to the proof.

CHAPTER SEVEN

'The extreme anxiety of having so much property in building'

Absalom's relations with his cousin Thomas Watkin had never been very close. It is probable that, from the first, Thomas resented Absalom's arrival as a boy to share his home in Whit Lane. He may well have resented also his father's respect for his nephew's business acumen and the substantial legacy Absalom received upon his death. Thomas had not been particularly successful in business. Perhaps he inherited the family temperament without its ability. Perhaps he was unlucky; it may be that his health was delicate. Tuberculosis was a common scourge of the time, but the number of those in the family who died of it seems to have been above average.

Occasionally Thomas and his wife Mary came to dinner with Absalom. In 1822 Absalom had taken them both to see his new houses and Thomas knew that he was looking for fruitful areas for investment. In February 1823 Thomas dined at Woodlands Terrace and it was probably then that he proposed a business deal. Thomas's father owned land not only in Audlem, near Nantwich, but possessed also a small cottage in the village of Bonsall in Derbyshire. Thomas suggested that he should sell Absalom his life interest in the cottage and that when the summer came they should go together to Derbyshire so that Absalom could have a look at it.

That was satisfactory. Much more deeply so was Absalom's election as a member of the Literary and Philosophical Society of Manchester. Apart from the Royal Society, the Literary and Philosophical was the oldest of its type in the country. It had held its first meeting in 1781 in a room adjoining Cross Street chapel. In 1804 it moved to a beautiful house in George Street, not far from Piccadilly. It was fairly exclusive and at the time of Absalom's election the membership was confined to sixty people. He attended his first meeting and was disappointed. Besides, his wife's mother had just died and the winter cold and household gloom made him irritable.

February 9th, 1823. Found at dinner time that we had no beer in the house but such as was too thick or too new to be drunk. And this too with such ample means of having everything comfortable! Mr and Mrs Hedley called. It is the first time I have seen the lady. She talked of <u>screwing</u> a dog if it should attempt to bite her and appears to be a woman of little education and perhaps <u>shrewish</u>.

She was not the only one.

March 1st, 1823. Talking with Elizabeth at night of the extreme anxiety of having so much of my property in building – she told me that 'I could sell the present house and build a row of cottages with the money and live in one of them myself!'

Absalom became so dejected that he was driven to peruse some passages of Arnold *On Insanity*, and the Sunday reading of Blair's sermon *The Duties of Middle Age* did nothing to regulate his spirits. However he had not forgotten Northenden, and one spring afternoon went there again with Grime and Andrew, reading some of Akenside's poems as he walked. They all had tea at the Boathouse, but the pretty servant girl was no longer there. On inquiry they learnt that she had married a carter at the mill. Grime and Andrew expressed their regret in their usual bad French, and Absalom felt sad to think that such a pretty creature had not done better for herself. After tea they walked to Didsbury.

March 23rd, 1823. From Didsbury we came by the high road to Manchester. The evening was beautifully fine: the robins and throstles were singing as if in emulation of each other. The moon when we left Didsbury was just rising and calm and soothing.

In April he got himself sworn in at the New Bailey as a special constable for Broughton and performed his first duty on Kersal Moor one morning from seven o'clock until noon. But he felt tired out. His hand hurt him and he consulted a Manchester surgeon who told him the trouble was due to the bad state of his digestive organs. The bad state of his mind would have been a truer diagnosis. Absalom wished to rise in the world, he thirsted for recognition, to be accepted as a man of parts in politics, literature and business, but the pressures which necessarily accompanied the execution of his schemes were too much for his highly nervous temperament. When he said he needed peace and tranquillity and was happiest working alone in his garden, he spoke the truth. But that could hardly lead to worldly success.

The Whitsun holiday spent at home with the family was a disaster and Absalom felt very low at first when he started out with Thomas Watkin and William Makinson in the *Lord Nelson* coach to Derbyshire. He intended to examine his newly acquired cottage at Bonsal. Away from home he relaxed gradually and his energy came surging back. He had not visited Derbyshire for six years, not since his expedition with Grime and Andrew just before his daughter was born. They got out of the coach at Buxton.

May 22nd, 1823. We walked towards Bakewell. The country varied, in some places beautiful and romantic, and others extremely rude and bleak. We got wet through after walking about five miles and were glad to turn in at a paltry ale house near Toddington. We got tea at Ashford-on-the-Waters and went on through Bakewell to Haddon. We saw the interior of this venerable mansion, being attended by the same elderly woman in the very same gown and gloves, as when I was here with Grime and Andrew in 1817.

Next day they had a long steep walk through Darley to Bonsal, where Absalom took possession of Thomas's cottage. It was let to a Mr Wigley for £6 a year. They walked from Bonsall to Matlock Bath because Absalom was determined to see again the vast caverns beneath the Heights of Abraham. After tea they felt tired and travelled by chaise to Edensor near Chatsworth, where they intended to spend the night. A bottle of madeira and an excellent supper of trout and asparagus greatly cheered them up, but Absalom's high spirits were soon dashed. Picking up a local paper before he went to bed, he happened to read an account of the death of Miss Hardy, the girl they had met on Thorpe Cloud in 1817.

May 23rd, 1823. It struck me as being not a little singular that when I was in Derbyshire with Grime and Andrew we should have met with Mr Hardy and his daughter and that now in revisiting the county, I should unexpectedly meet with an account of her death. Her youth and vivacity have been frequently recalled to my mind since I first saw her and Andrew has frequently been joked on the subject of his unskilful gallantry when descending from Thorp Cloud in her company.

Early in June the first bricks for yet another house at Broughton were laid by his daughter and Edward. The further venture worried him, but he found solace and deep contentment working in his garden, lovingly listing each plant in flower.

June 11th, 1823. Turk cap lily, pansies, rhododendron, flag iris, columbines, peony, red everlasting, wallflower (fading), single white rocket, heath flower, stone-crop, strawberry, sea-pink, London Pride, orchis, spindle-tree, laburnum, yellow jasmine, monthly rose mullein, white stock, perennial lupin, Siberian iris.

He enjoyed taking little Edward for walks through the fields, and in the evening helping the children to colour one of the prints in their story book. He thought how foolish it was to have possessions which vexed more than they contributed to comfort. He was made for tranquillity but lacked patience. His wife refused to sing when he asked her but did so readily enough at her brother's house. She gave him badly baked bread and ale that tasted as bitter as quinine; the plates and teacups were dirty, all prepared 'à la mode de Makinson'.

He was plagued by that family. In August William took him aside after the meeting of the club and had the audacity to insinuate that Absalom had cheated him by selling him a share in the new building development for more, not less, than its real worth. 'Such has almost always been the reward which I have received for endeavouring to oblige or serve the relations of my wife.' Worse was to come.

August 16th, 1823. This evening, while I was at the meeting, between eight and nine o'clock, <u>my wife</u> was met near the market place partially disguised in a grey cloak which she has not worn for some time. All the neighbourhood of the market place is, at that time of the night, thronged with the lowest and vilest of people, with drunkards, prostitutes and thieves. Yet at such a time did she choose to quit her home and family and walk nearly a mile and a half in the wet, and at night, and alone, to be seen in a situation from which a decent woman would shrink with abhorrence. The alleged occasion of this journey was her wanting some hops and some figs, either of which could have been procured quite as well on Monday!

After that little Edward was unwell.

August 20th, 1823. His <u>mother</u> told me this morning that, <u>on Saturday last</u>, he had swallowed a small brass nut, belonging to a spring-latch. This occurrence she has kept secret from me until now.

The child recovered, and on Sunday Elizabeth read aloud Paley's sermon *Our Knowledge of One Another in a Future State*. That was the last thing Absalom wanted. They were both incapable of understanding each other in this one. Absalom had married a pretty girl, by no means uneducated or a fool, but not one whose interests were his. She was by temperament careless, slapdash, generous, affectionate and not very truthful. His horizons were immeasurably wider because the intelligence and imagination that had prompted his extensive reading had made them so.

It would be cruelly unfair to see Elizabeth through her husband's eyes alone. She was still young and must have spent most of her married life in domestic drudgery. It seems that Absalom employed only one servant girl. He came home every day at noon for a meal and expected another in the evening. Elizabeth had to look after him together with three small children. Before long she would have another child and her mother-in-law would become bedridden. She had no running hot water, no labour-saving devices, nor convenience food. The housewife was expected to brew her own beer and bake her own bread. Before the invention of synthetic fibres, washing, drying, ironing and mending the family's voluminous and elaborate clothes together with the household linen, was a very laborious task indeed. As recorded in his diary, Absalom's reactions were sometimes intemperate to the point of hysteria. Elizabeth could just about manage her home; what she could not manage was a deeply frustrated man in the prime of life.

Very little was needed to alter Absalom's mood suddenly and completely. In the autumn, after the plasterers had begun to decorate the cornices of his new house, he made arrangements to go to Haslingden, near Accrington, to visit some friends of his called Hawarth, who were in business there. His wife walked with him to the coach intending to return home but when it arrived, on impulse leapt inside and decided to go with him. Presumably she sent a message back to his mother.

They reached Haslingden and stayed at the Bull's Head, the next morning out of curiosity attending a sale of land there. The sale was conducted in a shockingly disorderly manner; during the transaction the company drank as many as thirty-three large bowls of punch. Unfortunately the beds were damp and Absalom got up with a headache. The Hawarth's weaving shed turned out to be a model of industry.

September 26th, 1823. Mr T. Hawarth told us that a girl of sixteen years old in his employ, once wove in one week, ten of 4/4 stout cloth, each piece being thirty yards long. She worked from six in the morning till nine at night. This is ninety hours a week and if we deduct four hours and a quarter for meals, will average three and a half yards of cloth woven every hour.

They had now been joined by Joseph Makinson and together set out to walk to Masbury.

We dined with Mr Barnes of Hare Clough. We had some excellent roasted pork, some damson tarts and some of the best milk I ever tasted. We were all hungry, ate heartily and talked gaily. We then went to see Richard Bothwell who has a farm near Hare Clough. He received us with a hearty welcome, brought out basin full after basin full of rum and milk, till we one and all declared that we could drink no more. As we passed Barnes's he came out; another bowl of rum and milk was produced which to make it more palatable was enriched with spices. We drank it and commenced our return in high spirits and with much gaiety. Thus passed one of the most cheerful days of my life.

A few weeks later Absalom was woken in the early hours of the morning by two of his warehouse men.

October 13th, 1823. They came to inform me that some person had attempted to break open the warehouse's door and had succeeded so far as to get off the padlock. I went with Clough to the warehouse and found the lock indeed off and a little man who was in liquor had been found lying on the cellar steps, in custody of the watchman. But the man turned out to be one of the singers at St Stephen's church, who had been rather merry with a friend and had nothing on him but a music book and a musical pitch fork. It seemed most probable that the lock had snapped in consequence of the little fellow falling violently against it, so after we had ascertained that nothing had been stolen, he was suffered to depart.

Drink was always a problem. The workmen at Absalom's house had recently taken so much that they failed to turn up at all for two days. That was all the more worrying since Absalom had just sold his mother's investment house for £500 and the fixtures for £10.

In December their new house was almost ready but Absalom needed the Revd John Clowes's consent to excavate more gravel to make up the road. He went early one morning to Broughton Old Hall with Joseph to call upon him. Mr Clowes was not yet up so they walked round the garden and into the hothouses. Clowes had a magnificent collection of orchids, one day to find a home at Kew, but what Absalom noticed was a geranium nine or ten feet high and in full flower. They admired the lake and were turning towards the house when its owner emerged.

December 6th, 1823. He asked us to go into the house. We did so and he led us through a small hall into his breakfast parlour. It is a low room wainscoted with oak rubbed very bright and having two windows which look into the garden. The carpet was rich and the whole room kept with extreme neatness. We endeavoured to prevail on Mr Clowes to let us have the gravel for the remainder of the road but did not succeed and as his breakfast was on the table and his egg getting cold, a circumstance which he intimated to us by lifting it once or twice, we left him after a short conversation.

As the day for their second move in under two years approached, nerves got more and more on edge.

December 17th, 1823. I found at night that the cistern had been suffered to overflow into the necessary, not withstanding my repeated cautions to Elizabeth on the subject. It is in this way that almost everything to which I wish her to attend is neglected. In the midst of extreme exertion on my part, I find in my wife only careless, sluttish, imprudent conduct.

They moved just before Christmas. It took them two days and on the first night Elizabeth so bungled matters that they were all forced to sleep on the floor. Absalom's library was put in place at last and although they had visitors on

Christmas Day, after they had gone Absalom had a happy time sitting alone reading *Evelina*. Probably Elizabeth had never sat down at all. Absalom did not see the matter in that light. Against his natural instincts he worked himself to the bone attending to his cotton business and his houses. He was doing his duty; it was up to his wife to do hers.

Instead of that she was 'a shuffling liar', for ever canting about religion while guilty of gross neglect and mismanagement. The children's toenails were so long that they were growing into the flesh, their clothes had holes in them and, to add to his troubles, William Makinson's wife came round one evening and tearfully asked him to lend her husband money so that they could invest further in the Broughton property boom. It was awkward, but he was not in a position to diminish his capital. William himself then arrived and after protesting that it was a matter of no consequence, pressed Absalom for a loan of £200. His wife, he told him, cried when she talked about it, but he had said to her: 'Never mind lass, we shall manage some way, I'll warrant thee.' Absalom agreed to help him.

Next day he learnt how to get really rich and did not like it. He had been for a walk over Kersal Moor with Grime and in returning stopped at Mangnall's bleach works. Mr Mangnall was frank about his business methods. Piecework meant profit. A 'bowk' was the vessel used for bleaching or dyeing.

March 28th, 1824. He told us that he had now all his work done by piece and that in consequence he got twice as much work done in the same time and with the same number of hands as he did at his commencement. He told us that his men worked night and day. That his bowker would begin at two in the morning and work till ten at night, in which time he would bowk two bowkings, for which he was paid five shillings and fourpence. The next day the same man would bowk one bowking, beginning at two in the morning and giving over about eleven in the forenoon and for this he would receive two shillings and eightpence. His whole weekly wages therefore would be twenty-four shillings. This Mr Mangnall called by <u>comparison</u> extravagant wages. The work is laborious, so that the sweat runs down the man's face while he is employed in it and he [Mangnall] is all the time surrounded by them. Mr Mangnall observed that his men worked harder than the West Indian slaves, 'but then,' said he, 'it is free labour'.

Free labour – 24s. for an eighty-one hour week in appalling conditions and Mr Brougham, now in Manchester acting on behalf of the Waterworks Company, was said to have been retained for a fee of 250 guineas.

Trade continued to worsen. The boom of the last three years was plainly over.

April 17th, 1824. I conclude from what I hear and experience that business is really bad and that increasingly great production of cloth is gradually filling the market and slowly ruining the manufacturers. I expect bad times.

But in Absalom's garden the leaves of the pear tree were unfolding and the daffodils and primroses, the periwinkles and the dog-toothed violets were out. The apples, cherries and plums would soon follow. All that beauty and he was imprisoned in his warehouse. Why did he not retire now? He wrote his thoughts down on a separate piece of paper.

The building property which is in the possession of myself and my mother and which has cost me more than £1,000, will produce after making a liberal allowance for repairs and losses, a clear annual income of £50. By expending £1,000 in cottages I may expect to receive a further annual income of £100.

After doing this I have probably as much more money as would be sufficient to build a comfortable house for myself. Such a disposal of my property would therefore put me in possession of an income of £150 a year [about £7,500 in 1990 values] and a house subject to ground rent only.

By a calculation I have made, I believe that I and my family could live comfortably on an income of £150 a year. I do not mean that I could spend as much money as I do now in books and superfluities, but that everything necessary to my comfort and theirs might be obtained with that income.

I should be master of my time – I could employ five or six hours a day in study and the remainder in gardening or active and laborious exertion. My health would, I believe, greatly improve, my spirits and temper would be amended and I should live more to my own satisfaction as an accountable being and I should not despair of producing, in twenty years, if my life were continued, a work which would reflect no discredit upon its author and might add something to his property.

He would be able to attend personally and constantly to the education of his children, prepare them to act with propriety and principle, so that a healthy and happy youth could be followed by a mature age of honourable exertion.

But why quit business at all? Why leave a trade in which my success (considered in relation to the means) has been extraordinary? And in which it is probable I may, upon the whole, continue to do well and may finally leave to my children the means of a respectable subsistence, with the advantage of an established business?

He could not resolve the matter and wasted an afternoon watching from his bedroom window the ascent of Mr Saddler's balloon. It was released two-and-a-half hours late but at last they got a good view of it and saw it rise with steady grandeur until it was lost in the clouds.

Absalom's birthday was a Sunday, so he had to spend it at home. It served as a focus for his discontent.

June 27th, 1824. I am today thirty-seven years old. The year which I have completed has been singularly unhappy. I have suffered from ill health, great nervous dejection, the pressure of harassing business and the increasing difficulties of the times. At home I have no support or sympathy but cant, negligence and folly.

John kept them all awake crying at night, the sugar Elizabeth put out with his coffee was so dirty that he refused to touch it and when he tried to remonstrate with her all she did was to burst into tears and leave the room. Absalom retired to a quiet corner with Arnold's *On Insanity*.

Autumn was early. It comes as a recurrent shock to realize that Broughton was still in the country.

September 1st, 1824. Already the autumn tints begin to appear on the leaves. This season of the year in fine weather is very beautiful. The deep blue skies, the clear atmosphere, the full foliage and changing colour of the trees, the gay tints of the autumnal flowers, the cheerful brown of the corn fields, the song of the robins and the verdure of the meadows and pasture all combine to soothe the mind and infuse pleasurable ideas.

A few weeks later he attended a meeting of the select vestry of the townships of Broughton and Kersal. The proceedings distressed him. The vestry raised money for the poor in the form of a rate and had the power to disburse it.

September 17th, 1824. The case of a Mrs Dobson was mentioned at the meeting. She is seventy-four and was formerly housekeeper to Mr Cape. She cannot sew or do anything towards getting a living. She has an allowance of three shillings a week from the town and pays one shilling and threepence or one shilling and sixpence a week for her lodging! She has repeatedly applied for some additional relief and sixpence a week more was now granted. Mr Burge observed that her present situation was best for her, as it would humble her, she having been a very proud woman! It may be so – but God preserve me from being poor.

He must be careful. There could be no further talk with William Makinson about spending a year in France or Italy. He must carry on for the sake of the children. In fact, he was rather perplexed about them. *Robinson Crusoe* had been read aloud to them in the evening but its effects were unexpected – they now spoke about killing savages as a matter of course.

They had moved again and found the new house astonishingly damp. The walls of the parlour, the bedroom and the back lobby were quite wet and the furniture covered with moisture.

On Christmas Day Absalom had a dispute with William Makinson, who insisted that women's minds were in every way equal to those of men. On 1 January 1825 they walked to Northenden together to visit Joseph Johnson, now living there.

Johnson's attempts to distance himself from responsibility for what had happened at Peterloo and to minimize his links with the local radicals had been unsuccessful. He had been sentenced to a year's imprisonment together with other Manchester reformers, including the weaver Samuel Bamford. Bamford's account of their experience vividly brings home to us the strange mixture of humanity and barbarity which characterized the course of justice then.

Earlier, suspected of treason, Bamford had held a very courteous conversation with Lord Sidmouth and the rest of the Cabinet. The population was small, and proceedings amateur compared with the impersonal regulations of our own time. There were no 'Black Marias' or police stations in our sense of the term. The prisoners, although in irons, travelled in ordinary coaches and ate and drank merrily enough together with the rest of the company when they stayed at inns *en route*. Johnson and Bamford served their sentence at Lincoln Castle and both were allowed to have their wives to stay with them, although Johnson felt bitter because after his wife returned home he was refused permission to visit her on her deathbed.

Hunt blamed the severity of his own prison sentence after Peterloo on the fact that Johnson had invited the atheist and republican Richard Carlile on to the platform with them. He also accused Johnson of breach of faith because he had handed over some of his private letters to the government. In his turn, Johnson denounced Hunt and defended his own conduct both at Peterloo and at his trial. Absalom was not sympathetic; he did not care for the political opinions of either man.

At dinner his wife served him with melted butter the colour of brown ochre then expected him to eat an ill-dressed, filthy apple pudding sprinkled with brown sugar full of black lumps for which he had paid 18d. a pound. But despite the pudding, the neglect, the untidiness and the cant, that winter he got her with child for the last time.

CHAPTER EIGHT

'What can be stable with these enormous towns?'

Grime was getting on in the world. He held an important position in the New Quay Company and, now a widower with two daughters, returned that spring to live in Manchester.

The Mersey had always been navigable as far as Warrington and in the middle of the eighteenth century an attempt was made to give Manchester direct access to the sea by means of weirs and locks. This was successful, but the greatly increased trade between Manchester and Liverpool demanded better navigation of the Irwell. In 1823, therefore, another company was formed, with Grime as its agent. He came back to Manchester in a confident, bragging mood, declaring to Absalom that *'nemo me impune lacessit'* ('no one attacks me with impunity') was his present maxim. Such boasts were dangerous. The market was dismally flat.

One evening Thomas Watkin's son, John, came round to Woodlands Terrace.

May 13th, 1825. He is about seventeen years old and is much what I was at the same age. He does not much like business and is writing a tragedy, the action of which comprises three years and of which one scene is in England, another at Rome and a third in Venice. He asked my advice about his studies and I recommended him to apply to history, geography and English composition and to take pains to acquire a good <u>plain</u> English style. Finally I exhorted him to mind his business and keep a diary.

Absalom's own epic on King Alfred had never been written. It had dissolved like most of his dreams, destroyed by the warehouse and a wife who left mouldy hops in the sieve.

June 15th, 1825. Sold only four pieces in all the day. I have been in business eighteen years and never since I begun, have I sold so few pieces on Tuesday and Wednesday as yesterday and today. Going into the cellar when I came home at night, I found the candle-box which I had some time ago very particularly directed to remove, still lying spoiling in the cellar. Spent three hours watering the garden.

His garden was his joy and his solace. Sometimes he locked its door so that he could work there alone, at others he got the children to help him.

June 10th, 1825. Gardened from a quarter before three in the afternoon till near seven o'clock. It was very hot and I kept close to my work, my little Edward helping me manfully. I was tired, perspired much, but felt better for the exertion and am convinced that a course of such exertion in the open air would do me a great deal of good.

Not long afterwards their third son was born and they called him Alfred. Absalom was thankful to get away for his autumn break with Joseph Makinson and very glad that they chose to visit Rostherne, a small village between Altrincham and Knutsford which has a beautiful lake or mere close by the church. They walked there – Absalom, Joseph and Joseph's son Thomas – and as the light faded stood in the churchyard looking at the mere by dull moonlight. From the village came the sound of handbells ringing. Next day they returned to the church and looked at the monuments. Absalom was much struck by one to the Egerton family. They walked most of the way home.

At the end of November, the very day after they had been together to see the Chinese Jugglers, who had come to Manchester with their act, his wife began to feel unwell. She fell down in a faint and Dr Agnew was called in. Her condition worsened. Absalom's diary entries were brief.

November 26th–December 17th, 1825. Elizabeth worse. Erysipelas in the face and much fever. Remained all night with Elizabeth. Elizabeth worse. Up most of the night. Felt a fear of the result and felt the value of my wife to the family. Elizabeth worse, delirious. Attended to her very carefully. Elizabeth worse, not expected to recover. Very unhappy. Up most of the night. Occupied with Elizabeth. She is very weak tonight but pulses are lower. Still occupied with Elizabeth. Elizabeth getting a little better. Elizabeth improving, assiduous at the warehouse. Elizabeth rather worse this evening. Elizabeth gets very slowly better.

Erysipelas is a contagious disease popularly known as St Anthony's fire. Elizabeth was to remain subject to a milder form of it until the end of her life. The market was wretched. There was 'no money, no confidence, nothing but sacrifices and stoppages'.

January 4th, 1826. Rose late from having been kept up very late and been much affected by the discovery of my base wife's neglect of her accounts. She cannot tell what has become of the money which is deficient. Quite unfit for business. Thomas Crewdson and Company, the bankers, stopped payment.

There are other considerable failures and such difficulty and distrust in business as I never before witnessed.

As banks failed and credit became harder to obtain, some of his wife's family began to feel the pinch. It is difficult to disentangle exact relationships and to know the occupations of all the Manchester Makinsons at this time. Elizabeth's brother Joseph was a commission agent, her brother William was also in business but would soon become a schoolmaster like his father. There were at least two John Makinsons. One was a thriving attorney in Market Street, the other a classics teacher.

February 21st, 1826. It is one of the worst markets, perhaps the very worst market, I have ever experienced. Nothing can be sold but to great loss and little at any price.

All round was distress and embarrassment. Early in March Joseph Makinson called.

March 1st, 1826. He told me that he had one of his bills returned, that it was in the hands of an attorney, that he should be arrested if it were not taken up, that he could not raise the money, that Brooks the banker had refused to help him for some time, but had at length said, 'If Mr Watkin will endorse the bill I will help you.' I did it for him, but God keep me from ever having to solicit a similar favour from anyone.

If Absalom had seen little of Thomas Watkin and his family over the years, he had seen even less of his aunt, the widow of Thomas's father, Absalom's Uncle John. She had gone back to Audlem with her husband when he had retired from the cotton business and after his death had married again, which most probably accounted for the lack of communication between them. Her second husband was a local farmer called Mountford, who had rather too quickly snapped up a comfortably-off widow and in any case may have been considered to be socially a little beneath her. Something must have happened to improve relations because that spring Absalom's aunt, Mrs Mountford as she now was, arrived in Manchester together with her friend Mrs Stoneley, to stay with Mrs Thomas Watkin.

There coming involved Absalom's family in a round of social engagements. They dined together, went to the theatre, and at Woodlands Terrace enjoyed a lively tea party which included Mrs Mountford, Mrs Stoneley, Mr and Mrs Thomas Watkin and their three children, old Betty Watkin, Absalom and Elizabeth and their children. Mrs Stoneley had left her husband behind at Nantwich. She was a pretty woman. After tea they played blind man's buff 'with a good deal of glee' and kept it up until nearly ten o'clock. The visit invigorated Absalom. He started to ride over Kersal Moor in the early morning and felt better for it.

Contemporary Protestantism was attached to the Christian calendar with the slenderest of threads. Even someone as devout as Absalom treated Good Friday as a secular holiday. That year he rode over the moor before breakfast, gardened for two hours, continued Byron's *Childe Harold* and then set off to walk to Prestwich with Grime and Andrew.

March 24th, 1826. We got some warm ale and brandy and some bread and butter at Whiteheads. We all drank too much and then talked foolishly with too much personal jesting. They got tea with me and we joked Andrew unmercifully about his age.

Two weeks later Absalom heard that his cousin Thomas Watkin was dangerously ill. He died a day or so after and Absalom's tranquillity was shattered. The clerk at St Stephen's made a mistake about the day of the funeral and they were obliged to wait in the church for two hours. Moreover, troubles that had nothing to do with domestic problems were a cause for anxiety. Unemployment, deprivation and general distress had exploded into violence at last.

April 25th, 1826. Yesterday there was a tumultuous assemblage of weavers and other persons out of employment at Accrington and Blackburn. Many of them were armed with pikes and at both places power-looms and machinery were broken to pieces.

The same thing happened at Bury, where a number of people were killed by the soldiers. The trouble spread quickly to Manchester.

April 28th, 1826. Riotous assemblages of people have taken place today in Manchester. Mr Beaver's power-loom factory was set on fire last night and today shops have been entered and provisions and money have been taken by force. This afternoon a great number of persons have been robbed by the mob who surround well-dressed persons and demand money. I had a narrow escape myself near the New Cross. Mr Bramhall, who was with me, was obliged to part with some money.

'What can be stable with these enormous towns?' Lord Liverpool had exclaimed in 1819, 'one serious insurrection in London and all is lost.' The situation now, however, was not quite as dangerous as it had been then. No radical agitators came forward to inflame the masses with a programme for political reform. On the whole, the disturbances were the natural eruptions of men who could not find a decent living. Trade was so slack that in May Absalom found that he was worth £60 less than he had been in January. A meeting of the Club at Mr Kershaw's house cheered him up, but then Elizabeth's accounts were so wildly wrong for the hundredth time that despairing of speech, he wrote her a note imploring her to mend her ways.

The market got even worse. He could do no business. One day in midsummer after tea he walked despondently with little Edward nearly to Prestwich. Together they sat on the chains at the entrance to the road by the brook which separated Prestwich from the moor and silently watched the sun sink in the west.

John Watkin now had his father's estate at Audlem to settle and needed Absalom's help. In June they went together on the coach to Nantwich where they called on the Stoneleys before walking the six miles 'through oceans of sand' to Audlem. They arrived there about eleven at night to find the Mountford household already in bed.

Audlem was a typical Cheshire village with cobbled streets, a fine church built on high ground and a pleasant butter market. It was surrounded by flourishing small farms, fields and scattered cottages. Besides other property, Thomas Watkin had owned an eighteenth-century house with an orchard and farmstead on the village outskirts.

Next morning Absalom rose early and went alone into the churchyard. His Uncle John and John's father were buried on the south side of the church, on a slope leading down to the road. The graves are long gone and the inscriptions with them, the tombstones hidden under grass shorn by the lips of the motor mower. But time had not yet done its work and Absalom was able to read the following verse:

> This stone out of true respect;
> To him I loved I here erect;
> Whose life I prized; whose death lament
> But yet must learn to be content.

The next day was hot. Absalom spells Nantwich in the old way.

June 19th, 1826. Rode on Mr Mountford's tall horse to Namptwich to get a letter off by the coachman. Breakfasted with Mr Stoneley and then went with him and looked first at the inside of Namptwich church and then at the process of making salt. Rode back to Audlem under a burning sun, the effects of which were much augmented by the reflection from the sand.

After dinner he helped Mr Mountford with his accounts and then went to collect some of John's rents.

We met Mr Groom, the village lawyer, who insisted on our tasting his ale. We went back with him to do so and having first examined his garden and seen his pinks and a wasp's nest, which the owners have built on one of his gooseberry trees, we went into his kitchen to taste his ale. Here a scene presented itself of a most comic kind. His housekeeper came in, took part and a considerable part, in all the conversation and in short, behaved with all the ridiculous effrontery which in comedies we see exhibited in the too familiar housekeepers of foolish old bachelors.

The fine weather continued, and next morning Absalom and his aunt got up at half-past five to meet Mr and Mrs Stoneley and Miss Anne Stoneley, who had walked the six miles from Nantwich for the festival of the Audlem Female Friendly Society which was to be held that afternoon.

June 20th, 1826. After breakfast we walked with Mr Mountford, Stoneley and John to the mill and back through the meadows. Went with Mr and Miss Stoneley and John into my aunt's garden. We sat some time in the bower and chatted pleasantly. After dinner we went up to the market place to see the procession of the Female Friendly Society. After seeing the procession we went to the church and heard a sermon adapted to the occasion.

They all had tea and then went out again 'to see the dance on the green in honour of the establishment of the Friendly Society'.

It was kept up for about two hours and was a very agreeable sight, but the dancers were more grave than I expected. A Miss Bailey was in my opinion the best dancer. The motion of her body and still more of her arms was uncommonly graceful. Mrs Stoneley was conspicuous in the dance, her tall and elegant figure being shown to great advantage by a dress of violet coloured flowered crêpe over white muslin. After supper we had some drinking and smoking and got into that quiet chat which is most agreeable in company. It was morning when we went to bed.

Despite that, Absalom got up at five next day and walked by himself in the fields.

June 21st, 1826. Then in the garden and sat in the bower alone until breakfast was ready. The early morning was uncommonly beautiful and the freshness of the air delightful. Notwithstanding my great loss of rest and the unusual quantity of liquor which I had taken, I felt well. After breakfast we took leave of my aunt and Mountford and set out for Namptwich. I walked at least a quarter of a mile before I offered Mrs Stoneley my arm. She accepted it. John gave his to Miss Stoneley and we walked in this manner to Namptwich. The morning was very hot, the flies troublesome, the way long and the walk fatiguing. We made the best of it, talking of such subjects as they occurred, sometimes generally, sometimes apart. Mr Stoneley, after the fashion of husbands, stalked on before his wife. Mrs Stoneley and I got into talk on the subject of matrimonial differences and I quoted Cowper's beautiful lines:

> 'Not to understand a treasure's worth,
> Till time has stolen away the slighted good,
> Is cause of half the unhappiness we feel,
> And makes the world the wilderness it is.'

She assented eagerly to the truth and beauty of the remark. We got to Namptwich about eight o'clock and breakfasted again at the Stoneley's. At half-past nine we left Namptwich in the coach and had a most wearisome, hot ride to Manchester.

John fancied himself in love with Anne. Absalom was undoubtedly attracted to the older woman. Back at home the glorious summer continued and heightened feelings sharpened his appreciation of natural beauty.

July 17th, 1826. Walked with Elizabeth after tea to <u>our</u> lane. The evening was uncommonly beautiful, the moon brilliant, everything still, the leaves of the trees not moving, now and then the hum of a beetle and sometimes a distant noise of a coach on the road or of children shouting broke the silence. I felt all the beauty of the scene and was thankful; but my heart continually reverted to sad and strange thoughts, and as I write this on my return, and while all the delicious softness of the place and the hour is strongly impressed upon my imagination, I feel deeply and hopelessly sad.

The following Sunday he took Edward and his daughter for a walk.

July 23rd, 1826. Got home at tea time to find that the tea which my wife had promised to leave for us had been entirely neglected and even that the water had been put away. Found that John had only dirty or ragged night caps and that he had no buttons to keep up his trousers.

A week later he went into the garden alone and looked at the night.

July 31st, 1826. There is no wind, the leaves are still, the sky dark blue and thickly gemmed with stars, the Great Bear brilliant, the Milky Way conspicuous – the clocks in succession strike eleven, the watchman is heard, wheels rattle at a distance, water falls in Mr Beddome's garden, crickets chirp all round, dogs bark now and then, a cow lows at a distance, the sky is lightest in the north. Nature is as beautiful as ever.

Absalom read a paper on manures to the Club, Davies one on arsenic; he heard a sermon that went on for two hours and discovered that his wife was brewing beer with water from the cistern and not, as he had asked her to do, from the spring.

However, when he went to see about his cottage at Bonsal at the end of September he took Elizabeth with him. They arrived at Matlock at twelve and as soon as they had made arrangements to stay at the hotel, went for an hour and a half's walk and, nothing daunted, immediately after dinner set out to walk to Bonsal, returning in the dark. After attending the service at Matlock church next morning, they went back to their hotel for dinner to find a gentleman from Sweden had joined the company. Carving was then a much esteemed accomplishment but not one Absalom was skilled at.

September 24th, 1826. I feared that I should have some difficulty in escaping an attempt at carving, but I got off very well by lifting up the cover of the potato dish and declaring that to be the dish which I always succeded best in carving. The dinner consisted of a couple of fowls, a hare and some roasted lamb, with a plentiful addition of pudding and tart.

The Swede spoke excellent English and was most talkative.

I learnt that botany is not so much attended to in Sweden at present as it was in the time of Linnaeus and for some time after. Poetry, he said, was the fashionable study now. There is a Swedish bishop now living who is so celebrated as a poet that translators from France and Germany reside at Stockholm for the purpose of translating his works as fast as they appear. I enquired the subjects of his poems and found that they were chiefly of an amatory and romantic character. 'When he composes,' said the Swede, 'I suppose he lays aside his mitre.'

They had a pleasant ride home but looking after the children had been too much for his mother. Absalom drew up plans for yet another house to be built on some more land he had acquired at Broughton. The pressures mounted.

October 29th, 1826. My children, notwithstanding the great expense at which we live, are in rags. No sufficient care is taken by my wife. I fear that I shall be brought down by the constant unhappiness of my home.

He was therefore extremely gratified after a meeting of the Literary and Philosophical Society to be urged by his friends Kershaw and Davies to give up business and devote himself to literature.

December 1st, 1826. Davies told me that Mr Baxter had said of me that he had never supposed me to be a man of talent as a writer and speaker, although he had known me many years as a trader, in which capacity he had found me to be a clear-headed man and equal in integrity to any man.

Next day Mr Kershaw spoke to him again on the subject, going so far as to say that he would be answerable for his success. Perhaps after all he should retire. He walked to Northenden to see Joseph Johnson about some property for sale there. He was getting on friendlier terms with Johnson, who had helped him to get some American trees from Cobbett.

December 11th, 1826. I found Johnson well known to almost everybody about Northen and apparently respected. He told me that on his return to Northen from Lincoln Castle the people were surprised to see the number of books he brought with him and as he read much and kept no company, they looked upon him as a sort of conjurer and came to him for advice and information on all subjects.

By 'conjurer', Johnson meant a man of exceptional cleverness.
    Absalom's New Year resolutions were detailed. As far as business was concerned he determined to be regular in his accounts so as to know exactly where he stood.

December 31st, 1826. On Tuesday make out the dunning list; enter, and if possible, post up the goods received. Wednesday, enter goods kept in the ledger. Thursday, put money and sales. Friday, goods to be kept posted. Saturday and Monday, make out accounts current and finish things left before.

He would write four speeches and six lectures and one paper for the Literary and Philosophical Society. But he must avoid too much sedentary application.

I propose to do all I can to improve my health. I will take as much exercise as I can. Keep as cheerful as I can. Avoid long continued thought on any one subject. Sometimes omit study for a week altogether. Avoid too much feeling. Restrain passion.

These resolutions were not long made before his wife told him that he was able to go out two or three times a week and spend money but he complained if *she* so much as asked for threepence. She was 'a *vile liar*'. Trade did not improve and there were fears in some quarters that the workers might combine together in defiance of the law and bind themselves by oaths to demand higher wages.
    Since Mrs Thomas Watkin's husband's death, her family visited Woodlands Terrace regularly. Through them Absalom heard that Mrs Stoneley and his Aunt Mountford had come to Manchester. He went round straight away to call and next day they all went off to see Dacrow's equestrian performance. Dacrow rode

three horses at once but since the tricks were all of that kind they became tedious. Kean's *King Lear* was a different thing altogether.

March 7th, 1827. Mr Kean is said to be much enfeebled, but his performance was exquisite. The effect which he gave to the words, 'Aye, every inch a king', I shall never forget. He was equally happy in pronouncing the words, 'But I am old now', and indeed in several other passages, but the two I have mentioned touched most on my memory. His restoration to sanity and his recognition of Cordelia was a fine piece of acting.

Mrs Stoneley's presence and the break in routine gave Absalom new life. At his house they had tea parties followed by blind man's buff and Mrs Stoneley, sourly observed by Elizabeth, kept them all up till after midnight teaching Absalom to play whist. Aunt Mountford particularly wanted to see their old home in Whit Lane and one afternoon she, Absalom and an old servant whose name was Martha, took the coach and walked there from the turnpike.

March 14th, 1827. We found the house inhabited by three poor families and the garden in the utmost disorder. 'Next week,' said one of the inmates, 'the whole building is to be made into cottages.' We walked round the garden, Martha pointing out to me the spot which when a boy was my garden, and she, I and my Aunt looked for different objects with which we were formerly familiar. The bower, the sundial, the grass walks, the Siberian crab-trees, all were gone. The beech trees are felled and the tall cherry trees have been taken away.

It was a momentary check to his spirits. They saw Mr Young in *Hamlet*, drank hock with Grime, and for a day or two Absalom felt affection for his wife, a feeling no sooner remarked upon than shattered by her negligence and falsehood. The excitement began to make him feel ill. Hallworth returned from America and gave them a very interesting account of Niagara Falls, but the Good Friday game of blind man's buff was a failure. Mrs Stoneley had gone.

CHAPTER NINE

'The bells of Audlem'

The parting was not to be for long. Absalom was planning another expedition to Audlem to coincide with the annual meeting of the Female Friendly Society. In June he set out, this time taking with him his wife and Edward. They left in the *Royal Nettle* at two in the afternoon and arrived at Nantwich at about half-past eight.

June 16th, 1827. I ordered a chaise and while it was getting ready just called upon Mrs Stoneley. She went with me to the inn to see Elizabeth and then I, Edward and Elizabeth set out in the coach for Audlem. Elizabeth was unwell from the motion of the coach. She became very sick and we had an unpleasant ride to Audlem which we reached about eleven o'clock. At my aunt's they were all in bed, but were soon roused. We got tea.

Next day was a Sunday and Absalom got up early and took Edward for a walk over the fields and in his aunt's garden. On their return from church they found that John Watkin and Anne Stoneley had arrived from Nantwich.

June 17th, 1827. After dinner we walked through Audlem and went to look at John Watkin's fields. My wife stopped at the Baptist meeting house. John, Anne, Edward and I went on. We got into one of the fields, Edward and Anne ran after the butterflies and the dragonflies. John was dejected because she had refused him a kiss. There had been some little courtship between John and Anne; the girl exhibited a degree of coquetry in her treatment of him which amused me not a little. After tea we walked to Mr Morrey's. I drank rather more than usual, had joked a good deal with Anne and was in high spirits. Mr Morrey showed us his garden. We had something to drink and I sat some time in the little verandah at his front door, joking and laughing with Anne who appeared to delight in teasing John by being more familiar with everybody else than with him. As I sat, I could not help contrasting my feelings with those which I had endured in the same seat twelve months before; I was then unwell and extremely dejected, now, in unusually high spirits and in good health. Let me learn, <u>at last</u>, never to despair. We left Mr Morrey's to take a walk through the fields. We went back very merrily to my aunt's. Anne and John were the last.

They had a day to spend before the festival and the weather still held.

June 18th, 1827. Walked after breakfast with my wife and John, Anne and Edward towards Adderley. We read several pieces of poetry as we went along. Returned to my aunt's and sauntered about the house and garden till dinner. After dinner we walked through Audlem and through several fields in which poppies, columbines and yellow iris were growing. After tea we went to look at the canal which they are cutting near Audlem.

The morning of the festival dawned bright and clear and the four of them walked over the fields to have a word with Mr Mountford, who was ploughing. While he was grumbling about the wild mustard among his corn, they heard the church bells ring out over the meadows.

June 19th, 1827. We stayed in the fields until the bells of Audlem, sounding tingle-tum, tingle-tum, and the distant sound of the band of music which was approaching the village announced to us that it was time to return. We got back and had immediate recourse to bread and cheese and porter. Mr and Mrs Stoneley had arrived during our absence and joined us soon after our return. We went into the garden with them. John gave us some tunes on his clarinet and I talked more and faster than usual.

Mr Morray and Simcock the tailor, memorable for his dancing on the Green last year, were an addition to our company. As for the tailor, he has married since I was last here and appeared to have lost nearly all of his vivacity. Mr Mountford, in most unusual honour of the occasion, had cleaned himself and put on his Sunday clothes and we sat down to a good dinner with good appetites and cheerful faces. My wife and Mrs Stoneley did the honours and seemed to emulate each other in smiles and attentions. After dinner my wife's smelling-bottle and my snuffbox amused the noses of the good company and it was time to go to church before we thought about it.

We went to church and heard a tolerable sermon from Mr Breakspear and I observed with attention the beauty and fashion of the neighbourhood assembled to do honour to the annual meeting of the Female Friendly Society of Audlem. It was a pleasing sight. The church was filled principally with the young and well-looking and cheerful countenances, good clothing, smart ribands and a profusion of evergreens and flowers gave to the whole thing a very animating and enlivening effect. But I do not think or feel as the majority of mankind appear to do.

I looked upon the assemblage attentively and with interest; I even noticed some of the most attractive so carefully as to retain a picture of them and their situation in church in my imagination. But when I had done this my thoughts passed to the future destiny of the individuals before me, to considerations of human mortality, and to the saddening reflection that all the animation and liveliness which I beheld must terminate in the silence of the tomb. I diverted these reflections which only made me sad to no purpose by taking a few notes of Mr Breakspear's sermon. The service ended, we left the church and the Female Society went in procession through the village in the midst of a shower of rain, accompanied by a band of music.

Absalom watched the progress of John's courtship of Anne with interest.

During most of the day she had worn a flower in her bosom which he had presented to her and he had gallantly placed in the buttonhole of his waistcoat a sprig of love-lies-bleeding. Her flower was fading and he had gathered a rose bud which he gave her to replace it. Unluckily the stem was covered with aphids and when she took it, she discovered them and exclaiming 'It's all over insects,' threw it petulantly on the table.

When they were about to set out to see the dancing on the green, John offered Anne his arm and was refused. Vexed, he took his love-lies-bleeding from his buttonhole and in his turn threw it on the ground. When they returned from the dancing they played blind man's buff.

Mr Mountford was induced by the women to join us and throwing off his coat, fell to it heartily. We played till we were all very warm and then rested. After a while we discovered that the music was to be heard very agreeably in the croft and going out to listen, ended by dancing to it till a smart shower put an end to the playing and drove us into the house. Stoneley and his wife had intended to return to Namptwich that evening but the rain induced them to remain. We sat therefore in the parlour talking, drinking and smoking with an easy familiarity which if not very animating was yet sufficiently agreeable. John too was a source of great amusement to us. He had not forgotten the rejection of his flower and he sung for us such pieces as were calculated to express his emotions while we laughed at the importance he seemed to attach to them. It was late when we retired to rest.

The Stoneleys left next morning but this was no grief to Absalom since they had planned to meet the following morning at Nantwich to make up a party to explore Beeston Castle.

June 20th, 1827. John made some earnest but ineffectual endeavours to get Anne to remain at Audlem. We called upon the Misses Buttris, John's tenants at the large house and then walked in the meadows. We met with Groom, the lawyer of the village, who walked with us through the meadows and treated us with a constrained civility which he no doubt thought very condescending. When we parted with him we went to look at one of John's fields called 'The Thornhills'. We went round it, sometimes talking, sometimes singing, till we were all hungry.

After dinner I, Elizabeth, John, my aunt, Mr Bickerton and Edward, had another long ramble. We went up the Adderley road and then into the fields along the line of the canal which is being made in defiance of mountains of loose sand, up and down which we had to labour. Leaving the canal, we went through the fields to 'The Thornhills' again, over some gates and some truly Cheshire stiles and got home at tea time quite ready to eat and drink again. Tea over, Elizabeth and I went to Anne Malpas. Her husband was at home reading the Bible. I liked his countenance which was open, serious and manly. My wife talked to him seriously and we sang a hymn or two before we left them.

The next day was the one fixed for their expedition to Beeston Castle.

June 21st, 1827. Rose early and looked out upon the morning sun with satisfaction. Walked in my aunt's garden and took a farewell look at the bower and flowers. Put a sprig of thyme and a fine pansy into my bosom and gathered a rose bud for Elizabeth. Breakfasted and after breakfast Elizabeth, my aunt and I and Edward left Audlem in the chaise. We had a pleasant ride to Namptwich. Arriving, we had second breakfast at the White Lion which made its appearance with a celerity which did credit to our hostess.

She, of course, was Mrs Stoneley. They then went to see the salt-works again and to the church. While they were there John came to tell them that the chaise and gig were ready. Beeston Castle was five miles distant. Anne could not join them, but despite that, a chaise alone was not big enough to take them all. Somebody, probably Absalom, so arranged matters that Elizabeth and Edward were asked to go in the gig driven by Mr Stoneley while Absalom, Aunt Mountford and Mrs Stoneley travelled in the chaise with John accompanying them on horseback. Absalom was free to continue his flirtation with Mrs Stoneley.

Aware that conversation is not infrequently interesting or tedious according to the manner in which it is commenced, I did not lose time in repeating that it was a fine morning or in sagely remarking that we were likely to have a pleasant ride, but giving Mrs Stoneley a tap on the bonnet to awaken her attention, I told her that I expected her to be very entertaining and that if it was not so, I would certainly disgrace her for ever by going to sleep in her company. She laughed and asked how <u>she</u> could be very entertaining? I answered that for her to be pleasing it was only necessary for her to desire to be so and that if she was not, I should be quite certain that she was only dull out of spite. I added that if she was so, I would certainly either go to sleep or do all I could to make her angry. She laughed and said if I once saw her angry

I should never wish to make her so again. 'Oh yes,' said I, 'that I should. I am very fond of thunder and lightning.' 'Well,' said she, again laughing, 'you shall have none today, for I shall not be angry at anything.'

Mrs Stoneley proved to be very knowledgeable about the country through which they were passing, telling Absalom the names of the places and the owners of more remarkable houses.

After proceeding a few miles Stoneley drove over a dog which was in the road but I believe without doing it any considerable injury. We did not see the accident but John, who witnessed it, mentioned it to us through the window. I expressed my sorrow, but Mrs Stoneley said 'The dog should have kept out of the way.' I have noticed before in her indifference to animal suffering and I took the opportunity of speaking to her on the tenderness which ought to prevail in the female character. Luckily John at this moment offered me a collection of poems which he had in his pocket. It contained Ledyard's 'Praise of Women' which I got Mrs Stoneley to read, making her notice particularly the beautiful verse beginning:

> Alive to every tender feeling,
> To deeds of mercy ever prone.

Mrs Stoneley read aloud well and was so gratified when Absalom informed her of this that she took the opportunity to repeat her performance both on the way to Beeston and on their return. The journey was now nearing its end; the castle was glimpsed from the road.

As the castle is occasionally seen from the road at some miles distance, Mrs Stoneley was on the look out for it and at length told me to look at it. I did not at first discover it, being perhaps not very solicitous to do so. 'Do you see it?' said she. Instead of looking at the country, I looked at her and replied 'I see a charming prospect, but really I cannot see the castle.' 'Why, look there, there it is.' I still looked at her and repeated 'The prospect is charming but I perceive nothing like a ruin.' She perceived my meaning, smiled and said with pretended petulance 'Well, if you won't look, I won't show you.' 'Very well,' said I, 'I am quite satisfied with what I see.' We talked in this manner for some time and at last I allowed myself to see the castle.

Beeston is a hilltop fortress perched high on a five hundred foot crag rising from the Cheshire plain. Seen from the road it is not very impressive, but once through the gatehouse the massive grandeur of the inner ward built on its high sandstone rock is spectacular.

The ascent is steep and rough but we were all well and in high spirits. I was particularly pleased with the enthusiastic ardour of my little Edward. If this boy is not spoiled by the folly of those about him, he will assuredly prove superior to the herd of mankind. An old woman who lives at the foot of the hill has the care of the ruins and had come up with us to open the gate which supplies the place of the castle door. From her Edward learnt the situation of the deep well and came to me with sparkling eyes and a countenance full of smiles to tell me he had found it.

They were now at the summit and looked eagerly at some of the finest panoramic views Absalom had ever seen.

Standing at the highest point of the ruin which is at the steep perpendicular end of Beeston Hill, you see the course of the Mersey with Liverpool in the distance and Chester apparently, or comparatively, near. Then turning a little towards the castle gate, you see the Welsh hills and catch a faint indistinct view of Wrexham. From the gate you have below you the vale of Cheshire, with hills and woods and innumerable fields spreading to the boundary of the horizon. Passing by the gateway a little to the left, you look over another part of the vale and across De La Mer Forest to the hills of Staffordshire.

Mr Stoneley pointed to some lofty trees in that direction. It was from there, he said, 'that he brought his mistress'. Mrs Stoneley was in fact at that moment taking out the provisions.

She summoned us to sit down on the grass and partake of some cake and wine which she had taken care to bring from Namptwich. I do not know whether the wine was really the best I have ever tasted, or whether it was the brisk animating wind which played about us, the beauty of the day and the scene, the real and considerable improvement of my health and spirits and the exhilarating effect of agreeable company combining to make it appear so, but never did I drink two glasses of wine which appeared to me so delicious and never did I drink 'Many happy returns of the present occasion' with more glee than with one of those glasses at my lips. Our company appeared to feel equally pleased, but my wife who has an unhappy knack of being grave at improper seasons, did her best to damp the extra cheerfulness of the moment by observing, with a solemn air, that it was very unlikely we should all of us ever meet again at Beeston Castle.

Full of wine, happiness and energy, Absalom got up and suggested they should climb one of the towers. John and Edward were anxious to follow him. Mr Stoneley climbed one tower, then said that his head would not allow him to pass over the top of the gateway to the second.

John, Edward and I went over and lay down among the grass and stonecrop which grew upon the summit of the ruin. John took out his clarinet and played 'The Fall of Paris' and I lay in a state of such entire absence of all painful or stirring thought that for a few minutes my eyes closed involuntarily and I had great difficulty to avoid going to sleep. John was in a similar state of delicious drowsiness and if my wife had not called to us from below, we should in all probability have snored in concert.

The descent was steep and caused Mrs Stoneley to tremble. They chose a different route down, one that led across fields to a neat rose-covered cottage whose owner looked after Horsley Bath. Horsley Bath was a basin of pure water fed by a spring which gushed out of the rock. It had an ancient undressing house clothed in ivy to one side of it and above the spring an inscription in Latin describing the water's medicinal properties. They then had a meal at the inn near the castle where they had eaten before they started the climb and returned to Nantwich in the same manner as they had come.

Their energy was extraordinary. Back at Nantwich they accompanied Aunt Mountford for about a mile along her road to Audlem, then under Mrs Stoneley's direction, went to see an Elizabethan house in a remarkable state of preservation which stood at the entrance to the town. Supper was a delicious meal spoilt only by John's sulkiness because of Anne's refusal to walk along the Audlem road to see Mrs Mountford on her way home.

I suppose it must have been my increased health which produced the impression, but from whatever cause, it is a fact that the <u>white</u> wine which Mrs Stoneley almost insisted upon my drinking rather too freely, appeared to me most excellent. 'I shall be drunk,' said I, in answer to her request that I would fill my glass, 'and instead of going to Manchester, somebody will have to nurse me tomorrow.' 'I should like to see you drunk,' was her reply. 'I should not mind spending a day over you.' This appeared to me rather a strange declaration and Stoneley, who sat beside her, did not in my opinion, <u>look</u> quite pleased. It is not impossible that I might have sat too long and drank too much, but my wife kindly reminded me of the morrow and we went to bed. And thus ended one of the most agreeable days of my life.

He rose late with a headache. The household was gloomy.

June 22nd, 1827. Stoneley complained of indisposition and his mistress said she had been up at six o'clock and gone to bed again. She looked ill. After breakfast I went with Edward and Stoneley to look at his garden. Returned and waited till it was time to go to the coach. When I offered my hand to Mrs Stoneley as I was leaving the room, she said 'Must we part here?' 'No,' said I, 'come with us to the coach.' She <u>ran</u> for her bonnet and taking my arm on one side, as Elizabeth did on the other, we walked down to Farrar's. As we went along Mrs Stoneley very kindly invited Elizabeth to repeat her visit to Cheshire next year. We took leave of her and Mr Stoneley at the coach.

They reached home between four and five in the afternoon and as soon as they were alone Absalom told Elizabeth how John had made love to Anne by the hollow tree on the morning of the festival, the details of which he had used shorthand to write in his diary.

She received this proof of my confidence with a very ill grace and has ever since made it the occasional subject of ill-natured and unworthy reflections. She has also teased me into compliance with her absurdly curious desire to read my account of this journey.

CHAPTER TEN

'Would it not be better that the increase of the labouring classes should be prevented?'

In August 1827 Richard Carlile came to Manchester to stay with Joseph Johnson. Carlile was a prominent and uncompromising radical. He had been severely treated by the government for publishing Tom Paine's works and for disseminating his own periodical, *The Republican*, serving a six-year prison sentence in Dorchester Gaol. He had not long been released.

Absalom very much wished to meet him, not because he agreed with his views, which in his opinion were unreasonable and mischievous, but from curiosity to see an unusual person and one, moreover, who possessed a firmness of purpose he himself would have given much to have been born with. He wished, too, to discuss Carlile's atheism, to find out if there were any arguments against the existence of God which he had not heard or could not meet.

Carlile was with Johnson at his house in Northenden. Accompanied by Grime, Absalom went over there on 12 August and in effect interviewed him for nine hours, probably taking notes in shorthand. Four days later he met Carlile again at Grime's house. He wrote down these conversations a few days after they happened and showed them to the participants who declared them to be a correct account of what took place.

Richard Carlile is about five feet four inches high and well made. His hands are beautifully formed. A rheumatic affliction from which he suffers a good deal renders walking painful and difficult. He has light brown hair, slightly curling. His head is finely shaped and his countenance open and expressive. His eyes, which are rather dark, are full and lively but the muscles under the eyes have the swollen and dark appearance which usually indicates mental suffering. His mouth is pretty, the lips plump but not thick and the teeth regular and white.

Carlile was the son of a Devonshire shoemaker. He had not had much formal education and was liable to make grammatical mistakes. Absalom noted that he remarked that professional people were frequently unable to take open air exercise because with them business was 'a *prima facie* object'. Far from being violent or hectoring in discussion, he had a mild manner and never spoke loudly or lost his self-possession throughout the whole of their talks.

The first subject they discussed was birth control. Carlile had advocated its use in his publication *Every Woman's Book*, where he had urged the use of a contraceptive sponge, and proclaimed it as 'the most important discovery ever made'. It was already in use, he asserted, by the privileged; he had been told of an English duchess who never went out to dinner without one. Carlile now told them that the plan for such a book was made at a meeting of political economists and reformers which included Francis Place, James Mill, David Ricardo and Robert Owen. They had all agreed that the degraded and miserable state of the labouring classes could be remedied only by reducing their number and that this could be achieved best by frustrating the usual course of nature in the intercourse of the sexes.

After all, Carlile now argued, such a practice did not destroy life, it only prevented it. It lowered the rate of infanticide, enabled delicate women to avoid the incessant childbirth that often ended in death; allowed those people with a low income, like clerks in government service, to lead a decent life without the anxiety and suffering they so often endured. As for the labouring classes, surely, looking at their present state of degradation, was it not better that 'their increase should be prevented till the diminution of their numbers should compel their employers to give better wages and constant work?'

> He added that sexual intercourse was necessary to the healthy state of female life; while marriage with its usual consequences, was very often impracticable; and sexual intercourse without marriage and followed by the natural results, destroyed the reputation, the prospects and frequently the moral character, of the female. A female in the existing state of things, had, he said, very often no alternative but either to die by consumption or other disease in consequence of her abstinence from illicit pleasure, or to preserve her health at the risk of losing reputation, character and prospects; and was perhaps induced by the dread of this latter alternative, after having acted indiscreetly, to go on to greater crime and become the murderer of her own child. By the use of the means he recommended all this evil would be prevented.

This was objected to by Grime or Absalom in much the same terms as Charles Darwin would employ fifty years later. 'If it were universally known that the birth of children could be prevented,' Darwin wrote in 1878, 'and this were not thought immoral by married persons, would there not be great danger of extreme profligacy among unmarried women and might we not become like the "arreoi" societies in the Pacific?'

> To teach the means of gratifying the sexual appetite with impunity was to loosen the bands of moral obligation to obtain an imaginary benefit. The evil

effects of such a state of things were pointed out to him and the consequence in domestic life of conduct so dissolute were insisted upon at length. In particular it was demanded whether a man who married a woman who had acted in such a manner previously to marriage, could look upon his wife as any other than a prostitute, or could feel for her, or expect from her, a proper attachment. He answered that the sexual intercourse of a young woman with her lover was not prostitution and that, especially if not followed by pregnancy, the knowledge of it ought not to be any objection to her marriage with another. He added that he knew of two instances of persons who had even married prostitutes and the women, in both cases, made excellent wives.

However, under pressure, he admitted that 'a woman who had yielded to the solicitations of her lover and afterwards married another man, would be not unlikely to repeat the fault after marriage and he allowed this to be an objection to his scheme.'

He was then asked whether the best part of society, meaning by the best the most moral and intellectual, would not be adverse to his scheme, whether they would not be disgusted by its tendency to debase the imagination, to reduce the passion of love to a mere animal gratification, to increase immensely the amount of lewdness among females and to destroy, by what actually took place and if possible, still more by what was suspected, the happiness of marriage. He was individually appealed to as to his own feelings on the subject of having reason to suspect the chastity of his wife and reminded that the highest happiness of marriage consisted in the mutual belief of each party in the faithfulness and exclusive attachment to the other.

He admitted the force, in his own case, of the appeal made to him. He said that although he had no reason to question Mrs Carlile's fidelity, the idea of such a thing had sometimes occurred to him while he was in confinement and she living in London. That his determination, had she departed from her duty, would have been to separate from her. He added that Mrs Carlile had always had a great aversion to the preventative plan and a great dislike of Francis Place as the author of it. 'We have never adopted it,' said he, 'it has not been necessary; indeed Mrs C. declares she would rather have a hundred children than submit to it. But when I was a journeyman tinplate worker getting twenty-five shillings a week, if we had begun to have children fast, I should perhaps have been glad to adopt the means of preventing their increase.' The best part of society, he knew, would agree with his wife but the scheme was intended, not for them, but for the lowest and most degraded classes as a means of preventing greater evils than it produced.

This conversation, Absalom remarks, involving as it did so many topics upon which it was very difficult to speak both clearly and inoffensively, was carried on in a uniformly decorous manner. The next subject needed little prompting. The tale of Carlile's flight from the field of Peterloo was to him as important and probably almost as frequently repeated as Charles II's story of his escape after the Battle of Worcester.

'I was on the hustings, which were formed of two waggons placed side by side, but at such a distance from each other as to allow of a person's getting up or down between them. There were four women on the hustings besides Mary Fildes. When the Yeomanry were approaching I assisted the four women to descend and having done so I followed them myself – at that moment the pressure of the crowd forced the waggons together and my hat was caught between them, my head escaped! Now, was not this Providence?' As he said this he laughed and then continued – 'I got under the wagons and into the adjoining street. A woman was standing at the door of her house and allowed me to come in. Her husband was at his work. I had to remain till he came home and then to send him to buy a hat before I could leave the house.'

It is surprising to us that Carlile thought it necessary to remain in hiding until he could be provided with a hat. At that time, however, all men of whatever class, wore hats out of doors. Not to have done so would have made Carlile as conspicuous as a person today walking the streets in bare feet. Some years later Friedrich Engels noticed that any worker in Manchester too poor to possess a hat made himself a low, four-cornered cap out of paper. Carlile continued:

I took a place for London, and then went to the Star Inn, paid my bill and got my luggage. I had ordered a coach to take my trunks and myself to the Bridgwater. When I came out of the Star, a coach was at the door and I got into it, directing the coachman where to drive. It happened that this was not the coach I had ordered and I had scarcely got to the Bridgwater before there was a hue and cry after the gentleman who had come from the Star in the coach. As my name was on my trunks, I expected that the police were after me, but it was only the coachman of the coach I had ordered demanding his fare. I got into the London coach and found my companions quite afraid of being stopped and plundered by the radicals. On this subject I had no fears. It would have been sufficient, had anything taken place, for me to declare my name. When we were out of danger a loyal old gentleman, one of the passengers, insisted on my drinking "down with Hunt." We got safe to London and I was the first to publish an account of the affair at Peterloo, for which I was prosecuted.

Carlile concealed his passionate hatred for Hunt who, at his own trial, with tears trickling down his face, had denounced Carlile. Carlile now said that he thought

Hunt clever and courageous but not a man of principle. If he had been, he would not have lied at the York trial, making out that he did not know him when they were once on intimate terms. When Carlile spoke of William Cobbett, for the first time Absalom thought he detected a certain 'insidiousness' in his remarks.

> He said there was a mystery hung over that part of Cobbett's life which intervened between his return from Canada and his going to the United States. That Mrs Cobbett and her daughters always spoke well of her, [Mrs Cobbett] as a person of property and good family but the most probable account was that, when Cobbett married her, she was a servant at Fulham. He added 'It is reported that Cobbett is not on good terms with his family – that he does not eat with them but takes his meals in the seed-house.'

One might have thought that that was enough for a single day, but the question of the existence of God had not yet been touched upon. What followed was desultory, more of a preparation for further discussion.

> Carlile said 'I was for a long time a deist. Sherwin was the first person whom I ever heard declare his disbelief of a deity and when he did so, I said to myself "this is a very wicked young man." It was not until after some time and further examination that I adopted his opinions.'

The argument from design was appealed to, surely the structure of the eye necessitated an Intelligent First Cause? No, in Carlile's opinion, the eye was adapted to the purposes of vision and man had applied it to those purposes. 'There was no design in the business.' What then of the constitution of the sexes, that complicated combination of parts all tending to one end, the continuation of the species? Carlile admitted this to be a strong argument but not conclusive.

> Carlile said we knew nothing of the mode in which the species was continued and were completely in the dark as to the causes producing our children; that we had no will in the business and sought only to gratify ourselves in sexual intercourse. To this it was answered that although in the dark as to some parts of the process of generation, we had full knowledge of other parts and of so much as clearly evidenced intention and contrivance.

It was further objected that the fact that mankind was generally impelled to sexual intercourse by a desire of self-gratification without reference to the propagation of the species, proved not only that we were creatures of an intelligent being but actually under his government, since we were perpetually fulfilling his will in continuing the species without even intending it.

Carlile gave no definite answer to this but after some time admitted that there was a Supreme Power: 'But it is a blind power and cannot act otherwise than it does.' Shortly after he added: 'I am an accident – one of the many forms of being which might possibly have existed.'

Absalom was not satisfied. He did not think he was an accident. The subject was too close to his heart to be discussed lightly. The following Thursday they met again, this time at Grime's house. Absalom started the topic at once by saying that Carlile had asserted publicly that he did not believe in the existence of God. This flustered Carlile. He denied it. All he had done was to call for proofs of God's existence, he had asserted nothing.

'Yes, sir,' it was replied, 'you have asserted it publicly and in print, and here is your own book, Every Man's Book, which contains the assertion.' He said that 'the book was written hastily and in a very short time in reply to William Allen – my friends thought it proper he should be replied to and I did it. It was written in a very short time.'

The argument from design was discussed once more at length. At the end of it all Carlile gave his definition of the term 'God': God is a chemical action through matter producing all that exists.

Towards the end of the month Absalom took the boys to Kersal Moor to see how the blackberries were ripening.

August 23rd, 1827. We went over the Moor and ascended the hill near the workhouse. Then we got upon the high hill above Drinkwater's Wood. The boys went about in the field to examine how far the blackberries were from being ripe and I lay on the summit of the hill and looked at the prospect. It is more than twenty years since I first saw it and I involuntarily looked back upon the events that have taken place in my life during that interval. Upon the whole perhaps I have had more than an average share of the good of human life in that period. <u>Yet I am not satisfied</u>. How difficult it is to know in what happiness consists. How much more difficult steadily to pursue it.

On the way back he met a friend and together they discussed the nature of the felicity of heaven.

Absalom's teeth continued to give him trouble.

September 22nd, 1827. Kept awake by toothache. I got the tooth pulled out about noon and again observed that the pain of the operation is very endurable. Perhaps all pain is so if steadily faced. I noticed during last night, while I was unable to sleep from pain, that my imagination and reasoning powers were rather more vigorous than usual.

He had tea and then spent the evening with Johnson. The children were with him, other children were there too and both Absalom and Johnson became cheerful by observing their cheerfulness. The mood was soon shattered.

September 29th, 1827. Elizabeth in the scullery began to saw a leg of mutton with the saw literally covered with rust and dust. Convinced that it is in vain to hope from such a woman for a house kept in good order or even tolerably clean. Went in deep sadness to the warehouse and applied as well I could to business. In the middle of the forenoon Mr Spencer came to invite me to his house on Tuesday, adding that Mrs Spencer would be glad to see Mrs Watkin. Alas! how can I either decline or accept such an invitation. If I decline it, I offend a man whom I sincerely esteem and whose company I love. If I accept it, how can I invite him, Mrs Spencer or any other person possessed of a well-ordered home to my dirty, ill-managed, expensive dwelling?

Hardly had Mr Spencer gone than Mr Baxter arrived and proposed a business partnership with Absalom and a Mr Marshall. The pleasure and pain of it all released a flood of resentment.

I could not listen to Mr Baxter without great pleasure and still greater pain. My home and the misconduct of my wife rob me of half my powers, deprive me of a great portion of my time and drive me to conduct which degrades me in my own eyes. Yet in spite of all the evil influence under which I shall perhaps at last sink, I have frequently proofs such as these, that I am respected by those who know me.

A Turk named Mr Heket-yan was admitted a member of the Literary Debating Society and made a speech distinguished by shrewdness and humour on the subject of the interference of Russia, France and England in the affairs of Greece. As the year moved slowly towards Christmas Absalom took fencing lessons, read Shelley, walked in the winter moonlight, laughed at an Elizabethan book on farming for asserting that stale cabbage seed produced radishes, resolved to reconcile himself to the disorders of his home and the peculiarities of his temperament and was just attaining some kind of spasmodic equilibrium when Thomas Potter invited him to become editor of the *Manchester Gazette*.

CHAPTER ELEVEN
'My principles are too honest, my opinions too moderate'

Thomas and Richard Potter were rich men and well known for their liberal views. Their father had been a draper and small farmer at Tadcaster. When the shop was sold the capital was used to start a cotton warehouse in Manchester which, through hard work and a flair for business, flourished exeedingly. Both brothers supported reform and had helped the editor of the *Manchester Guardian*, J.E. Taylor, to launch his paper in the liberal interest.

The editor of the *Manchester Gazette* was then Archibald Prentice. Prentice was a prominent member of the loosely knit group of reformers to which the Potters, John Shuttleworth, Taylor and Absalom belonged. He had started out in the muslin trade and with the financial backing of like-minded friends and a loan from the bank become the proprietor and editor of the *Gazette*.

Prentice's views were to the left of Absalom's. He was a Benthamite radical and, full of hope and faith in reform, had launched his paper in June 1824. He was defeated by a combination of trade depression and his own lack of administrative skill, and now found himself in financial difficulties. Potter had invested in the *Gazette* and must have thought that a change of editor might save the paper. Absalom had the reputation of being a sound business man, a liberal and someone who knew how to write. He was many other things as well, but this Potter could not have known.

Absalom was pleased to be thought of in any literary connection but, above all, he was cautious. Change frightened him. Besides, there were other considerations. Potter had said that although he was confident of Absalom's success, he would nevertheless guarantee him against loss. The *Gazette* was a weekly. It is not clear if Absalom would have carried on his own business at the same time as editing the paper. In any event, his chance had come, but he foresaw all sorts of difficulties and troubles. He sat in his warehouse and drafted what might be his first editorial.

December 10th, 1827. This literary labour, to which I applied vigorously for two hours, made me very sensibly unwell. I walked home by Tetlow Fold but although better from the exercise, still I was not well. So much for the effects of literary labour! Such occurrences as this make me feel that I am utterly incapable of severe mental labour. And is fame then to me impossible?

December 11th, 1827. Determined to abandon the idea of becoming editor of the Gazette. My health is too much impaired and, I believe, my principles are too honest, my opinions too moderate, and too reasonable, for a successful prosecution of such an undertaking.

A visit to Joseph Johnson's the day before to dine with an acquaintance of William Hazlitt had done nothing to encourage him. Hazlitt, it seemed, was a dissolute, intemperate fellow, living unhappily with his wife, sheepish in appearance but eloquent and interesting after wine and the eighth glass of brandy and water. Absalom decided to refuse the editorship.

Potter came round to the warehouse and again pressed him hard. Absalom gave in.

December 15th, 1827. Wrote to Potter offering to undertake the Gazette on condition that I have the uncontrolled management and am allowed on all subjects and on all occasions, to express my own sentiments in my own way. They will not like my resolute independence and they think I want what they call 'nerve'. We shall see.

He was right. Five days later Potter withdrew the offer.

December 20th, 1827. Potter told me that the idea of making me editor of the Gazette was given up. 'You know,' said he, 'it would be a terrible thing if somebody got hold of it that was not decided in his opinions and they think you would not be decided enough.' I expected the matter to end in this manner: by <u>decided</u> they mean <u>decidedly of their opinion</u>, and my resolute demand of entire liberty and giving my own sentiments in my own way, has convinced those who were most anxious to put me in possession of the paper that I am not the man for their purpose.

Nor was he. Absalom's decision was a wise one and his assessment of the situation shrewd. The Potters did not like resolute independence, as J.E. Taylor had discovered the year before. Finding the Potters personally cool to him, he wrote to inquire the reason. It was, Richard Potter replied, not to be wondered at if they did not 'feel so cordially' towards him as formerly since the views he was expressing in the *Guardian* had 'materially softened'. Taylor's answer was dignified and independent and had Absalom known of it, he would have thoroughly approved. The brothers, Taylor pointed out, were saying in effect that they were ready to be friendly only so long as he remained an instrument to forward their views. Absalom was well out of it. Like Taylor, he would never have forwarded any views as his own unless he believed in them. Life would go on as before.

In the new year of 1828 he attended a curious meeting of the Literary and Philosophical Society.

January 25th, 1828. The stomach of Dempster, who died in consequence of swallowing a table knife <u>nine</u> inches long, was exhibited together with the remains of the knife. The man lived two months after the accident and might apparently have recovered but ventured <u>by coach</u> from Carlisle to London. He got no further than Middlewich and there died. The haft of the knife was entirely destroyed and much of the substance of the knife itself eaten away during its continuance in the man's stomach.

That winter Grime was very much occupied with the affairs of the New Quay Company but his industry was to lead to one of the worst disasters ever witnessed in Manchester up to then. His firm were building a large barge to be launched on the last day of February. It was the first time that a fully rigged barge or 'flat' had been ceremonially launched on the Irwell, and Grime, as principal agent of the company, determined to make the most of it. The spectacle was to include a military band, yards of bunting and the firing of guns. Most importantly of all, Grime's elder daughter, Elizabeth, was to name the vessel.

It was a leap year and the day appointed for the launch of the *Emma* was 29 February. A large crowd assembled on both banks of the Irwell, flags fluttered, the band played from the quay and, dressed in white, Grime's two daughters stood ready at the bow. Grime himself welcomed people on board, but after a time realized that the boat was becoming overcrowded and ordered the ladders to be removed. This was done, but unknown to him and out of sight, a single ladder was left in place. More and more people climbed up it until there were some 300 on board. The boat had a flat bottom and an empty hold and her mainsail was set. She was not only dangerously overloaded but those on board were unevenly distributed.

At one o'clock Grime gave the signal, Elizabeth named the boat and amid loud cheers and the firing of guns the *Emma* slid into the river. Accounts of what happened next vary. Some said that no sooner had the boat hit the water than she listed to port, or larboard as it was then called, and that the people on that side rushed across to the supposed safety of the starboard side, already crowded with people listening to the band. Other witnesses reported that the boat went forward too quickly, hit the Salford bank and then heeled over.

Whatever the truth, it took only a moment for the *Emma* to turn over completely on that side with her mast on the river and water pouring into her unsecured hatches. A cry of horror went up from the crowd and the shrieks of those on board were terrible to hear. A number were sucked down into the hold, others were trapped beneath the stern, many more were thrown into the water and struggled and choked for breath in the filthy depths of the Irwell. Some people managed to scramble up the bank on the Salford side, some swam to safety, others were rescued by men in the crowd, some of whom dived into the water without even removing their coats.

One such man rescued a person and once back on the bank sensibly divested himself of nearly all his clothes before succeeding in saving thirty more. Another exerted himself so strenuously that he had a fit and nearly died himself. Another, an excellent swimmer although he had only one arm, inexplicably ignored the people struggling in the water and rescued the floating hats instead. This he did by swimming out, putting a hat on his head, then throwing the hat on the bank before turning round to save another.

Forty people were picked up by boats. Grime's daughters were thrown into the water on the Salford side, where one of them was saved quickly. The other was longer in the water and remained critically ill for some days. We do not know how Grime escaped.

Fortunately, neither Absalom nor any of his family were on board. Most likely Grime had seen to it that they had a good place on the company's premises by the Manchester bank, because Absalom says he was an eye-witness of the launch and saw the 'oversetting and the sudden destruction' of forty-one people. Unluckily the catastrophe so stimulated his pen that he wore himself out describing it in letters to his friends and had no strength left to write it out all over again in his diary.

Final estimates of the death toll varied between thirty-eight and forty- eight. The bodies in the hold were got out by means of drag nets and grappling irons. Those in the water on the Manchester side were taken to the rooms above the New Quay stables where Grime worked, and those on the Salford side were first laid out in a field and then taken to the King's Arms or to Dr Kay's house. Dr Kay, Dr Carbutt, the surgeon Dr Jordan and many others spared no efforts at resuscitation. That they were successful in four cases is astonishing considering some of the methods employed.

People were rubbed vigorously, put into hot baths, brandy was injected into their stomachs and attempts were made to inflate their lungs by making incisions in their windpipes and using bellows. Two people are reported to have been saved by these means. Alternatively, the jugular vein was opened to 'unload the congested cavities of the heart', or shocks of 'electric fluid' were applied to the heart and diaphragm. As a last expedient, Dr Kay suggested that a person's blood, or failing that, the blood of a dog, should be transfused into the patient's vein. Two dogs were reported to have been bled to death for this purpose.

On the very day the *Emma* foundered, Prentice appeared before the Bankruptcy Commission. Business was stagnant, he had found himself unable to repay the money advanced to him for the *Gazette* and declared himself bankrupt that January, only a month after Potter had asked Absalom to edit it.

Prentice went from meeting the commissioners to the premises of the New Quay Company where he saw the dead bodies laid out, wet and livid. So unhappy and despairing was he, he afterwards confessed, that for a moment he almost envied the victims; at least they slept sound after life's fitful fever. The mood did not last nor his lack of occupation. The *Gazette* was soon incorporated into the *Manchester Times* and Prentice became once more a newspaper editor.

Grime's daughters had escaped death. Mrs Thomas Watkin was not to be so lucky. Tuberculosis was in the family and that winter she had to watch her daughter Mary grow steadily weaker from the disease. Mary was John Watkin's sister. She was not yet sixteen.

March 16th, 1828. Went in the afternoon with Elizabeth to see Mary Watkin. Poor girl, she is without hope of recovery. Alas, what a change since last August. She called on me then and was the picture of health and vivacity. Unwilling to depress her, I said to her this afternoon, 'You must make haste and get better that you may go with me to Matlock.' She asked 'When will that be?' 'At midsummer,' replied I. She looked at me intently for some time and then said, 'If it please God I should get better, I shall be very happy to go with you.'

The following day she died.

March 18th, 1828. Went in the evening to see Mrs Watkin. Saw poor dear Mary. Her face has the sweetest expression I ever saw in the face of a dead person. A sweet smile still dwells round her mouth, no line indicative of care, anxiety or suffering is to be seen upon it. It is the very countenance of innocence and peace. Her lips are a little parted, her eyes only just closed seem to intimate that she is about to awake from refreshing sleep or delightful dreams and that she will speak as soon as she awakes.

Absalom's spirits were as always mercurial and Mary's death caused them to fall fast. Towards the end of April he took Edward for a walk to Prestwich Clough.

April 26th, 1828. It was one of the most beautiful evenings I have ever beheld. We had got to the entrance of the Clough when Prestwich bells began to ring. We went into the Clough just as the day began to depart. The scene was beautiful – the sky glowing on one side so as to throw out Prestwich church and the rising ground very strongly and the moon in the opposite part of the sky, which was without a cloud. The little stream which runs through the Clough was unusually full and flowed with a rushing sound. Edward and I gathered each a large handful of anemones as we went along. The bells brought to the boy's mind Moore's song 'Sweet Evening Bells' and he began to repeat it. The lines were in my thoughts at the same moment and I was pleased to hear him. I recalled the days of my youth and recollected that I had listened to those bells and walked in this wood while yet a boy. I could feel all that the poet describes but I did not feel that life is less valuable or less pleasurable than it was then. I know more, I feel more, I have more means of enjoyment and if I could recover my health and possess a home, I should hope more than ever. We left the Clough with our bouquets of wood anemones and walked home observing the moon and the stars and the changes in the sky and we talked of the universe and of its Author and I was happy.

Unfortunately soon after this the children caught whooping cough and life became depressing again. His wife and family went to Bolton for a fortnight's change of air and Absalom was left to read *Werther* in peace. On the return of the family from Bolton something happened that made him even more certain than ever of the utter hopelessness of expecting happiness in his marriage. They had gone with their friends Mr Kershaw and Mr Davies to look at another friend's garden.

May 30th, 1828. There is in Mrs Potter's garden a small rustic hut, formed by excavating part of a bank. The path is first <u>over</u>, then passes this hut as you descend. Davies and my wife were before us and had entered the hut as we passed over it. I stood on the top looking at the lodge, they were talking and Elizabeth called out 'Where are you?' I replied 'I am here, just over your head.' 'What,' said she, 'peeping are you?'

The vulgarity of the reply pierced Absalom to the heart. His cry of outrage expressed the gulf between his wife and himself. At first sight the outburst which follows seems absurd. However, it must be remembered that Elizabeth's remark was the typical *badinage* of their shared background, the very thing Absalom's innate fastidiousness was trying to escape from, which was why it triggered the same kind of violent reaction that her walking alone at night in the market had provoked.

I had the presence of mind sufficient to reply to this <u>imprudent</u> or <u>impudent</u> speech, which was heard by Mr Kershaw and John Hall, 'No, I am looking at the prospect' but I felt and still feel, while I live, the folly and impropriety, and to the utterer of it, the degradation of such a remark. A woman is estimated as she estimates herself and she who makes such a remark to her husband when she is in the company of another person, has no right to complain if she is considered as inviting such familiarities as husbands must either not see or if they happen to <u>peep</u>, must wash away in blood. I do not suppose that my wife was guilty of any bad intention but the gross impropriety of her conduct gave me the greatest pain. I told Elizabeth at night my opinion of her conduct and had reason to regret my openness.

He was thankful to get away with Grime for a day's excursion to Buxton on the first of June. He got up at three in the morning, walked to Grime's house and breakfasted with him, leaving for Buxton in his gig at about six. When they reached Buxton they had a second breakfast before walking in the Crescent. Absalom had the eye of a novelist.

June 1st, 1828. Grime and I had much interesting conversation but I felt the usual difficulty of supporting a <u>tête à tête</u> of over six or seven hours. We dined at the Grove Inn. A rich clergyman from the neighbourhood of Sheffield was at the head of the table, next to him sat Mr Haycock, the Duke of Devonshire's steward. The lower end of the table was taken by a Mr King, a sort of half Quaker, whose full Quaker young and rather pretty wife sat opposite to me and was very civil in the Quaker style to everybody. By her side was her husband's brother, a young, large nosed and coarse featured semi-Quaker with whom she principally conversed and now and then rather frivolously. Between her and Mr Simpson, the clergyman, were a gentleman and a lady, well-fed, well-dressed, middle aged, somewhat consequential and speaking little. [Next to them] sat Mr Heywood of Manchester, short, fat, a good carver and every now and then inquiring in a scarcely articulate grunt 'If he should have the pleasure of assisting anybody?' Those persons with Mr Grime and three others who scarcely opened their mouths except to put something into them, made our dinner party. The dinner was good. I ate and listened.

The clergyman was the chief talker. He spoke mostly to Mr Haycock, but without neglecting anyone. He is apparently about sixty, tall, rather corpulent, with a full pale face, unmeaning eyes and an air of easy gentlemanly self-possession. He carved well and helped everybody with polite attention, talked of his carriage, his servants, his son, his cheese, his garden etc., as men do who are in good humour with themselves and wish to be considered persons of consequence. Occasionally he complimented the landlady on her cookery and then invited the fair Quaker and afterwards the other lady to take wine with him. Heywood amused me by the truly comic grunt in which he addressed Mrs King when he told her 'he would be happy to take wine with her.' Dinner ended, Mr Simpson returned thanks very ungracefully and gave 'The King' afterwards 'The Duke of Devonshire, the Lord of the Manor'. When these toasts had been drunk, the ladies retired, the rest of the company rising and bowing as they retired, a ceremony I never saw at a public table before.

Not long after their return an awkward thing happened at a meeting of the Club held at Woodlands Terrace.

June 5th, 1828. Davies, who had dined with Tom Burgess, was intoxicated when he came. He brought the Revd Mr Remington to the meeting and challenged Jervis to box on the grass plot.

At length the matter was settled and the company assembled to listen to Mr Hallworth's paper on 'Instinct and Reason'.

This finished, the cigars and liquor brought in, we were soon in a state of friendly excitement, had a round of papers and parted at nearly half-past twelve, in great good humour with one another. Mr Remington drank freely of brandy and water, smoked cigars adroitly, talked with much self-complacency and appears to have a good deal of information but uses low expressions. He talked of spewing and told us that spirits and tobacco acted upon him as diuretics etc. and with much composure, indeed extreme self-possession is, I think, a man of coarse manners. I should not like to be intimate with him.

Hallworth now wished to return to America with his son but was unable to get together enough money for the passage. Absalom collected £18 for him with the help of Davies and Kershaw. It was the least of his worries. He was beginning now to lose blood from his bowels and he put the trouble down to constant uneasiness about the state of his home. He needed a rest and when William Shuttleworth, John Shuttleworth's brother and a minister of the Methodist New Connexion, invited him and his wife to stay at Hanley he gladly accepted. Towards the end of June they set out together in the *Independent Potter*, Absalom reading the *Quarterly Review* during the journey.

They spent the next day with their host in a close examination of Ridgeway's pottery works but the following one was a great disappointment. Absalom had not forgotten Mrs Stoneley. He had planned an expedition to Audlem, stopping at the Stoneleys at Nantwich on the way.

June 21st, 1828. But the morning was very wet and the thunder kept every now and then growling about and threatening more. I sat in Shuttleworth's room and looked at the descending rain and the gloomy sky and sighed at the contrast between this day and the bright and beautiful morning on which I had journeyed to Beeston. Long did I hesitate, often look at the sky and very slowly and most reluctantly determine to write to Namptwich instead of going thither. At last I wrote and made up my parcel and went out with Shuttleworth and found the postboy from Newcastle and just as the thunder gave the last loud peal that I heard that day, delivered my parcel into his hands and abandoned the hope of seeing Beeston or the fair fields and sweet roses of Cheshire for at least another year – perhaps for ever!

The Shuttleworths were not well matched. William had married a young and pretty woman not altogether suited to be a minister's wife. Discussion of the evidently unhappy marriage put life into Absalom's own. Elizabeth and he were by themselves in the coach for part of the way back to Manchester. They had left soon after six o'clock in the morning.

June 24th, 1828. We had an opportunity for unreserved and affectionate

conversation which we did not neglect . . . We got to Manchester by about
twelve o'clock and putting ourselves and our boxes immediately into a
hackney coach, we drove home without delay. I was struck, as I have often
been after a short absence from home, with the strange appearance of objects
with which I was perfectly familiar. The boys came running to meet us as the
coach drove up to the gate and as I took their hands and saw their smiles and
looked at my little house and garden and contrasted what I saw with what I
had seen in the possession of others, I <u>felt</u> I had much to be thankful for.

The mood was fleeting. Before the evening was out he was suffering from a
violent headache and disorder of the stomach. Hallworth came to say goodbye.

I shook hands with him at the gate of my garden when he left us and we
parted most probably for ever – at least in this world. Poor fellow, he has
virtue and talent but not the sort of talent which is wanted. He had no
address, no management. May what I have seen of him and his sufferings
make me doubly cautious and induce me to bestir myself with more vigour
than ever to escape a similar fate. I have noticed with concern the state in
which Mr and Mrs Shuttleworth live together. She is flippant and he is surly.
They have ceased to respect each other. Their son William is a boy of
nervous and stupid disposition and to him Shuttleworth is improperly severe.
Alas! How many are the ways of being unhappy!

He heard Mr Grime's daughters play the piano and Mr Allin preach on the
Seraphim before leaving for Halifax where his own daughter was staying with the
Listers. Brook and Lister had been Absalom's debtors in 1815, the year of his
business failure. Mr Lister was a surgeon. Why and in what manner he had been
involved in Absalom's affairs is obscure. At all events, Absalom wished to see how
his daughter was getting on and travelled by coach to Halifax, arriving there at five
in the evening.

July 24th, 1828. Mr and Mrs Lister and my daughter were still at Baildon,
but Hannah, the servant of Mrs Lister, got me some tea quickly and in a style
of elegant simplicity which I did not expect even at Mrs Lister's. While it was
preparing I fell asleep on the sofa on which I had reposed after the toil of one
of my marches among the hills during my difficulties in 1815. I revolved in
my mind as I got tea the events of the thirteen years which have elapsed since
that period – the labour, the anxieties, the success – my present ill health and
my depressing apprehensions. I got rid of these thoughts by noticing the exact
order and cleanliness of the little parlour in which I sat, but as that brought
the contrary state of my home too strongly to my mind, I had recourse to
Brougham's speech on the State of the Law of which I read several pages. I
was reading it by the window as it grew dusk when Mr Lister came to the

door. We supped. He gave me an account of the loss of his patient and of the unpleasant situation in which he had been with his partner Mr Dawson. He spoke also of the death of his daughter and of her amiable conduct and was affected to tears. The room in which I slept was prettily papered and the furniture, which was good but not extravagant, was in the highest state of polish and cleanliness. Again I mourned over the state of my own home.

The journey back was enlivened by an elderly, talkative woman who got into the coach at Middleton.

July 25th, 1828. We entered into conversation and she gave me the history of her early life. She was a barmaid at an inn in Bury, had saved about £100, married a young fellow whom she described as 'rather low, broad-set, fair complexioned and very nice looking' who, after living with her seven weeks and getting possession of her money, left her in consequence of its being discovered that he had another wife and two children living at Leeds. By this fellow she had a child and she related in the Lancashire dialect but with great pathos her feelings and conduct after having been thus deceived. 'Yet,' said she, 'I could na be quiet – after my child was out of my arms and I were in my old place again, I could na keep off, but I begun acourting again and so I were married to the mon who is now my husband.' She then spoke of her children, one subject to fits and not right in his mind, of the trouble she had, of her loss of health and of the change that had taken place in her since she was young and slender, active and very 'breet', telling me how trouble had made her nervous and how resignation had made her more comfortable, that it was all the will of God and all for our good, if we chose to let it be so. I asked her if she would have hanged her deceiver if she could. 'I were very glad that he geet away. He were,' she added, 'a very genteel young man, but could na settle, he were too fond of a breezy life.' She had never seen him after he left her but had heard that after imposing in the same manner upon a young woman at Bullock Smithy, he had finally returned to his first wife.

That summer the country was eagerly following the trial of Corder for the murder of Maria Marten in the Red Barn, an account of which Absalom read for an hour at the Griffin during a pause in a walk through the fields he had taken with Alfred when he should have been at work in his warehouse. It was agitated too by something of more importance – the movement for the repeal of the civil disabilities imposed upon Roman Catholics. Feeling ran high in certain influential circles in Manchester.

Now editor of the *Manchester Times*, Prentice made justifiable fun of the anti-Catholic Emancipation meetings with their lurid references to the Massacre of St Bartholomew's Day and the fires of Smithfield. 'In the reign of Mary two hundred and seventy persons were burnt to death, including five bishops,' the Presbyterian Prentice quoted a Mr Folliot announcing at a meeting at Knutsford.

> Think of that – think of that; and twenty-one clergymen – think of that. There were also eight laymen and eighty-four tradesmen; and now listen you husbandmen – a hundred husbandmen were burnt – aye, made beefsteaks of. Think of that, farmers of Cheshire. How would you like to be made beefsteaks of? Think of that –

Absalom had thought of that. He shared the widespread fear and ignorance of Roman Catholicism and probably did not realize the Catholic origin of the Anglican prayers he now so much appreciated. However, he had been brought up as a Protestant Dissenter and both he and many of his friends had reason to detest intolerance and bigotry.

CHAPTER TWELVE
'Your garden, citizen, if you choose'

Much to Absalom's joy, in November 1828 John Thelwall returned to give another course of lectures. Absalom was doggedly loyal to Thelwall, the man who had had such an influence upon his mind when it was yet unformed and ignorant. He went to a lecture on *Hamlet* and sadly remarked that only fourteen people were present. Undaunted, and despite some anxiety about an illness of his mother, he attended them all and was delighted when his friend John Shuttleworth, William's brother, invited him to his house to meet the speaker.

John Shuttleworth was also in the cotton trade and at this time a more active reformer than Absalom. It was he who had been at Peterloo and given evidence against the Yeomanry. Some people thought that he and Absalom were the two most effective public speakers in Manchester. Absalom was more refined, as a contemporary put it, Shuttleworth more energetic and powerful.

Thelwall was then sixty-four. Absalom thought of him as an old man and marvelled at the energy of his body and mind, at his sensibility and the force with which he still expressed his feelings.

Mr Thelwall occupied an arm chair on the right of the fireplace and the first thing that struck me was the easy and graceful manner in which he filled the chair. This is a thing few people do well and which little and slender people usually do ill. When we came in they were talking of Bonaparte and Mr Thelwall half expressed a wish that he had fallen at Waterloo. It was asserted that he had sought death but had been compelled to leave the field by those around him. Mr Shuttleworth contended that he had shown the superiority of his mind by the manner in which he had borne his reverses.

The conversation at length shifted to the reformer Horne Tooke, with whom Thelwall had been intimate in his revolutionary days. He said that Tooke was one of the most delightful companions he had ever known and at his own table had the power of rendering himself exquisitely agreeable. His dinners were not principally at his own cost. Some of the guests sent wine, some game and some other things and in this manner an elegant table was kept without much expense to the master of the house. This applied only to Sunday dinners at which his two natural daughters never appeared though they made all the pastry that came to the table.

He had what he called a <u>cold</u> dinner on Wednesday, to which none but his most select friends were invited and at which his daughters and their mother were present. The young ladies were accomplished, understood music and had been taught engraving by Sharpe, who resided some time with Horne Tooke for the purpose of giving them instruction. They were also exact housewives, having been carefully initiated into all the branches of domestic management. I was curious enough to ask what sort of woman the mother of these girls might be. 'One of the most made-up dolls,' said Thelwall, 'that I ever saw.' 'Tooke,' he added, 'was often pressed to marry. "Mr Tooke", said one officious friend, "you should take a wife." "Take a wife," was the reply, "well let us see, pray whose wife shall I take?"'

'Tooke,' continued Mr Thelwall, 'had a great mind, I don't know why, to have me for a son-in-law. He always called me "citizen". You are aware that he had a son who gave him a great deal of trouble. He said to me one day, "Citizen, what I am going to tell you must never be repeated while I live. Yesterday I parted with my son. I have sent him to India. I put a £100 note into his hand and I said to him, 'This is the last money I will ever give you, this is the last time I will ever see you, neither will I ever hear from you again. If you write, I will put your letter unopened into the fire and if any of my friends shall, at any time, mention your name to me, I will forbid him my house and never see him again.' Now, citizen, I have no son, why should not you be my son? The chambers my son occupied at Cambridge are my property and shall be yours if you like. I will procure for you the patronage of the Bishop of Bristol and secure you the means of support while you are at college and such patronage as will ensure your advancement afterwards."'

'He then,' proceeded Mr Thelwall, 'invited me to his cold dinner and introduced me to his daughters and their mother. The young ladies were accomplished but my heart was already engaged; I was indeed on the point of being married. Going not long after to see him at Wimbledon, I found him at work in his garden and said to him, "You take a great deal of trouble, Mr Tooke, to embellish your garden." "Your garden, citizen," replied Tooke. "Your garden, if you choose."'

Mr Thelwall praised Tooke highly for his firmness and presence of mind. He said that when he, Thelwall, and the other persons who were tried with Tooke were going with him from Newgate into court, 'following him,' said Thelwall, 'like chickens following a hen,' Mr Kirby, the keeper of Newgate, said to them, 'Not so fast, gentlemen, there is no occasion for being in a hurry.' 'No occasion for hurry,' said Tooke, 'pray don't let us make a toil of a pleasure.'

Mr Thelwall had once or twice met Thomas Paine at Tooke's table.

Paine was a man who spoke little, but every now and then made a shrewd remark. He was also a mild tempered and humane man. Tooke on the contrary, loved strong measures and had no great tenderness for human life. One day when Tooke was talking of the blood which must be shed to effect such a change as was desirable in the government of the country, Paine said to him, 'After all, you are still an aristocrat at bottom, nothing will satisfy you but blood, nothing but blood.' Tooke used to say that he had made one grand mistake in his life: he had given communities credit for too much sense and individuals for too much virtue. 'Aye,' said Mr Shuttleworth, 'it was but one mistake, but it was a wapper.'

Mr Thelwall then passed to Charles James Fox.

He said that as a speaker, he was, until warmed by his subject, as tedious and clumsy as Lord Holland, but when roused powerful, though never elegant.

William Pitt the Younger was a fine example of what art and education could do and undoubtedly the first of second-rate speakers.

His enunciation was wonderfully distinct. No syllable was lost in his delivery. He did not say Parlament, but Parliament. In listening to him you were astonished at the perfection of his periods. Of Burke, he said that his delivery was thick, hurried and spluttering, but his language beautiful and all that he said rich in metaphor and illustration. Burke was a very laborious writer and corrected and re-corrected with astonishing perseverance.

As Christmas approached the social round quickened. Grime had evidently recovered from the *Emma* disaster. He opened a bottle of burgundy after a meeting of the Club and, not to be outdone, Absalom offered them all a glass of hock. On a Sunday not long after this Grime gave an entertainment at which Thelwall was present and Absalom observed the other guests closely, in particular a Mr and Mrs Goadsby.

December 7th, 1828. We had some lively chat and some music, part sacred, but principally of a lighter kind. I was struck with the contrast between Mr and Mrs Goadsby. He, thin, pale and wanting some front teeth, apparently about fifty, with a look of insignificant amiability, saying little – she, perhaps thirty-five, plump, with dark eyes, a nose rather turned up, a very pretty mouth, complete self-possession and a rather graceful deportment, taking little notice of her yoke fellow, smiling at the company and talking moral reflections with Mr Grime. 'What the devil,' said Johnson with his usual deliberate manner, as we walked home, 'what the devil could induce such a man as Mr Goadsby to marry such a woman as that?'

Entertainment had to be returned.

December 15th, 1828. Mr Thelwall, Mr and Mrs Spencer, Grime and Johnson dined and spent the day with us. This is the first formal dinner I ever gave and I and my poor heedless wife were of course guilty of innumerable blunders. Yet the thing passed off tolerably well. I got a bad headache by sitting too long and drinking too much and went to bed almost determined never to have another dinner party.

Three days later Grime gave a far grander party than Absalom's. Eleven gentlemen were present, the meal was sumptuous, music was provided and Absalom did not go to bed until two in the morning. Nervous exhaustion followed.

December 18th, 1828. This week I have been more in set company than almost any week of my life. It is pleasant enough, if one had no business to attend to and were able to take a full part in the company. I am not fit nor qualified to do so. Add to this that the enjoyment of elegant society so possesses my thoughts that I am unfit for the labour of business. When I return to it I still think of the company, still dwell upon the conversation and linger when I should be active and neglect that to which I ought to attend.

On the last day of the year he poured out his feelings into his diary. No one else would listen to him even if he had been inclined to speak. It was the voice of despair. He does not mention the fact, perhaps he did not even remember it, but in the coming year he would be forty-two, the age in his 'Plan of Life', written in 1810, when he had imagined himself returning home from his extensive travels abroad in good health and full of knowledge and experience.

December 31st, 1828. I close this year in great dejection. Home I have none. Dirt, rags, a mean appearance, a table wretchedly provided, linen but half washed, a disgusting mixture of finery and beggarliness, such is the home I purchase by the expenditure of a large sum of money. A sum of money, sufficient to produce every comfort, is regularly required in the tone of a tax-gatherer and as regularly produces a disgraceful and disgusting house table. My mental capacity, my ability for study, for company and above all for business, sink under the unceasing disappointment which I purchase at so high a price.

Grime wished to see his daughters well married and started 1829 with yet another lavish dinner party. Absalom did not altogether approve. We do not know the cause of Mrs Frost's sadness.

January 15th, 1829. We had a splendid dinner, wine, cards and music, but no conversation. I was amused by the evidently great effect produced by Mr Grime's plate and furniture on the minds of the ladies. I noticed the polite dignity of Mrs Goadsby and the <u>endeavour</u> to please of Mr Grime. I noticed, too, the air of sadness of Mrs Frost and the sighs which, from time to time, involuntarily escaped her. As to Mr Grime, his laugh, not I fear a laugh of genuine pleasure, still rings in my ears. Finally, I am convinced that splendour and happiness are not usually connected.

A remark of his wife rankled. He had spoken to her about her bad example to the children. 'And what,' she had replied, 'do you do for them? Read Humphrey Clinker and swear in their presence.'

Absalom had not seen much of Thomas Potter since the affair of the *Gazette* but at the end of March he called upon him about some business matter and found him in an expansive mood.

March 21st, 1829. He took me into his private counting house and began to talk to me confidentially about himself and the New Bank in which I had some shares. He said that when he began to work his father was barely solvent and that in twelve years, he, Mr Potter, had made almost £15,000 which, said he, in a place like Tadcaster, in a draper's shop and with a bit of land, was not doing amiss. 'I worked hard and I don't think that in the whole of the twelve years I spent £4 a year either on the lasses or in drink or diversion of any kind though I had the till to go to at any time.'

On Good Friday Absalom joined Grime and Joseph Johnson for a walk to Northenden.

April 17th, 1829. In a little field at Piperhill in Northen we found the sweet white violet in flower, covering the banks as it does in Bromley in Kent. I gathered the flowers and some of the roots. We dined at the Boat House and [after our return] stopped for more than an hour at Grime's and drank some champagne which is about as good as well made currant wine. I got home at about ten o'clock having passed an innocent, happy healthful day at the expense of two shillings and eightpence halfpenny.

Prices were low because wages were. The Potters had succeeded and a few like them. To a far lesser degree so had a large number of people like Grime and Absalom. But for hundreds who had prospered in Manchester there were thousands who had neither the intelligence, perseverance nor opportunity to get even a decent living.

In early May Absalom watched the phrenologist Dr Spurzheim dissect a human brain, found anemones, wild garlic and yellow saxifrage in Broughton and saw the swallows flying low over Drinkwater's Grounds. On the day he accompanied his daughter to her dancing lessons at Grime's house, the hand-loom weavers rioted. The mob broke looms, set some factories on fire and plundered shops. It was the despairing cry of a class created by one invention and destined to be deprived of its livelihood by another, a people whose skills would increasingly and for ever be made redundant by technology.

CHAPTER THIRTEEN

'Mr Cobbett is five feet ten inches in height, robust and even lusty'

Mrs William Shuttleworth seems to have been an attractive woman. Evidently Absalom thought so. That June she came to visit her mother-in-law, old Mrs Shuttleworth, who, like John Shuttleworth, lived in Manchester. She came to stay at Woodlands Terrace together with her son. Absalom took her and Edward for a walk on Kersal Moor before tea.

> **June 12th, 1829.** After tea we amused ourselves for some time by observing the people who were returning from the Moor. We used a telescope for part of the time. The females who discovered our observation smiled and seemed pleased, the men were all dissatisfied and some expressed their dissatisfaction in coarse language. We had some wine. Mrs Shuttleworth and I had a walk alone to the bottom of the New Road, up and down once or twice. We walked with confidence and interest. The night was beautiful and I received such proofs of her esteem as affected me very sensibly. She is not fit for her situation as a Methodist Preacher's wife. Her disposition is gay and sportive and she dislikes the formal and affected gravity to which her situation condemns her.

They walked together every day with the rest of the family and one June evening again ventured out alone.

> **June 18th, 1829.** We went through the fields. We talked with friendly confidence and Mrs Shuttleworth even took the liberty to scold me for some parts of my conduct during the time she has been with us. I made her a jocular promise of amendment and we stayed out so long that on our return my wife was sulky and scolded me and pouted a little at Mrs S. It was however but a passing cloud and we sat up late with a good deal of pleasure.

The following day Absalom went to a meeting of the Club at Jervis's house.

> **June 19th, 1829.** While I was at the meeting Shuttleworth came to our

house and scolded his wife furiously for having been so much with us and so little with his mother. He was surly too with my wife and, as I was told, railed at them until they wept abundantly.

The next day both Shuttleworth and his wife left for Hanley.

June 20th, 1829. Before they left I drank to Mrs Shuttleworth and wished her 'much happiness among the pots'. 'I shall have none,' she mournfully replied, 'I don't expect happiness.' She then drank to me and wished me as much happiness as it was possible for me to have in this world.

Absalom still hoped for his fair share of it. He was determined to return to Beeston Castle and not long after the Shuttleworth's departure took his wife and Edward in the *Hark Forward* to Tarporley and put up at the Swan.

June 24th, 1829. After tea we took a chaise and went to Beeston. We arrived a little before sunset and got into the Castle itself just in time to see the last beams of the sun convert the Dee and the Mersey into sheets of flame. We sat down at that point of the ruin which projects over the perpendicular side of the rock and drank the health, first of Mrs Shuttleworth, then of absent friends. I climbed to the top of the tower over the gateway. I do not intend to visit Beeston any more and the probability that I was taking my last look had no small influence on my mind.

They drove to Horsley Bath, which they reached just in time to have light enough to see it.

It was as beautiful as ever. The house covered with fine roses, the garden full of beautiful flowers and the clear water of the spring gushing into the basin and passing out of it with an agreeable rushing sound. The evening was still. There was a low twittering now and then from the birds and this, with the sound of the water and that of our voices, was all that broke the silence of the place.

The owner of the house, who was perhaps fifty years old, told them that in all his life he had never been more than forty miles from his home. The following day they took a chaise to Nantwich.

June 25th, 1829. It was a lovely summer's morning. Our ride was agreeable except from the ill humour of my wife. We stopped at Namptwich to dine and then called at Stoneley's. The master and mistress have not altered since I last saw them, except that Mrs Stoneley has a more sedate look and a touch of sadness below the eyes. Anne is much improved. She is taller, has more colour and her eyes have more vivacity and expression. Mrs Stoneley went with us in the chaise to Audlem. It rained, my wife became sick and our ride was unpleasant. We got to Audlem and to my aunt's. Mountford hobbled to meet us, my aunt was fetched, tea prepared and we made ourselves as comfortable as we could. It still rained. Something, I know not what, made me feel nausea and giddiness. I went out into the garden in spite of the wet. The little bower at the bottom had been destroyed and the seat removed. This vexed me. I gathered two roses and went into the house. We stayed till eight and then set off in the chaise to return.

The idyll was over. He was to return to Audlem only twice more in his life; the last time in the cold January of 1838 when there was snow on the ground and his Aunt Mountford lay dying.

In Manchester civil unrest was just below the surface. Troops were stationed on Kersal Moor and held elaborate military exercises which included a sham fight. A detachment of infantry, horse and artillery took possession of the Moor and were attacked by 'the enemy'. Cannon were brought up and cavalry sheltered behind the grandstand where once 'coffee, tea, chocolate, strawberries and cream' were provided every Wednesday and Friday during the summer months. The noise was considerable and Absalom took Edward to enjoy the fun. More worrying to Grime were rumours about the new railroad.

If goods were moved in trucks by steam engines at great speed along rails, then how could river transport compete? The New Quay Company might be forced out of business. In any event, the volume of traffic along the Irwell might be considerably lessened.

Grime was not alone in his anxiety. The railways might well turn out to be a success and what then would happen to horses? Stationers' windows in Manchester were full of pictures of half-starved horses leaning over railings and looking wistfully at a passing train. He and Absalom hired a sociable and went to Peel Green to see the new railroad cuttings. The rails had been placed on a high embankment and Absalom, who was not in the transport business, admired the view from the top.

Others might be feeling the pinch, but despite his fears he was doing quite well. He bought yet more land in Broughton and was busy again with surveyors and builders. Although fourteen years had passed since his dealings with Brook and Lister had ended in near disaster, still Brook had not paid him all he owed. Absalom wanted to settle the matter and to use any money he got from Brook for a new cottage in Camp Street. In September he took the *High Flyer* to Bradford, reading the *Wealth of Nations* as he went.

September 24th, 1829. I was well and ate with more relish than usual. Set out on foot for Baildon. In the course of a long conversation I <u>extracted</u> from Brook that he owes to X and to me about £1200 and that he cannot pay

half-a-crown in the pound! As I believe Brook to be an honest man and have
in the last fourteen years been a considerable gainer by my business with him,
I thought it right to tell him that I would take for my debt what he was able
to give, and thus I lost at a stoke £250 [about £12,500 in 1990 values].

At night, alone in his bedroom, he looked out at an almost cloudless sky, then
stretched his legs luxuriously along the clean and dry sheets. Once he woke and
heard the clock strike three and got out of bed and looked at the still brilliant sky.
At five Brook came in carrying a candle. When Absalom set out half an hour later
an autumn mist was swirling down from the moors, obscuring the houses and
making the cobbles slippery, but it was the prelude to a beautiful day.

Whatever the precise nature of their business, neither of Absalom's two
brothers-in-law, Joseph and William Makinson, seem to have been financially
sound. Absalom had already bought some building land to help Joseph and now
William suggested that he might do better to give up business altogether and
become a teacher. He said that his present income was £350 a year. He had six
children to house and feed. If he built himself a large house at Pendleton they
could all live there. He could then take in twenty pupils at £3 a quarter and
manage well enough. Later he followed this course with some success, eventually
presiding over a Gentleman's Academy in Lime Place, Broughton.

At a party at the Medcalf's the Potters were present and James Potter, whom
Absalom had not met before, told the company about the slaves in Jamaica, where
he had lived for some years.

November 11th, 1829. The slaves work from day-dawn to sunset with an
interval of half an hour for breakfast and two hours for dinner. Mr Potter said
that marriages are not common, men and women live together by consent.
The slaves have each a provision ground and are allowed one day a fortnight
to cultivate it. The owner finds a hut and gives to the slaves six salt herrings
every fortnight and clothes annually. The slaves keep hogs and poultry. Land
in Jamaica is not capital, slaves are the capital. The land is worth little,
although so fertile that the labour of one day in a fortnight will maintain a
family. To cultivate the soil personally would degrade a white man.

According to William Cobbett the workers in England, suffering from want and
brutalized by the Poor Law, were little better off than Potter's West Indian slaves.
Absalom had planted some cuttings from Cobbett's American apple trees in his
garden but he had never met him personally. In January 1830 Cobbett was
stumping the country on behalf of parliamentary reform. He had come to
Manchester and was staying with Johnson at Northenden. Absalom now met him
there on two occasions. He probably took notes when he got home and expanded
them later. He possessed a remarkable memory. He wrote his account, not in his
diary, but like the other long entries, in a separate notebook some of whose

contents were eventually published as two pamphlets by his son Edward.

January 3rd and 10th, 1830. Mr Cobbett is five feet ten inches in height, robust and even lusty, but not corpulent. His appearance is that of sturdy rural respectability and his deportment, although not awkward, is yet not graceful. His complexion is ruddy and his countenance open and expressive but his grey and rather small eyes give to his face, especially in some positions of the head and when he is speaking of some clever act of his own, an expression of keen penetrating shrewdness and even of cunning. His forehead is high and very little wrinkled and he has a full head of very white hair, which, as his appearance discovers no other mark of decay – even his teeth remain entire and unusually white – appears so little to belong to his healthy and florid countenance that a stranger is almost irresistibly induced to ascribe it to the use of hair powder. His enunciation is clear, distinct and correct, his voice musical and his speech discovering not more than enough of the peculiarities of the southern counties to accord with his rurally respectable appearance. Mr Cobbett's dress is that of a substantial yeoman or gentleman farmer, with however a thorough cleanliness of person not always to be found in that portion of the people of England.

Cobbett was accompanied by one of his sons and a daughter.

Mr John Cobbett is a slim, thin-visaged young man, civil and intelligent, but without any striking exhibition of peculiar talent. Miss Susan is a pretty, dark haired and dark-eyed brunette, modest but not bashful and rather pleasingly attentive to what is said by others than forward to speak herself. Both these young people are very attentive to their father and apparently proud of him. He, on his part, behaves to them with evident affection. It may not be improper to notice here that Mr Cobbett has provided for the future of each child the copyright of one of his publications. Miss Cobbett is the proprietess of his English Grammar, which produces £300 a year and Miss Susan is the owner of Cottage Economy, from the sale of which she nets about £180 a year.

Mr Cobbett was a model of temperance.

On the first day of my seeing him he took, in the course of seven hours, about a glass and a half of port wine, not as an indulgence, but as a medicine. Instead of tea he took milk and water and ate nothing except two or three apples from dinner time until ten at night.

Absalom had an instance of Cobbett's characteristic warmth of feeling, 'the source, perhaps, of much of the excellence, as well as the defects, of his character'.

Several years ago, when Mr Cobbett returned from America and was coming
from Liverpool to Manchester [bearing the bones of Tom Paine] Mr Johnson
went to Irlam to meet him and was present when the letter of the Borough-
reeve and constables of Manchester, forbidding his entry into the town, was
delivered to Mr Cobbett. To this circumstance Mr John Cobbett referred and
reminded his father that Mr Johnson was in the room with them when the
letter was received. 'What,' said Mr Cobbett, laying down knife and fork and
starting on his feet, 'were you there? Give me your hand, my boy,' and
forthwith he extended his hands not across merely, but along the table and
shook the hand of his host with a right English squeeze.

Cobbett had been accused of egoism and violence but this might be accounted
for by considering the warmth of his temperament and the circumstances he had
had to face.

His life has been a life of battles. He has been opposed, many times single-
handed, by a host of opponents, the hirelings or zealots of almost every party.
His really great talents have been underrated, his facts have been
misrepresented, his really correct reasoning scouted, his motives questioned and
his conduct vilified. It was to be expected and it has been the case, that the man
thus assailed, conscious of his superiority, has turned round on his assailants, has
answered scorn with scorn, contumely with contumely, abuse with abuse and
having worsted his antagonists at their own weapons, has left them no resource
but to cry out against his superior ability in coarseness and egotism.

His conversation was agreeable.

His own remark 'It is not possible for me to be dull' is not less correct than
expressive. He has considerable comic power and his voice and countenance
are, in his narrations, equally flexible. He speaks deliberately, but not slowly.
The hearer does not wish him to speak faster and is never tempted to help
him with a word. In argument he listens patiently and replies definitely in
clear and perspicuous language; nor did I observe any tendency to a
disposition to take an advantage of his opponent, or even to evade the force
of an argument.

The talk was unavoidably political for the most part and much of it related to
Robert Peel's reform of the currency, about which he held strong views. He was
doubtful about the value of free trade. He had an acquaintance who was a market
gardener at Fulham, supplying Covent Garden with early vegetables and fruit.

But now, on the principle of free trade, the French run over from the
opposite coast and supply it. Of course they get the custom which he had

previously. But do they buy your manufactures? No such thing. They take the value of their produce to France all in silver. See then, what you have got by your free trade. You have injured the business of an industrious fellow countryman, robbed three or four labourers of the means of subsistence, increased your poor rate and diminished the number of your customers – and all this to enable a parcel of Frenchmen to carry so much sterling money out of the country.

He was asked if he were an advocate for the Corn Laws.

Certainly not. I don't think the Corn Laws, as some people do, the great cause of all our sufferings. I think if my measures were adopted, the landlords would want no Corn Laws, because I believe that this country would then be able to grow corn with any country, but I was never friendly to the Corn Laws. When they were first proposed I was the only person who petitioned against them. I was a farmer and my yard was full of wheat ricks, but I did not like the law and I petitioned against it.

England, Cobbett thought, owed its superiority to the industry of its people.

Let any man go to America, or to France, and see how the people work and let him compare their application with that of the people in this country, and then he will understand the real cause of the superiority of England. There is not a country in the world the people of which are at all to be compared with the English for steady, continued industry and willing submission to lawful authority. It is the habit of the people and runs through all ranks and is, in my opinion, owing in a great degree to the laws which regulate apprenticeships. There is nowhere such prompt and willing obedience as in England. In France and Italy the servants who wait at table do not refrain from taking part now and then in the conversation and if you are travelling in an open carriage, the fellow who stands behind it will lean over and address his observations to his master and those who are with him. In England this is not thought of and would not be suffered. Certainly it is to the superior industry and the equally superior habit of obedience that the superiority of England in manufacture is to be ascribed.

Cobbett may have been an egoist, a hot-headed fool, or a mischievous visionary but at least he was sincere. The same could not be said of his host. Later on that year, Johnson 'ingenuously enough' confessed to Absalom that he did not wish for reform or revolution until he had made his own fortune. 'I had not been six months a radical,' said he, 'before I was disgusted with the radicals.' Nevertheless, he did very well out of them. Admirers of Cobbett, Orator Hunt and Joseph Johnson had collected enough money to buy the three of them an annuity with a reversion to the survivors. Fortunately for Johnson, both Hunt and Cobbett died in 1835 and he lived to enjoy the triple annuity until his death, a dedicated conservative, nearly forty years later.

As a committee member of the Commercial Clerk's Society, Absalom frequently had to arbitrate in business matters. A man named Ridings had been expelled from the Society and now asked to be reinstated.

> **January 13th, 1830.** We agreed to reinstate poor Ridings as a member of the Society. When I was a boy in my uncle's warehouse in Back Square, Ridings was a man of about thirty and with John Walker next door. How little could he then think that the boy with whom he sometimes amused himself could live to receive his acknowledgements, <u>his humble acknowledgements</u>, for devoting a few hours to the examination of his conduct with a view to prevent his being excluded from the Clerk's Society.

He felt under pressure. First he had to extricate Johnson from a tedious dispute he was conducting in the pages of the *Guardian* about Peel's Specie Bill and then William Harvey, one of the 'small but determined band' of Manchester liberals, took him aside and asked if he would draft a Petition to the House of Commons on behalf of the people of Manchester to ask for parliamentary reform.

It was not strictly accurate to say that Manchester was completely unrepresented in Parliament. It had its two County Members and for a long time they had sufficed to protect its interests. But now Manchester was the second most important town in England commercially, so it was patently absurd for it to have no direct representatives at Westminster. Absalom stayed up writing the Petition until two in the morning. On Easter Sunday he attended the christening of a former servant's baby at the Old Church and was amazed to see how many children were baptized at once.

> **April 11th, 1830.** There were perhaps three hundred children christened at the same time and the variety of squalls and the varied appearance of the children, the parents, the sponsors etc. constituted a scene sufficiently grotesque. Not a word of the service could be heard by three fourths of the assembly. Mr Wray, the officiating minister, was very liberal in aspersing the faces of the children and the place, from the crowd of persons assembled, was very hot. A child with the baptismal water still lying in drops on its face was brought by the godmother to its father, a simple looking, young country fellow. He looked at it and observing the drops, exclaimed, 'Eh, bless it! How it swats.'

Absalom's cousin, the impetuous John Watkin, had got himself into trouble.

> **May 20th, 1830.** In defending some women employed at Mr Harter's Mill

from the violence of the turn-out weavers, he was himself assaulted. In self-defence he drew out his penknife and stabbed three persons. He was apprehended, lodged in the New Bailey and brought up the next day before Mr Foster on a charge of stabbing. The evidence however proved that his life was in danger and the charge was dismissed.

Fear of poverty never ceased to haunt Absalom.

May 28th, 1830. Attended the meeting of the Commercial Clerk's Society. Poor Ridings was put on the superannuated list with an allowance of five shillings a week and the same allowance was continued to old Mr Dettleson. Dettleson could not be satisfied without coming into the room to thank us. He is sixty-six years old, gouty, ruptured and destitute, although formerly in the receipt of a handsome income. The sight of him and Ridings was a valuable lesson. I never before knew the value of five shillings a week.

Mrs Shuttleworth stayed with them again and hardly had she gone than five-year-old Alfred fell seriously ill.

June 6th, 1830. Rose unwell, having been kept awake all night by Alfred who is unwell. Mr Nursaw, who has seen him this morning, says it is a severe attack of scarlet fever and has ordered leeches to be applied. The poor child is delirious and very restless. We had great trouble in the application of the leeches from his struggles and cries. Alfred worse at night. Leeches applied behind the ears and cloths dipped in cold water laid on his head. He has been put into a warm bath once or twice during the day and tonight has taken a powder composed of calomel and ipecacuanah.

The next day the child gained possession of his senses.

June 7th, 1830. He recognizes his mother and me and has kissed us repeatedly, like a fond child who awakes from a long and sound sleep. Of the occurrences of yesterday he appears to have no knowledge. Alfred is worse at noon, he is again delirious and his throat worse. His hair has been thinned to render the cold water more effective and a blister applied to the back of his head.

Two days later the doctor declared that he was out of danger. That was a great relief but Absalom's mother remained unwell, he himself was still losing blood, he could not get on with a historical romance he was writing about Peter the Hermit and, to add to it all, his daughter caught the scarlet fever. On Sunday Joseph Makinson and his daughters came round and sang Job's Anthem in the parlour. Even through his anxieties Absalom thought their wry faces comic. But the anthem was opportune.

That July, five days after the funeral of George IV, just as Absalom was about to go upstairs to bid his mother goodnight, his wife came in and said that the old lady was dying.

July 20th, 1830. My mother died about half-past eight o'clock this evening. She had been up in the afternoon and was thought to be better. Yesterday, although very feeble, she had the full possession of her faculties and blessed the children when they bade her goodnight. This evening, just as I was going to see her, they were coming downstairs to tell me she was dying. I did not expect it. I went into the room and heard her laborious breathing and held her hand and looked upon her face and in a few minutes, a long sobbing expiration of the breath, not apparently painful, only laborious, closed her sufferings and her life. Her sufferings she has borne with patient resignation. Her life has been one of unostentatious usefulness. Alas! my mother. To me she was ever the truest and kindest of friends and to her care and her example I owe everything useful or valuable in my character. I owe her also my education and my property. Her failings were over-anxiety and a degree of suspicious querulousness which <u>now</u> appear to me very excusable. I have not been a bad son, but she deserved a much better. I feel that I might have made her more comfortable. I feel that I ought to have done so, I lament that I did not. Alas! I have lost one, the only one, who loved me with a disinterested affection and the business of whose life it was to promote my welfare.

I saw my father die when I was about ten years old and was convinced by what I saw that <u>dying, mere dying</u>, is not terrible. I have now, at the age of forty-three, beheld the death of my mother and the conviction is strengthened. Death in both cases appeared to me to be rather the coming on of a troubled sleep, than painful. My mother looked younger and if I may use the word speaking of a person of seventy-four years old, handsomer after death than she had done for years. Her face was much less wrinkled and the outline of her features in consequence more youthful. In early life her appearance must have been very agreeable.

The shock, the weariness and the grief intensified Absalom's resentment against his wife. Convention decreed that a death in the house rendered it necessary for white blinds to be drawn down over the front windows. One pair only could be found and these were too dirty to be put up. They had to be washed, dried and ironed but during that time the windows would be bare, a shame to the family, a needless disgrace when he was giving Elizabeth 'enormous sums' just to keep the house in order.

Absalom wished his mother to be buried at Prestwich, by the church whose bells rang out over the brook to Broughton. He walked there with Edward but was refused permission; only those who lived in that parish could lie in that churchyard. She would have to be buried a little farther to the east, at Cheetham

Hill, a village two miles from Manchester; a pleasant place of green fields and lanes, half-timbered farmsteads and a handful of comfortable houses built by rich merchants.

Old Mr Makinson attended the funeral at St Mark's together with his sons, Joseph, William and John. Absalom was there together with his three boys and Mr Grime. He was 'a good deal affected'.

What followed was absurd, macabre and sad. It must not be imagined that in those days bed bugs were to be found only in the houses of the poor and dirty. They were ubiquitous and extremely difficult to get rid of, as any reader of the letters between Thomas Carlyle and his wife knows very well. That the infestation at Woodlands Terrace had been allowed to get so bad was partly the fault of Elizabeth but Absalom's violent reaction to it was more an indication of his highly nervous state than a normal response to a not unusual problem.

July 27th, 1830. Intending to obviate any dislike which might be entertained to sleeping on the bed in which my mother died, I directed that it should be got ready for me. Clean sheets were accordingly put on it and I went to bed about eleven o'clock. I lay some time reflecting on the past but having lost a good deal of rest lately and had a fatiguing day's work, I was sinking into repose when my slumber was retarded by a disagreeable tingling and smarting in different parts of my body which continued to increase. I rubbed myself and turned from side to side and in a while, felt something alive on my forehead which being crushed by my finger, I found by the smell to be a bug! From my neck and then from my hand, I had to remove a similar annoyance. I lay sleepless and uneasy until daybreak and with the first light discovered to my astonishment, disgust and rage, that the bed and the curtains were swarming with bugs. I called my wife from her room and having made her witness the effects of her neglect, I destroyed more than twenty bugs on the pillow and one side of the curtain and several on my nightshirt and then having stripped and washed myself all over, I went to another bed to try to get an hour or two's sleep before I went to town. I could not sleep for some time. I reflected that my mother, deprived of the use of her lower extremities and unable even to turn without assistance, had lain on the bed I had quitted and on that bed had died.

A few days later he went to bed at twelve o'clock.

August 2nd, 1830. When I got to bed I found the under sheet so damp that it clung to my legs and I had a slight return of the tingling which I had experienced when I lay in that nest of vermin, the bed on which my poor mother died. I could not sleep and rose in the morning unwell and unrefreshed. I inquired what sheets I had slept in and if they had been aired. To my astonishment I found that the sheet on which I had slept was one of

those from my mother's bed, the very sheet on which I had killed the bugs,
which had lain in a heap since July 27th. I was enraged to the highest degree.
I cursed the unfeeling hypocrite and was at last provoked to give her a box
on the ear.

He regretted the act even as it was done, not because his wife did not deserve it
but because in hitting her he was degrading himself.

CHAPTER FOURTEEN

'High above the grim and grimy crowd of scowling faces a loom had been erected'

Absalom's wife complained to her brothers about his treatment of her and William sent a letter round to Absalom's warehouse announcing that under existing circumstances he could no longer associate with Mr Watkin. To this Absalom returned a severe reply which must have been effective, for the following Sunday his brother-in-law shook hands with him after the service at Oldham Street Chapel. Ten days' holiday at Runcorn did them all a great deal of good, although the 'incurable negligence' of his wife nearly caused them to miss the coach home.

Coaches would gradually become a thing of the past. No change in Absalom's lifetime was so revolutionary as the coming of the railways. His journey from London to Manchester as a boy in 1801 was restricted to the pace of a horse. It took him roughly the same amount of time as it would have taken a Roman commander or a medieval king. At his death the journey was accomplished in a mere fraction of the time.

Five years before, in the year of Alfred's birth, a single steam engine driven by Stephenson had drawn thirty-four carriages of a gross weight of ninety tons. The train, preceded by a signalman on horseback, had moved off at about twelve miles an hour and attained fifteen miles an hour on a favourable part of the line. That particular train had run between Stockton and Darlington, but once the experiment proved workable and it was realized that if such a weight could be pulled by a single engine then more engines could draw heavier loads, and that human beings as well as goods could be carried safely in a similar manner, the revolution in transport was inevitable.

It was obvious to others besides Grime that the carriage of goods between a manufacturing town like Manchester and the port of Liverpool was of prime importance, and plans had been made for a railway link between them before the opening of the Stockton and Darlington line. The railway directors had offered a prize for the best engine. This had been won by the Stephenson brothers with the *Rocket*, an improved version of the engine that had opened the Stockton and Darlington line. Surveying the route and laying track had alerted people in the neighbourhood of Manchester for a long time to what was going on, but it was not until the summer that they were informed that the opening of the railway, to include a ceremonial ride between Liverpool and Manchester, would take place on Wednesday, 15 September. The occasion was to be marked by the presence of William Huskisson, the MP for Liverpool, Sir Robert Peel, and the greatest attraction of them all, the Prime Minister, the Duke of Wellington.

The Duke was staying nearby with Lord Wilton at Heaton Park and on the Sunday before the ceremony Absalom attended Divine Service at Prestwich church in the hope of seeing him. He was not disappointed. The Duke was then sixty-one.

September 12th, 1830. He is a mild looking, thin, long-faced, pale, elderly man, with hair completely white but with a look of ability and animation quite at variance with the idea of his being an <u>old</u> man. I noticed him attentively. He does not look well when his eyes are cast down, as in reading, but when his head is elevated and he looks to one side, with a rather quick motion of the head and eyes, his look is noble. He did not use spectacles.

The following evening Absalom walked down to look at the railway warehouse and by chance met Andrew on the bridge. Since his departure from the Club they had seen little of each other, but they had shared a portion of their youth. It was their last recorded meeting.

Grime had kindly got places on the New Quay Company's stand for the family to see the procession of trains pass by on the track from Liverpool to Manchester.

September 15th, 1830. The assemblage of people was very great. We waited as patiently as we could a long while and at length came the engine with Lord Wilton for a surgeon for Mr Huskisson. As nobody was aware of the accident which had befallen that gentleman and as the time for the appearance of the procession was already much exceeded, this engine was considered as a precursor of the procession and when, after a short stay, it dashed back again, there arose a doubt as to whether the procession would take place at all and after a while the rabble became very tumultuous. Stones were thrown, the constables driven back and the railroad, which had hitherto been kept clear, was covered with people.

Everyone was puzzled and tired, besides, the weather was wet and thundery.

After some time and rather unexpectedly, the carriages containing the directors with the Duke of Wellington made their appearance. They moved rather slowly along, without music, and the crowd of course, made way but from where we stood some stones were thrown. The Duke stood in the front and replied to the partial but hearty shouts with which he was greeted by touching his hat with his finger and slightly moving his head sometimes to one side, sometimes to the other.

What was intended to have been a happy occasion had turned into tragedy. There was no music because the carriage the band had been travelling in had been requisitioned to bear away the mortally wounded Huskisson, his wife and attendants. The sequence of events becomes clear only when the arrangements are understood.

It had been agreed that the trains should start from Crown Street Station in the morning, run to Manchester and return to Liverpool in the afternoon. Both lines of the railway were to be used, the trains running side by side in the same direction.

The day before the opening Liverpool had been invaded by hundreds of eager spectators. It was almost impossible to get accommodation and the streets were blocked all night with carriages unable to get into the inn yards. The invited guests were asked to be at the station by ten o'clock. The station was gaily decorated with flags and the women were wearing bright dresses. 'Such a scene,' an onlooker remarked, 'as might be made up by a combination of the Lord Mayor's Show and the Epsom Races.'

. On one line stood the carriages forming the train for the directors and the distinguished guests. The Duke of Wellington's carriage had been decorated in a Moorish manner, with gilt pillars supporting a crimson canopy. A car in the Grecian style was designed for the band. The engine which drew the Duke's train was driven by George Stephenson himself. On a parallel line stood a procession of six trains, all decorated with silk flags and containing some hundreds of ticket-carrying passengers. Trumpeters were stationed throughout the trains, all of whom played in succession 'See the Conquering Hero Comes' as the Duke's carriage moved slowly forward after the firing of the starting cannon.

Absalom's party waiting at Manchester could not of course have known it, but when the trains stopped for water at Parkside, a station between Liverpool and Manchester, Huskisson got out. According to the reporter for *The Times*, he was standing a little way from the rails and talking to some other passengers when the *Rocket* came up unobserved behind him. If he had stood still he might have been safe, for as the reporter pointed out, no engine can move off the rails. Unfortunately in the agitation of the moment he ran forward, then finding no escape in front, went across the line and while attempting to climb the steps into another carriage, was knocked down by a door and fell into the path of the *Rocket*. He managed to get his head and breast out of the way but the wheels went over his left thigh, squeezing it almost to a jelly, breaking the leg in two places and tearing out a large piece of flesh leaving the muscles bare from the ankle nearly to the hip. With his wife hanging over him in an agony of tears, the poor man was taken to the rectory at Eccles, a village about four miles outside Manchester, where he died.

After the wounded Huskisson was taken away, it was debated whether the procession should continue to Manchester or turn back to Liverpool. Wellington and Peel were for turning back. Mr Hulton, the magistrate who had ordered the

Hussars into the crowd at Peterloo, told the Duke that an unprecedented concourse of people were assembled at Manchester and there might be rioting if the procession failed to arrive. The borough-reeve strongly urged them to proceed and so did the directors, who feared for their invested capital unless the practicability of the venture was demonstrated.

The situation was delicate. Wellington may have been a conquering hero, but as Absalom's limited observation shows, to many of the working classes he represented a hard-hearted and repressive government. Indeed, when he eventually reached Manchester that day, the deputy constable told the magistrates that he could not be responsible for the Duke's safety or the peace of the town. Nor at that time were the railways universally liked, they were part and parcel of that machinery which had thrown so many out of work. The borough-reeve may have feared that the waiting and frustrated crowds might tear up the railway line.

The engine drawing Wellington's train had left with the wounded Huskisson, so two engines on the parallel lines were attached to the director's train by a long rope and thus ingloriously was the Duke towed into Manchester, the band silent and the trumpeters dumb.

The young Fanny Kemble felt the sad contrast between the joyful departure and the sombre arrival. Given a seat with her mother on board one of the trains and flying 'swifter than a bird' between enormous masses of densely packed people waving hats and handkerchiefs, her spirits had risen to 'truly champagne heights'. After the accident all was changed. The sky darkened as they approached Manchester. Fanny wrote:

> High above the grim and grimy crowd of scowling faces a loom had been erected at which sat a tattered, starved-looking weaver, evidently set there as a <u>representative man</u> to protest against this triumph of machinery and the gain and glory which the wealthy Liverpool and Manchester men were likely to derive from it.

A few weeks later Absalom took the nine-year-old John to the railway line at Eccles. Huskisson was dead, but standing under the lime trees they watched another train make its way into the future.

Absalom's mind was preoccupied with the past. He had returned to his study of the Crusades and he spent some time at the warehouse writing a paper on the character of Peter the Hermit before attending the anniversary dinner of the Society for the Preservation of Ancient Footpaths, of which he was a founding member.

The town of Manchester was covered by a pall of smoke, its innumerable chimneys, a later traveller was to complain, each bearing on top 'a troubled pennon of darkness', the lurid gloom spreading like a murky blot over half the firmament. This was an exaggeration even when it was written and in 1830 Manchester was still surrounded by beautiful country – meadows, cornfields and woods, for the most part all within a radius of a mere two miles from the Exchange.

However as wealth increased and families moved farther out, a race of men Prentice called 'tyrants of the field' came into being. Richer than Absalom, these people imagined that what ran through their land must belong to them and in order to protect their privacy they started to close or divert old footpaths. A series of skirmishes between angry owners and public-spirited townspeople prompted the foundation of the Society. After dinner Absalom introduced the sentiment: 'The pleasant walks of our youth and may they be preserved to enfeebled age.' The applause that greeted this speech excited him. He did not drink too much but sufficient to make his head ache.

Grime did not wish to move farther out of Manchester and was steadfast in his course of regular entertaining. That autumn he managed to get the fashionable Siamese Twins, Chang and Eng, to his house for the evening. The twins were exhibited by a Captain Coffin, and Absalom was curious about them.

October 20th, 1830. The Siamese youths are twins, nineteen and a half years old, and united by a cartilaginous and fleshy substance from the lower part of the breast of one to the corresponding part of the other. As there is an arterial circulation through this connecting substance, it is supposed that it would not be possible to divide them without endangering their lives. It also appears that having never known any other state and having learned to accommodate themselves to it, a separation, even if possible, would not be desirable. Their tastes are nearly similar and they are capable of rapid and easy motion. Apparently they enjoy excellent health and they seem to be happy. As for the possibility that one may die before the other that, from the great sympathy between the state of their stomachs and in their general health, is an event not <u>likely</u> to occur, so that for anything that appears, they may continue to enjoy this strangely united existence during a long life. They play at chess, draughts and whist with different partners.

Absalom stayed until two o'clock in the morning, supping, drinking and playing cards. He was getting overtired. Peter the Hermit preyed on his mind and one evening he stayed awake to past midnight preparing what he intended to be an extensive lecture on the subject to the Literary Society. Unfortunately on the day itself he got wet through in walking to work and had to go about all day in soaking clothes.

November 16th, 1830. Suffered in consequence a violent pain in the head. Attended the meeting of the Literary Society and delivered a speech maintaining that the First Crusade was a just and necessary war and that the consequences of the Crusades were beneficial to Europe and to mankind. I spoke for nearly two hours, often with considerable embarrassment, always too diffusely – but I have reason to believe that my speech made a strong impression.

Still weary, he was doing his accounts two evenings later when Joseph burst into the house.

November 18th, 1830. As I sat writing Joseph Makinson came in and told me he was <u>ruined</u>. That Samuel Emden of London had stopped payment and that he had guaranteed Emden's accounts, <u>without security</u>, to the amount of £22,000 or £24,000!!! I have often warned him against trusting Emden. As I have taken his bills upon Emden to the amount of £340, I shall in all probability be a heavy loser in this affair. Joseph is, he says, worth £5,000 and thus at one stroke, down goes the fruit of the labour of years.

After hearing of his brother's failure William was taken ill, stricken with apprehension over the state of trade and fears for the future. Grime too was in an anxious state. He had been bitten on the finger by his cat, which died the next day, and he was convinced that he would get rabies.

December 2nd, 1830. The cat was opened and appeared to have died from inflammation of the bowels. The black spots in the stomach and bowels which are found in rabid animals were not found in the case of poor Tom. Indeed he had shown no sign of madness but had bitten his master accidentally, in taking a bit of kidney which Mr Grime was giving to him and at which he made a hasty snap in consequence of the approach of the dog. Still it is thought advisable to employ some measure of precaution against infection. The finger was cauterised, wrapped up and ordered to be kept constantly moistened with a solution of chloride of lime and a mercurial course sufficient to affect the mouth is to be carried out.

George IV had died that June. In July the French drove the last of the Bourbons from the throne and installed a constitutional monarch in his place. The revolution in France, the demand for parliamentary reform and discontent with the Poor Law were among the many factors that produced a weakened Tory majority at the General Election, which by custom followed the death of the sovereign. In November Wellington resigned and a Whig administration was formed with Lord Grey as Prime Minister.

The question of parliamentary reform could no longer be shelved. Agitation gathered strength throughout the country. Cobbett and Carlile were laying about them in the popular press; an army of artisans headed by the French tricolour had marched on St James' Palace; and Lord Stanley's seat at Preston had been successfully contested by Orator Hunt.

Nothing had yet been done with the Petition Absalom had drawn up at Mr

Harvey's request. Although the agitation was growing in Manchester, the movement was hindered by the extremism of the radicals. Moderate reformers there were working for redistribution of seats and an extended franchise, but the radicals wished to give the vote to the working class, so were advocating universal male suffrage, the ballot and even annual parliaments. There was no possibility of containing the reforming impulse within a single organization because the hopes, fears and aspirations of sectional interests were so widely different.

The moderate party in Manchester feared that the radical's unrealistic and undesirable demands would effectively prevent any progress being made at all. Towards the end of 1830 Absalom attended a meeting of like-minded friends at the York Hotel in King Street 'to consider the propriety of a public meeting to promote reform in Parliament.'

December 13th, 1830. This meeting I had been specially invited to attend. Mr Greg was in the chair and Mr Mark Philips, Mr Harbottle, Mr Potter, Mr Baxter etc. were present. It was quite evident from what was said that there were serious apprehensions entertained as to the disposition of the working classes and a fear of their interference produced an evident disinclination to a meeting <u>at present</u>. It was resolved that a meeting was desirable and a committee was appointed to consider when it should be held and what resolutions should be proposed. <u>I said nothing</u> but was appointed with the others to be of the committee.

Absalom often walked with the children up Cheetham Hill to visit his mother's grave and on Christmas Day 1830 went there alone. Soon afterwards he had yet another reminder of the uncertainty of life.

January 7th, 1831. Today I had the pleasure of returning to Mr William Riley his gold watch which he deposited in my hands in August 1827, as security for £8 which I had lent him. When I was in difficulties in 1815 Mr Riley was a kind friend and now that he is down and I have risen, it is right and my duty to show that I remember his kindness. Therefore I forgave him the £8 and returned the watch, which had been his former wife's, having been given to her on their wedding day.

Despite this, the need for the strictest economy had again taken hold of Absalom. He had tea with a family called Coddington and Mrs Coddington told him that her mother never required more than £2 a week for household expenses for a family of *seven* people.

January 2nd, 1831. Out of this sum she paid for everything except rent, taxes, schooling and liquors. Kept always a plentiful table, clothed two of the children, which she estimated to cost ten shillings a week, and could still save money so as to have always £8 or £10 on hand. Soap, candles, brushes etc. she estimated at eight shillings a week.

A few days later Grime sent for him. Absalom found him in a state of great excitement, brought on, he was convinced, by hydrophobia caught from the bite of his now-dead cat. He was bled, Absalom spoke calmly to him and gradually he became more composed. The physicians diagnosed not hydrophobia at all but inflammation of the stomach and bowels, and ordered forty-nine leeches to be applied to his abdomen.

Manchester's achievements owed little to the aristocracy or initiatives from the government in London. They were the consequences of self-help and hard work on the part of a group of people who sincerely believed both in economic liberalism and that the lot of their fellow men could and should be improved. Up to now, extreme diffidence had prevented Absalom from taking any prominent part in public affairs but as a result of the agitation for parliamentary reform he found himself being edged forward slowly towards the front of the stage.

The machinery of local democracy was cumbersome, painstaking, and because it was a genuine consultative process, far more complicated than the outsider might imagine. First of all, a number of preliminary meetings were held by the requisitionists, that is, those who were asking for a public meeting. At these preliminary gatherings, like the one Absalom attended on 13 December, a committee was elected which then drew up the resolutions to be put before the public meeting. Sometimes these public meetings resulted in an actual Petition to Parliament or pressure on the county members. Their purpose was to remedy or improve local conditions where they could, or to draw attention to the town's opinions on national issues.

In early March 1831 Lord John Russell introduced the government's Reform Bill in the Commons. It went further than many people anticipated. The Ministry intended to provide once and for all a more equitable and sensible distribution of seats and to introduce a uniform franchise. This bold approach served to spike the radical's guns.

One hundred and sixty-eight seats were to be abolished and a number of new seats created, among them Manchester, which would be able to return two members to Westminster. The untidy and unjust diversity of the old franchise was to be swept away. In the boroughs every householder who occupied a house whose rental value was not less than £10 a year was given the vote. In the counties, where those who owned property worth forty shillings a year already had the vote, it was to be extended to certain lease and copyholders.

These proposals were far too extreme for the Tories and did not go far enough for the ultra-radicals, but they were well received in the country as a whole. The intention of Absalom and his friends in Manchester was to put pressure on Parliament and the King by demonstrating the strength of provincial feeling in the Bill's favour while the debates were going on in the House.

March 5th, 1831. Went as one of the deputation of the requisitionists for a public meeting on the subject of Reform, in company with Messrs Potter, Baxter, Mark Philips, Greg, Shuttleworth and Hunter, to the Town Hall to present the requisition to the Borough-reeve and Constables and receive their answer. After some conversation, they agreed to call a meeting. This is the first time I have taken any part in public business and I felt somewhat embarrassed.

Mark Philips was the son of a prosperous local merchant and the chairman of Grime's New Quay Company. He lived in a beautiful house in the village of Stand, near Prestwich. The proposal for a public meeting was accepted and Absalom spent Sunday writing the resolutions for it which were submitted next day for the approval of the requisitionists at yet another meeting. He was asked to draw up the Parliamentary Petition.

March 8th, 1831. Wrote a Petition to Parliament in favour of the Ministerial plan of Reform and an Address to the King on the same subject. Attended the meeting of the committee for arranging the business of the public meeting. My Petition and Address approved and adopted. My attention to these things has occupied too much of my time, I have been greatly excited and suffer from it.

Mr Burt, the borough-reeve, took the chair at the Town Meeting.

March 9th, 1831. The meeting was very numerous, it is said there were more than two thousand people present. Looking down from the hustings it was one continued pavement of faces. My resolutions were passed unanimously. I seconded the fourth (which was moved by Mr Lloyd, the barrister), and addressed the meeting. I had then been standing more than three hours on the hustings which were much crowded and when I stepped forward to speak I found that I had almost lost my voice. I was however heard with attention and got through an unpremeditated speech of five or seven minutes without disgrace.

He went on feeling tense and overexcited and longed to be left in peace. Unfortunately his very success deprived him of this. He had to attend a meeting to press for the inclusion of Broughton in the Manchester franchise, to draft the Petition and Memorial for them and then to draw up another on behalf of the inhabitants of Flixton. It all took up time he should have devoted to his business. The Footpath Society now asked him to write three Petitions on their behalf. He felt mentally worn out.

April 19th, 1831. Went afterwards to the warehouse where I stayed till past eleven. Came home, made out the dunning list and wrote this entry.

There was one cause for rejoicing. Grime, recovered from his hydrophobic disorder, had achieved what he had set out to do. His daughter Elizabeth was married as advantageously as could reasonably be expected and was now the bride of Mr Thomas Goadsby, a future Mayor of Manchester, whose father's look of insignificant amiability had caught Absalom's attention the year before. Still greater glory was in store for her which in the nature of things, Mr Grime never lived to see. As a widow, Elizabeth was to marry Alderman Heywood, present the city with its statue of Cromwell and in 1877 to witness Sir Joseph Heron hand her husband the golden key by means of which he unlocked the doors of the imposing new Town Hall to the sound of trumpets.

A series of lavish dinner parties followed the wedding. Champagne flowed, the silver sparkled and sumptuous food was served on fine china. Absalom found it all tedious and moreover had to waste 6s. on the hire of a coach. He pruned his gooseberries and got four seats put down in the garden, one for each of his children. That same evening he returned to the warehouse to do some work. It was a beautiful night, the moon and stars bright in the spring sky. 'How cheap a thing is happiness.'

CHAPTER FIFTEEN

'If this Reform Bill passes who will not go down on his knees and thank God he was born in England?'

Thanks to the Irish MPs, the Commons passed the Reform Bill by a majority of one early in the morning of 23 March. Before the Bill could get to the Lords the Government was defeated on an amendment and the King dissolved Parliament. The General Election followed only a week later and was conducted in an atmosphere of intense excitement. It was a peculiar election, not solely because of the speed with which it followed the dissolution but because the proceedings, like a referendum, were dominated by a single issue. The slogan 'The Bill, the whole Bill, and nothing but the Bill', swept the Government back into office with a greatly increased majority.

The summer was glorious. Parliament did not meet until the end of June and for the moment there was little public business to be done. Absalom enjoyed the races on Kersal Moor with particular zest, partly because of the weather and partly because after they were over he was expecting Mrs Shuttleworth to pay them another visit. She arrived and was with them only a day when on returning from a walk in the fields, he found John Watkin had brought Mrs Stoneley and Anne to see them.

Absalom's wife and Mrs Shuttleworth were immediately on guard, the one protecting her own, the other a potential rival. Absalom thought Mrs Stoneley looked older and even sadder than when they had last met at Nantwich. After she had left he went with Mrs Shuttleworth for a walk alone in the garden and when he came indoors his wife took him aside and scolded him for paying too much attention to her. Irritated, he took himself off to read some passages from *Werther*.

A fairly large dinner party was planned for the following day. Mrs Thomas Watkin, her son John and her daughter Frances, the sister of Mary who had died of consumption, were to come over with Mrs Stoneley to meet Mrs Shuttleworth together with three more friends. At first all went well. They had 'a pleasant and cheerful time' until dinner.

June 1st, 1831. In the afternoon we walked into Mr Richardson's garden and because Mrs Stoneley took my arm and walked with me a few times up and down the shady part of the walk without showing any sign of dislike to my company, Mrs Shuttleworth, who it appears was observing us, very charitably concluded that Mrs Stoneley had a bad design upon me and chose to be offended because she had not got all my attention. Returning to our house we had tea and after tea, a walk to Kersal Moor. Mrs Shuttleworth would not go, but although I avoided taking Mrs Stoneley by giving my arm to Mrs Whitworth, I found that I was suspected of being too fond of her company. After supper the Whitworths left and about midnight Mrs Watkin, John and the Stoneleys. Mrs Stoneley, in the kind judgement of Mrs Shuttleworth, exhibiting no small reluctance to leave me. As I had drunk more than usual, I did not ask Mrs Shuttleworth to take wine after they were gone, and thus gave another great offence to that lady.

These entries began and ended in shorthand. Mrs Stoneley had announced her intention of returning to Nantwich on the morrow. Next morning, however, she and Anne paid a visit to Absalom's warehouse.

June 2nd, 1831. As the Stoneleys had expressed their determination to leave town this morning, I was not a little surprised, while looking over some returns, to see them enter the warehouse with Frances Watkin. They stayed some time and Mrs Stoneley, in walking round the warehouse, spoke of the habits of intoxication into which her husband had fallen and of his inattention to business, with a little too much of contrast between him and me.

As soon as Absalom returned home he saw that news of the warehouse visit had preceded him. His wife wore an air of injured innocence and Mrs Shuttleworth said that she was about to leave the house.

When I handed her into the coach I was at once puzzled and moved to laughter at the comical air of haughty determination with which in answer to my 'hope that we should see her again', she – who forty-eight hours before had hung on my arm and talked to me of her friendship as we walked in the fields – now repeated 'Goodbye sir. Goodbye sir.' All mystery was however at an end as soon as I was alone with my wife.

Elizabeth was extremely angry. Mrs Stoneley was a wicked woman, an absolute 'fiend', she had sought Absalom even in his warehouse, she had designs on him, while his partiality was evident, he had slighted her dear friend Mrs Shuttleworth that very day at dinner and at last night's supper by neglecting to drink wine with her. Absalom was not sufficiently involved to care. Mrs Stoneley and Anne had already agreed to join them for a trip on the new railway tomorrow. Elizabeth must make the best of it.

It seemed at first that the day would pass quite pleasantly. It took them an hour and three-quarters to reach Liverpool on the train and the novelty of it overcame any awkwardness. Unluckily their return journey was delayed by the Newton Races, so that when they got back at last to the Star inn at Manchester they found that the coach for Nantwich had already left. When she heard this Mrs Stoneley had a fit of hysterics, 'so violent as to oblige them to take a coach, and after they got to Mrs Watkin's, she became so outrageously ill as to frighten everybody about her'.

Next morning John Watkin called round at the warehouse and gave a fearful account of their guest's health. He said that Mrs Stoneley was in bed and could not possibly leave Manchester.

June 4th, 1831. In the afternoon I went to the Star to see Miss Stoneley go off. To my great surprise there also was Mrs Stoneley, paler than usual and a little dejected, but with no signs of illness. 'I thought you were dying?' 'You see,' was her answer, 'I am soon well again.' Then taking my hand she said, 'If you had known how ill I was when I had hold of your arm in King Street – but I am well again now.' They got into the coach and just before it went off she held out her hand and I said 'you will have a pleasant ride.' 'I want something else to make it so.' 'What?' 'To be as we were on the railroad.' 'Oh,' said I, 'my wife is not here, but here is John, take him with you.' John said something about the impossibility of his leaving Manchester and the coach drove off.

The weather continued beautiful and Absalom enjoyed it to the full. He walked with Mr Spencer and J.E. Taylor, the editor of the *Guardian*, to places then in the country, now so built over as to be unrecognizable by any of the three.

June 12th, 1831. We went to Pendleton and got some brandy and water at the Bowling Green between the Liverpool and Bolton roads. This green is a very pleasant spot. Leaving it we went by the riverside to Agecroft and passing over the bridge came to the road leading to Mrs Byrom's house. We went down this lane, which is a private road, and passing Kersall Hall, Mrs Byrom's house and Mrs Royle's farm house which is in a quite secluded spot, came out through the fields at Mrs Wolfendale's farm on Kersal Moor.

The good weather continued.

June 13th, 1831. Pleased with the beauty of the garden when I came home in the evening. Went after tea with Edward and John through Tetlow Fold to my mother's grave. The evening was delightful. The walk did me good. I came home better and have been writing two hours since my return without weariness.

June 14th, 1831. Happening to get out of bed at four in the morning, I saw the sun rise over Picton's hay shed. The previous state of the sky was beautiful and the rising of the sun magnificent. I <u>felt</u> the power and goodness of the Creator.

On his forty-fourth birthday Absalom walked home by Tetlow Fold with Edward.

June 27th, 1831. We went into the chapel yard at Cheetham Hill and sowed pansies and heart's ease on my mother's grave. As we came along the lane, the rain having ceased, the wild roses shed fragrance, the insects were humming in the beech trees and Prestwich bells came sweetly, now loud and now faint upon the breeze.

If the Reform Bill was passed, Broughton and Salford were to form one constituency. Absalom went round with Richard Potter to canvass votes for Brotherton, one of the proposed candidates. It was a novel experience. Everywhere they went they seemed to be well received and often invited in to take wine. Absalom noted with grief how elegant, tidy and clean the houses were compared with his own and the difference struck him to the heart. He needed a change and determined to go as soon as he could to Derbyshire to see about his cottage at Bonsal. His daughter Elizabeth was now nearly fourteen and they went together, travelling by the *Nelson* coach to Matlock and then walking to Bonsall, picking stonecrop and wild thyme as they went.

Absalom was disconcerted to hear his daughter describe the cottage as 'a mean little place'. He took her to Chatsworth, which pleased her rather better, and then hired a chaise to take them to the village of Eyam. Eyam was famous because when the Great Plague of Charles II's time broke out in one of its cottages, in order to contain the infection William Mompesson, the Rector, succeeded in persuading his parishioners to isolate themselves from the rest of the country. The resulting loss of life in Eyme itself was very great and the wisdom of Mompesson's heroic action has been questioned.

July 3rd, 1831. We looked at Mrs Mompesson's tomb, visited the caves in which her husband used to preach during the plague, went into the public house to get something to drink and there I saw a picture of the Virgin and Child which I bought for twenty-seven shillings.

This was an unusual thing for a Protestant of his background to have done. The change did not do Absalom as much good as he had hoped. Ten days later the bleeding from the bowel started again. The anxiety about this, weariness caused by the drawing up of resolutions for a public meeting to be called to relieve the distress in Ireland, difficulties with the workmen who were building on an extension to his house, or some sharper, hidden reason, prompted an outburst of bitterness and near despair.

July 11th, 1831. Extremely unwell in morning, bleeding and in great pain, but suffering more from the unfeeling hypocrisy of the artful wretch my wife, who not only did nothing to assist but everything to hinder me. I solemnly determine henceforth to regard her as my assured enemy. God grant me power to suppress my feelings.

One night he came home by Cheetham Hill and accidentally met Elizabeth on the path. They went back together and it was 'an unhappy walk'.

Very little, usually simple pleasures and small triumphs, was enough to raise Absalom's spirits. One evening in September he went to a meeting of the Club at Jervis's.

September 2nd, 1831. We left at half-past ten. It was quite cold. I had on linen trousers and felt chilled. I quitted my friends at Pendleton and came home by the suspension bridge. The night was fine and starlight. The view up and down from the suspension bridge was beautiful. From Pendleton to our house I met only one person, a man, who was singing as he went along the road to Lower Broughton.

Towards the end of September the Commons passed the Reform Bill and it was taken to the Lords. Well-grounded fears of the intransigence of the Upper House decided pressure groups throughout the country to prepare resolutions intended to influence the decision. A public meeting in Manchester agreed to present a Petition drawn up by Absalom in favour of the Bill.

September 22nd, 1831. Attended the public meeting in the Manor Court Room to consider the propriety of petitioning the House of Lords to pass the Reform Bill. It was crowded and very hot. There was some good speaking. The resolutions and the petition which I had drawn up were passed unanimously. I seconded one resolution but made no speech being determined to attempt no public display at present.

The debate in the House of Lords began on 3 October and lasted for five days. At the request of the Manchester Reform Committee Absalom had drawn up a placard to be exhibited immediately the news of the Bill's rejection by the Lords was received. The division was taken at an all-night sitting between 7 and 8 October. On that morning the reforming press published their newspapers with black edges. The Lords had rejected the Bill by an even larger majority than had been anticipated. The following day was Sunday.

October 9th, 1831. About six in the evening Mr Baxter and Mr John Shuttleworth came up to our house bringing the London Courier containing an account of the rejection of the Reform Bill by the Lords. Their object in coming was to get me to write some resolutions for a public meeting on the subject. Employed till late in writing the resolutions.

On Tuesday there was more writing to be done.

October 11th, 1831. A very dull market. Sad and full of anxiety. Wrote at the warehouse immediately after dinner an Address to the King to be proposed at the Public Meeting of the Requisitionists at the Town Hall. The Resolutions and Address adopted.

The placard he had already prepared was posted at the Town Hall. The inhabitants of Manchester were invited to assemble in the Riding School, Lower Mosley Street to

consider the propriety of presenting a dutiful and loyal address to His Majesty, at this alarming crisis, for the purpose of assuring him of their devotion to his person, and of their unshaken determination to give His Majesty and his present government all the support in their power, and also of imploring His Majesty to take such decisive constitutional proceedings as shall counteract the pernicious consequences which may result from the rejection of the Reform Bill by the House of Lords, secure the passing of that important measure into a law, and thus preserve the peace and secure the future welfare of the country.

What the moderate reformers always feared now happened. From early morning people gathered in the street outside the Riding School. When the doors were opened at eleven o'clock a mob of about 4,000 poured inside and clamoured for the meeting to be adjourned to Camp Field.

October 12th, 1831. Attended the public meeting on the Rejection of the Reform Bill. It began at eleven o'clock in the Riding School but was immediately adjourned to Camp Field by the will of the rabble. The Borough- reeve left the chair and the meeting altogether in consequence of this adjournment.

There was no help for it. Gathering support as it went, the mob proceeded to Camp Field. Estimates of the numbers vary. Absalom thought there were between 80,000 and 100,000 people present at the height of the demonstration; 40,000 more, Prentice was later to point out, than had gathered at Peterloo. Some carts from Grime's New Quay Company were hastily converted into hustings and the borough-reeve having refused to have anything more to do with the matter, Mr Thomas Potter was persuaded to take the chair. He climbed on to the cart with Absalom, Prentice, John Shuttleworth, Mark Philips and others and from there attempted to move the resolutions Absalom had drawn up and which had previously been agreed upon.

In every sense it was difficult to get a hearing. They were in the open air, the audience was huge and not disposed to acquiesce in counsels of moderation. John Shuttleworth had a good voice and was both heard and listened to fairly quietly until he suggested that the King should create new peers. According to Prentice, at this there were cries of 'no more peers, we've had enough of them'. It was the turning point. From then on the Reform Committee lost control of the meeting.

An operative moved a radical amendment urging the King to support universal suffrage, annual parliaments and vote by ballot.

> Our leaders battled with them until four in the afternoon and all that time did we stand on our wagon, squeezed, elbowed, threatened and in danger, in the midst of a furious mob. At last, after protesting against it, Mr Potter was compelled to put a mangled version of our Address praying for annual Parliaments, universal suffrage and vote by ballot and we left the ground, tired, baffled, exhausted and chopfallen but congratulating ourselves upon having escaped personal violence and avoided endangering the peace of the town.

They ought not to have been baffled. Absalom thought that the meeting had been disrupted deliberately by the rival Political Union of the Working Classes, an organization that ran parallel to, and often opposed, the more moderate and broadly based Manchester Political Union formed the previous year. He was right. Prentice reported a significant exchange that Absalom may not have heard. Someone on the platform begged the meeting to support the men who were fighting their battles in Parliament and received the reply that they would fight their own battles.

Poverty, bad working conditions and social inequality brought the masses together, not concern for the Constitution or respect for the £10 householder. As Richard Fryer, a Wolverhampton reformer, pithily remarked the year before: 'All fiddle-de-dee about Old Sarum – stick to repeal of the Corn Laws and vote by ballot.' After a meeting in Manchester addressed by the indefatigable Hunt, effigies were burnt, not of kings, lords or bishops, but of Richard Potter and the manufacturer Hugh Birley. The working classes in the country as a whole had not yet grasped that the Reform Bill offered them nothing immediately. But Manchester was the heartland of informed radicalism, there a strong body of opinion existed which refused to fight the battles of the middle classes for them. The Reform Committee took fright.

October 14th, 1831. At the committee meeting of the Reform Committee it was determined that no expression of public opinion in favour of the Reform Bill should be attempted at present <u>for fear of the radicals</u>, but that a letter should be written to Earl Grey to account to him for our being quiet.

Absalom thought this cowardly. He considered that they should not allow themselves to be bullied by the radicals but send their own address to the King as originally planned. His advice was not taken, and with other committee members he was asked to draft a letter to the Prime Minister which in the end he had to write by himself.

October 15th, 1831. Met the sub-committee at the lodgings of Mr Melly in Fountain Street. We examined the letter from the Committee to Lord Grey which I had prepared. With a few additions it was adopted and Mr Melly undertook to copy it for the approval of the general Committee in the evening.

There was a further difficulty. What was to be done about the radical address Potter had been forced to put to the Camp Field Meeting? The radicals were pressing Potter to say whether the committee would or would not be party to the amended address. If Potter signed it, it would appear that he agreed with its terms. If he did not sign it, he might be in breach of the rules that regulated the conduct of a public meeting.

We counselled him to sign it if the rules of public meetings required him to do so, but not otherwise. It was finally agreed that a statement of the circumstances should be drawn up and submitted to those gentlemen in the town who were most conversant with the rules of public meetings and that Mr Potter should abide by their decision. Pym and Curran, two leaders of the Political Union, came while we were deliberating. Mr Heron drew up the statement which they allowed to be correct and they were desired to come again at four in the afternoon to receive Mr Potter's answer. Mr Philips, Melly etc. went to consult the authorities on the subject. I went to my business.

The legal mind is always reluctant to commit itself.

Some time elapsed before Mr Atkinson, the attorney, could be found and when he came the form of Mr Potter's answer could not be decided upon. Mr Potter became impatient, swore he would never attend another public meeting but 'stay in his warehouse and mind his business.'

In the end Potter refused to sign the radical address despite some threatening noises from the two delegates of the Political Union. The committee was recovering its nerve. It put Absalom's letter to Lord Grey aside and decided on another address to the King.

October 18th, 1831. Attended the meeting of the Reform Committee at night. Mr Dyer, Dr Kay and myself appointed to draw up an Address to His Majesty. C.J.S. Walker, who was present and tipsy, told the Committee that they ought to have appointed me only to draw up the Address, that they knew that I should have all the trouble and that I ought to have the credit. This vexed Dr Kay and <u>did me no service</u>.

Dr Kay was the physician who was said to have attempted to transfuse dog's blood into human veins at the time of the *Emma* disaster. He is known to history as Sir James Kay-Shuttleworth because some years later he married an heiress and added his wife's name to his own. A keen reformer, he and Absalom were to cross each other's path frequently. C.J.S. Walker came from an old Manchester family of liberal sympathies. His father, who had been borough-reeve at the outbreak of the French Revolution, once had his house and warehouse attacked by a 'Church and King' mob and had been tried for treason.

Like Potter, Absalom was becoming tired of it all. He composed an address in his warehouse but did it badly. Sure enough, neither Dyer nor Dr Kay had prepared any draft for consideration. The rumour that Parliament was about to be prorogued was widespread. The King together with Queen Adelaide returned to London from Windsor and William Cobbett compared their coming to the return of Louis XVI and Marie Antoinette to Paris in 1789.

The comparison was incorrect but not altogether absurd. People were rioting in the streets of London, a mob released prisoners from Durham Gaol and Nottingham Castle, the property of that notorious borough-monger, the Duke of Newcastle, was burnt to the ground. With good reason, popular feeling against the Established Church was growing also. Twenty-one of the bishops who sat in the House of Lords had voted against the Bill, seven had abstained. If they had voted the other way the Bill would have passed and the Lords Temporal would have been routed. Bishops were booed in the street and burnt in effigy, and during serious riots in Bristol the episcopal palace was burnt.

Rumour was right. Parliament was indeed prorogued, but only to the end of November. No one knew what would happen next. William IV might not be persuaded to create the large numbers of peers necessary to pass the Bill nor was it likely that Lord Grey and other members of his Cabinet would wish to dilute the members of their own order with such a considerable rush of new blood.

Self-interest is society's regulating force. The industrial middle classes as a whole wished for the Bill because their economic interests required direct representation. The idealists among them sincerely thought distress could be alleviated by political measures; that a man's labour would be protected from exploitation not by aristocrats and borough-mongers but by themselves, the middle classes sitting in Parliament. 'If this Reform Bill passes,' the painter Benjamin Robert Haydon was writing in his journal, 'whose breast will not broaden and heart swell, who will not go down on his knees and thank God that he was born in England?' The working classes, apathetic until spasmodically roused, were for the most part shouting down the warnings of Hunt about the restrictive franchise and allowed themselves to become victims of self-deception and mass hysteria. What the activists among them really wanted was not the Bill many of them were screaming for, but direct political power.

The annual dinner of the Commercial Clerk's Society was approaching and the arrangements for it had to be discussed in the leisurely fashion most arrangements in Manchester were then conducted. For that purpose Absalom supped with the other members of the committee at the Half Moon in Chapel Walks and enjoyed cod, hare, cold roast beef with cheese, butter and celery for a shilling a head. The dinner itself was a grander, far less enjoyable affair, attended by about 200 people including Mr Heywood, the county MP, Mr Foster the Magistrate, the borough-reeve, constables and churchwardens.

November 24th, 1831. Everything went off well. The company were excited but fell into no excess. The chairman, Mr Heywood, and the vice-chairman, Mr S. Fletcher, both filled their office with ability and £163 was subscribed in aid of the Institution in the course of the evening. I had to acknowledge the honour done to the Committee when their health was drunk and delivered a speech, not a long speech, which the newspapers say was 'appropriate', 'excellent', 'eloquent', and which the company greeted with applause. They cheered when it was ended. Several persons whom I never knew before drank to me and shook hands with me, but I was both pleased and amused when Thomson, the solicitor of the Society, made his way to me and shaking me warmly by the hand said, 'When I write anything to you I shall say "My dear Sir,".That with me means everything.'

But it did not mean everything to Absalom. Business was slack, many were out of work and firms were failing – one of which owed him nearly a thousand pounds. He had security for most of the amount but nevertheless felt nervous when he heard two days later that another business that owed him £40 had stopped payment. The matter was made far worse by his wife, who told him that his losses and anxieties had been sent to humble him and he should expect more to come. 'Damn her,' he wrote in the margin of his diary.

He walked to his mother's grave with the children and saw that Alfred had a large hole in the heel of each stocking. So low did he become that he thought it wise to consult his physician, who once more prescribed a mixture of calomel, ipecacuanha, sarsaparilla and chinchona. He advised Absalom to rest at home for a little time. Rest at home indeed! That was the last place he could rest.

In January 1832 Mrs Stoneley suddenly put in an appearance.

January 16th, 1832. Surprised, when I came home at noon, by finding my aunt and Mrs Stoneley at our house. Our house is dirty in the extreme and my wife who hates Mrs Stoneley, was in more than her usual Hibernian bustle. Mrs Stoneley looks better than usual, more healthy, more serene. Her object in coming to Manchester is to purchase some articles of furniture for Anne Stoneley who is about to marry a schoolmaster, a Mr Robinson, rather too fond of drink.

John Watkin would have to find another wife.

Cobbett was lecturing again in Manchester and Absalom spent an entire evening talking to him about farming. Cobbett advocated small farms and rekindled in Absalom his longing to move farther into the country. He successfully opened the Literary Society debate on Monasticism between the eighth and twelfth centuries but either that or vexation about the disposal of the *Manchester Times* aggravated his complaint and he spent some gloomy hours consulting Salmon's book called *The Protrusion of the Lower Bowel*.

After chapel on a Sunday in February he walked with the boys to Eccles and they were all very cheerful over wine and water and Eccles cakes at the White House. The respite was temporary, a glimpse of a filthy and untidy bedroom at home plunged him yet again to the edge of despair. If he could find any way of living apart from his wife without injuring his children he would take it.

One evening towards the end of March when Parliament was still wrangling over the Reform Bill, he walked home with Edward by Tetlow Fold.

March 19th, 1832. The wind was high and sharp but to me singularly refreshing and invigorating. I had suffered from headache all day and the free air drove it away. I had been depressed and became full of spirits. I listened to the noise of the wind among the trees, observed the distant lights, always brighter in windy weather, then noticed the gradual appearance of the stars and felt, as I had not felt for some time, the pleasure of living in the open air. Assuredly it is my duty to myself so to arrange my affairs as to pass much of my time out of doors and as free as possible from <u>harassing cares</u>.

Absalom's forebears had farmed their land in Cheshire at least since the time of Charles II. It was in his blood. He had already made up his mind to move away from Broughton. The winds and the sky and the crops in their season were absolutely necessary to his whole existence. He could not leave his wife and perhaps he would be bound to the warehouse until the very end, but he could set a distance between Manchester and himself, retreat into the real country and at least attempt to live that life he had so vividly imagined while speaking to Cobbett.

CHAPTER SIXTEEN

'We talked all the way of the similarity between the state of England <u>now</u> and that of France at the commencement of the Revolution'

Dr Kay had other matters on his mind besides the Reform Bill. The dreaded Asiatic cholera, a particularly virulent disease that could kill with terrifying suddenness, had reached the Continent the previous winter and in the early spring of 1832 spread to the British Isles. It was strongly suspected that cholera was transmitted by contact with infected human excrement and that people living in insanitary conditions with no proper lavatories or access to clean drinking water were therefore highly susceptible to the disease.

In Manchester a special Board of Health was set up to take precautionary measures in anticipation of an epidemic. Dr Kay was its secretary. Kay had been trained at Edinburgh under Professor Alison, the pioneer of environmental medicine, and was well aware of the likelihood of an acute outbreak in the town. Indeed no one could have been better informed. He was medical officer of the Ancoats and Ardwich Dispensary, situated in the poorest and most densely populated part of Manchester. The Board of Health had ordered an investigation into the state of the streets and houses in all fourteen police districts. Each district was divided up into sections, each the responsibility of two or more unpaid inspectors who made house-to-house visits. The results of this survey had been carefully tabulated. It was the first time that the actual conditions in which a large urban population lived had been scientifically examined.

Set in a contemporary context, Manchester may not have been much worse than many other manufacturing towns, what made it different was the speed and scale of its industrialization. Central Manchester was by this time almost exclusively inhabited by small shopkeepers and the working class. It had no systematic drainage and its unpaved lanes, alleys and courts were frequently soaked with sewage and piled high with garbage. The 'Rookeries' of the Deansgate area with their back-to-back tenements were loathsomely wretched. Squalid, damp, dilapidated and generally without privies, their inhabitants were ill-fed, ill-clothed and a prey to disease, and respectable people did not venture there.

Sometimes pork butchers would pay tenants a pittance to make use of a small area at the back, where putrescent garbage and refuse would be flung out to feed the animals. As yet there was no control of slaughterhouses in Manchester. Abbatoirs were situated in the poorest and most filthy part of the town and the bloody drainage from them, often impregnated with animal matter, ran down the streets and stagnated in the ruts and resulting pools. The River Irk was clear a mile or so upstream, but towards the centre of the town it was black with refuse from dye-works and tanneries, and thick with sewage, filth from the bone-works and size manufacturers and drainage from the gasworks.

Out of the 687 streets inspected, 248 were totally unpaved, 53 were partially paved, 112 were 'ill ventilated', and 352 contained heaps of refuse, stagnant pools and excrement.

Out of the 6,951 houses inspected, 2,565 needed whitewashing, 960 needed repair, 1,435 were damp, 452 were ill ventilated, 939 needed their drains repaired and 2,221 were without privies.

There were more than 267 lodging houses for paupers. More than half the women had to depend upon charity at the time of childbirth and more than half the children died before the age of five. There were, to use Dr Kay's own description, a thousand 'haunts of intemperance', that is to say gin shops, beer houses or taverns. The borough-reeve had taken observations on eight successive Sunday evenings outside a certain gin shop and in forty minutes an average of 112 men and 163 women had entered it.

It cannot be wondered at. Two years later, in 1834, the Manchester Statistical Society calculated that almost 15,000 people lived in cellars. We know from Mrs Gaskell that they were not all squalid, but a large proportion were below the level of the unsewered streets. Dark, noxious, and often pestilential, they were popular not because they were necessarily cheaper to rent than rooms above ground, but because they offered more independence from the landlord and space to carry out some trade.

When the cholera reached epidemic proportions in London but before it got to Manchester, the Evangelicals pressed for a day of fasting and supplication. Some scoffers called it 'a farce day', but whatever real confidence in the efficacy of prayer and self-denial the Government entertained, it did not wish to alienate a large segment of its supporters by appearing irreligious. It therefore announced that a National Fast Day should be observed on Wednesday 21 March.

Absalom took the opportunity to walk to Northenden with Joseph Johnson and Edward. Northenden he knew and liked and Johnson had told him about a property for sale there.

March 21st, 1832. We got there at half-past one, after a very pleasant walk. Went to look at the little estate belonging to Mr Torkington which he wishes to sell. There is an ill-contrived, cottage-looking house with a barn and a stable. The situation beautiful, about a quarter of a mile from the church, on a little knoll overlooking the surrounding country and commanding a fine view of the river. The estate consists of six fields containing about seven statute acres of land. Two of the fields are water meadows at the foot of the knoll on which the house stands. The other fields occupy the knoll and part of the ground on the other side of the road, which is narrow and indifferent, to the house. The land will keep three cows, summer and winter. The garden is tolerable but much remains to be done to make the place as I should like it. It is let to Mr Badcock for £40 a year and the price asked for it is £1,100. Upon this property, it being his own, a man might live and bring up a family. The land is some of the best in Northen.

The fast does not seem to have been observed very strictly for they had a good tea at a Mrs Sidebottom's clean and well-ordered house in the village. It was ten o'clock by the time they reached home and Absalom was struck by a house kept in a very different manner from Mrs Sidebottom's. He made but a routine protest, his mind was elsewhere, committed to Northenden, the farm and schemes for improvement.

William Makinson was about to give a course of lectures on Animal Mechanics and had gathered the family together so that he could try out his first talk. Absalom thought he sounded far too much like the preacher he still was. He himself had caught a cold but neither that nor a further financial loss prevented him from going forward with the Northenden venture. The family went over to inspect the place and Absalom concluded that the house was much better and larger than he had imagined at first. Grime, himself toying with the idea of buying a property at Coniston, gave his approval to the scheme. On 9 April, the day before the Reform Bill was put before the Lords for a second reading, the legal formalities were completed and Absalom became the owner of the property he decided to call Rose Hill.

We know what Rose Hill eventually became with its pillared porch and grand entrance, its billiard room, reception rooms, library, servant's hall, kitchens and greenhouses. It has been called a typical merchant's house. But it was never like that in Absalom's lifetime. The place he first saw was comparatively small. It had two moderately sized reception rooms only and so few bedrooms that when guests came to stay, the family had to share rooms. Until Absalom built a cottage for the gardener and his wife, it had no accommodation for outside staff.

Absalom intended to buy more land, and the children and he went over there again with the surveyor.

April 30th, 1832. Went with Mr Irwin, my daughter and Edward to Northen. We took a coach to the White Lion at Withington and walked the rest of the way. Our object was to get the ground measured which I have bought. While they were measuring it I and the children walked about and looked at every part of my purchase. My daughter had not seen it before. She was pleased with it and Edward more desirous than ever to commence farming. We counted more than a hundred young trees, mostly poplars, which have just been planted and forty-seven apple and pear trees, many of which will have a great deal of bloom. We dined at the Boat House. After dinner I went again to the farm. As I walked towards it, I involuntarily reflected on the change in my mode of life which would result from removing with my family to Northen. On their account, and on my own, many circumstances have to be carefully considered. We got tea at the Boat House. John Watkin had come over in the afternoon and as he had not yet seen the place, I sent Mr Irwin, my daughter, Miss Johnson and Edward to meet the coach and went with John Watkin again to the farm. The evening was beautiful, the place looked more than pretty.

Possession, however, could not be immediate. Not only was there a sitting tenant in the person of Mr Badcock, but a great deal needed to be done before they could move. Since it would be so long before they could leave Broughton, Absalom had no hesitation on that score about taking up the appointment of senior overseer of the poor for the district. It was interesting to go round other people's properties in Broughton to assess them for the Poor Rate. He was struck again by the elegance of everything, in particular the well-kept gardens and the fine paintings and furniture enjoyed by the Revd Mr Clowes at the Old Hall. His daughter read aloud to him some of Cobbett's *Advice to a Father* while he was employed on his accounts. His wife *promised* to alter her conduct for the better, they saw a poor man who had hanged himself from a tree in the lane and Grime predicted that the country was fast approaching a crisis.

Indeed it was. The Reform Bill had passed its second reading in the Lords by nine votes, but on 8 May the Government was defeated on an amendment and Lord Grey asked the King to create fifty new peers, the number necessary to pass the Bill as it stood. The King refused to create more than twenty, whereupon Grey and his colleagues thankfully resigned.

The news did not reach Manchester until early in the morning of Thursday, 10 May. Business was suspended. According to Prentice, fear of insurrection paralysed the home market and foreign traders countermanded their orders. Shops were closed and groups of workers gathered in knots to condemn the iniquity of the faction which was attempting to frustrate the will of the people. Absalom was asked immediately to draw up a Petition to the Commons asking the House to adhere to the Bill and to grant no supplies until it was passed. He set about his task at once. The arguments had been well enough rehearsed and he finished that same afternoon. Events then moved fast.

It has been claimed that Manchester's Petition was the first ever to ask the Commons to stop supplies until grievances were redressed. It was read to the Reform Committee and approved unanimously. An hour later two placards were posted up stating where the Petition would be placed for signature. By six o'clock that evening 24,000 people had signed it. Richard Potter, John Fielden and John Shuttleworth, who had been assigned to take it to London, then set off in a post-chaise amid the cheers of the crowd. News of the swift measure taken by Manchester soon reached other places, and those who were still in ignorance of it were informed at the changing of horses.

Crowds gathered at Macclesfield and Leek, and when Derby was reached at midnight the coach was surrounded. They drove through Loughborough and Leicester during the night but Northampton was reached in the early dawn and at every stage between there and London the coach was greeted by welcoming crowds. They got to Palace Yard soon after eleven, having done the journey in seventeen hours. The deputation then went to Westminster Hall and placed the Petition into the hands of two Members of Parliament, Mr James Heywood, the county member, and Mr John Wood, who represented Preston.

The Manchester Petition was by no means the only one. The City of London together with Birmingham joined the protest in the same terms as Manchester and when, out of a sense of duty, Wellington accepted the King's request to form a ministry, it was rumoured that people were arming up and down the country. This was not so, but the atmosphere was certainly extremely tense. The King and Queen had been advised to retire to Windsor and on their return to London, according to Croker, the royal coach was pursued by a jeering mob from Hounslow to St James's Palace.

Absalom was harassed. On top of public business he was on the Committee which was seeing to the disposal of the *Manchester Times*. This was eventually sold to Prentice and Cathrall with the copyright and all its stock-in-trade for £550. Now he was asked to write the resolutions for a public meeting to be held on the ill-fated St Peter's Field on 14 May.

In Manchester, the split between the moderate reformers and the Radicals was deep. The situation was explosive. The Radicals remained determined to press forward with their demand for annual parliaments, manhood suffrage and the ballot. The working classes had not been directly involved in the meeting so hurriedly called when the news of the Government's resignation reached the town. It was important that they should be able to express their opinion, but in such a way that no riots ensued. Absalom spent most of Sunday composing the resolutions, then when he had finished a note arrived from Thomas Potter asking him to prepare an address to the King. He felt tired out and went to bed without doing it.

Next morning he got up late and still weary had to force his wife to mend the children's clothes before they could leave their beds. Potter came round to ask about the address as Absalom was shaving. He wrote it after Potter's departure and then took it round to the Reform Committee at the Town Hall only to meet further difficulties.

May 14th, 1832. The Radicals sent a strong deputation of ill-looking,

conceited fellows, headed by Elijah Dixon and Hetherington to say they
would oppose us unless we united with them in a deputation about universal
suffrage, annual parliaments and vote by ballot. After some jangling however
they consented to waive this if we would withdraw my Address and
substitute one brought by Mr Fielden which declared that every man of full
age and unstained by crime had a right to vote. This was conceded, I thought
imprudently.

John Fielden was a partner in a large-scale cotton manufacturing business in
Todmorden, Yorkshire. A radical and ardent disciple of Cobbett, after the passing
of the Reform Bill he became one of the members for Oldham. He took an active
part in the movement for limiting the hours of labour and was the author of an
influential pamphlet called *The Curse of the Factory System*.

It was not Fielden but Mr Walker, whose half-tipsy comments some months
ago had ruffled the Committee's feelings, who took the chair at the meeting on St
Peter's Field. It has been estimated that one-third of the people at Peterloo in 1819
were women and children. Now there were only men. Walker was flanked by
flags inscribed 'The Rights of Man' and 'The Ministers and Reform'. Absalom
noticed that two flags having figures of the King and Queen were turned upside
down.

The meeting was not very large – not more perhaps than ten thousand
persons. All went off quietly and my resolutions and petitions and Fielden's
Address were voted with loud cheers.

To Absalom's surprise Dr Kay called at the warehouse in the afternoon. Kay was
overworked and under great pressure. Two years later he was to have the first of
his breakdowns. The long-awaited cholera had reached Manchester that May. Kay
was acutely conscious of the lack of contact between the higher and lower social
classes in Manchester. He felt that it was not the commercial system itself that was
to blame but the *moral* degradation that accompanied it. Depravity and poverty
went hand in hand. It was the compelling duty of the better classes to break the
bonds which so viciously bound together immorality and want.

Kay now told Absalom that he had conceived the notion of a Political Union.
In what way this was to differ from the existing Political Unions, which were
already split between the moderates and the radicals, is not clear. In any event, Kay
persuaded Absalom to go along with him to Potter's counting house where a
meeting of reformers had already gathered. Absalom followed Kay there, met
Fielden and others and talked. He found to his dismay that they had already
committed the proposed Political Union to universal (male) suffrage. He felt that
this was premature and that the mass of the people were not yet sufficiently
educated to be entrusted with the vote.

That same evening the debate in the Commons proved conclusively to the

Duke of Wellington that his attempt to form an alternative administration had failed. In Manchester a weary Absalom retired to a quiet corner to read *Kenilworth*. It is a measure of his exhaustion that he soon started once more to rearrange his library, a task he always found therapeutic.

He doubted if there could be a political union among people with such diverse aims and went reluctantly the following morning to meet his new associates at the York Hotel and found that the Political Union was now to be called 'An Association to Promote Reform'.

The workers' party was led by a man named Elijah Dixon. Dixon was a prominent radical and an advocate of universal suffrage. Two years before Peterloo he had been arrested on a charge of high treason, taken in irons to London and appeared before Lord Sidmouth at the Home Office. He worked as a spinner, a milkman and a pedlar before starting to manufacture pill boxes. So successful was he as a capitalist that he turned to the timber trade and died as head of a prosperous firm of match manufacturers finally taken over by Bryant and May.

> **May 15th, 1832.** A deputation from the working classes, headed by Elijah Dixon, attended this meeting and he, as their spokesman, told the meeting that the working classes would combine with us to obtain the Reform Bill, but only on the ground of our helping them to obtain something further. He said that the 'sperrit' of the age was an advancing 'sperrit', advancing towards perfection, that the greatest degree of this 'sperrit' existed in England and that it was possessed in the highest degree by the working classes in and about Manchester. The superior classes might lead, if they thought proper, or they might not; but if they did not, they would find that the working classes could do without them. The younger part of the working classes were more enlightened than any other. They were either out-and-out radicals (republicans) or else co-operatives. He concluded by saying that at present an acknowledgement of the right of all men of mature age and unstained by crime to a vote in the election of the members of parliament would satisfy The People and they should be content to waive that right until the Reform Bill should be obtained and had been tried, but with the understanding that the acknowledged right should be ultimately conceded. I left the meeting as soon as this speech was concluded, but have since learnt that a committee of five persons, Baxter, Shuttleworth, R. Potter, R.H. Greg and myself, was appointed to draw up a declaratory resolution and to frame rules for the government of the Association.

Absalom felt he was in a false position. Luckily others too were having second thoughts.

> **May 19th, 1832.** Met the committee of the projected Reform Association. With the exception of Mr Fielden (Mr Potter being absent) they see, I think,

that the project is injudicious. Fielden is a thorough Radical and wishes for a <u>Radical</u> Union.

But Grey was back in office. Surely the Bill could now be passed without the assistance of people like Elijah Dixon? It could, but not without recriminations, a steady undertow of bitterness and unresolved conflict.

May 21st, 1832. After dinner I went and called on Mr Greg who told me that the Committee, with the exception of Mr Fielden, had agreed that no Association was now necessary. At Mr Greg's request I attended the meeting at Hayward's Hotel. There was a large attendance of Radical delegates but a small one of the Moderates. Mr Shuttleworth, Mr Greg, and Mr Baxter announced that the Committee thought the Association unnecessary and were immediately charged with inconsistency and desertion. An angry altercation followed. Fielden took part with the Radicals and read his proposed rules for the Association. Much noise and some threats from the Radicals followed and it was finally agreed to defer the final consideration till Monday, May 29th. I was merely a spectator of all this and came away sad. No union with such men as the leaders of the existing clubs is possible. They seek for confusion and want only the countenance of the wealthy to produce it.

The French Revolution indeed had cast a very long shadow. Conversation was gloomy on the previous Sunday walk to Northenden with Grime and Edward.

May 20th, 1832. We talked all the way of the state of the country and of the similarity between the state of England <u>now</u> and that of France at the commencement of the Revolution. As we went along we looked at the many pleasant homes which are to be found in this part of our beautiful country and <u>shuddered</u> to think of the dreadful change which civil commotion would produce. Mr Badcock, strange to say, had been thinking of revolution and told me that several other persons in the neighbourhood had similar apprehensions!!

They need not have worried. At three in the afternoon of 5 June the news reached Manchester that the Reform Bill had passed its third reading in the House of Lords. There had been no need to create new peers. The reluctant King had pledged himself to create as many as were necessary and the threat was enough.

June 5th, 1832. Flags were hoisted, huzzas uttered and the bells set a-ringing and firearms and cannon were discharged in all parts of the town.

Absalom had tea with Grime and they stayed up past midnight discussing recent events and wondering what effect the Bill's passing would have on the state of the country.

CHAPTER SEVENTEEN

'Met the factory people going to their work and noticed the children'

As part of the celebrations for the passing of the Reform Bill, the well-known aeronaut Mr Charles Green released into the air a balloon which was shaped and painted to resemble Lord Grey. More than that, he himself ascended to the height of some 3,000 feet and from there freed a goose which after some initial hesitation recovered the use of its wings and flew off quite safely. After rising still higher into the sky, Green then released a parachute with a basket containing a cat. That too landed safely in a field and was restored in good health to its usual home, the gasworks.

Mr Green's choice of animals was as appropriate as his method of propulsion. The agitation for the passing of the Bill had generated a lot of hot air and those of the working classes who had imagined that they would profit immediately had been geese. One adult male out of seven in the United Kingdom had a vote and in England and Wales one in five. The population of Manchester and Salford was 182,812 in 1832. The number of voters on the register was 4,293. Nevertheless, if the immediate benefits were not obvious, the reform was a real one. The whole system of representation had been altered.

Absalom was involved in a court case that caused him a little disquiet. A friend of his called George Parott had had some money stolen from his house and Absalom was needed as a witness. At the end of June he spent the day with the Parott family at Stockport.

June 20th, 1832. I dined and got tea with Parott and saw for the first time his new wife, a smiling, polite and not ill-looking woman of about thirty-six, he being probably at least thirty years older. She is of a respectable family and had sufficient property to live genteelly, but a woman beyond thirty is easily persuaded to accept anything that can give her a home and save her from being an old maid.

Before the case came on, an unpleasantness had arisen in Absalom's own home. Mr Burd took him aside and told him it was reported in the neighbourhood that he was 'too intimate with his maidservant!' The idea was preposterous. Absalom spent a flustered evening with Linnaeus, *The North American Review*, Pulleyn's *Etymological Compendium* and *Childe Harold*. Next day Mr Burd took tea at Broughton and Absalom was able to satisfy him that the report was utterly false.

The Parott case was heard at Chester and Absalom had to wait about the entire day and spend the night at an inn before the trial began.

August 7th, 1832. The trial of Peter Anderson and Margaret Wainwright for the robbery at Mr Parott's house and for receiving the property came on late in the day. The prisoners were convicted. The lad, he is only seventeen, transported for life; the woman for fourteen years.

Rose Hill was often in Absalom's thoughts and before his visit to Chester he walked to Northenden with Alfred, a long way for a child not quite seven years old.

August 3rd, 1832. We found my tenant Mr Badcock sitting in the barn cutting the turnips. He told me he had got about five tons of hay from the two meadows. The crop of onions, carrots etc. are very heavy and the fruit trees <u>laden</u> but everywhere neglect in every part. The rain fell heavily and all looked so dismal that I never liked it so little before. I saw enough to convince me that with proper management the place could be extremely productive.

They took a sociable home and Absalom drank two cups of tea before setting off to the Albion Hotel to meet Count Plater, a member of the late Polish Diet. Absalom was there for three hours and after his return read a book about Egyptian antiquities far into the night. No wonder he was tired and what he called his 'complaint' returned. He had to write a Petition to the House of Commons against the power of Justices of the Peace to stop footpaths without an appeal to a jury. Then he was asked to write another on behalf of the Poles, which Taylor insisted upon altering. That done, he composed an address to the shopkeepers of Manchester urging them to associate for mutual defence in the exercise of their right to vote at the coming election.

Rose Hill was his abiding joy. He went there with the children and filled his handkerchief with ripe apples. The following Sunday evening he went again.

September 23rd, 1832. One of the most beautiful autumn days I ever saw. The evening was delightful and I hope I was grateful as I stood <u>in my own fields</u> and saw the abundant produce and thought of the progressive accomplishment of my early wishes. Returning to the Boat House we were surprised to find my foolish wife, Mrs Soulby and Miss Barber, who had followed us to Northen! We got tea, obtained a lodging for Miss Barber and then at half-past eight set out on a beautiful star-light night, on our return.

We saw the Aurora Borealis as we came along.

October brought bad weather.

October 13th, 1832. Went in the afternoon with Edward and Joseph Makinson to Northen. We had a very pleasant walk there. We stopped till it was dark. The rain fell heavily and wind was strong but we borrowed a lanthorn and went merrily over the first two meadows but in the third we found Mrs Badcock standing on the bank of the river absolutely bewildered by the darkness and the storm. We could do no less than give her the lanthorn and then indeed had a difficult and perilous walk on the bank back to the lane.

Joseph Makinson had suffered a slight seizure, perhaps brought on by his financial crash. His affliction gave a strange cast to his features but he was evidently recovered because he enjoyed going to Northenden and four days later accompanied Absalom again.

October 19th, 1832. In crossing the ferry, Joseph Makinson, who was assisting at the rope, fell backwards into the river which is about five yards deep. Being able to swim he kept up till we got hold of him and pulled him into the boat. He was stripped and clothed in some old garments of the landlord's which were much too big for him and being well dosed with brandy was not much worse for his ducking.

That was not the only trouble to befall the family that autumn. A month later a relation named Elizabeth Makinson had to have her leg amputated. She bore the operation well. Absalom watched it performed before spending a pleasant evening at the Club.

On 12 December 1832 the bells rang early from the Collegiate Church to announce that at least some of the people of Manchester could vote for their own member of parliament. Strictly speaking, this was not the first election in Manchester. Under the Protectorate the town had had the distinction of sending that zealous soldier and native of the place, Lieutenant-Colonel Charles Worsley to Westminster; the very man who had removed the Mace from the Speaker's Table when Cromwell turned out the Rump.

At this time by no means all seats were contested. In most constituencies the candidate was nominated unopposed. The first election under the Crown in Manchester was, however, a bitterly fought contest. The importance of the town was shown by the number and quality of those wishing to represent it, the deep divergencies among the electorate were equally evident.

There were five candidates: the local man, Mark Philips; S.J. Loyd, an eminent London banker; Poulett Thomson, vice-president of the Board of Trade in Lord

Grey's administration, a free trader and a disciple of Jeremy Bentham; Hope, an aristocrat who had been put up by the Tories; and lastly Cobbett, put up by the New Cross Radicals. The Prentice group supported Philips and Poulett Thomson; to keep them out some Tories made an alliance with the Radicals and voted for Cobbett.

Elections could take more than one day. The proceedings were still rough and ready and did not all follow the same pattern. There was no secret ballot. The list of electors was compiled by the overseers of the poor from the ratebooks. The hustings were platforms on which were placed compartments rather like the booths for Punch and Judy shows. There was one booth for each candidate and some of his supporters and a central booth for the officials. If the nomination of a candidate was agreed upon by a show of hands, then he was considered to have been elected. If the election was contested, the proceedings took longer. Either on that day or the one following, the electors went to an appointed place to sign their names in their chosen candidate's book.

Past and present mingled on that first election day in Manchester. The hustings were erected in St Ann's Square and the crowd was rowdy and a little hilarious. The borough-reeve presided. He occupied the centre box together with other manorial and clerical officials who included churchwardens and sidesmen from the Collegiate Church. This box was flanked on either side by those of the five candidates and some of their supporters.

The beadle rang his bell and asked for silence, then the borough-reeve took the oath and the candidates were nominated and seconded from the hustings. The noise was tremendous. The beadle rang his bell incessantly for silence but to no avail and the borough-reeve's voice was so effectively drowned by shouts, hoots and hisses, particularly from the Cobbett mob, that part of the proceedings had to be conducted in dumb show.

Salford was still a manor of the Duchy of Lancaster and a separate constituency. The morning after the Manchester nomination, Absalom voted in Broughton for his friend Joseph Brotherton, one of the Salford candidates, before hurrying to the Manor Court Room in Manchester, where the voting was taking place and where, as a Poor Law official, he had to be prepared to act as a sworn commissioner should the need arise. Brotherton won the Salford seat. A partner in a prosperous firm of cotton spinners started by his father, he had retired early in order to devote himself to the public good. He was a pastor in the Bible Christian Church, a branch of the Methodists whose members abstained from both flesh meat and alcohol.

Mark Philips and Poulett Thomson were victorious in Manchester and after Christmas Absalom met them both at a dinner given in their honour at the York Hotel. Poulett Thomson had a sepulchral voice and awkward manner, his speech went on for two hours so that neither Richard Potter, Dr Kay nor Absalom had a chance to deliver the ones they had been asked to prepare.

Towards New Year's Eve Absalom's father-in-law died.

December 30th, 1832. My wife's father died about ten minutes past six this evening aged seventy-five years. He has suffered much during the last three weeks. Thus we have lost a kind-hearted and affectionate relative. We never know the value of such persons until after they are gone.

Rose Hill was the partial fulfilment of Absalom's dreams. It provided some sort of escape from his wife, his warehouse and the ugly, crowded, dreary streets. Walking to Northenden in the sharp crisp January air he felt thankful to be alive. The improvements and the planting absorbed his imagination and pacified his spirit. Yet his very happiness, the contemplation of the sky, his own fields and the gradual transformation of the house pointed a constrast his conscience could not accept.

His life was difficult, he had worked hard and against the grain for what he had got, but he did not dare compare his lot with that of the great mass of the people in Manchester. The more he read, the more he saw, the worse the factory system as it was then organized appeared to be. But he owed a substantial part of his income to it. Cloth as well as investment property had enabled him to buy the fields and the orchards of Rose Hill, his library and his pictures.

He investigated some factories for himself and after one visit an operative lent him *A Brief View of the Medical Evidence on the Factory Question*. He was much affected. The system was abominable, particularly in relation to children, who began in the mills from the age of seven or eight and were expected to work the same hours as adults for six days in every week.

With reason the matter was referred to as the factory *question*. It was difficult to say who would support restrictive legislation and who would not. Some Radicals opposed it, as did John Bright, Henry Brougham and at this time, Lord John Russell, Robert Peel and Thomas Macaulay. This opposition was not by any means just a matter of callousness, self-interest or the consequences of an alliance between the gentry and some of the working classes against the manufacturing party who had succeeded in getting the Reform Bill passed. All these factors played a part but there were practical and economic objections to restricting working hours by law, particularly in the cotton industry.

Because of the diversity and complexity of the processes required to produce cloth, children could be extremely useful and were often exploited by the operatives themselves. The 'piecers', the people who joined the threads broken by the spinning process, were usually boys and girls employed by the spinners, who kept them hard at work in order to increase their own wages. Those employed removing waste cotton or 'fly' from the machinery were also frequently children. The number of children employed was so large that it was difficult to organize mill labour in such a way as to limit work for people under a certain age to ten hours and to leave the time for adults unrestricted. Further, if the hours in which a man could work were curtailed by law, it was said that production costs would increase, goods would be more expensive, demand slacken and unemployment rise. Besides, if the operatives had to work shorter hours because the children and young people did, naturally they would be paid less and a reduction in wages would hardly be popular or contribute to social harmony. Lastly, it could be argued that the operatives were free agents, not requiring government protection like children, and that under the guise of restricting the working hours of those who could not help themselves, the reformers were in fact interfering with the free play of economic forces.

Absalom understood the objections and was not in favour of a universal eight-hour day as suggested in some quarters. But those Richard Oastler called 'little white slaves' had to be liberated. He canvassed his friends – Kershaw, Hadfield, Dr Kay and others – asking them to support the Bill to shorten the hours of factory children, introduced by the Tory Michael Sadler. Only Dr Kay refused. He had his reasons, as Absalom, who had just read Kay's celebrated pamphlet entitled *The Moral and Physical Condition of the Working Classes Employed in the Cotton Manufacture in Manchester*, understood very well.

When Friedrich Engels wrote *The Condition of the Working Class in England* his intention was to expose the poverty of the proletariat in order to demonstrate the logical necessity of revolution. Dr Kay wished not for revolution, but to shock people into reform. He had collected his material partly from the investigation carried out by the inspectors from the Board of Health before the cholera epidemic, partly from personal observation as medical officer in the slums and partly from information provided by the Manchester authorities.

Kay was almost obsessively moralistic. His pamphlet was written with a controlled intensity which when he was referring to the barbarities of the Manchester Irish, that 'mass of animal organization', sometimes toppled over into near hysteria. So strongly did he feel about the 'moral leprosy of vice', the sloth, drunkenness, ignorance, sensuality and irreligion of many of the working class, that his attitude towards poor relief was ambivalent to the point of being contradictory. He wrote:

> If the only test of the application of this fund be <u>indigence</u>, without reference to <u>desert</u> – be <u>want</u>, irrespective of <u>character</u> – motives to frugality, self-control and industry are at once removed and the strong barrier which nature itself erected to prevent the moral lapse of the entire population is wantonly destroyed . . . The wages of the worthy are often given to encourage the sluggard, the drunkard and the man whose imprudence entails on the community the precocious burden of his meagre and neglected offspring.

Society had decided that even the most worthless indigent should be kept alive, but the amount of relief bestowed ought to be determined by a man's deserts. Those wilfully indigent through dissipation or idleness might be refused help altogether. He trembled at the thought of applying an unmodified Poor Law to Ireland, it would turn that country into a vast infirmary.

He admitted in his introduction to the edition of his pamphlet Absalom was reading, that had investigations been undertaken in other towns, Manchester might have compared favourably with them. His figures and tables, however, were confined to Manchester and showed the appalling conditions in which large numbers lived.

Those engaged in cotton manufacture rose at five, and worked in the mill from six to eight o'clock. They went home for half an hour or forty minutes to a breakfast of tea and bread. They returned to the mill and worked until twelve, when they had an hour for dinner. After a miserable meal, consisting mostly of potatoes and bacon fat, they went back to the mill and worked until seven o'clock or later. Their evening meal consisted of bread and tea, the last often laced with spirits. The wages of the English had been reduced by the Irish, who had taught the people of this country how they could live like savages and yet keep alive. The youngest child in a mill earned 3s. a week, the best female spinner 21s. and the average wage was 9s. 6d. a week.

It is interesting that Dr Kay did not consider that these hours of labour in themselves injured the health of the population. The evil consisted in the combination of long hours with moral and physical degeneration. He believed passionately that it was useless to improve conditions without at the same time giving instruction in religion and morality. There was no point in reducing the hours of labour unless accompanied by a general system of education; the time gained would be wasted or misused, spent in sloth or dissipation.

So Absalom went ahead without Dr Kay's encouragement. One gets the impression from the diary that they did not like each other. In early February Absalom asked the borough-reeve to requisition a public meeting. He then wrote a Petition for a Ten Hours Bill and obtained the approval of his fellow requisitionists for it.

February 11th, 1833. Attending the preparatory meeting of the requisitionists on the Ten Hours Bill. My Petition and resolutions adopted by a very thin meeting.

February 13th, 1833. Attended the final preparatory meeting for the requisitionists of the Ten Hour Bill. All arranged, but no help to be got from the very rich. They do not like to come forward on this occasion.

Absalom implies that they had been active enough on behalf of the Reform Bill. The *Manchester Guardian* reported indeed that on the day of the actual meeting the Dining Room was only half full.

February 14th, 1833. Attended the public meeting in the Exchange Dining Room on the Ten Hours Bill. All our resolutions and the Petitions, passed unanimously. The meeting was not very numerous. I acted as clerk to the Borough-reeve, who was in the chair and moved the third resolution.

Those who were asking for this reform, Absalom said, should not talk about *humanity*. What they were seeking was but an act of bare *justice*. And why did they seek it? Here Absalom and Dr Kay were in agreement. 'That time may be afforded to the children for their intellectual, moral and religious instruction, without which life has no value.'

For Absalom life had value, the improvements at Rose Hill were coming on well. He pruned the young poplar trees 'while the last rays of the sun were beaming and the throstles were singing merrily' but the very success of his enterprise and the happiness it promised continued to make him more sensitive to the plight of others and more conscious of the fragility of human affairs. On the anniversary of his insolvency in 1815, he blessed God for all his benefits and read Blair's sermon *On Fortitude*.

He was remarkably energetic whether on his own or public business. In March he had to go to Lancaster on a legal matter and on the way back spent the night at Preston.

March 29th, 1833. Rose at four, but did not get off till half-past five. Met the factory people going to their work and noticed the children. <u>Saw the sun rise gloriously</u> and got to Yarrow Bridge where we breakfasted about seven. We took a chaise to Bolton and thence to Manchester by coach. I got home about half-past twelve and being much tired, went to bed. At half-past two they brought the letters from the warehouse and I found that it was necessary for me to go immediately to Liverpool to see Mr Hardman. I rose, went to the warehouse and at five o'clock I and my ledger were on the way to Liverpool. I got there about eight o'clock. After tea at the Royal Hotel, I took a coach and went to the workhouse. There I made out my account with the Parish, saw Mr Hardman, paid him the balance and returned to the inn.

The next morning he got up at eight o'clock and had his breakfast.

March 30th, 1833. I bought two books and then went to the workhouse. Sat for some time with Mr and Mrs Hardman. He is very ill and cannot live long. His son and daughters are not yet prepared to earn their own living and his property is nothing but a life insurance of £2,000, out of which there will be debts of some hundreds of pounds to be paid. Mrs Hardman, when we were alone, spoke almost despairingly of the probable situation of the family in the event of Mr Hardman's death. I left Liverpool by the railway at twelve and was in Manchester soon after two.

Rose Hill was taking shape, a man was doing the brickwork at sixpence a yard, a landscape gardener employed, Cobbett's seeds sown and another road made over the fields to the house. Soon they would be able to move, but expectation was clouded by Absalom's knowledge that his wife would have to go with him.

CHAPTER EIGHTEEN

'To erect a barrier beyond which in this country human suffering cannot pass'

In June 1833 Absalom went with Edward to see if all was well with his Derbyshire cottage. Together they visited Chatsworth, stayed at the hotel at Matlock and from there one early morning Absalom climbed the Heights of Abraham alone. He was sad and discouraged, for once his spirits were not raised by the magnificent view of the River Derwent far below, the tree- covered hills and the summer sky. The path to the top led to a hexagonal seat.

> **June 2nd, 1833.** Some writing on the seat caught my eye. I read 'Persevere and thou shalt attain the summit.' I accepted the words as a <u>prediction</u> and went cheerfully to the hotel.

It was a resolution more easily understood than acted upon. Rose Hill was a joy but also an anxiety. Mr Badcock accepted the noise and inconvenience of the building works almost too readily, he showed no sign of moving. The Rector of Northenden was an absentee but Mr Hornby, his curate, was kind and helpful and negotiated the sale of some glebe land. The parish of Northenden, he said, extended for five miles and its population was 1,420. Mrs Hornby was amiable too. Once Absalom spent half an hour alone with her in the rectory drawing-room while waiting for her husband. They spoke agreeably about gardening, travelling, Scott's novels, education, roses, sweet peas and the new annual just on the market, *Clarkia pulchella*. The contrast between Mrs Hornby and his own wife and between other elegant, well-managed households he visited in Northenden served to intensify his own domestic unhappiness. He was vexed to the soul by Elizabeth's filth, her mad behaviour in thunderstorms, her banging of the shutters and fits of vulgar passion. Once more he drew up a plan for the regulation of her day, once more she promised to adhere to it.

Thomas Potter invited Absalom to dine.

> **July 19th, 1833.** We had a good dinner – ice, fruit, etc. and a hearty welcome but dining in this way is always disagreeable to me. I do not enter readily into its formalities, nor is it pleasant to me to sit still and take wine.

We went round Mr Potter's garden and grounds which are pretty. He is a most industrious man and justly pleased with the wealth he has acquired, but every state has its vexations and I can see that he has his.

The Factory Act was stalling. That summer Lord Ashley, who was not yet Earl of Shaftesbury and therefore still in the Commons, had brought forward a Bill that was objected to by its opponents as dishonest, its real intention being to lower adult working hours under the guise of protecting children. Lord Althorp, the Leader of the House, then put an amended Factory Bill before it.

This Bill, which applied to all textile factories (save in some of its clauses to the manufacture of silk) forbade night work to anyone under eighteen. 'Night' was defined as half-past eight in the evening to half-past five in the morning. It forbade the employment of children under nine, restricted the work of children under thirteen to forty-eight hours a week with a limit of nine hours in any one day, and the work of young people between thirteen and eighteen to sixty-nine hours a week, that is to say, twelve hours a day and nine on Saturday. Inspectors were to be provided to enforce the new regulations and children under thirteen were to go to school for two hours every working day. The funds for this were to be deducted from their wages. The Commons had authorized the employers to make a contribution but this provision was deleted in the Lords after a motion put forward by Lord Salisbury.

The Bill fell far short of the demand for a ten-hour working day. Nor was it designed to protect the employment of children in other industries, where they were often exploited even more mercilessly than in the textile mills. Many reformers were disappointed, including Absalom who drew up a Petition against it. But despite objections from one side to its timidity, from the other to its liberality, the Bill was passed and the Factory Act came into force the following year.

All through the summer Absalom's family had been going backwards and forwards to Rose Hill, sometimes spending the night on improvised beds.

September 1st, 1833. Went to Northen with Thomas Makinson and Edward in the afternoon. The evening was beautiful and the walk from Kennedy through Northen enchanting. Never did our little peaceful village, or my little place, look more lovely. Walked about in the moonlight.

September 2nd, 1833. Came with Edward, Thomas Makinson, Miss Barber and my daughter to Manchester. We started late and walked too slow and I was too late for my affairs in Manchester. We read some poetry before we left Rose Hill.

A week before Christmas Absalom went to a dinner given by the Manchester Reform Association in honour of the two new Members of Parliament for the borough, Mark Philips and Poulett Thomson, later Lord Sydenham. Absalom had been asked to reply to the toast: 'The Working Classes of the United Kingdom and may their unrivalled industry and skill never fail to receive adequate remuneration.' The composition of the speech does not seem to have worried him as much as usual but on the evening itself anxiety almost overwhelmed him and he wished himself anywhere but where he was.

December 19th, 1833. We had a good dinner but the room was crowded and distressingly hot. It was past eleven before I was called upon to speak. When I got up on the bench I would gladly have been away. I was tired, as were all the company, my head ached and my thoughts were confused. When I rose, the company applauded for some time. I was thus able to collect myself.

He started, was loudly cheered, and proceeded calmly. It was a clever speech, a sincerely balanced appeal to self-interest and philanthropy likely to go down well with his audience. His opening remarks were greeted with cheers.

Of the importance of the working classes to the general welfare we are all, I am sure, deeply sensible. We feel that the real evidence of national prosperity must be sought not in the luxury and splendour of palaces but in the plenty and comfort of cottages. We know that it is by the condition of the laborious many, not by that of the privileged few, that good or bad government of a country must be estimated.

However, Absalom continued, ignorance of the real position of the working classes in society, could lead only to mischievous results. We must not ascribe the production of national wealth exclusively to them. The accumulation of wealth in a community does not result from the labour of a particular class, however important, but from the combined exertions of the whole. The unions they themselves had formed were lawful and praiseworthy when they confined themselves to legitimate and proper purposes. Unfortunately, some put forward schemes which not only inconvenienced others but harmed the workers themselves. Absalom now turned to Robert Owen and his socialism.

Cobbett's joke that the aim of the Evangelicals was to teach the poor to starve without making a noise was amusing but demonstrably false. Owen, however, was one of the few early nineteenth-century philanthropists who was not religiously motivated. When he was very young he made up his mind that all received forms of religion were untrue and a hindrance to progress. From that conclusion he never moved until towards the end of his life when he succumbed to spiritualism and believed that he was receiving messages from Jefferson, Shakespeare and the Duke of Kent.

Human beings, Owen maintained, were not responsible for their actions since their characters were formed by their environment. Hence the extreme importance of placing a child under proper moral and social influences. Like many others, evidently Absalom was repelled by Owen's open hostility to religion and put off by the nature of his schemes for the radical reorganization of society on socialist principles. Yet on one level both Absalom and Owen had much in common and if ever there was need for the forces of humanity to stand together it was then. Absalom failed to appreciate what was good in Owen's schemes just because he perceived so clearly that his 'new world', even if achieved, would but replace one evil by another. Owen, he said, intended his Society for National Regeneration 'to be merely preliminary to what he calls the formation of a new world by the reconstruction of society upon scientific principles'.

A world, gentlemen, in which religious observances are to be abolished, laws unnecessary and places of punishment unknown; in which also the duration of marriage is to depend upon the agreement of the parties and to prevent inconveniences the children are to be the property of the state . . . To tell you, gentlemen, that this commonwealth will never exist is certainly unnecessary, but admitting for a moment the possibility of its existence, what, I would wish to ask, would be the consequences to the working classes?

Would it not reduce the skilful and prudent to the level of the careless and ignorant? Would it not take away all stimulus to exertion by extinguishing all hope of reward? Would it not impose upon all men a new and intolerable species of slavery and degrade the human race to the condition of the inferior animals, who perform instinctively a certain round of operations and eat, sleep and die?

Will any man of the working classes deliberately assist in forwarding a scheme, the end of which is to take from him the right of working for himself, or receiving the reward of his own labour – which is to make him a mere tool in the hands of a company, without whose consent he may not drive a nail or thread a needle?

However, Absalom continued, it was not ignorance alone but suffering that induced the working classes to listen to such visionary schemes, it was suffering that gave them a tendency to combine for dangerous purposes. In Manchester they all lived in the middle of a dense population. The condition of the working classes was continually under their notice. Only too often unceasing industry was accompanied by hopeless poverty, the very existence of which demanded an investigation into its causes and prompt application of those remedies it was in the power of the legislature to apply. He was here interrupted by loud cheers. What he went on to say has a disturbing if familiar sound to twentieth-century ears.

As far back as the coronation of George IV in 1821, the *Manchester Guardian* had vigorously blamed the Irish for much of the disorder of that day. The immigration of the Irish poor, it said, had inflicted a deadly blow upon the health and comfort of the working classes in Manchester. The Irish had unstable characters, were indolent, filthy, totally regardless of order, cleanliness and comfort, their communities a nucleus for the generation and diffusion of fever and human miasma.

The *Guardian*'s words might be considered as mere journalistic exaggeration, but someone supposedly as measured as Dr Kay used terms that were scarcely more flattering. He had compared the Irish immigrants to animals, to savage tribes debased alike by ignorance and pauperism, an inferior race whose colonization of this country had pernicious effects. He was still writing the same thing thirty years later.

Friedrich Engels, who had a working-class Irish girl as his mistress in Manchester for years, owed a great deal to Dr Kay's statistics and closely followed what Kay said about the Irish in his own *Condition of England*, first published in 1845. They were 'uncouth, improvident, and addicted to drink. They introduce their brutal behaviour into a section of English society by no means noted for civilized habits or moral principles.' Few people asked how it came about that this particular race was so degraded, or why they were in such a pitiable state that they were forced to seek a miserable living across the water.

It is extraordinary, and a lesson in the myopia of the well intentioned, that Absalom and his liberal friends who felt so deeply about the wickedness of Russia's treatment of the Poles and who would so loudly applaud the efforts of the Hungarians to free themselves from Austria, did not perceive what was happening on their own doorstep. So obsessed were they with the notion that Ireland was a natural part of England that they simply could not grasp the plain truth that she was a conquered country whose native inhabitants had been massacred on a large scale, whose lands had been confiscated and given to strangers, and whose religion an alien race had attempted systematically to stamp out.

However, many who were blind to the political dimension of the problem felt keenly the condition of the people. Absalom used far more moderate language than the *Manchester Guardian*, Dr Kay or Engels.

There is one large portion of the working classes of the United Kingdom which is doubly unfortunate, inasmuch as the individuals who compose it are not only wretched themselves but the authors, wherever they come, of wretchedness to others – I speak of the labourers of the sister island – men deserving of all praise for their industry and for the light-heartedness with which they have long borne the evils of their situation, but who have yet, from the state of their own country, been the involuntary, but most active agents in deteriorating the circumstances of the English workmen. (Hear, hear.)

To make his point Absalom then went on to refer to a village which was undoubtedly Audlem, the peaceful place where his ancestors had been born and he had spent so many happy summers.

There is in an adjoining county, at the distance of about forty miles, one of those pretty, clean and cheerful villages, surrounded by orchards and cornfields, the frequent occurrence of which every Englishman regards as one of the most pleasing features in the scenery of our lovely country.

Irish labourers, Absalom explained, were employed there to help cut a canal. When the work was finished they offered their services to the local farmers for low wages and as a result quarrels broke out between the natives and the newcomers.

Still the Irishmen remained and to all that was said or done to them, this was their constant reply: 'You may kill us, if you please, but we will not go. Here we can get potatoes and straw. We cannot get them in our own country and while that is the case, here we will remain.' The consequence has been that some of the English workmen have been compelled to leave their birthplace, the condition of those who remain is worsened and with their condition their moral character – depredations have become common – the once quiet and comparatively happy village is the scene of commotion and discontent and the English labourer has been degraded or exiled because his brethren in Ireland are destitute of the protection of a Poor Law. (Hear, hear and cheers.)

He was well aware of the objections to the Poor Law, Absalom continued, but for all that could be said against it, it had been a blessing to the unfortunate.

This I am aware, is not the place for a discussion on the subject. It is sufficient now to remark that the obvious effect of the Law is to erect a barrier beyond which in this country human suffering cannot pass. In Ireland people are not surprised that children and men, and even women, should be seen in public in a state of nudity and whole parishes have, as we know, been exposed to death by starvation. In England this not been, and while the Poor Law exists, cannot be the case – (cheers) – not that we are more humane than our fellow-subjects, but with us the rights of humanity have been embodied into law and the law takes care that our eyes shall not be accustomed to the sight of female nakedness, or our hearts hardened by the constant spectacle of unalleviated misery. What then, are the destitute labourers of Ireland and their English brethren who suffer from that destitution entitled to expect from the hands of a reformed parliament? On behalf of the working classes I answer, 'Poor Law to Ireland' – (loud cheers) – the extension to that unhappy country of the great charter of the destitute.

For his peroration Absalom turned directly to Philips and Thomson.

To you, gentlemen, the representatives of the borough-representatives, be it remembered, of many thousands of industrious Irishmen who reside in it – I commend in the name of humanity and sound policy, an attention to this great measure. By the wrongs of our Irish fellow-subjects, by the sufferings of our own most worthy labourers upon whom those wrongs have been severely visited, I entreat you to lose no time in urging the adoption of a system of parochial relief in Ireland.

The applause was prolonged, the speaker heartily congratulated by the two MPs, the London papers reported the occasion, but it was to no avail. In 1838, more in the hope of preventing further Irish immigration than solicitude for the poor, a limited form of the Poor Law was applied to Ireland. It had to be limited. The natural reluctance of the possessing classes to give something for nothing, to blame the unfortunate, to condemn the hungry as improvident or lazy, was in Ireland compounded by racial hostility and the sheer impracticability of providing relief on a scale the situation demanded.

Absalom had not understood the magnitude of the problem. Enormous sums would have been needed for the building of sufficient workhouses and for outdoor relief even on the scale provided for by the Poor Law Amendment Act. In Ireland poverty and destitution were too widespread to admit of outdoor relief and until the great famine of 1845, it was declared strictly illegal. After that Dr Kay's grim prophecy was fulfilled. Ireland was indeed turned into a vast infirmary.

CHAPTER NINETEEN

'Mr Watkin of Rose Hill'

Much to Absalom's joy his tenant, Mr Badcock, left Rose Hill in March 1834. At last, after almost two years of going to and fro, sleeping on mattresses on the floor, coping with burst pipes and overflowing cisterns, with builders, decorators and gardeners, he was about to live in the house of his dreams. Preparations for the move began in earnest. Rose Hill had to be cleaned out and sixteen rats were killed. Woodlands Terrace had to be emptied, a load of furniture was sent to Northenden by the cart and was followed by another and a few days later by a third.

The day Absalom had looked forward to for so long did not turn out quite as he had imagined.

March 21st, 1834. Most of the things sent off to Northen. Returned to Rose Hill in the evening. My wife and daughter came to Rose Hill in the omnibus about eight o'clock. It was a lovely moonlight night. The bells were ringing and as the omnibus came down the lane to Northen the boy played some tunes on his bugle. I felt as I walked down to meet them and looked at my little place, an elevation of spirits, soon to be checked. My wife met me with more than usual Irish hurry and was impatient to hide herself in bed.

The truth was that despite his severe strictures upon Grime, Absalom himself had begun to collect some silver. Nothing ostentatious to be sure, nevertheless some quite respectable spoons, candlesticks, snuffers, cream jugs, punch ladles and sugar tongs. These had been placed in a special basket.

At last it came out that all our plate had been packed in a basket, that the fool had had the special custody of this basket, that she had given it to she knew not whom, to put she knew not where – and that it was missing!!! The omnibus was emptied and the basket was not there, the goods were examined, it was not amongst them – she <u>hoped</u> that it had been put into the wagon, but the wagon did not arrive. We waited till midnight and then Battersby and Edward went to Cheadle in search of it. They did not meet it and could hear nothing of it. It was about two in the morning when we went to bed, worn out, unhappy.

Battersby was the gardener. Early in the morning news was brought of the missing things.

March 22nd, 1834. The joiner brought word that the wagon load of goods was standing at the ford mouth – that the carter had in vain endeavoured last night to make his horses cross the water and had returned with them to Manchester, leaving William in charge of the goods. This was about eleven at night and from that time until six in the morning no person had passed towards Northen, so that there had been no opportunity for William to make us acquainted with his situation.

Absalom sent horses to bring up the wagon.

In the tail of the wagon, stuck amongst some other things in the most careless manner, was the basket with the plate. The wretch delayed so long to get breakfast ready that I was too late for the omnibus and had to walk to Manchester amidst clouds of dust. I returned to Rose Hill in the afternoon and stayed up too late. And thus ended my second day at Rose Hill.

It took some weeks for Absalom to get things in order, decide on the placing of the furniture, to arrange his library, make up his mind where to build the cottage for Battersby and generally adjust to the rhythm of a new life.

It was more tedious and required more organization than he had thought to live so far from his work. His wife complained that she missed her old friends and did not find the people of Northenden so congenial. Various parties were given to introduce them to their neighbours, the Alcocks, the Whiteleggs, the Albistons, the Sumners and the Harrops. They took tea, danced the quadrille and played cards but Mrs Hornby was now only condescendingly polite. Perhaps rumours of the Methodist New Connexion had reached her.

On a beautiful day towards the end of May Absalom travelled in a sociable to Rostherne with his daughter and Edward, Mr Mordacque, Mr Davies and others. Sociables were rather uncomfortable, the seats so arranged that the passengers faced each other with the consequence that one was dragged sideways through the air.

May 23rd, 1834. From the church we went to the sign of the White Hart, there in a pretty arbour in the garden formed of Dutch beech trees, we got bread and cheese, porter and brandy and water. Then we went towards the mere and being invited to pass through the garden of the large house below the church we came, by a succession of agreeable walks, to the little bathing house at the end of the mere. We were all well and in good spirits and I was pleased to see Mr Mordacque form two pipes of the reeds which grew upon the margin of the mere and observe him and Davies <u>piping</u> while Greaves was looking for the best point of view from which to make a sketch of the church and mere. When he had finished he left the mere and just below the church we met Mr Albiston with a haversack at his side, smoking a short pipe.

Part of Absalom looked at the world through the eyes of an intelligent child. He had, as one of his friends remarked, 'a bottom of innocence'. He was always happiest in simple surroundings and doing simple things. The weather held and the first haymaking at Rose Hill was a great success. Friends came for the day together with some of the family: William and Joseph Makinson, and John Watkin with Mary Brierly, the girl he intended to marry.

May 29th, 1834. A hurrying and agreeable time. About eleven o'clock they began to load the hay. I got the joiner, bricklayer and labourer into the fields with Darbyshire, his three sons, Battersby, the two Whittles, Tommy Whittle and Mrs Hewitt. They worked and drank heartily and at half-past nine the hay was all in the 'hay-shade'. They drank a parting pint and shouted, or rather 'whooped' three times and then proclaimed aloud that Mr Watkin of Rose Hill 'had gotten his hay bout rain'. They then 'whooped' again and the children in the village 'whooped' in return. I read several pages Tristram Shandy.

Joseph Makinson bought the hay for £18, just as it stood, paying himself for the cutting, trussing and carting.

Sunday was the day most people from Manchester came to Rose Hill and it was the day Absalom most liked to keep for himself. Dr Carbutt was perhaps an unbeliever, Grime still faithful to the chapel.

June 22nd, 1834. Dr Carbutt, Mr Mordacque and Mr Grime spent the day with us. We went to church in the forenoon and heard a curious sermon by Mr Hornby on the character of David. Dr Carbutt and Grime talked and did not behave quite well in leaving the church. [After dinner] we walked by the riverside and back by Carr Lane. Dr Carbutt talked bitterly of others. He is evidently unhappy. They left early and as I walked about after they were gone, I thought with sadness of the voluntary unhappiness of man. Religion is absolutely necessary to happiness.

The trouble was that they had far too many visitors.

July 4th, 1834. At home all day, suffered from flatulence. Mr Mordacque came about eleven and stayed till past five. My old associates in debate, Pownall and Bradley, with the son of the former, came about three. We waited for dinner till past four and then had cold meat and peas half boiled. They left about eight. I was glad to be alone.

That month misfortune struck Joseph yet again. The wonder is that he had anything left to lose.

July 24th, 1834. About half-past five in the afternoon Joseph Makinson sent for me. I went. He told me that Vogel had stopped payment and owed him between four and five thousand pounds!!! He asked me to go with him to London. I consented. At eight we got into the Knutsford Mail. We got to Knutsford about half-past ten. Took places in the Liverpool Mail for Birmingham. Travelled all night.

They reached Birmingham at half-past six in the morning.

July 25th, 1834. Breakfasted. Got places in the Tally Ho! for London. Travelled all day. We got to London about seven in the evening, tired, heated, unwell. We put up at the Swan with the Two Necks, Lad Lane. We got tea and then went to call on Vogel at Finsbury Circus.

As they were looking round, who should they meet but Grime, presumably on the same errand.

He was staying at the same inn as ourselves. Vogel was not to be seen. We called twice, left a letter for him and returned to the inn. We talked a little with Grime and went to bed.

July 26th, 1834. Rose in good health, breakfasted, spent most of the day in looking after Vogel and getting a docket struck against him. Found time to look at my old habitation, school house and places of play. I looked also at the churchyard of St Benet's, Paul's Hill, in which my father was buried.

The next day was Sunday. Absalom went to St Paul's with Grime and had his handkerchief stolen on the way. He left London at seven o'clock in the evening travelling in the mail with Mrs Thomas Goadsby. He does not tell us anything more about Vogel or whether Joseph or Grime got any money back.

Edward was now nearly fifteen and already working in his father's warehouse. John, who was nearly thirteen, now joined them for all or part of the week. Later he would reproach his father for not giving him a better education.

Absalom loved Rose Hill and was to do so more and more, but the increased responsibility and the incompatibility between him and his wife intensified his nervous anxiety. He was also nearly always exhausted because he stayed up reading until the small hours in an attempt to make up for time lost both at the warehouse and at home. Towards the end of August Mrs Mordacque and her two children came to stay and after they had gone to bed Absalom spent most of the night devouring the *Memoirs of Madame Roland*. Not surprisingly, the next day he could not stand more than a morning's work. When September came he spent an evening at Davies's with Mr Audubon the naturalist, read *Sense and Sensibility* and at last went off for a short holiday at Hayfield in Derbyshire with some friends from the Club.

September 25th, 1834. We got there about ten at night and put up at the George inn. The beds were clean and dry and we slept well till four in the morning, when we were roused by Mr Jervis, who came to tell us that we might remain in bed as it was raining very hard and the ascent of Kinder Scout would be impracticable. We were going to sleep again when the sound of a strange disagreeable musical instrument, accompanied by the announcement of the hour, recalled us to consciousness. It was an operator on a 'cow's horn', who was going through the village to awaken the work people.

In November the news reached Manchester that the King had suddenly dismissed Lord Melbourne.

This was a distortion of the truth. The fact was that on the death of his father, Lord Althorp had become Earl Spencer and therefore removed to the House of Lords. Althorp had been Chancellor of the Exchequer and Leader of the House. Melbourne doubted if the government could survive without Althorp in the Commons and offered to resign.

William IV, who disliked the Whigs, was at Brighton. He eagerly accepted his Prime Minister's tentative resignation and gave him a letter for Wellington at Apsley House, inviting the Duke to take office. Melbourne had more or less dismissed himself but that was not how the matter was perceived by many in Manchester. The Whigs, it was thought, had been turned out by the exercise of arbitrary power. In fact it was the last time a monarch would decide whether or not an administration should continue.

The careful, clumsy, local machinery started up. Thomas Potter called a meeting on the dissolution of the Ministry. Absalom attended and agreed to write a resolution and an address to the King for the proposed public meeting. The proceedings did not go as intended. The rifts between the parties in Manchester were too deep and passionately felt for a single resolution representing all views to be adopted. Those Radicals who despised the moderation of the Whigs made an unholy alliance with the Tories.

November 27th, 1834. I stayed an hour and got much heated by the crowd. The radicals, assisted by the Tories, succeeded in carrying an adjournment to Stevenson Square and there carried resolutions of their own, thanking the King for having turned out the Whigs. I did not go to Stevenson Square, but walked [back] to Northen, reflecting on the state of affairs and resolved to be quiet and to mind my own business, unless circumstances should <u>demand</u> the exertion of all honest men.

Wellington was a caretaker Prime Minister only. He soon handed over to Peel, who took office but was unable to secure a majority at the General Election which followed. It seems strange to us, but at that time the result of a General Election did not mean the automatic fall of the minority party. It was for Parliament, not the electorate, to eject a ministry. Not until April the following year, after he had been six times defeated in the House, did Peel resign and Melbourne return.

As the days shortened towards Christmas, it was time for Absalom to do his accounts. That 'foolish muddler' his wife had, of course, got hers wrong. He took down his books and calculating from them wrote in pencil a list of his expenses for the past year which he slipped between the pages of his diary: Meat £60; Drink £30; Coals, candles and soap £10; Rent, taxes and wages £50; Clothes £40; Sundries £10; Jaunts and stops away from home £20; Wear and Tear £20. This made a total of £240 for the year's expenditure (about £12,000 in 1990 values). By 'meat' Absalom meant food in general.

The realities of living so far away from his work in the winter were more unpleasant than he had imagined. His fields were under water, frequently he had to work all the day in wet shoes and then in January 1835 the snow came.

January 22nd, 1835. The road impracticable from the rain having frozen under the snow. Sent for the sociable. It is now past eleven and the sociable not here and I sitting by the fire while my business in Manchester is standing still. This is living in the country.

The well-known traveller and MP for Sheffield, James Buckingham, came to lecture in Manchester. Absalom read some passages in *Travels in Mesopotamia* the evening before he and the rest of the Club attended the talk. Buckingham's philosophy summarized a great deal of what Absalom and his fellow liberals believed in and shows how much they accepted the worth of their world.

January 30th, 1835. The whole Club from Davies's to Mr Buckingham's lecture. It was a good one. From the ancient prosperity of Palmyra he deduced the advantages of Free Trade and concluded by exhorting his hearers to avoid the errors of antiquity, to cherish free institutions and to extend education accompanied by moral and religious instruction, to labour to make the mass of the people happy, and <u>individually</u> to determine to do <u>something</u> to preserve and increase the greatness and happiness of our great and happy country. After the lecture I introduced John and Edward to Mr Buckingham.

For some time both Absalom's wife and daughter had been urging him to give a dinner party, their first formal entertainment at Rose Hill. When the weather improved Absalom consented and one March morning his daughter excitedly accompanied him to Manchester. Together they ordered provisions and other things necessary for the occasion, all the time Absalom vexed to the heart by the expense. The market was bad and he ought to have been getting business but instead he spent time at the warehouse studying 'The Art of Cutting up a Pheasant' in *The Cook's Domestic Duties*. The day came.

March 5th, 1835. Prepared for our dinner party at half-past five. I had a hired waiter, Hanson, who understands his business well and laid the cloth and arranged the sideboard to admiration. At half-past five came our guests, Messrs Hornby, Harrop and Davy. These with Thomas Makinson made our party. Mr Hornby brought his man. The dinner was well served and except that I perseveringly called the leg of lamb the shoulder, I do not know that we made, I and my wife, I mean, any noticeable blunder. The dinner cost me above £7 for the eatables and wine; and in extra furniture, plate, glass etc. at least £12 more. Foolish expense!

He could not afford such things. That was the road to bankruptcy, poverty and ruin. His complaint returned and was not helped by the washing that usually alleviated it, nor were his spirits raised by sitting quietly alone by the kitchen fire with the newspaper. He spent a restless, painful, anxious night and to reassure himself took stock of his assets.

March 7th, 1835. I have taken stock and find that, after all my foolish and wasteful expenditure, I have still £540 in my business. My property therefore stands thus: In business = £540; Mrs Haworth's house = £600; Mrs Soulby's school = £800; Mr Harrison's house = £500; Cottage at Bonsal = £80; Stable in Broughton = £65; Cottages St George's Road = £95; Houses, offices and land at Rose Hill = £1,600; Battersby's cottage = £100; Total = £4380. My furniture, books and plate and farming stock cannot be worth less than £700, so that my total property is at least £5000 [about £250,000 in 1990 values]. Bless the Lord, oh my soul, and forget not all His benefits.

The next month Absalom wrote a sad note in the margin.

April 28th, 1835. I have discovered an error of £240 in the stocktaking. I have not above £300 in my business. Alas!

He could not throw off a bad cold.

March 8th, 1835. Rose late, very sore and unpleasantly, rather than painfully unwell. Walked round the garden after breakfast and was pleased. At home all day. Fell asleep in my chair in the afternoon, the disposition to do so increases upon me and ought to be repressed. I am an old man.

He was not yet forty-eight. That was Sunday. Monday was worse.

March 9th, 1835. In the afternoon rain, followed about four by one of the heaviest falls of snow, for the time it lasted, and composed of the largest flakes, that I ever saw. From half-past four to seven we had a complete hurricane. At home all day, quite unwell.

His life was slipping away. Business was bad, his cough was troublesome, his piles painful, and on occasions he did not get home until the small hours of the morning. He read Tucker's *On Death* and some part of the Book of Job. But spring was on its way.

March 29th, 1835. Walked two or three times round my little domain and was pleased. All is improving and when I can sit down quietly by the kitchen fire, nothing appears to be wanting except a more grateful heart and a wife who would be clean and speak the truth.

His cow calved, and the snowdrops, the yellow and then the striped crocuses, and the primroses came up in his garden, followed in time by the fruit blossom. He read passages from *Don Juan* again and had Bloody- Roger potatoes set in the east bank. One evening in April, coming home from work at four o'clock, a neighbour asked him in to admire his garden.

April 2nd, 1835. Just as we entered, there was a peal of thunder in the west. His garden is beautiful, the walls covered with peach and nectarine trees in full blossom, the ground skilfully laid out and all in high order. The distant thunder grew louder and before I had reached the end of the wood which extends from the termination of the kitchen garden almost to the ford and is prettily intersected by walks, the rain was heavy and the storm at hand. All the way to the boat I had rain, thunder and lightning. I crossed the river, the storm increasing. In the churchyard the lightning appeared to descend into the old yew tree. From the churchyard to our house the storm was terrific. Lightning almost unintermitted, thunder incessant, heavy rain, violent hail and unusual darkness. I was soon wet through from the shoulders downwards, in spite of my umbrella. When I got home I found the lower part of the house abandoned. My wife, John, Alfred, Mary and Fido were all together in my daughter's bedroom in great alarm.

A few weeks later Edward undertook his first public duty and acted as 'check clerk' at the by-election that followed Poulett Thomson's promotion to President of the Board of Trade. He was re-elected and Absalom was invited to the dinner held in his honour at Hayward's Hotel. No one had told him that he was expected to speak.

April 29th, 1835. I stayed until eleven o'clock and a little before I left I had to introduce the sentiment 'National Education'. I was exhausted by the heat, the cheering and the great excitement. I was also unprepared. However, I got on the table and <u>talked</u>, but not well, for about five minutes. I escaped disapprobation and was even applauded but I will never, if I can avoid it, speak again in public without careful preparation.

The next day the papers referred to his 'truly eloquent, sound and enlightened speech'.

May 2nd, 1835. Now the truth is that with the exception of a very few sentences, it was a poor, commonplace, indifferently expressed effusion, unworthy of the subject, the place or the occasion, but I have acquired a sort of reputation for speaking and my want of preparation escaped rebuke.

As spring turned to early summer his spirits alternated between joy and dejection, hope and near despair. Rain had brought on the garden. Apples, pears and cherries were in bloom, the wind blew the grass like the waves of the sea, the laburnums and white lilac were almost out. He heard the cuckoo, read the *Memoirs of Harriet Wilson* with much interest and thought himself happy until the bad market plunged him into gloom.

Absalom's was a private diary. In it he poured the hopes and fears he was unable to communicate to his wife or indeed to anybody else. It served as a safety valve. To the outside world plainly he appeared as a much calmer person than the man revealed in the journal. Nor may his relations with his wife have been quite so bad as he made out. The real Absalom is probably to be found somewhere between the diarist and the public figure.

May 12th, 1835. A very bad market, did very little and was much depressed. All appears to be against me at present. We have a large stock of goods which I cannot sell. I have invested the greater part of my little property in land and buildings and so far as my expenditure in alterations at Rose Hill is concerned, very foolishly, because the money I have sunk there I <u>want</u> in business. My business capital I have reduced to little more than £300, so that I depend on the assistance of Jones and Co to enable me to go on. Assistance which is expensive and of course diminishes my profits. Then my health is bad and at home I have no comfort. I live in a pretty place it is true, but the house is ill-managed, untidy and expensive.

Haymaking had come round again.

June 6th, 1835. Assiduous, but feeble at the warehouse. My hay was got on the stock about eight in the evening. I don't think there will be more than four tons, which I estimate to be worth £16. The expense of mowing, getting and leading, including drink, in which I have as usual been foolishly liberal, is not less than £6 ten shillings, so that my clear gain will not be above £9 – a poor result. Stayed up till near three in the morning. At two I went into the garden and walked about more than half an hour. The morning was <u>delicious</u>, warm, dry, refreshing, the birds tumultuous in song and all nature full of joy. How much pleasure I lose by not rising early and going to bed early.

When Absalom speaks of 'leading', he is using the northern dialect word for carting the hay.

It took him about two hours to walk from Rose Hill to his warehouse. He was finding it inconvenient living in the country without a carriage of his own, so he bought a second-hand sociable from the man in the village who hired them out. It was slow and the first morning he used it did not get to Manchester until a quarter to ten.

He was troubled by the behaviour of his children. They were rude and indifferent, and Edward was particularly difficult now that he was becoming so independent. He made excuses about stocktaking in order to stay late in Manchester. In reality he was enjoying himself with his friends, often not coming home until twelve at night. Absalom's daughter, Elizabeth, was now approaching her eighteenth birthday, a grown-up woman.

They had arranged a simple birthday celebration for her, entertaining a few family friends to tea, together with Joseph and his daughter Hannah. Unfortunately, Hannah was a pretty, lively girl, to whom Absalom had paid particular attention in the past. This had aroused all his wife's jealous instincts and she had already told Absalom that her visits to Rose Hill must not be encouraged. Nevertheless, Hannah was invited not only for the birthday party but for the night. The tea was a success and afterwards the younger guests amused themselves in the garden and among the mown clover until eight o'clock when some of them left.

July 31st, 1835. Joseph, Hannah and I walked home with the Misses Sumner and returned by Sharston Hall and Carr Lane. The evening was beautiful, a rich glowing western sky, the moon a week old and the sky without a cloud. The air, too, was cool, refreshing and fragrant, bringing the scent of the recent hay. Our walk was very pleasant. Joseph kept exclaiming 'beautiful!' and Hannah declared that to breathe such air on such a night was indeed to live and to be happy.

Joseph's seizure, three years earlier, had affected not only his face but his hearing. He was so deaf that it was sometimes easier to communicate with him in sign language. Now, sitting with him and his daughter by the rockery, Absalom began to do so. Perhaps the silence made his wife suspicious. When Absalom went indoors for a moment he was met with a torrent of reproaches. He withdrew and spent the rest of evening alone reading *Othello*. Next morning, not finding breakfast ready, he went into the garden.

> **August 1st, 1835.** Hannah had been there for a few minutes and we walked to the seat, where we sat some time looking at Worthington's mowers. In a minute or two my precious wife came along the walk. I called to her, but as soon as she saw Hannah she turned back and ran into the house. When Hannah and I had walked round we went in and were received by my wife with the looks of a fiend and expressions the most revolting. Hannah and her father returned to Manchester in the sociable. Edward came in the ten o'clock omnibus and was charged by his mother to tell me 'that she was very unhappy'. 'About what?' 'About his cousin Hannah.'

At that inopportune moment Mr Hornby called.

> As soon as he had gone my wife came out and demanded an explicit answer to this impudent question. 'Is your conversation with Hannah perfectly pure or not?'

Some emotion, whether anger, shame or disgust, we can never know, made Absalom continue his diary in shorthand. He sat up late alone for the second night running, this time reading *Dix Ans d'une Femme*. Joseph may have been deaf but his daughter certainly was not. Two days after the visit to Rose Hill, Hannah called at the warehouse.

> **August 3rd, 1835.** She told me that she was going to Rhyl with Miss Barber who has taken a house there and intends to take lodgers during the bathing season and to keep a school. Hannah is to be a sort of housekeeper in this establishment which is, I think, as unlikely as possible to succeed, Miss Barber being notoriously maladroit in domestic affairs. Poor girl! She has no comfort at home and is therefore willing to take any offer which takes her away from home.

He advised her to go to Rhyl for a fortnight to try it out.

The same historical quirk that had deprived Manchester of the franchise meant that it possessed neither a municipal charter nor a corporation. It remained in principle still feudal, run by officers of the Manorial Court together with people called improvement commissioners. Early in August Absalom was asked to write a Petition to the House of Lords in favour of the Municipal Corporations Bill and also a Memorial to Lord Melbourne on the same subject.

The Municipal Corporations Reform Bill, now obstructed by the Lords, proposed to transfer the powers of the old town corporations to councils elected by male ratepayers of three years' standing. As matters stood, this legislation could not apply to Manchester. However, provision had been made for the incorporation of towns wishing for it but only after Petition to Parliament. Absalom was by now a practised hand at writing Petitions, nevertheless the task was tedious and he was mocked by the glorious weather.

One Sunday in August when he had completed his task, he walked with the boys nearly as far as Gatley, returning by the river where they found the enchanter's nightshade. The bells of Northenden began to ring and the moon rose above the hills. The night was clear, at once moonlight and starlight. Absalom felt the richness of the air, his corn was nearly ripe, the dahlias, hollyhocks and monkshood were in flower, the lime trees beginning to fade and the mornings to get misty.

No beauty can obliterate pain. A fortnight later he had a severe attack of his complaint. He put it down at first to eating unripe plums, then to the castor oil he had taken. But as he lay tossing and turning all night in agony, he knew he must get some more expert advice than anything Manchester then could offer. In early September 1835 he made his will, got it witnessed and left Rose Hill with his daughter at six o'clock in the evening to catch the *Bee Hive* coach for London.

CHAPTER TWENTY

'I told him that if he remained it must be on condition of behaving with propriety'

After travelling all night Absalom and his daughter Elizabeth arrived in London at three o'clock in the afternoon of the following day. The specialist Absalom intended to consult was Mr Salmon, author of the book on protrusion of the lower bowel. Before breakfast on the morning of his appointment he walked alone to Paul's Wharf and looked at his father's grave in St Benet's churchyard. The medical examination proved painful but was not so bad as he had feared since no instrument was as yet introduced into the rectum.

Mr Brotherton, the MP for Salford and Broughton, kindly got Absalom and Elizabeth tickets of admission to the Royal Gallery so that they could see William IV proceed to the House of Lords on his way to prorogue Parliament. Before the ceremony Brotherton took them round the House of Commons.

> **September 10th, 1835.** He showed us every part, new and old. Then, after putting Elizabeth into the Speaker's chair, he showed us into the Royal Gallery and left us. The Royal Gallery is the passage by which the King, after leaving his carriage, proceeds in state to the House of Lords. It is a beautiful place and we had a very good sight of the King and the procession, there being few spectators in the gallery. The King is a healthy looking, red-faced old man. He was dressed in the uniform of a naval officer and looked like a bluff old sea-captain.

Absalom's next visit to Mr Salmon was most unpleasant. An exploratory instrument called a bougie was passed up the rectum and a stricture found about six inches up. The pain was great but, although it still hurt him to walk, the next day he spent some hours prowling round his childhood haunts. He was struck by the number of vines growing up against the houses. Salmon had arranged three more appointments and the following was the worst. The bougie was kept up the rectum for eleven minutes and caused so much pain that Absalom had to spend the rest of the day in bed.

He took a mercury pill, and in an attempt to relax before his next visit to the doctor, went to the Haymarket Theatre to see *Clari, or the Maid of Milan*. He could not hear a word of the first act because of the shouts of the audience which had been led to expect a performance of *Hamlet*. On his last visit to Salmon, a size-seven bougie was passed up the rectum and held there for four minutes of considerable suffering.

Before he left for home Absalom returned once more to St Benet's and this time went inside the church. He had not seen its interior since he was fourteen, the year he set out for Manchester. It was the church of his last days in London as a boy and his father's coffin had been placed before its carved wooden Holy Table. Like its near neighbour, St Paul's, it almost miraculously survived the incendiary bombs of the Second World War and has been beautifully restored. Absalom noted the changes since he had last seen it, left before the end of the service and spent some time searching for the house of a child who had been his earliest friend, a boy named William Sheppard.

He had never been away from home for so long before. He found on his return that the wind and rain had altered the appearance of the garden and that it was also difficult to get back into his old routine. He was faced almost at once by the trouble and anxiety of moving his place of business. He had traded in Cannon Street since he had set up on his own, now he moved his warehouse to the High Street.

Throughout 1835 and 1836 he suffered greatly from his complaint. One Saturday night he stayed up reading a pamphlet about Ireland and Daniel O'Connell until four in the morning, hoping that the pain would subside or that he could bear it better employed reading than lying in bed. The next day was St Valentine's Day.

February 14th, 1836. Did not rise till one o'clock. Read several pages of Boswell's Tour to the Hebrides. Much pleased with the place as I walked about the garden from four to five o'clock in the afternoon. The birds were singing and the western sky lighted up by the setting sun, while the snowdrops, aconites, cloth of gold crocus, wall flowers, primroses, polyanthuses, the first flowers of the mezereon and the catkins of the hazel already enliven the garden. This is the anniversary of our coming to inhabit the cottage in 1833.

He added in the margin of the page: It is <u>now</u> my duty to cease to think of distinction and to be grateful for a quiet sufficiency.

He undertook to act as one of the overseers of the poor for Northenden, took part in a debate with Cobden about the relative merits of Russia and Turkey, sat in the kitchen watching the day fade gently into night and took stock of his cellar. He had fifty-one bottles of sherry, twenty-four of port, six of Bucellas, thirty of brandy and two of Rousillon '86.

In July he spent an hour contentedly in the kitchen garden.

July 23rd, 1836. We are now alone having had one or more with us for three months. Spent an hour gathering red currants. I found that I had got about five and a half pounds. I was struck with the abundance of everything. Gooseberries, currants, raspberries, apples, all fine and all in abundance. The other crops equally so. I felt grateful and desirous to show my gratitude by an innocent and useful life. God help me to do so.

Unluckily, two days later Hannah Makinson paid them a visit.

July 25th, 1836. Walked three times round the garden with Hannah. My wife called to us from the door and the window and accused us of an improper intimacy. After we came in Hannah demanded an explanation and there followed a scene of most disgraceful violence on the part of my wife.

In early October Absalom had a most unpleasant row with Edward. What occurred was not unexpected. The boy was just seventeen, quick, intelligent, ambitious and impatient of his father. When it happened Absalom had not long had dinner at the Dog with Grime and Jervis. They had talked about the money market and discussed the state of trade.

September 23rd, 1836. I felt, while we were talking, my own inferiority as a man of business to either of my friends, but especially to Grime. Considering my natural disadvantages, my unhappy home, my depression, my ill health, it is a wonder that I have succeeded even to the extent that I have.

Edward had poked a sensitive nerve, pulled a rough finger along an already tender place.

October 9th, 1836. When Edward came down this morning he behaved very insolently both to his mother and to me. I spoke to him sharply about his behaviour and his coming down so late. He said other people could lie in bed and be attended to. I asked what he meant. He shuffled. I insisted upon his telling me. He answered that he meant nobody. Angry at the lie, I gave him a box on the ear. He looked at me furiously and said I should remember it. To this threat I replied that he might leave me whenever he pleased, that I would suffer no such insolence and that if he thought it would be for his good to go elsewhere, I would promote his interests as much as I could, but that while he stayed with me, he should behave properly.

After breakfast I took him into the parlour and there carefully explained to him my plans for the good of the family. I represented to him that in doing all he could for the common interest, he was in fact working for himself and I added that if he thought he could do better elsewhere, I wished him to do so.

I told him that if he remained with me it must be on condition of behaving with propriety and that in the future, when he forgot what was due to me, I should avoid any passionate expostulation and merely tell him, if at the warehouse, that he was wanted below, if at home, in the other room. That rather than submit to improper treatment from any of the children, I would close the doors of the warehouse, leave them to do what they could for themselves, and live upon, or eat up if need be, my property. He heard me with attention, appeared to be <u>a little</u> affected, but made no reply.

Absalom knew he needed working capital and there was every appearance of a difficult and dangerous time ahead in the commercial world. One morning not long after his row with Edward he sent John out to Jones and Lloyd to ask for a bill of £300. Jones sent it but warned Absalom that the balance owing was too high, his bills were out of all proportion to the returns on his account. Absalom decided that the best thing for him to do was to take out a mortgage on Rose Hill.

October 24th, 1836. Having ascertained that I could get the money I then went to Mr Lloyd and was received with smiles because I showed that my circumstances were good and told him of my intended mortgage.

It was a complicated business. The Northenden property was examined by the trustees of the lender, then Absalom had to pay £10 or £12 to have an abstract of the Rose Hill deeds drawn for the attorney. He began to feel the truth of the old saying that if you want to know the worth of money try to borrow some.

He sprained his foot in jumping over some calicos in the warehouse and had barely recovered from this mishap when Mrs William Makinson arrived there. She was in distress. The matter was an awkward one. Many of the details remain obscure and what we do know is puzzling. It seems that her son, John Makinson, was in custody at Lancaster waiting to be examined by the Insolvent Debtors Court. The money for which he was imprisoned was owing to Absalom. His mother now begged Absalom to go and speak up for him. Absalom consented.

November 11th, 1836. At home till eleven o'clock, then went to Manchester and at two o'clock left in the Umpire for Lancaster. Mr Gill, the Independent minister of Turton, got into the coach at Pendleton and with him I had a good deal of interesting talk, although I had never seen him before. At Darwen we stopped some time to have one of the lamps glazed. Then we proceeded and were going not improperly fast when, about half a mile from Darwen, the coach suddenly swung round on the side on which I sat and the next moment came to the ground, smashing the window and the lamp on that side and throwing the coachman, the outside passengers and the luggage that was on the top of the coach violently to the ground. We in the inside, lay very quietly at my request, till we had ascertained that the horses were quiet and then, one by one, cautiously extricated ourselves so as not to tread upon and hurt one another.

Absalom was cut and bruised but not seriously. The coachman had been thrown out on the back of his head, the outside passengers were filthy from the muddy road but no one was dangerously hurt.

As the coach was so much damaged as to be incapable of being moved, one of the horses was detached and a passenger went on it to Blackburn to get another coach. I, and the lady who had fallen with us inside and three male passengers, walked on to Blackburn which we reached after a long, tiresome walk through the mud, at about eight o'clock. I ordered tea and in about three-quarters of an hour the coachman with the rest of the passengers arrived in an old lumbering omnibus, the only conveyance that it had been possible to procure. In this thing we all went on slowly and with difficulty to Preston. It was too late to get any further and there I remained all night.

Absalom left Preston at six o'clock next morning, which was the day of the hearing, reaching Lancaster at nine. He went immediately to the Insolvent Debtors Court.

November 12th, 1836. It was some time before John Makinson was called up and I had leisure to observe the gross frauds that were attempted by the insolvents and the suspicion and irritability which this had produced in the mind of the Commissioner. When John was called and I had been sworn, the Commissioner, Mr Reynolds, first inspected me with his spying glass and then desired me to leave the court while John was examined. In a while I was called in and at first with evident suspicion, then with civil consideration and at last with entire confidence in my veracity, was examined at much length as to my debt and motives for sending John to gaol, his character etc. I found by the result that John had made a false statement upon oath. He was severely reprimanded by the Commissioner but finally discharged 'out of consideration to his relations and in the hope that he would alter his conduct for the better and learn to speak the truth.'

I left the court feeling the weakness of human nature and convinced, more than ever, of the need we all have to pray 'Lead us not into temptation.' May God keep me from the necessity which leads man to falsehood. I dined at Miss Noon's. I had a delicious steak, a cranberry tart, a jelly, and half a pint of sherry, with some good cheese, for three shillings and sixpence, and sixpence which I gave to the waiter and for which, it being twice the usual gift, I had a smiling alacrity of attention. The perfect cleanliness of tablecloth, knives, glasses etc., made my dinner a treat. I reflected with sadness that such a dinner, even such a dinner, was unobtainable at home.

His wife's signature was needed to complete the mortgage. Absalom received £2,500 and had to pay his attorney £57 for preparing the deeds. He was plunged into gloom again, gloom not dispelled even by an unexpected sale of 10,000 pieces of calico in a week. John had caught some of his brother's rebelliousness. He behaved so badly at the warehouse that Absalom dismissed him, whereupon Edward declared himself unwell and Absalom had to work alone. John soon became bored at home and he pleaded with his father to let him return, promising never again to give him trouble.

In the new year Absalom had to go over to Broughton to see about the rent for Woodlands Terrace.

January 13th, 1837. I called on Mr Harrison who agreed to pay me £40 a year, instead of thirty-six guineas from next March for his house. It looked so well that I wished that he had resolved to leave it that I might be able to return to it. Now I feel the inconvenience of living at Northen. I am unwell and my horse is lame and the expense of keeping and paying for our conveyance by the omnibus is too great for my income. I find also that the time I spend in going to and from Northen deprives me of many opportunities of improvement and even interferes greatly with the proper prosecution of my business. I ought perhaps to return to Broughton and yet I am much attached to this place and have spent so much money on it and like the quiet seclusion it affords me so much when I am at it that I cannot think of leaving it without pain.

The previous July Absalom had had to go to Altrincham to see the Poor Law commissioner in order to be briefed about the proposed changes in the Poor Law, not yet introduced into the North. Now, as one of the overseers of the poor at Northenden, he needed a magistrate's signature for the amount of the Poor Rate and walked over to Cheadle to obtain it from the High Tory rector, Mr Trafford Leigh. He was snubbed and minded it.

January 21st, 1837. I went to the Rectory and was admitted into the lobby by a servant in livery. I sent in my name and the Rector, a chubby-faced tall young man came out, took my book and left me to look at the lobby while he went out to sign it. It was soon done, he returned. I thanked him and bade him good morning with the usual civil addition. My return was a very aristocratic 'Good morning to you,' and he turned away, leaving me to let myself out.

The Literary Society debated republicanism. The question: 'Could a republican government be established in Great Britain with safety or advantage to the commonwealth?' was briskly discussed on the part of the opener and other young members with evident leanings to republican schemes.

The market was bad, a number of firms in America failed and as the late cold spring turned to glorious summer, news reached them that American banks were suspending specie payment. But the recent rain made the country look fresh and full and rich. The limes, horse-chestnuts, maples, elms, oaks and beech were in leaf, together with the ash and the balsam poplar.

On 20 June William IV died at Windsor, and at Kensington Palace Lord Melbourne kissed the hand of an eighteen-year-old girl. Four days later, at the request of the borough-reeve, Absalom wrote a loyal address to the young Queen Victoria.

CHAPTER TWENTY-ONE
'It is now one o'clock and at four the operation will be performed'

Never had the garden looked so beautiful. The roses were in full bloom; scarlet moss, white glove, Madame D'Arbrey, Susette and Tuscany. The borders were bright with sweet williams, lilies, Canterbury bells, poppies, pansies and mignonettes. Yet Absalom saw it all through a haze of pain. His condition had worsened considerably. He spent long anguished hours in violent pain from tenesmus, or severe straining, in such agony that he found it difficult not to cry out. Lying down gave him no relief and when he was up he crawled rather than walked. Mr Occleston the surgeon was called out from Manchester. He gave Absalom opiates and a syringe to inject himself.

> **July 21st, 1837.** At six worn out with pain and want of sleep. I got some coffee and wrote a letter. Then I lay still but could not sleep for weakness, soreness, pain through the left chest and in the legs. Mrs Watkin read to me Scott's account in the Life of Napoleon of the Battle of Waterloo. I felt dreadfully weak and depressed but was insensibly interested by the narrative and shall I think always remember it. About twelve I fell asleep and I slept <u>stupidly</u> till six in the evening, awaking very weak and with a bad headache. I got up, shaved and crawled into the garden but had neither strength nor appetite. I durst not attempt to relieve the bowels at night, indeed there was no desire. I slept but indifferently although I had taken an opiate.

From now onwards Absalom usually refers in his diary to his wife as 'Mrs Watkin'. The following Sunday he got up well and cheerful, enjoyed his breakfast and then injected himself.

> **July 23rd, 1837.** Tenesmus followed for eight hours. During most of this time I could do little but apply my hand to resist the tenesmus, now lying down a little, now crawling rather than walking about. Still the pain was not so violent as on Thursday. I could endure it without crying out and in the evening I was able to sing [a hymn]. Much struck with the poetical beauty of the Book of Job in our reading tonight.

The next day he felt a little better.

July 24th, 1837. Walked about in the garden and round the meadows. Went at four in the afternoon with John, Alfred and William Shuttleworth to Northen church, looked at the organ which they are putting up, went into the belfry and ascended the steeple. The day being clear, the view was beautiful. I saw what I believe to be Mow Cup rising beyond the first range of hills, almost directly in front of our house. I walked up and down the church for some time alone.

He had done too much and paid for it with a sleepless, painful night. Hannah Makinson came to help but Absalom's wife had another fit of jealousy and was discovered reading his diary which she had abstracted from his desk. The opiates gave him some relief, he was able to show Dr Smith, the High Master of Manchester Grammar School, round his garden and even to get to town to record his vote in the General Election that followed the accession of the new sovereign. He voted for the two Whig candidates, Mark Philips and Poulett Thomson. The Tories nominated Gladstone without his consent and he came bottom of the poll. Absalom had two votes. He was able to vote for the Manchester MPs and also for those who represented South Lancashire.

The relief was temporary. After an injection the pain was less violent but it was enough to render his life absolutely miserable. Camphorated oil, laudanum, turpentine and hot bran were applied to the base of the spine. Joseph Johnson and his daughters came to visit him and the following day he heard a piece of bad news.

July 31st, 1837. Walked about the garden and then applied to my accounts till dinner time and was well and cheerful. Just as I had finished dinner John came in with a letter from Mr Grime in which he says that he had only on Saturday discovered that his sufferings had arisen from enlargement of the heart which must soon prove fatal and desiring forthwith to see me on important business. I was much affected and sent a reply by Battersby immediately.

Occleston came over and once more examined the bowel. This time he declared that ulceration existed and that an operation ought probably to be performed almost at once. He called in a colleague, the well-known surgeon Joseph Jordan. Jordan had built a school of anatomy at his own expense and his lectures there led to the formation of the Manchester School of Medicine. His grandfather was credited with starting the art of calico printing. Absalom had to undergo yet another painful examination. Jordan agreed with Occleston. That day was Saturday, the operation was fixed for the following Thursday, to take place in the bedroom at Rose Hill.

Absalom stayed at home on Sunday morning and enjoyed the garden. In the afternoon he went to church.

August 6th, 1837. Never did the service affect me so much as on this occasion. The state of my health, the uncertainty of the future, my sense of God's mercy and of my own unworthiness, all combined to produce an unusual impression and to convince me more than ever of the necessity of religious consolation in times of affliction. One verse in the 32nd psalm, which happened to be the first appointed for the evening service, particularly struck me: 'Great plagues remain for the ungodly; but whoso putteth his trust in the Lord, mercy embraceth him on every side.' The roses are now almost over, but the dahlias and hollyhocks are coming to supply their place. The weather is beautiful and I have enjoyed the day, although the boys trouble me with their violence, rather however, from thoughtlessness than bad intentions.

All operations then had to be endured without anaesthetics and in the knowledge of possible serious infection. On the day it was to be performed, Absalom got up at seven o'clock.

August 10th, 1837. Asked help from Heaven and felt deeply the words 'Like as a father pitieth his children, so the Lord pitieth them that fear Him, for He knoweth our frame, He remembereth that we are dust.' God grant that I may never lose the purposes and feelings of this hour. Wrote a codicil to my will and got it witnessed. It is now one o'clock and at four the operation will be performed. May my Creator and Preserver be with me, enable me to bear it and bless the result and if my life should be continued with renewed health, may He enable me to devote the residue of my days honestly and heartily to His service by regular discharge of all my duties to all to whom I owe them. Two o'clock. I have been round the garden. The trees grow, the flowers bloom, the fruit invites the hand. I have lived fifty years which have been crowned with mercies and in life or in death I will exclaim 'Bless the Lord, oh my soul and forget not all His benefits.'

The doctors did not arrive until nearly five o'clock. They brought with them two more colleagues, Mr Greaves the surgeon, and a Dr Phillips. Phillips examined Absalom yet again and agreed with the others on the necessity of an operation. Mr Greaves himself was to die many years later from blood poisoning caused, it was said, by pricking his hand during an operation.

I undressed to my drawers and stockings and lying down on my left side at the foot of the bed, with my back to the window and pressed against the bed post and taking hold of Mr Greave's hands, I was ready for the operation. Mr

Jordan then introduced the knife, guarded by his finger, into the rectum and made an incision about an inch and a half long, laterally against the left buttock, through the bowel and the sphincter muscle, so as to divide the latter. He is a steady and skilful operator, but the bowel, which has for so long been liable to prolapsus, rolled under the knife and had to be cut through doubled. Still the operation was not very painful and it was over in two minutes. I was forthwith put into bed, while the medical gentlemen went down to tea. Immediate faintness, fluttering, depression and a sense of soreness were the consequences of the operation. The night wore away in faintness and a sense of pain and about morning, I slept.

He got up the following afternoon about two o'clock and shaved.

August 11th, 1837. At about five Mr Jordan, Mr Greaves and Mr Occleston came. I had a motion with a good deal of bleeding and it appeared to be quite certain that the sphincter was fully divided. Feeling tolerably well, I asked Mr Jordan if I might walk downstairs and he encouraged me to do so. I sat with him and the others some time, talked of antiquities, of Nelson's monument in St Paul's etc., became excited, reached some volumes, folios, of Montfaucon, out of the bookcase for Mr Jordan to look at and before they went felt weak and tired.

He went to bed.

As I began to undress and got off my coat and waistcoat, my head became giddy, a cold sweat covered me, the extremities were cold, the figures on the paper and on the carpet became indistinct, I appeared, if I may so speak, to be hurrying away from my body and limbs. The children applied camphorated spirits to the nostrils and to the hands and face, gave me hot brandy and water and rubbed and fanned me for nearly a quarter of an hour, so long did the fluctuation between consciousness and unconsciousness continue. When it was over I was undressed and put in to bed. The children rubbed me for a long time, but the night was one of painful weakness and I did not sleep till morning.

It is difficult to establish with certainty the exact nature of Absalom's complaint. He continued to bleed but never again records the acute pain he endured before the operation, which must therefore be looked upon as at least a partial success.

His recovery was slow and hindered by the arrival of too many well-meaning visitors. Contrary to expectations, Grime did not die immediately. He came with his daughter to stay at Rose Hill and there was further excitement when the daughter of their former neighbour at Broughton, the schoolmistress Mrs Soulby, got engaged to Thomas, the eldest son of Joseph Makinson. Thomas was a graduate of St John's College, Cambridge, and now in holy orders. He and his future bride intended to emigrate to New South Wales.

The immediate crisis over, Edward began to be troublesome again. He was rude and rebellious and made a scene before Absalom and Grime set out to dine with Richard Cobden. Probably he considered himself quite old enough to accompany his father. Indeed, he was later to become a closer colleague of Cobden than Absalom ever was and eventually to publish his letters and reminiscences in his book *Alderman Cobden of Manchester*. But for the moment he suffered all the frustration and bitterness of a clever boy ignored by the older generation simply because of his age. Cobden lived in a large old house in Quay Street, afterwards the first home of Owen's College.

September 8th, 1837. We had a good dinner and a kind reception and talked agreeably. Mr Cobden, who was in Egypt a few months ago, is of the opinion that the condition of the Irish peasantry in Connaught is worse that that of the Fellahs under the rule of Mehomet Ali. He thinks also that the agricultural labourers of France are better off than ours. Speaking of Mr J.S. Loyd and his unsuccessful attempt to get into Parliament for Manchester notwithstanding his abilities and the influence of his wealth, Mr Cobden, adverting to the prejudice against Mr Loyd which had been produced by the questioning of Mr Prentice, observed, 'Prentice should have been bought over.' 'Not,' he added, 'that I mean to say our friend is for sale, but he should have been won over – such things are to be done – he should have been consulted, that would have been enough.' A glance from Mr Grime told me that he, as well as myself, had noticed this remark and not long after Mr Cobden's man entered the room and told his master that a person from Mr Prentice wished to speak to Mr Cobden about a paper. Mr Cobden apologized for leaving us and went to him. Now Prentice eulogizes Mr Cobden in The Times and as I have no doubt, has been consulted. In this manner reputation is maintained and the way to distinction is smoothed.

After dinner Cobden showed them a number of skulls he had taken from a tomb at Memphis and when Absalom got home he found a letter from Edward apologizing for his conduct, a sensible and well-written letter that gave his father real pleasure. Mr Occleston paid a professional visit and examined Absalom's rectum.

September 15th, 1837. The ulcer looking healthy but not healing, he applied caustic. The sensation, for about twenty minutes, was that of burning, painful but endurable. Afterwards it became a cold pain but not so intense as I have often suffered. The pain continued most of the day. Employed as well as I could for the pain, in my accounts. Our hive, the old stock of bees, was taken last night by Goodier. There is but a small quantity, perhaps seven pounds, of honey and a fair quantity of wax, but it is our <u>own</u> and there is a great charm in that little word.

With the approach of winter came the usual surge of civic activity in Manchester.

At the beginning of the nineteenth century the idea that elementary education should be free, universal, compulsory and secular was accepted by very few and smacked of the French Revolution. By the end of the century there had been a reversal in public attitudes, a change as far-reaching in its way as the coming of the railways. Elementary education became free, universal and compulsory. What it did not become was secular.

To most people the notion of secular education was not only unfamiliar, it was an abomination. Man was a religious being. It would be wicked to allow children to be brought up without knowledge of religion and even worse for them to be instructed in an erroneous one. The reasoning was sound. Since religion is concerned with the nature of man, religious error is indeed far worse than any mistake about the observable processes in the physical world. But truth about that world is more easily obtained.

At first the Protestant Reformation had a disastrous effect upon education. A large number of schools were swept away altogether and their endowments seized by the Crown. It has been stated that neither Henry VIII, Edward VI nor Queen Elizabeth I founded a single school, at the most they rescued a handful from the general ruin and got the credit for the generosity and piety of others.

Manchester's own Grammar School was founded in 1515 by Hugh Oldham, the Bishop of Exeter for

> the good mind which he did bear to the county of Lancaster, where the children had pregnant wits, but had been mostly brought up rudely or idly and not in virtue, cunning, education, literature and in good manners.

Two years before, Absalom had written an Address to the Trustees urging them to apply some of their funds to the education of the poor and indeed the education there was originally intended to be free: 'There shall be no scholar or infant of what county or shire soever he be of, being a man-child, be refused, except he have some horrible infirmity, infective.' In Absalom's time this particular school was a fee-paying one. His own boys did not go there. Probably this was because he intended them not for the professions, where a predominantly classical education might be useful, but for business. The decision, however, was to have some unfortunate consequences.

There existed another ancient school in Manchester, Chetham's Hospital, founded in the year of King Charles I's execution, for the free education of poor boys in the neighbourhood. Unlike the Grammar School, this remained free but it was small and taught boys from six to fourteen only, who were then apprenticed to some trade. There were a few other endowed schools in Manchester but they were small and unimportant. Apart from these, children who were taught at all received their education from private schools of varying quality, from Sunday schools run by unselfish volunteers, or from the two rival scholastic institutions provided for the education of the working classes.

The two institutions were both religious and both disagreed with each other. The British and Foreign School Society was non-sectarian. It taught the Bible but no doctrine. It drew its support from the Whigs and the Nonconformists. Lord John Russell was its vice-president. The other society had a longer title and a more restricted field. It was called The National Society for Promoting the Education of the Poor in the Principles of the Established Church. It taught the liturgy and doctrines of the Church of England.

The Factory Act was the first assertion of the right of the state to compel children to be educated. That same year the first faltering steps were made towards providing it. In the summer of 1833 an almost empty House of Commons voted £20,000 for educational purposes, the money to be divided equally between the 'National' and the British and Foreign School Society. One condition only attended the grant: it was not to be paid until at least half of the total cost of building a school had been raised by public subscription.

The Factory Act had decreed that children working in factories must attend schools provided by their employers for two hours a day. Each Monday they were expected to produce a signed certificate stating that they had done so. Yet these were children of between nine and thirteen who might have been working up to eight hours a day and were hardly in a fit state to learn even if had they been properly taught. Some factory schools which Absalom himself was to visit were conscientiously run, but since the manufacturers had to finance them out of profits supplemented by the children's wages, many served little educational purpose but were useful as a check on the statutory hours of labour.

A great industrial town like Manchester sucked in thousands and thousands of labourers from the surrounding country and from Ireland. We know something of the squalor in which these hordes lived. What we may not realize is that without schools the children of working parents were left to roam about the streets unsupervised.

It has been pointed out that the nineteenth century was not the unique age of child labour as is popularly supposed; it was the age of child unemployment. The children of the poor had always been put to work, but before industrialization they did so in a family environment, in contact with adults. Many children were indeed employed in Manchester factories but still more were not, either because they were under the legal age of nine or because the work was not suited to them. Mill wages naturally tempted women to go out to work. Babies were often farmed out, children put in the charge of an older member of the family or simply left to fend for themselves. They were the nineteenth-century version of 'latch-key children'.

In 1834 that pioneer of social investigation, the Manchester Statistical Society, had formed a committee to investigate the situation in the town. Despite the valiant efforts made by voluntary societies and by the poor to finance education out of their own pockets, the returns revealed a deplorable picture. One-third of the children in Manchester did not receive education of any kind. Only ten per cent of the existing schools reached even a reasonable educational standard. Therefore, although Absalom had not yet recovered fully from his operation, when Cobden asked him to speak at a meeting on education to be held in the Theatre Royal he felt it was a matter of such importance that he could not refuse.

The object of the meeting was to urge the Government to make provision for the 'mental improvement and moral training' of young people throughout the entire country. Its supporters were numerous and held divergent religious opinions. According to Cobden, among those present were nine MPs, thirteen magistrates, the secretary of the Manchester Literary and Philosophical Society, thirty-eight Churchmen, thirty-eight Unitarians, twenty-three Independents, fifteen Methodists, eleven members of the Society of Friends, nine Baptists, one or more members of the Scottish church, Roman Catholic, Moravian, and the Scotch Secession Church and a single Swedenborgian. If the newspaper reporter's description of the gathering as 'wholly unparalleled in the annals of our history' is perhaps a little exaggerated, nevertheless the scene was striking enough.

The Theatre Royal had been turned into a banqueting hall, the pit and the stage levelled and the entire place was bright with oriental hangings and brilliant gas lighting. Mark Philips took the chair, Lord Brougham sent a letter of approbation and Samuel Wilderspin, the pioneer of infant education, stressed that children must be managed by love, not fear. The most important speaker of the evening was the Catholic MP for Waterford, Thomas Wyse, who made a strong plea not to allow denominational differences to hinder access to education. This was loudly applauded but as events were to show, far from easy to put into effect.

Absalom had decided to speak shortly and on an agreeable aspect of the subject under discussion.

October 26th, 1837. At four o'clock, in a very indifferent state of health, I went in the sociable with my wife and daughter to Manchester. I went to the meeting at the theatre at half-past six and contrary to my wishes, was placed at the President's table with Mr Philips. The theatre was crowded, above four thousand persons being present, including several hundred ladies. Mr Wilderspin, Mr Wood and Mr Wyse addressed the meeting at great length and then at eleven o'clock I proposed 'The ladies who have honoured us with their presence on this occasion and may the importance of that early education to which we are indebted to females be duly appreciated.' I spoke for about ten minutes and was followed by Dr Gerrard, Mr Matieson, Mr James Heywood and Mr Simpson. The speech of Simpson was an ebullition of mortified vanity at having been called upon so late and was accompanied by some very improper advice – 'Agitate! Agitate!' addressed to the working classes.

They got back to Rose Hill at two in the morning and Absalom remained downstairs reading until four. His energy was spasmodic, Cobden's constant. At the recent General Election, Cobden had stood for Stockport but came bottom of the poll. His failure was attributed partly to the fact that he was a stranger to the borough, and partly to the machinations of the Tories. To show their confidence in him, Cobden's supporters decided to give him a present of plate and had got 17,000 people to contribute a penny each for that purpose. A ceremony was arranged to take place in Stockport towards the middle of November. At six in the evening Absalom drove over with his friend and neighbour Mr Alcock.

November 13th, 1837. Two thousand five hundred persons were crammed into a huge tent pitched in a field belonging to Mr Orrell. O'Connell and his son Morgan were present. A tolerable cold dinner was eaten with much difficulty and crowding. There was singing, speaking and shouting in abundance and we did not leave till one in the morning.

Daniel O'Connell was then sixty, perhaps his finest work for Ireland had already been done. Absalom, so concerned for the Irish poor, remained indifferent, not to say hostile, to the political dimension of the problem. He had never seen O'Connell before.

He is a man of large size, with a broad, vulgar, cunning Irish countenance and is a clever, cool, slow speaker, just fit to lead a mob.

CHAPTER TWENTY-TWO

'He spoke of human life as an inexplicable mystery'

Preparations for a Christmas party at Rose Hill were begun and, as the day approached, became almost an obsession. As always, half of Absalom detested the entire business. Yet he enjoyed being hospitable and wanted the occasion to be a success. As activity intensified he felt the pressure of the family and insisted that they left him alone to read in peace at half-past eight in the evening. Richard Cobden had just distributed five thousand copies of his vigorous and amusing pamphlet entitled *Incorporate Your Borough!* Signed 'A Radical Reformer' it was being sold at twopence a copy and Absalom was anxious to see what he said.

Cobden was in business as a calico printer. He had been summoned to attend the Court Leet as one of the jurors and afterwards been given a ticket for a free dinner at Sir Oswald Mosley's expense. Cobden professed a dislike of the aristocracy and was particularly touchy about patronage. The absurdity of the situation struck him forcibly. A great town like Manchester still under the feudal system? Subject to the medieval antics of a manorial court with a borough-reeve, constables, beadles, ale tasters and muzzlers of mastiff dogs?

The borough-reeve, Cobden argued, had to be resident in Manchester, an increasingly difficult stipulation as most of the middle classes had moved out to the suburbs and there was an unwritten law that he must not be a shopkeeper. Moreover, since the Collegiate Church was entwined with the governance of the town, churchwardens and sidesmen having certain civic duties in relation to the rates and poor relief, it was impossible for the borough-reeve to be a Nonconformist. High Church and Tory he had always been and High Church and Tory he would remain unless something was done to rectify a ridiculous anachronism.

Peterloo, Cobden said, was the consequence of Tory squires coming into the town and letting off a troop of fox hunters disguised as yeoman cavalry. This was funny but inaccurate. The local government of Manchester then was dominated by cotton traders who had more to lose by the disturbance than fox hunters. But Cobden was enjoying himself. Peterloo, he asserted, would never have happened if Manchester had been incorporated.

Why? Because the united magistrates of Lancashire and Cheshire who then entered the town to hold their bench at the Star Inn, take command of the police and order the soldiers to cut down and trample upon unarmed crowds, would in such a case, have no more jurisdiction over Manchester than Constantinople.

Absalom finished the pamphlet and agreed with its main argument. Manchester should have its own elected town council. He himself had drawn up the Petition for incorporation in the summer of 1835. Peterloo was a long time ago. His daughter Elizabeth had been only two years old, his wife about to give birth to Edward. Now they were grown up and agitating about the party, scribbling lists of guests, discussing the food and, most important of all, trying to decide how the house was to be arranged for the occasion. An evening party meant dancing and dancing meant space. Eventually it was agreed that since the parlour and dining room were really too small for dancing, the only suitable room was Absalom's bedroom.

He spent the day of the party at home helping to move out the beds and chests of drawers and supervising the carrying of the piano upstairs. There was a great deal of fatigue, fluster and irritability but somehow they managed to be ready to greet their guests at five o'clock. Many local families were there, the Alcocks, the Sumners and the Whiteleggs. The Manchester contingent included Mr Occleston and his wife and certain selected Makinsons. They were about thirty altogether.

January 11th, 1838. With great toil we were ready at five. We had dancing for the young and cards for the old and supper, which all took when they liked, and the evening ended about three in the morning, all appearing to have gone off well. I drank too much and slept ill and suffered from weariness and headache and my daughter was extremely tired and unwell.

He woke up next morning with a hangover.

His old friend, the former schoolmaster Mr Hallworth, was still alive and wrote to him from Sag Harbour in Long Island. Mrs Thomas Watkin wrote too but her letter came from Audlem and brought bad news. Aunt Mountford was very ill with dropsy and not likely to live. Absalom set out for Cheshire next day. He arranged to meet John Watkin in Manchester and to go part of the journey by railway train. In those days the Manchester terminus was Liverpool Road station. The station stood in rural surroundings in open fields away from the town. Those who wanted to travel could obtain a ticket at the booking office in Market Street and be conveyed from there in an omnibus to Liverpool Road.

January 25th, 1838. Rose a little before six. Left home at seven. Got to the railway station by half-past eight and went in the Grand Junction Railway train to Crewe. Much pinched by the cold. We got to Crewe about a quarter before eleven. Walked to Namptwich. Took a chaise and went, John and I, with Mrs Stoneley to Audlem.

It was over ten years since they had heard the distant approach of the festival band from the summer fields and the church had been bright with silks, muslins and trimmed bonnets. Absalom sat with Aunt Mountford for two hours. He found her very ill but not yet dying and advised her to make her will. Mountford came to the inn where they were staying.

He drank, and cried, and prosed for a couple of hours and then went home well filled. The selfish old fellow laments the approaching death of my aunt because he will with that event be deprived of the house that has so long sheltered him and of the income, her income, upon which he has lived.

He awoke to snow and paddled through it next morning to say goodbye to his aunt who had had a bad night and felt worse. They returned to Nantwich by the chaise. By 'car', Absalom probably meant a hackney carriage.

January 26th, 1838. It snowed all the day and the ride was chill and appeared long. We drove to Stoneley's and breakfasted again. Then, by car, to Crewe. We waited twenty minutes and then the train came up and we set off for Manchester. It was a starving ride to Manchester. We got there by two o'clock. Called and sat an hour with Mr Grime in his office at the New Quay, which was strongly scented by the perfume of the goats from the stable underneath. He gave us a long account of his symptoms and sufferings, he is evidently hypochondriac, takes no exercise and lives low and is therefore depressed and unwell. How thankful I ought to be that I am still able to take free exercise notwithstanding my complaint. Pleased with my home when I got back.

In early March they had a day of wonderful weather.

March 5th, 1838. I spent the day in looking after the getting and spreading of the gravel, in pruning a few trees and reading some pages of Howitt's Life in Rural England. I was quite satisfied with my situation and grateful for my mercies and like the birds, the cats, and the dogs I enjoyed the beautiful weather and my own existence.

Three days later he was cast down to the depths. Business was very bad, his own especially, and the precariousness of life was brought home to him by something that happened at the committee of the Commercial Clerk's Society.

March 9th, 1838. Old Mr Gabriel Spencer whom I have known in business

London febuary 24 1806

Dear Son

I am happy it was so ordained
you should be unimployed for two hours otherwise
I find I should not received so long letter it may asear tedig
to you but its not thought so by me But I am fully Convinced
by its Content that my thoughts are Confirmed I am nearly
three times your age you must Alow me to be a little juge of
youthfull follys I was apprehensive your thoughts was too
much engayed to learn musick I never wish you to atempt
any thing you have an aversion to but its polite and useful
in Old Age if we are disapointed of what we expect or engage
in buines and it do not answer many gains thar livelihod
by musick and learning was I mistres of A good education or
musick how comfortable I should live you ask if any one was
happy a wish you give me further reason to suspect you pray
my dear Son what little strang entrovdanary uneasynes has
found the way to your brest what plagus or crofses has render
this motly lif of yours unhappy to make you think its not
worth having you say miserably Cheated you are young but
uppon my honer there is Something verry misteries in your letter
write poems on the Beautys of the suntary I rather
think its to dispell the thoughts of Som favourite Object as you
desire my thought on love my dear Son if you think on love
as I have don that will never cause you to wander for happy
nefs my thoughts was always thus and let yours be the Same
if we are disrespected by the object we love thank god for his
good nefs in preventing us from Obtaining our desire look to
god and he will direct us he is a mercifull father to us all
if you ask any thing of me or have romited any fault or
are in danger of doing Wrong do I not grant it if its not
hurtfull and forgive you your faults and direct you in the
rite way if poisible then how much are we to blame to murm
er at disapointments When the good god knows What is best
for us if god maks you rich thank him for his goodnefs that
he has blefsed and Chose you for his steard if poor and oblodged
to work hard and live hard thank god for it for if we was rich
we mith be wicked and be in everlasting torment hereafter

Letter from Absalom's mother to her son, London, 24 February 1806
(continued overleaf)

god is A deserner of the thoughts and intents of the heart
nuither is there any Creature that is not manifested in his sight
but all things are naked and open unto the eys of god but what
ever will happen to us you may depend on it if we live a
godly life and serve god as we ought nothing Can hurt us long
if I am sick or poor or in any trouble when I pray to god you
do not know what Comfort and happyness I poses think how
good god is to you. you have a good education never want money nor
victuals never work hard have friends to Conven with all these
things ought to make you happy, I am verry sorry you have
the head ack do drink Coffe or Cammomile in the morning
thank god I am verry well as I hope you are all an

and I hope if ever you pluck roses you will ware glovs that the
may not prick you to hurt your feelings I think its dangerous
to fix our thought on any thing I always say I should like it if pleas
god and if I am disapointed it is what pleas god never be unhappy
at any thing if we know how to give good gift to our Children
how much moore do our heavenly father know how to give good
gifts to us if we examin the scriptures there is a Comfort for every
trouble and according to your former writings you know the
scripture better than me and I hope will practise them more
I Can only say with the poor Publian the lord be mercifull to
me a wicked siner

and I Dearly think if I had emus to live so as I Could read
my bible as I ought that I should not be unhappy one houre
except for my sins if you was well and your I should be
as Charfull as any old woman for religeon was never
desined to make our pleasurs less therefore drive
all nonceence from your mind dispell those gloomy sighs
till ever you see any person either man or woman that was
as I positively think you are in love but what they ware
laughed at that is there recompence but I hope you have
to much good sense to be posesed of those follies
So god almighty bless you and be not ashamed to let me
know the meaning of your letter; mind all Comp^ts

    I remain your Loving mother and pray to god
for your happyness hear and hear after
                                    B Watkin

(continued opposite, top)

P.S you see I wrot the day I received yours By the twopeney post I am sorry to put you to the expence of paying for the letters always let me know how you go on with your aunt I hope you will never neglect your astore Business and always be just and honest

Absalom in 1821 aged thirty-four, by Minasi

Nov 5 None of us got up till 10, & all were in consequence too late for church. We spent an unpleasant squabbling forenoon. Breakfasted between 11 & 12 & dined at 1/2 past 4. Made some notes for a speech. Felt a great deal of mental incapacity. My powers of mind are certainly impaired.

Nov 8 A vad worklet, hurried, unsuccessful, unhappy. The Lit. Soc. I opened the debate. 'Do great talents, or acquirements conduce to the happiness of the possessor?' in a very hesitating, bungling manner. I made a tolerable closing speech. I felt they all feel now, that I am inferior to what I was 5 years ago.

Nov 9 Unwell & unbecile at the ale. But did some business.

Nov 10 Shunned my post, but not very badly, in shrugging over some calices in the ale. Mrs Wm Matt. called at the ale. to tell me that, unless I go to Lancaster, to appear in the insolvent debtors' court next Sat, John Matt. will be but back for 5 months, I consented to go.

Nov. 12 At 6 left Preston in a one horse chaise. [Reached Lancaster at 9. Attended the insolvent Debtors' court.] It was some time before John Matt. was called up, & I had leisure to observe the gross frauds, that were attempted by the insolvents & the suspicion & irritability which this had produced in the mind of the commissioner. When John was called, & I madison sworn, the Commissioner Mr. Reynolds first inspected me with his spying glass, then desired me to leave the court while John was examined. In a while I was called in, & at first with evident suspicion, then with civil consideration & at last with entire confidence in my veracity was examined, at much length as to my debt, & motives for sending John to gaol, his character etc. I found by the result that John had made a false statement upon oath. He was severely reprimanded by the commissioner, but finally discharged 'out of consideration to his relations, & in the hope that he would alter his conduct for the better, & learn to speak the truth.' I left the court feeling the weakness of human nature, & convinced more than ever, of the need we all have to pray 'Lead us not into temptation'. May God keep me from the necessity which leads men to falsehood! I dined at Miss Nevis, I had a delicious steak, a cranberry tart, a jelly, & half a pint of sherry, with some good cheese, for 3/6 & 6d which I gave to the waiter, & for which, it being twice the usual gift, I had as melting alacrity of attention, & charity with the perfect cleanliness of table-cloth, knives, glasses etc, made my dinner a treat. Still I reflected, with sadness that such a dinner, even such a dinner, was unattainable. I left Lancaster at 2 in the afternoon. [Travels with an attorney.] Mr. Law, who has the character of being a foul-mouthed vulgar fellow, was during the whole of the journey, extremely civil & perfectly decorous. I did not get to bed till 2 in the morn - had a vivid night.

Nov 13 S Did not rise till afternoon. Unwell all day.

Nov. 15 Late at the ale. Unwell, unsuccessful. The market very bad. The Lit. Soc.

Nov. 16 Late but not idle.

Nov 17 Rose late & unwell.

Nov 19 Ass. but unwell & irritable at the ale. Cont. Mackintosh. His life is a lesson. His talents were thrown away for want of method & steady industry. If you my great grandfather a lesson, to a sad lesson, & have lived for more than you did. I have dissipated away all all the best years of life. Ed. W. 1924]

Nov. 20 S At church. Much interested by the service.

Nov 21 When I got back to R.H. I went round the garden, was struck with the beauty of my little place; & my [think] felt grateful.

Nov 22 Did little business & was depressed.

Nov 23 Went to Mr. with my wife whose signature was necessary to the mortgage. We gave the mortgage completed, & received £2500 & had to pay Loock & Parry a bill of £57 for preparing the deeds. [Party at Mr. Whitclegg's]

Absalom's wife, Elizabeth, in 1821 aged thirty-one, by Minasi

Absalom's mother in 1821 aged sixty-five, by Minasi

Audlem

Beeston Castle

Advertising the *Illustrated London News* in 1842

Northenden church and Boathouse inn

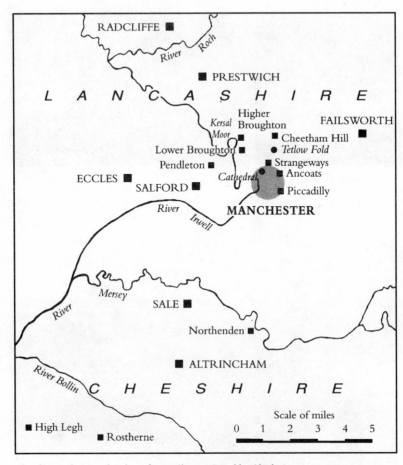

Sketch map showing the places frequently mentioned by Absalom

Membership certificate of the Anti-Corn Law League

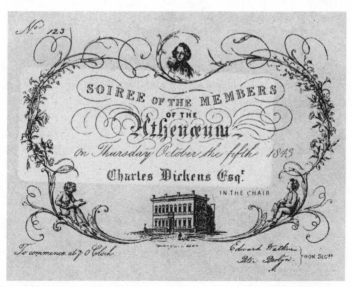

Ticket to the Manchester Athenaeum soirée with Dickens in the Chair, 1843

Rose Hill July 31. 1858

My dear, inconsiderate Alfred,

I cannot but give an immediate reply to
your painful letter, although that will necessitate
the sending of Robinson to Manchester.

It is true that I am spending freely at
this place, and making quite comfortable for
myself, and my successors: but allow me to
ask most seriously. What have you to do
with that? Not a farthing has come out of
your pocket, or shall be paid by you. The allowance of £30 a month, which you thought sufficient for me has not been taken. I have
yet about £180 in your hands to which I

Letter from Absalom to his son Alfred, 31 July 1858 (continued opposite) shall call as I want it. Of what then do you complain. Your exertions have not been overtried by me.

Your are in a bad temper, and you relieve yourself by vituperating me. For shame! Your complaints of your Mother, and your sister may be true, but they are ill-timed, and are my misfortune as well as yours.

I am anxious to see how I stand, and I shall know what I can do. I shall act as I have always acted — like an honest man and your Father

Absalom Mathers

Absalom in middle age, by William
Bradley

Absalom's son, Sir Edward Watkin, by
Hubert Herkomer

for nearly thirty years, applied for the allowance of five shillings a week on the ground of his having lost all his property and being unable to gain the expenses of himself and his family by the business he is able to do. <u>Claim refused</u>, he not being, in the meaning of the rules, in distressed circumstances. Alas! to what a situation <u>I</u> may be reduced in old age.

He stayed up until four in the morning reading Lockhart's *Life of Scott*. What a lesson! But how could he expect his own business to prosper when sometimes he did not get up till noon or if he did rise early was too exhausted through lack of sleep to attend properly to his work.

The question whether to incorporate or not to incorporate had split the town. On one side the Tories and Radicals formed a temporary and unnatural alliance to oppose the measure. On the other, the reforming party led by Cobden continued to press for its introduction. The Tories disliked any weakening of the bond that bound the town to the Collegiate Church and all it stood for. Besides, they distrusted the representational element in local government. They argued that the old system protected Manchester's citizens far better than the new, which served but to put the affairs of the town into the hands of a clique who would put the rates up. As for the Radicals, they thought Cobden could call himself a 'Radical Reformer' if he chose, but he was as much a capitalist as the rest.

Posters appeared in Manchester warning working men against the dirty tricks of the Whigs, and Cobden found himself obliged to address an enormous and rowdy crowd in the Town Hall. With the priggish blindness to external forms common to so many reformers, he assured his audience that fears lest incorporation would entail needless expense were groundless. Manchester would never go in for such baubles as 'maces, cloaks and chains'.

The Radicals were unappeased. Cobden was a 'mere spouter, to gain applause', the people of Manchester must resist 'the tyranny of the bloated rich and to trust not to the truckling, vile, base, bloody and brutal Whigs'. After more than four hours of tumultuous discussion the meeting eventually decided to petition the Queen in Council for a charter.

The anti-charter party straight away got up a rival petition and by employing professional canvassers who were paid three shillings a day with another three shillings for every sheet of forty-two names, they speedily obtained almost 32,000 signatures compared with the barely 12,000 on Cobden's. Nevertheless, his was a hundred yards long and taken by train to the offices of the Privy Council, who were left to decide on which side truth and justice lay.

After some months' deliberation the Privy Council decided that far more names had been forged on the Anti-Charter Petition than on the Pro-Charter Petition and at the end of November Manchester received its Royal Charter and became an incorporated borough.

The new borough council consisted of a mayor, sixteen aldermen, and forty-eight councillors representing fifteen wards, one-third of whom had to retire each year. Absalom went to a meeting of the Burgesses of the Collegiate Church and proposed his friend, Mr Kershaw, as one of the councillors for the ward. Cobden himself was elected an alderman and Thomas Potter the town's first mayor.

The lord of the manor however still continued to exercise his jurisdiction in some matters. Sir Nicholas Mosley had bought the manor of Manchester in 1596 for £3,500. In 1819 it had been offered to the town for £90,000 and refused. It was not until 1845, seven years after incorporation, that the Town Council bought the manorial rights from Sir Oswald Mosley for £200,000. Never again would tickets for a free dinner be distributed and by then Cobden was devoting his energies to reform on a wider stage.

Grime was worse and talking about his will again. Absalom sat with him for three hours taking down his testamentary instructions and attempting to soothe his spirits. Next day he went about the will to Grime's lawyer who said something that troubled Absalom.

April 26th, 1838. He spoke of human life as an inexplicable mystery. He said that we were certainly not sent here to enjoy life and that he would not live his life over again if it were in his power to do so – yet he has been a successful man.

Lord Grey's government had freed the West Indian slaves five years before, but a seven-year apprenticeship had been prescribed as a transitional period before complete liberation. During this period the negroes were bound to work most of the day for their masters. Absalom had been asked to speak at a meeting in the Town Hall to support the movement for immediate emancipation. The Radicals had other ideas.

May 3rd, 1838. A numerous meeting. Many ladies. I should have moved the second resolution but the radicals headed by that impudent rascal Nightingale, moved a long rigmarole about white-slave weavers and the New Poor Law and kept us in a state of <u>battle</u> for more than an hour. At last the Borough-reeve, Mr Brown, a poor creature, refused to put Nightingale's resolution and our motions were put <u>en masse</u> and carried, and the meeting ended.

Absalom returned thankfully to his garden, heard the cuckoo, dipped into the *Arabian Nights* and learnt with sadness of his Aunt Mountford's death.

For some time there had been talk about establishing a zoo in Manchester. Absalom liked the idea and was pleased when some fifteen acres in Higher Broughton were leased from the Clowes estate for the purpose. The zoo lay between Broom Lane and Northumberland Street, where the Greek church was later to be built. A joint stock company was formed to finance the venture and the buildings were designed to be more spacious and better adapted to the animals' natural habits than most zoos of the time. A lion and a lioness, three tigers, leopards, an elephant, a rhinoceros, monkeys, deer and many other animals and birds were assembled. A pit was dug for the polar bears and the park was carefully laid out with a large lake, arbours, rustic seats and an archery ground; all this within a mile and a half of the Exchange and at the cost of a shilling a ticket. Absalom was appointed one of the auditors.

He was especially interested in the zoo partly for its own sake and partly because it was sited so close to the haunts of his youth and early married life. He accepted an invitation to speak at the public breakfast arranged to mark the opening at the end of May. He took a lot of trouble, starting to write the speech at half-past eight on the evening before and finishing at about five in the morning when he went to bed for a couple of hours.

The ceremony did not begin until two o'clock in the afternoon.

May 31st, 1838. A large company, excellent music, and lovely weather and scenery. The breakfast did not begin till near two o'clock. It was eaten in a marquee, one hundred feet by forty and forty-five high. I spoke to the sentiment 'The Manchester Zoological Gardens: may they long be distinguished as a source of rational recreation and instruction to all classes of the inhabitants of this populous district.'

The Manchester Times gave him a fine spread and Absalom counted the number of his words carefully. They would fill about eleven pages of the first edition of Scott's novels. Sir Walter wrote at the rate of sixteen pages a day. His speech had cost him eight hours of labour, how hard Scott must have worked!

In June they had a deluge.

June 9th, 1838. Awakened at five in the morning by Battersby, the rain falling in torrents and the river rising rapidly and already over part of the glebe. My hay would all have been swept away, but my neighbours came to my help. By half-past eight nearly all the grass was carted up to higher ground. It was afterwards spread. The river rose almost to the top of the hedges.

It was at this time that Absalom's daughter began to complain of various illnesses which time would prove to be of nervous origin. Her joints ached and painful red blotches appeared on her skin. She came downstairs and lay on the sofa all day. Absalom put it down to rheumatism caused by sleeping all night with the windows open.

Absalom's cousin Samuel arrived to see them. He was the son of Absalom's uncle, Ralph Watkin.

July 22nd, 1838. He enlisted in the Thirteenth Dragoons in his sixteenth

year, was sworn in at Disbury, and sent to the Cape of Good Hope and has
been thirty years in Africa and the East Indies. He returns <u>a corporal</u> with a
pension of one shilling and sevenpence a day and a very good character from
the officers under whom he has served.

The Club still met regularly. William Makinson was inclined to drink too much
but at their last meeting Mr Greaves had read an interesting paper on the economy
of the debtor's side of Lancaster Castle. He had just come back from a three-
month residence there. Greaves was a magistrate, presumably he had been at the
castle for professional reasons. An installment of *Nicholas Nickleby* was read aloud
and Absalom was disturbed because the Master of Chorlton School had been
appointed by the Society for the Promotion of National Education at a salary of a
hundred pounds a year. The man had a wife and six children and had come all the
way from London for that pittance. The poverty of the schoolmaster, the exertion
of going round the village begging on behalf of a very old man he had found
almost destitute, or perhaps Mr Greave's account of the debtor's quarters at
Lancaster Castle caused Absalom to be seized by an attack of nervous terror.

August 18th, 1838. This week I have been unwell, excessively irritable,
bashful, incapable of getting on and very much depressed. I have had in an
extreme degree the old dread of the loss of my business and consequent
poverty.

Where was security to be found? A friend had just collapsed and died when
walking down Moseley Street. Joseph Makinson's wife had cancer of the uterus
and not even Arkwright's millions could guard against that. Edward was rude,
insolent and lazy and Hannah Makinson worried him.

September 30th, 1838. She tells me that Mrs Soulby wishes her to receive
the addresses of Harper Soulby. He is only nineteen and she at least twenty-
seven. She has hitherto only looked upon him as a boy and as to knowledge
of the world, he is nothing more. But marriage is so necessary to the
estimation of women in the eyes of the world, that perhaps if Harper
conducts himself properly, and she can esteem him, it may be better for her
to accept rather than to refuse him.

Absalom continued to work hard on a speech which he hoped to deliver at the
Manor Court Room to inaugurate an institution for the mental improvement of
the lower classes to be called 'The Parthenon'. When the day came once more the
Radicals attempted to capture the meeting.

October 1st, 1838. Walked to Manchester in the evening. Attended the
meeting. Mr Brotherton took the chair. A report was read. A Mr Dixon and

myself were heard with attention and then a fellow of the name of Hunt, an Irishman, got up in opposition supported by Nightingale, Richardson, Thomas Fielden and a large body of Political Unionists. A scene of great confusion ensued. Hunt was at last pulled off the table by a woman and Mr Brotherton declared the meeting to be dissolved. The intruders then put Broadie into the chair and talked about universal suffrage until midnight.

Many took it for granted that if violent revolution were to break out in England it would start in Manchester. It was, after all, the heartland of the industrial revolution, the pulse of radicalism, a town of abnormal growth whose prosperity was attributed by its enemies to chance and avarice, and by those who profited from it to hard work and piety. Radicalism in Manchester however, as the meeting about the Parthenon showed, was counterbalanced by other factors, including a strong middle and lower-middle class that held liberal but more cautious views.

That autumn two movements started to make themselves strongly felt in Manchester. Towards the end of September Feargus O'Connor, the Chartist leader, held a massive meeting on Kersal Moor. Some said that over a quarter of a million people were present. The demands of the People's Charter had been drawn up the previous year at the Crown and Anchor Tavern in the Strand. They were six: annual parliaments, universal male suffrage, equal electoral districts, the removal of the property qualification for members of parliament, the payment of members and the ballot. The suggestion that women should also be given the vote was rejected on the grounds that the proposal would not be taken seriously.

One of the speakers at the meeting on Kersal Moor was J.R. Stephens, a former Methodist minister. He declared that the Charter was not a political question but a knife-and-fork question, not a matter of ballot boxes but of bread and butter. To an extent that was true. The support for the Charter ebbed and flowed with the economic tide.

Yet at the root of it all lay something deeper; a profound and justified resentment at being excluded from society and treated as of no account. It was the howl of the underdog translated into political terms. Orator Hunt had been right when he made himself unpopular by foretelling that the Reform Bill would bring little immediate benefits to those who shouted most loudly for it. The trade depression, the New Poor Law, excessive working hours, pitiful wages and, above all, the stupid, selfish indifference of richer people in the face of human beings brutalized by want, ignorance and filthy surroundings: those were the roots of Chartism.

Some places had already established an Anti-Corn Law Association but oddly enough Manchester, the town that was to capture the movement, had not yet done so. However, on 24 September, the very day that the Chartists held their huge meeting on Kersal Moor, Prentice gathered a handful of men at the York Hotel, King Street, and together they formed an association which was to develop into the nationwide Anti-Corn Law League. Cobden had been abroad all September but he soon joined them and threw himself into the struggle for repeal. Absalom was not present at the preliminary meetings but very quickly became involved, remaining closely attached to the movement, in Edward's words, 'from its birth to its triumph'. In fact his first silent, tentative participation in public affairs as long ago as 1815 had been concerned with the imposition of those very Corn Laws.

He was soon put on the Committee of the new Association and on 3 December Cobden asked him, together with Prentice and J.B. Smith, to join him in drawing up an address explaining its nature and objects. The manifesto eventually produced by the four of them was measured, carefully reasoned and lengthy. It guarded against any exaggerated notions about the value of free trade and repudiated all ideas of privilege for the manufacturing class at the expense of others.

The address meant a great deal of hard work, the weather was bad and Absalom's teeth ached. One evening he returned home by the four o'clock omnibus and found his wife and Joseph Johnson returning at the same time. As they were crossing the meadows his wife acted with 'the grossest impropriety'. What she did we shall never know, but Absalom condemned her in his heart. He spent the evening listening to his daughter reading passages from *Antony and Cleopatra*.

Old Mrs Shuttleworth died aged a hundred-and-one and Absalom caught a cold at her funeral. He had hoped to spend the last day of 1838 quietly at home but when he gave business instructions to Edward and John they behaved with such unfeeling insolence that he left the house immediately for Manchester. He reached his warehouse at nine o'clock and remained there taking stock and setting all to rights until past eleven at night. Anything was better than the shadow of obligation to ungrateful children.

CHAPTER TWENTY-THREE
'Do you intend to be free men or slaves?'

One Sunday not long after Mrs Joseph Makinson's funeral, Absalom listened to a long sermon on the Deluge and calculated that even if he should live to seventy he had but two hundred and twenty months left. The next day he learnt that he had been appointed one of the first magistrates for the newly incorporated borough. Edward remembered how his father blushed and cried 'Bless my soul', when he heard the news.

Reflection brought anxiety. He had just learnt about the troubles of his old acquaintance Mr G.W. Wood, the MP for Kendal, President of the Manchester Chamber of Commerce. Chosen to second the Address on the Queen's Speech at the opening of Parliament, Wood had made a complete fool of himself by first painting a black picture of the injurious effects of the Corn Laws on trade and employment and then going on to describe the remarkably prosperous state of the country, particularly in the cotton industry. What terrible traps lay waiting for anyone even remotely connected with public life.

> **February 16th, 1839.** From thinking of him, I turned to myself. My elevation to the magistracy is perhaps unfortunate, as it will occupy time which I cannot well spare and turn on me public observation. But I cannot now decline the office and I therefore resolve to enter it with the greatest caution of which I am capable, taking time to understand the disposition and intentions of my colleagues, doing nothing rashly, saying as little as possible, acting in all things with quiet independence and labouring really to <u>know</u> what I ought to do.

His first act as a magistrate was to administer an oath on the Hebrew Scriptures to one of the Jewish community. That was a routine matter, he had not yet sat on the bench. Indeed there was a vociferous party in the town who were determined that there should be no bench for him to sit on.

Those who opposed the new regime remained obstinate. The charter was illegal. The Tories refused to stand for election to the council and when a council consisting only of Liberals was returned it was forbidden admittance to the Town Hall and had to retire to the York Hotel next door for its first meeting. An unpleasant quarrel broke out in the Manor Court Room when two of the old county magistrates challenged the authority of the borough magistrates to appoint overseers of the poor. So persistent was the opposition that it took over eight years to extinguish the old town offices and transfer all their functions to the new corporation.

It was a bad moment to indulge in municipal squabbles. As a member of the council of the Anti-Corn Law Association, Absalom had spoken recently to over 3,000 people in the Corn Exchange. But a greater number than that probably supported the Chartists. According to the *Manchester Times*, in 1837 over 50,000 workers were either unemployed or on short time and there was little reason to suppose things were any better now.

At first sight free trade appeared to be a more inviting banner to fight under than the six points of the Charter. One offered immediate tangible benefits in the shape of cheaper food and increased demand for manufactured goods both in the home and foreign markets; the other offered prosperity indeed but deferred until certain political demands were met. However, it was the very vagueness of the paradise which lay beyond their precise political demands that had led to Chartism's initial success. It gathered within itself the grievances of a multitude, giving collective expression to the hopes and resentments of men trapped within a system they could neither understand nor control.

It is little wonder that ideas of violent revolution were gaining ground. On Kersal Moor the previous autumn Feargus O'Connor had openly incited his followers to armed rebellion. Richard Oastler was advising the working classes to procure weapons and there had been torchlight meetings with men wearing tricolour cockades and caps of liberty. As winter gave way to spring the situation had worsened. The Chartist convention in London was captured by the extremists. It affirmed the right of every Englishman to bear arms and made plans for a general strike should Parliament reject the Charter.

Absalom read the life of the seventeenth-century regicide Colonel Hutchinson and pondered the question of civil liberty. Strafford and Laud were rascals and he blessed the memory of the Long Parliament. Yet what a sad picture of mob government did the Committee of Nottingham Castle present. After that he read the life of Madame du Barry

March 24th, 1839. This is a book very proper to read after the Memoirs of Colonel Hutchinson. The latter exhibits the evils of civil war passing into military domination and ending in an unreflecting submission to a worthless monarch for the sake of getting an <u>established and regular</u> government which would leave men to pursue their own affairs. The former exhibits the dreadful corruption of an old established despotism. Both exhibit the depravity of human nature. Both show how almost impossible it is to invest men with power and to make it even tolerably certain that they shall use it for the general good.

The government appointed Major-General Sir Charles Napier, later conqueror of Sind, to command the Northern District. He worked out a plan for defending the streets of Manchester against a mob of 100,000 men. A handbill circulated in the town ran: 'Dear brothers! Now are the times to try men's souls! Are your arms ready? Have you plenty of powder and shot? Have you screwed up your courage to the sticking place? Do you intend to be free men or slaves? Are you inclined to hope for a fair day's wages for a fair day's work?'

Manchester was not in a state of panic. The townspeople had General Wemyss's garrison stationed among them and not only a strong element of the steady, middle class in whose interests it was to maintain the peace, but a large proportion of factory operatives who were earning good wages. The lower classes had a pecking order like everyone else. The capture of the Chartist movement by the 'physical force' revolutionaries was not at all to the taste of the prosperous factory worker.

As usual, spring's coming brought Absalom a surge of happiness and hope. One Sunday in April he walked with his daughter and Alfred to Baxter's Shade and back through the meadows.

April 21st, 1839. Alfred brought a handful of polyanthus and I read some of the spirit-stirring poetry which I have copied out into the 'Perennial Kalendar', and I felt as if I were again young and as if the flowers and the buds and the poetry, and even life itself, had all the freshness of my first youthful impressions.

However the prospect of violence was becoming closer. On 4 May Absalom attended two meetings of the borough magistrates to consider what measures might be necessary to preserve the peace should Parliament reject the giant Petition in favour of the Charter which was now ready for presentation to the House. The Petition contained 1,200,000 signatures and was so large that it had to be rolled onto a bobbin-like structure. While it lay on its cart in London waiting for Thomas Attwood and John Fielden to hand it over, Lord Melbourne's government most inconveniently resigned over a matter that had nothing to do with the Charter.

The Queen was only twenty. Years later, as an old lady looking back on her life with the eyes of age and experience, she admitted that her behaviour then had been mistaken. But at the time it was different. Lonely, isolated, a victim of court intrigue, she clung to the fascinating and fatherly Melbourne with all the intensity of her emotional nature. On the government's resignation she summoned the Duke of Wellington who declared himself too old and deaf to be of any use as Prime Minister. There was nothing for it but to call upon Sir Robert Peel. What followed was the natural consequence of human vanity and obstinacy, an unclear constitution and genuine misunderstanding.

Victoria was an overwrought girl who thought herself abandoned. She cried and sobbed during her interviews with Melbourne and even with Lord John Russell.

She had been brought up among Whigs and detested the Tories; Peel's calm, reserved manner was uncongenial to her. He told her some changes in the Ladies of her Household would be required as a mark of confidence in his government. This provided Victoria with what she thought was an escape. *Some* changes would eventually mean *all* changes, every one of the Ladies of the Bedchamber would have to go. That could not be endured. They wished to treat her like a girl but she would show them that she was Queen of England. Peel withdrew and Melbourne was given a few more years to run.

Like the country as a whole, Manchester was misinformed and thought that Peel had refused to form an administration unless all the Ladies of the Household were dismissed. Absalom was applied to yet again.

May 11th, 1839. Employed in the afternoon in writing an Address to the Queen, praying her to appoint only such Ministers as will advance the cause of reform. This I did at the request of the Corporation of Manchester and afterwards I prepared another, a little varied in phrase, for the authorities of Salford. These Addresses were hastily got up in consequence of Sir Robert Peel having refused to take office unless the Queen would dismiss <u>all</u> the Ladies of the Household.

On Whit Saturday a crowd the *Manchester Times* estimated to be 20,000 and O'Connor's *Northern Star* to number 500,000, gathered for a Chartist rally on Kersal Moor. The authorities were having no repetition of Peterloo. General Napier was not fond of Manchester, which he described as 'the chimney of the world. The entrance to hell realized!' He held liberal views and had more sympathy for the Chartists than Absalom. But then he was not in trade. 'Would that I had gone to Australia and thus been saved this work, produced by Tory injustice and Whig imbecility,' he wrote in his diary that April, 'the doctrine of slowly reforming when men are starving is of all things the most silly; famishing men cannot wait.' He used his influence to prevent the Manchester magistrates from considering breaking up the meeting but before it took place went to some lengths to make it clear to the Chartist leaders that he and Wemyss would be on the spot and would not hesitate, if necessary, to employ both cannon and cavalry. In the event the demonstration was peaceful and whatever the inflated figures given by its organizers, lacked both the numbers and the *élan* of the great rally of the previous autumn.

Meanwhile the Chartist Petition, still rolled up on its giant bobbin, had not yet been presented to Parliament. The physical-force party among the Chartist leaders was making preparations for a 'sacred month' which would follow the expected rejection of the Charter. The sacred month was to include a general strike, which they called a 'national holiday', a refusal to pay rent, rates and taxes, a run on the banks and a refusal to patronize non-Chartist shops or to read hostile newspapers. Placards were distributed in Manchester calling for a meeting to protest against the introduction there of a 'damnable foreign police system' and local Chartists taunted the newly established borough force in the street with cries of 'Bluebottles' and 'Bourbons'.

On 12 July the Chartist Petition was at last presented to Parliament and the young Benjamin Disraeli made an interesting speech, half-romantic, half-perceptive. His swift, intuitive imagination seized upon an essential truth. The root cause of the trouble was the lack of interest each class took in the other's welfare – a state of affairs, of course, quite unknown before the passing of the Reform Bill. 'I am not ashamed to say however much I disapprove of the Charter, I sympathize with the Chartists.' As expected, the Commons rejected the Charter by 235 votes to 46. The 'sacred month' was proclaimed to begin on 12 August. It now remained to be seen if the proletariat as a whole could be pushed into revolution for political ends.

Three days after the Charter had been presented at Westminster, Mr Grime came to Rose Hill. He felt better than he had done for some time and agreed to stay longer. A few happy days passed in the enjoyment of the garden and the company of the boys, then one evening he fell ill. He got worse and became so weak that Mr Lacy, a doctor from Manchester, stayed by his bedside until very late. Neither 'old lant' nor 'red bottle' could help him now. This time his heart was really failing him and much to Absalom's distress he died early on the morning of 27 July, twenty-four years since that November evening in the year of Waterloo when he had drunk brandy and water while Absalom scribbled a draft of his will by the light of a candle.

His complicated testamentary depositions, however, long lingered to torment Absalom as their executor. The day appointed by the Chartists as the first National Holiday arrived at last. Absalom and his colleagues were prepared, but in the end nothing very much happened.

August 12th, 1839. At the Borough court all the forenoon. Several Chartists committed. In the evening with Mr Kershaw at the Allum Street Station. Went with him to disperse a meeting at the waterworks. Luckily the people ran away and nobody was hurt.

The Chartists themselves realized that a general strike was useless unless it was really general, that is enjoyed the support of a large majority of the working class. But the trade unions had distanced themselves from the movement; their support was vital and it had been lost. Throughout the country as a whole there were few disorders worth mentioning and in September the Chartist Convention declared itself dissolved. It was by no means the end of the Chartists, but it was the end of one phase of their activity.

Absalom had been deeply upset over Grime's death and he was worried by the losses he had sustained through the general depression of business. He felt on edge and in need of a change. He took his daughter to London, this time going there by train. He had been to London twice already that year. He does not say why he went but very probably it was to consult Mr Salmon about his complaint, which always returned when he was under stress. He visited Bromley with Elizabeth.

October 13th, 1839. A beautiful autumnal day. We had a very pleasant ride. The increase in the buildings between London and Bromley is astonishing and the alterations in Bromley itself are very great. Many houses have been rebuilt, roads altered, etc. We went to the church and joined in worship with a large and well-dressed congregation. After the service we looked at the churchyard and gathered some berries from the old yew trees I have so often climbed as a boy. We dined at the White Hart and I went to look for my old home on Wigmore Green, but a road had been carried that way and all was so altered that I could not find it and probably it has been pulled down. We walked a good way along the high road, through fine country, but I could recognize no part of it. I was struck with one advantage of a form of prayer, recollecting as I did in Bromley church that my family at Northen and multitudes everywhere, were engaged in the same service.

The day before he left for Manchester he went to St Paul's. It might be his last visit.

October 18th, 1839. Took a last look at St Paul's and the city and the river from the centre of the Iron Bridge. Went down to Paul's Wharf and up Benet's Hill, looked at my father's grave and passed through the Herald's Office Yard and by the pump at which I have so often drunk as a boy. All these I shall probably never see again.

In 1835 a new literary and scientific institution 'for the Advancement and Diffusion of Knowledge' had been suggested for Manchester. Its leading spirit had been Richard Cobden, then not long in business and on the threshold of public life. The title 'Athenaeum' was put forward for the new venture which was to have a reading room, newspaper room and lecture hall. Absalom was one of its directors.

The Athenaeum thrived and perhaps became overconfident. Before very long it embarked upon a new building, an ambitious structure designed by Barry which cost so much that the directors were forced to borrow and soon found themselves in financial difficulties. Absalom spoke at the official opening of the new premises and a few days later took some of the family along to a then fashionable 'soirée'.

October 31st, 1839. Attended with my wife and Alice Makinson, the Soirée given by the Essay and Discussion Society in the new Athenaeum. My wife was one of the six lady patronesses and five hundred and twenty ladies and gentlemen were present. A paper was read in the lecture theatre by Mr

Franklin on the question 'Has popular credulity diminished in proportion to the advance of civilization?' A discussion followed in which I was the first to speak. The discussion over, the company adjourned to the Library and the Concert room. Horrobin's band began to play and quadrilles and waltzes were kept up till three in the morning. It was a pleasant scene but I dislike the waltz more than ever. It is ugly and indecent. We left at half-past eleven, stopped half an hour at Mordacque's and got home about half-past one and Alice and I sat chatting by the fire till past three.

Mrs Soulby and her friend Miss Barber had decided to go out to Sydney to see Mrs Soulby's daughter, who had married Joseph's son, Thomas Makinson. It may be that they intended to settle permanently in Australia for there is no further mention of them in the diary. In any case, it was sensible to make a will before venturing on such a lengthy voyage and Absalom helped Mrs Soulby to draw up hers. A few days later they left for London on the first stage of their journey to Australia in the ship *Globe*. He was sad to see them go but nothing like so upset as he was by the next piece of family news.

December 1st, 1839. John is at home suffering from the impure embrace of some dirty strumpet. This is the result of suffering a foolish boy, with low and vulgar tastes, to remain in town at night by himself.

All his children save Alfred were an anxiety. The close companionship he had enjoyed with Edward as a boy had turned into hostility and irritation, and now they were all wasting time and money preparing for the largest party the family had ever given. His daughter was ill with the fatigue of it, Edward was 'brutal', the entire house in an uproar. Absalom escaped into the relative calm of Thomas Potter's business premises.

December 5th, 1839. Dined with the Mayor at his warehouse. There were six at dinner and our fare was excellent, potato pie, some good cheese and toast and water. After dinner a few glasses of good wine. I have seldom dined so much to my own satisfaction.

His own entertainment was a more lavish occasion.

December 19th, 1839. I got home about five and found Mrs Watkin as usual late, savey [sic] and careless, leaving all arrangements to chance and the exertion of others. I had to assist in cleaning out the closet of Edward's room, which was to be the ladies' dressing room after I came home and neither it nor the bedroom had been or were swept. The company began to arrive, as usual, before we were ready to receive them.

About thirty-two people came.

These, with our family, filled the house well but except at supper, not crowdedly. They danced and sung, ate and drank and Messrs Mountain, Alcock, Occleston and Davy played a rubber at whist and all went off tolerably well till the last of them left us about two o'clock. Yet there were some disagreeables. Alice was not well and the chalk with which the room floor had been ornamented was rubbed off in dancing and rose in clouds of dust as the dance proceeded, daubing the ladies' dresses and powdering the gentlemens' coats and trousers and discolouring all faces. I thought that Mordacque was not pleased to see his wife dance so spiritedly and some other faces betrayed a little uneasiness. Still most of them seemed happy and I was glad to see the Miss Faulkners enjoy the evening and Mrs Occleston look on with interest and Miss Mary Sumner's face radiant with smiles and Hannah Makinson looking well and happy.

Absalom did not get to bed until five in the morning and wondered again if it was all worth it. He jotted down some of the expenses and left the paper in his diary.

Twelve bottles of wine: £2 10/-; brandy: 4/-; muslin: 12/-; dyed calico: 4/-; extra help and food £1; at the Boat House: 11/-; spoons: £4 14/-; 4 decanters: £2 8/-; hire of lamps and glass dishes: 10/6; 2 quarts oil: 8/-; candles: 8/-; cakes etc.: £1 13/-; groceries: 17/5; flour: 1/-; beef, fowls, eggs etc.: £1 17/-; wood: 6/-; cards: 6/-; tissue paper: 10 pence.

That winter saw dancing of a different kind in the royal palaces and a charming, excessively handsome young man with beautiful blue eyes and a pretty mouth reminded his future bride of the joy they had felt flying together through the lovely ballroom at Windsor Castle. When spring came Manchester Corporation asked Absalom to write the loyal Address to the Queen on the occasion of her marriage to Prince Albert of Saxe-Coburg Gotha.

CHAPTER TWENTY-FOUR

'I have scarcely ever felt so much anxiety and fear for the future as I do now'

In early January 1840 Absalom enjoyed a fine display of the Aurora Borealis and sold more than 10,000 pieces of calico. Perhaps they were bought by the Anti-Corn Law Association for the decoration of its new hall.

Events had moved swiftly since that meeting at the York Hotel in September 1838. Richard Cobden and his colleagues possessed energy and organizing ability of a high order. They had successfully mobilized local support, formed a council and sent out missionaries to set up new Associations throughout the country. The following year, fortunately for him, Cobden was able to recruit John Bright for the League. Bright, the son of a Rochdale cotton spinner, was already involved in public affairs and was a friend of Cobden's. In 1841 his first wife died tragically young at Leamington. Cobden happened to be there and calling upon Bright, who was almost in despair, advised him once the first paroxysm of grief had passed 'to come with me and we will never rest until the Corn Law is repealed.' Bright accepted the invitation. If Cobden was the mind behind the movement, his was the imagination that stirred the masses with eloquence and moral fire.

Cobden owned nearly all the remaining unbuilt-up land in St Peter's Field. Since there was no suitable building in Manchester large enough to hold even half of the local Anti-Corn Law Association, he now offered sufficient ground on that emotive spot to build what would become known as the Free Trade Hall. By chance the site he offered adjoined a chapel of the Methodist New Connexion, one day to be converted into the Alexandra Music Hall.

A temporary wooden pavilion was erected, according to Prentice, the work of a hundred men in eleven days. One hundred feet long, and a hundred and five feet wide, it could hold over 4,000 people. The intention was to open it with a grand banquet attended by the local Association together with invited guests and delegates from all over the country.

On the evening of the banquet 3,000 people sat at tables placed from side to side of the hall. Hundreds more came in after dinner to hear the speeches. The hall was lit by twenty-four chandeliers bearing twelve burners each. Above the president's chair there was a device in gas on the wall. This consisted of the word 'JUSTICE' in letters a yard long. About 20,000 yards of white and pink calico were draped along the roof and walls, and the galleries were hung with deep crimson inscribed with mottoes in large letters. The one facing the chair and extending the whole length of the pavilion read 'Landowners! Honesty is the best policy'; the one on the eastern gallery 'Total and immediate Repeal', and that on the west 'A fixed duty is a fixed injustice'.

Daniel O'Connell was one of the invited guests and had been met at the railway station with loud cheers. The ladies had seats in the galleries and at five o'clock the celebrities entered the hall to the strains of a band playing the National Anthem. Prentice thought the scene was one of unsurpassed magnificence and beauty. Absalom was not so impressed.

January 13th, 1840. Dined as one of the Vice-Presidents at the Anti-Corn Law banquet. There were nearly five thousand persons present but the speeches were not worthy of the occasion. I stayed till near twelve and was much tired.

That was the first Free Trade Hall. In 1843 an even bigger brick building was put up on the same spot and in 1856 a third one in stone. This was destroyed by bombs during the Second World War and in 1951 the present building opened.

The League did not wish to cultivate its middle-class image. If it were to succeed in the large towns, particularly Manchester, with its vigorous Chartist element, it was essential to gain the support of the working classes. So an 'Operative Anti-Corn Law Association of Manchester' was formed, with Edward as one of its keenest spirits.

He early showed his manipulative gifts by organizing a second entertainment for those below the salt. The day after the one his father attended, 5,000 operatives sat down to another banquet in the same place. The radical Samuel Bamford was delighted. His experiences had made him acutely aware that the poor were usually shunned by the rich and the act of shunning had 'filled the working classes with a fierce contempt and hatred of anyone wearing a decent coat.' Now for the first time 'the two classes had come together to shake hands and to look manfully in each other's faces.' The middle-class Prentice saw it a little differently. The most striking feature of this vast assemblage, he wrote a trifle patronizingly, was 'the order, propriety, and general excellent demeanour of all the company' which reflected great credit upon the working classes of Manchester.

Prentice was tireless in League activities and came to stay at Rose Hill in order to speak at meetings in Gatley and Cheadle. At Gatley, Edward made his first public speech. Much to the annoyance of the Rector of Cheadle, the Revd E. Trafford Leigh, a local Association was formed in his parish. Trafford Leigh was the clergyman who had kept Absalom standing in his lobby. When Edward wrote to enlist his support for the League he replied that he was convinced that the repeal of the Corn Laws 'would ruin the middle class of gentry and reduce the agricultural labourer to the miserable condition of the Continental serf'. His opinion was not unusual, but not all the clergy shared it. Father Daniel Hearne, the Rector of the Catholic church of St Patrick in one of the poorest districts in Manchester, spoke on public platforms in support of the League. An early exponent of what today might be called liberation theology, he was rebuked by his superiors for taking part in politics and temporarily suspended from his priestly duties.

Absalom was half proud of Edward's activities and half critical because so much of his son's time, which should have been given to the warehouse, was taken up with political agitation.

May 26th, 1840. Read Edward's 'Letter to Sir Robert Peel on the Corn Laws'. It is a fair and conclusive reply to the very artful, shuffling speech, and does great credit to Edward's industry and argumentative powers.

If Absalom was proud of Edward, his daughter was causing further anxiety. He remained particularly fond of her, but the little girl who once so delighted him had grown up into a neurotic woman. Her plainly psychosomatic illness now took a new form. She was sick after eating. 'Alas,' Absalom wrote, 'hers is a life of suffering.' So this was to prove. Elizabeth was twenty-two and isolated with her mother at Northenden. Too rich to earn her living, even had there been any opening for her, she was not rich enough to enjoy a life of subsidized pleasure. Her brothers could exercise what talents they possessed in their own manner while she was confined to the domestic round. The one love affair that we know about went sadly wrong.

Absalom wrote a Petition to the Queen on behalf of the Females of Manchester praying for the repeal of the Corn Laws. He bought two fields from his neighbour, Mr Sumner, together with a road connecting Rose Hill to the highway for £340. It was a great price but unexpectedly in one week he had sold nearly 2,000 pieces of calico and nearly 3,000 bundles of twist.

The decade Absalom had now entered has gone down in fairly recent history as the 'Hungry Forties', that is to say a period of continuous and especial suffering for the poor. Exactly how hungry they really were is controversial. Dr W.H. Chaloner has pointed out that the expression seems first to have been used as late as 1904 in a circular letter written by T. Fisher Unwin, the publisher, who was collecting material for a campaign against Joseph Chamberlain's protectionist policies. Fisher Unwin had married Cobden's daughter, Jane. He was to publish the first edition of Absalom's diary and by chance to commission one of Absalom's great-grandsons, E.I. Watkin, to translate Elie Halévy's classic, *A History of the English People in the Nineteenth Century,* from the French. So much for the origin of the term. As for its truth, Sir John Clapham has shown that contrary to popular belief, the Industrial Revolution raised real wages and that even in the first half of the nineteenth century the working classes were materially better off than their forefathers. Chaloner has argued convincingly that after 1842 the standard of living in England was not only no worse than in the previous twenty years but better. It is interesting that Friedrich Engels, writing from Manchester at the end of 1842, remarked that the English worker had a standard of living that would have been the envy of his counterpart in France or Germany.

Yet it was not *felt* to be so. Charles Shaw was not a lone voice when he described the excruciating poverty which surrounded his childhood in the Potteries at this time. In 1903 he recalled the enormous improvements that had taken place since then and wondered how people could have endured the deprivations of his youth in much the same terms as we wonder how the poor put up with conditions prevailing in 1903.

Absalom's testimony is difficult to evaluate, partly because of the narrowness of his experience, partly because of his temperamental over-reaction to any sort of trouble. As a convinced Leaguer he was psychologically prepared to look for distress and to attribute it at least in part to the wickedness of the Corn Law. It must also be remembered that he was a magistrate, for the first time in touch with the concentrated misery of the law courts, that he was directly involved in the Chartist and related agitations that shook Manchester in the early part of the decade, and that the tragic Irish famine had a distorting effect upon the social conditions of the North-west. But when all reservations are made, the diary confirms the picture of a severe, prolonged if fitful economic depression.

His position as a magistrate meant that Absalom was in far closer contact with poverty, deprivation and human frailty than he had ever been before. In late February he spent several hours in court.

February 24th, 1840. I had to examine fifty beggars, about a score of drunkards and several Sabbath-breakers. The beggars exhibited such a variety of distress and destitution that I gave to the most pitiable of these unhappy creatures all the silver I had in my pocket.

He was as yet uncertain of himself. In April he was sent for in a hurry because the court was waiting and no magistrate had turned up.

April 9th, 1840. Among the cases which were brought before me was that of an Irishman who, in a fit of drunken jealousy, had struck violently the man of whom he was jealous and threatened to shoot his wife. Mr Maude had remanded the case to inquire into the man's sanity. Ollier, the surgeon, deposed that he was perfectly sane and his wife said that he was a very quiet man when sober. While she was giving her evidence, the Mayor came in, and a sort of jumble ensued between his examination and mine and finally he desired me to decide. Hastily, as I now think, I merely bound over the offender in £10 for three months at his own recognizance. On reflection, I felt that the period was too short and the security too little. I will never again decide on a partial hearing of the case, nor without some deliberation. The affair made me really uneasy.

The evident poverty rendered him even more so.

April 27th, 1840. About fifty cases [in court]. Two of extreme and hopeless destitution, a boy and a girl. Alas! How defective are the laws of this Christian country in Christian charity!

The intensity of his experience turned him to verse. Among his papers he left an undated poem entitled 'The Voice of Dearth'. It is perhaps more a tribute to his heart than to his literary skill.

From outside an ancient hall bright with tapers where a magnificent company is dancing in gold embroidered silks, comes the faint low sound of distress.

> A murmur like the fresh'ning breeze
> On summer's eve, that stirs the trees.
> Hark! 'tis the widow's feeble wail!
> Mingled with sighs of orphans pale,
> And children's sobs who weep for bread;
> While parents, groaning, hang the head.
> Listen, ye mighty of the earth,
> Oh! listen to the voice of Dearth.

Unheeding, the company continue to dance to the entrancing music. The arbiters of the nation's fate meet in grave debate but do nothing. No relief is given, the ports remain closed to the import of bread. Maddened with hunger, rage and despair, the people turn to bloody revolution. Those who scorned the voice of dearth die most miserably.

Soon after Easter, John brought the disagreeable news that Moss's were sending their goods to another firm to sell. That meant a loss of £160 a year. Absalom's firm had an immense stock which nobody wanted to buy. The business was in a critical state and yet the boys continued to neglect it for Anti-Corn Law activities. His daughter became ill again. She was bled four times with leeches but became so weak that Mr Occleston considered further advice desirable. Dr Robinson came out from Manchester and pronounced that there was no danger but recovery would be tedious.

When early summer came Absalom remained at Rose Hill helping to save his hay from the flooded meadows but felt he was giving a bad example and that he should have been at the warehouse.

May 26th, 1840. The mowing continued. We had besides the two mowers to whom I am to give £1 for the mowing, George Wallstonecroft to assist

Battersby in tedding. I gave them a gallon of porter – two shillings over my
bargaining which included <u>no drink</u> – and Mrs Watkin, pitying their wet
condition, added three bottles of homemade wine, made hot and sugared,
value two and sixpence.

The market continued bad, his stock still unusually large and the demand
extremely small.

May 28th, 1840. Really assiduous all the forenoon at the warehouse. Called
upon as many people as I could and <u>laboured</u> to do business but all to no
purpose. Much depressed and vexed because Moss's assignees sent a part of
their cloth to John Jones who professed to be able to get six shillings for it, a
price which I cannot obtain.

He gave his daughter £10 to put in her savings bank. She would be glad of it
when he was no more. It was a wretched market.

June 9th, 1840. We are overwhelmed with stock of about eight thousand
and fifty-five pieces for which we cannot find customers and shall probably
very soon lose half our consignment from our inability to sell the goods we
hold. I have scarcely ever felt so much anxiety and fear for the future as I do
now. One thing I resolve and that is not to engage in anything which shall
put to hazard the property I possess. I will keep on as long as I can get
expenses. When that cannot be done I will retire to Rose Hill and live with a
<u>severe economy</u>, spending as little as I can possibly avoid beyond my income
and so between my books and garden and my office, pass the residue of my
life <u>quietly</u> and without mean dependence, although enduring many
privations.

He spent the next day at home carefully calculating his expenses. Some idea of
them may be gathered from a loose piece of paper inserted into his 1839 diary.

Sociable and omnibus for seven years = £420. My illness, Elizabeth's and
family = £300. Education John, Edward, Alfred and Elizabeth = £200.
Parties for seven years = £70. Mortgage = £60. Bad debts = £300. Total =
£1,350. Plate and furniture = £100. Two cows, horse, sociable = £70.
Implements = £20. Books = £160. Total = £350. Shares Athenaeum =
£30. Do Zoological Gardens = £50. Corn Laws = £25. Total = £455.

He craved for simplicity, just to be alone.

June 13th, 1840. Enjoyed my tea very much after washing. I sat in my clean
comfortable kitchen, looking out upon the beautiful evening, the contrasting

foliage, the shadows of the trees on the meadows and the sun illuminating even the distant hills and I was consoled for all my anxieties and looked up with hope.

The Broughton houses had to be attended to.

June 15th, 1840. No business to be done. Went to Broughton in the afternoon. Mr Haworth wants the pump repairing, the wall patching and the house beautifying. Mr Harrison fears that he shall be obliged to leave his house, in which case I shall have to beautify – so that here is a pleasant prospect of half a year's rent being to be laid out. It is seldom that I have all my affairs at the same time going wrong, but at present difficulties and losses threaten me on every side.

Grime's will took up a lot of his time, so did the court, which he found crowded and hot and the smell of so many dirty people disagreeable. On his birthday he learnt that the Commercial Bank of England had stopped payment. He had shares in it. The week after he had to attend a meeting of the shareholders of the zoo which had been in financial difficulties for some time. Both Cobden and Absalom wanted it to open on Sundays, not at a time to compete with church services, but in the evening. However, the Sabbatarian lobby was too powerful and well organized.

July 3rd, 1840. Attended a special meeting of the shareholders of the Zoological Gardens. We are in debt and losing money. I supported a motion for opening the gardens on Sunday evening, which was carried by a show of hands but lost by ballot, the opponents of the measure having been canvassed for, and obtained, a number of proxies.

Edward took his sister off to Lytham for a holiday and Absalom heard of the failure of yet another important firm. 'Such was human prosperity! Such was human prudence!' But how foolish it was to torment himself like that. He reproached himself for not being able to control his imagination. He knew that in all probability he had enough to secure himself and his family from want. Then, most unexpectedly, he sold 1,700 pieces of calico and 100 pieces of sheet and began to feel hopeful again.

Towards Christmas a large dinner was held at the Corn Exchange to honour Sir Thomas Potter, knighted after presenting Manchester's Address to the Queen congratulating her on her escape from assassination on Constitution Hill.

December 10th, 1840. About eight hundred persons were present. The dinner went off well. I proposed the Corporation of Manchester and the principle of self-government. I was greeted by applause but I did not speak with energy and the hearers had been talked to so long before that they were inattentive.

He had a skin eruption on his face and had caught cold.

December 11th, 1840. Rose late, tormented by the eruption and hoarse with a cold. Thought <u>sadly</u> of myself and my speech, of my past life and future prospects. <u>I spent a bitter forenoon</u>. After dinner I arranged some books. Employment generally dissipates dejection. I became cheerful. Took tea with pleasure by the kitchen fire and spent a satisfied evening in reading Shakespeare.

He had to go to Manchester next morning.

December 12th, 1840. A <u>black</u>, cold, frosty day. Extremely troubled by my complaint and the eruption. Went to Town unwell and dejected, thinking my speech had lessened my reputation and that business would never mend, in a short time it behoved me to gather up the remnants of my fortune, reduce my expenditure and pass the rest of my life amongst little men. To my surprise, I find my speech characterized in The Guardian as full of eloquence and good sense, and The Times as 'distinguished by that beautiful and yet vigorous style which always characterizes Mr Watkin's addresses.' Kershaw, whom I saw in the afternoon, declared it to be the best speech that was delivered. As for business, as soon as I got to the warehouse we had some customers and made some unexpected sales. Then as to my reputation, I had in the afternoon an application on behalf of some persons I do not know, to request that I would decide a difference which they had mutually agreed to leave to me. How falsely do we often judge of ourselves and of the world in which we live!

The winter of 1840–41 was severe. The thermometer fell to fifteen degrees Fahrenheit. The river froze from the ford to the Boathouse and then snow made walking difficult. Spring came suddenly, bursting forth as if they were in Russia; snowdrops, polyanthus, aconites, white crocus and hellebore delighting Absalom in his garden.

On St David's Day 1841 he went to the Welsh dinner and heard Mr Roberts from Caernarvon play exquisitely on the harp. Absalom was now one of the directors of the Commercial Bank of England, entrusted with three others to wind up the whole concern and this took up much of his time. There was a good deal of infighting and jockeying for power between the old and the new management. Feelings sometimes exploded into physical violence.

May 5th, 1841. All day at the meeting of the General Board of the

Commercial Bank. A quarrel between Turner and Davidson. Davidson collared Turner and the latter struck him and threw him to the floor.

That June, Lord Melbourne's government was defeated on a vote of confidence. According to current constitutional practice, the government could either resign or dissolve. It chose to dissolve and in the General Election that followed, Peel and the Conservatives were victorious, gaining a clear majority of seventy-six seats in the House of Commons.

Parliament met again in August. Conservative majority or not, it was for Parliament, not the voters directly, to make or unmake ministries. Not until Lord Melbourne was defeated on an amendment to the address did he resign and Peel take office for the second time. Any real difficulties with the Queen were over. This time Victoria was resigned to Melbourne's departure. She had had the extraordinary good fortune to marry a young man wise beyond his years and upon whose guidance she would more and more depend.

Both Edward and John were deeply and excitedly caught up in local politics. Their concern for the prevalent distress was doubtless as sincere as their zeal for reform, but they were only twenty-one and nineteen, and the prospect of civil disturbance in the town was far more diverting than the warehouse. The fight in Manchester was a three-cornered one involving the Anti-Corn Law League, the Chartists and the Irish.

It has been pointed out that when it came to violent and absurd language there was little to choose between the three movements. O'Connor's inflamatory speeches and contributions to the *Morning Star* were notorious. O'Connell in his turn, could talk about the landlord's venison being sweetened with widow's tears and his claret dyed with orphan's blood. Cobden referred to the Corn Laws as baptized in blood, begotten in violence and perpetuated at the expense of tears. Other Leaguers predicted revolution, and one threatened the Queen with the fate of Louis XVI. Even Absalom's poem was explicitly menacing.

The organization of the League in Manchester had been very carefully worked out. The town was mapped into districts, each one with its own association and appointed leader. The workers' section was called the Operative Anti-Corn Law Association. Edward had been made chairman of a district and thoroughly enjoyed a violent scrap in Stevenson Square between the League, the Chartists and the Irish repealers. His father distanced himself from such activities, as did Mr Neild, the mayor.

June 22nd, 1841. Dined with the Mayor of Manchester at the dinner given by him at Mayfield to the Magistrates and Town Council. There were more than sixty persons present and the dinner was sumptuous. The dining-room was a temporary building, profusely adorned with flags, crowns, armorial bearings and letters in gas. Two large looking glasses were fixed to the sideboard. I had to speak, much to my annoyance, but thanks to the Town Clerk, I did pretty well.

Some months later Absalom stayed up until three in the morning preparing a speech to be delivered the following day. There were better ways of dealing with the situation than squabbles in Stevenson Square.

September 16th, 1841. Attended the Public Meeting in the Town Hall to consider the existing distress and the propriety of presenting a memorial to Her Majesty praying her not to prorogue Parliament until the cause of the distress and the restrictive laws have been considered. I moved the first resolution, spoke at first with difficulty, afterwards easily and was applauded. The meeting was large and nearly unanimous.

He walked with Alfred to Broughton by way of Cheetham Hill and Tetlow Fold. Although there were many pretty places left, he was shocked by the changes since he lived there. He did not reproach himself for the part he himself had played in this destruction of natural beauty, or appear even to recognize it. The cloud of smoke hovering perpetually over the centre of Manchester was spreading farther and farther outwards; shops, business premises and houses inexorably eating up the fields and woods of Absalom's prime. Before long Friedrich Engels would describe Manchester as a city 'which changes water into stinking slops', and his friend Julian Harney, the Chartist, called it 'a damned, filthy hole', declaring that he would be 'rather hanged in London than die a natural death in Manchester'. For all that, some of Absalom's 'pretty places' remained far longer than people might imagine. Even at the end of the century heather grew and blackberries could still be gathered on what was left of Kersal Moor and the walk through Drinkwater's Park to Prestwich was pleasant enough.

One Sunday in late autumn Absalom had a disturbing encounter at Rose Hill.

October 31st, 1841. While I was at home alone in the afternoon, a poor Irishman, the picture of famine, came into the stable yard. He told me that he came from County Mayo, that he had been in the 'fin country', that he had 'tuk the ague' and 'had been laid on his back' for three weeks and was still very ill and 'had not a farthing'.

Absalom helped him.

That winter distress in the manufacturing districts increased. A subscription had been got up to celebrate the birth of the Prince of Wales but because of the widespread misery the £2,000 raised was spent on blankets and warm clothes for the poor. Absalom stayed up to hear the bells ring in 1842, fearful for the future but delighting in the sound of so many bells from so many steeples ringing at once.

Faced by a serious financial crisis, that spring, Peel introduced his first budget. In his opinion a return to economic prosperity would relieve distress, not government interference. His problem was a familiar one.

To make up the country's deficit he had either to borrow vast sums of money or to increase taxation. As a temporary measure, therefore, he revived the income tax abolished immediately after the Napoleonic Wars. The amount contributed was sevenpence in the pound, and no one paid it who had an income of less than £150 a year. Influenced by his young Cabinet colleague, Gladstone, who had been converted to the principles of free trade, Peel also proposed a revision of the whole elaborate system of import duties and to reduce the range of tariffs.

Logically this was the time for the total abolition of the Corn Laws but Peel considered that to be a political impossibility. The landed gentry, he argued in agreement with the Revd E. Trafford Leigh, must not be destroyed, nor could the country's good be at the mercy of a foreign enemy in the time of war. A sliding scale of corn duties was introduced instead. This unhappy half-measure did not appease the League and from now on it stepped up its campaign.

The Chartists had not forgotten Edward's attack upon them in Stevenson Square the previous June. Internecine warfare in Manchester continued and that March another fracas broke out at a meeting in the Hall of Science. Several people were badly hurt and the furniture destroyed. Feargus O'Connor used his paper the *Northern Star* to accuse Edward of having actually incited the Irish to attack the Chartists.

Absalom was unhappy about his son. The boy was inattentive at the warehouse and spent far too much of his time on political activities. It might be a good idea for him to get right away for a short while. A trip to Italy with his friend George Wall was suggested and Absalom wrote to Cobden for introductions. Cobden, now Member for Stockport, was helpful but not deceived. 'I should be very glad,' he wrote, 'to be able to render any service in the way you wish to your son, Edward, for whose character, talents and energy I have the greatest respect. Am I correct in the supposition that you are actuated by a prudent desire to withdraw him for a short season from the vortex of political excitement into which his ardour has plunged him?'

In the May after Edward's return from Italy the Chartists presented a Petition to Parliament for the second time. It was another monster Petition, containing, the Chartists claimed, over three million signatures. Thirty bearers carried it on poles and so long was it that it had to be broken up and carried into the House in pieces. The Petition included a condemnation of the new Poor Law, a request for legislation to restrict hours of work in the factories, and a demand for one man, one vote.

Macaulay, not foreseeing that prosperity would enable the lower classes to emulate the middle, warned the House that universal suffrage would mean the end of private property and was therefore 'utterly incompatible with the very existence of civilization'. In the event, a motion that the Petition should be considered was rejected by 287 votes to 49.

Trade stagnation continued and was widespread. The *Manchester Times* spoke of hungry and half-clothed men and women stalking the streets begging for bread. It was said that Manchester soup kitchens dispensed as much as 10,000 gallons a day.

While a Dean of the Established Church praised the nutritional value of turnips and mangelwurzels, an Irish Chartist declared at Colne that 'ere three hundred suns, the Charter shall be gained, or a bloody revolution. Ere three hundred suns have set we shall have our Liberty or fill a glorious grave.' No wonder the League announced that revolt was imminent and Sir Charles Snow, the Manchester commissioner of police, suggested that the local force be issued with cutlasses.

In 1832 Absalom had drawn up the Manchester Petition begging Parliament to refuse supplies unless the Reform Bill was passed. Now Cobden was urging people to withhold taxes, and John Shuttleworth suggested that their leader should speak out in the House in such a way as to be sent to the Tower. It is doubtful if Cobden was prepared to be quite so self-sacrificing, but he was determined to increase the pressure. 'The government is very much alarmed at the present state of the country,' he wrote to Edward in June, 'and any disturbance in the country would, I think, force the aristocracy to conciliate the people. We are doing all we can to increase the uneasiness of the rascals.'

In the middle of July the Manchester Anti-Corn Law Association adopted Absalom's former tactic. They asked for signatures to a Memorial requesting the Manchester MPs to stop supplies since the country was on the eve of revolution. Manchester and Salford between them obtained over 70,000 signatures. Some people thought this treasonable, but as John Shuttleworth had earlier pointed out, the situation was critical. In the past the middle classes could be relied upon to help to keep the peace, but faced with injustice they might not now be so anxious to suppress violence.

As tension increased Absalom's mind once more turned back to the Civil War. Exactly two hundred years ago the King had set up his standard at Nottingham.

> **May 25th, 1842.** Continued Laud's diary. The courage with which he bore up against imprisonment and a protracted trial and his undaunted behaviour on the scaffold oblige one to respect him. Popular rage is blind. He ought not to have been executed, although he deserved death.

From there he moved on to George III and more recent troubles.

> **May 26th, 1842.** The squabbles between the parliament of George III and Jack Wilkes make one almost believe that the past times were a rehearsal for the present. Man has been always 'the animal man' – credulous, impetuous, quarrelsome, and occasionally insane.

Events endorsed his judgement. In the hot summer to come the entire industrial north would be ablaze.

CHAPTER TWENTY-FIVE

'The explosion has been so sudden that there has been no force adequate to the occasion with which to meet the mob'

Before the end of July 1842 the price of wheat had risen yet again. This was the moment chosen by the coalmine owners and the manufacturers to reduce wages.

Earlier in the year the Royal Commission on child labour in the mines had produced a report that showed the appalling conditions in some coal pits. On all fours, almost naked children of both sexes pulled loaded trucks through passages only a few feet high for as long as fifteen hours a day. They could be as young as five or six and some of them were unpaid pauper children sent from the workhouses. The disclosures were a shocking affront to the public conscience.

Lord Ashley had no difficulty in persuading the Commons to take action and the Mines Act was the first law ever passed to exclude women from a particular kind of labour. The Act prohibited altogether the employment underground of women and girls, set an age limit of ten to the employment of boys and provided inspectors to enforce the law. However the attempt to regulate children's employment led to familiar difficulties. Children were protected at the cost of reducing the amount of money earned by families as a whole. The mine owners were well aware of this and, either to provoke a strike and to show who was master or for some genuine economic reason, they lowered the weekly wage.

The motive for the reduction of wages in the manufacturing districts is also controversial. It has been suggested that the factory owners did it in order to foment industrial unrest and so bring pressure on the government to repeal the Corn Laws. That certainly was John Bright's intention in suggesting a lockout. Absalom was not the only merchant to feel the pinch and many manufacturers were in a precarious financial position. To reduce wages was the only course some of them could take to avoid bankruptcy, with its resulting further unemployment and empty factories. Richard Cobden was in an awkward predicament. 'On some terms or other,' he wrote after the Chartists had disrupted yet another League meeting, 'the masses must co-operate with the middle classes or there is no hope for us.' But how far did he want the middle classes to co-operate with the masses?

After some consideration he had dismissed Bright's plan for simultaneous factory closure on the ground that not enough manufacturers would agree to the idea and that in any case it would involve antagonizing too many of the operatives. His vehement nature, contempt for the landed classes and passionate sense of the injustice of the Corn Laws meant that part of him welcomed violence, or more accurately, as he hinted in a letter to Edward, the threat of violence as a means to force the government's hand. At the same time he was desperately anxious to distance himself from it, in his own words 'to try to set ourselves right with the moral and religious part of the community'. The backbone of the League was middle class. The middle classes did not wish to be associated with the Chartists or to accept any degree of blame for what happened. Absalom shows no consciousness at all that the language and policies of the League could have been in any way responsible for exacerbating the situation.

For the most part passive during the long years of hardship, the workers in fact had been incited by the Chartists and inflamed by the League and now were driven by hunger and despair into open revolt. The miners called a general strike, disturbances spread quickly from Scotland to the industrial North and into South Wales. A multiplicity of groups – the Chartists, the Leaguers, the Trade Unions, the Irish Repealers, the National Complete Suffrage Unions – all contributed to agitate the working classes, but at bottom it was the familiar knife-and-fork question and the rallying cry a simple one: 'A Fair Day's Wages for a Fair Day's Work'.

At the beginning of Absalom's account of the ensuing riots, there runs an undercurrent of reproof, a suggestion of unpreparedness and even lack of resolution on the part of the authorities. But the situation was extremely delicate. Some mayors in the large manufacturing towns in the North had stated that if riots broke out they would not allow troops to fire on the crowd. Yet if military support were refused the police alone would have to bear the brunt of civil disorder. The Home Secretary had not approved the issue of cutlasses, but in any case the police could not be expected on their own to control serious rioting although they were now a full-time constabulary under the control of the Justices of the Peace. In Manchester they were still 'the bluebottles', hated by Tories and Radicals alike, badly paid and largely recruited from the Irish.

On 21 July some 5,000 or 6,000 Staffordshire miners marched into Congleton taking food by force from the shops and houses before going on to Macclesfield, on their way sabotaging some collieries by pulling out the plugs in the boilers of the steam machinery. It was this action, repeated elsewhere, that led to the disturbances being called 'the Plug Riots'.

To the north-east of Manchester, in the working-class districts of Ashton-under-Lyne, Stalybridge and Dunkinfield, wage reductions had led to widespread strikes and mass meetings. Despite this, on Sunday 7 August, Colonel Wemyss, who had already sent a troop of Dragoons into Staffordshire and was in charge at Manchester, wrote complacently to the Home Office.

I am happy to state that all the information I have been able to obtain in Manchester indicates a considerable improvement in commercial affairs – the

Town is quite quiet, and unless the Chartists or <u>Other Agitators</u>, are concerned in this new Turn Out, in the Collieries – I trust we are not like to have any disturbance now, or on the anniversary of Peterloo – on the 16th, which is to be celebrated by opening a monument to the memory of Hunt, and a Procession, promised to be headed by Mr Feargus O'Connor . . .

The next day some 2,000 to 3,000 strikers marched round Stalybridge and, using violence where necessary, stopped all the mills before going on to Dunkinfield, Ashton and Hyde. When evening came it was decided to march on Manchester the following day, to bring all the mills there to a stop and hold a meeting at the Exchange. This intention was known to the commissioner of police, Sir Charles Shaw, who did not however inform any magistrate until nine-thirty next morning, when the mob was actually on the march. Absalom's implied criticism is not altogether unjust. There was a sad lack of liaison between the magistrates, the army and the police.

The stipendiary magistrate, Mr Maude, on receiving the information about the march, met Wemyss at the Town Hall, caused the Riot Act to be copied out, then rode with Wemyss towards Great Ancoats Street where the Ashton procession had just arrived. Two companies of the Rifles prevented further movement towards Manchester and a troop of Dragoons were placed along the end of Pollard Street. But the procession included a large number of young women and gave the appearance of being a peaceful demonstration. It was difficult to know how to act. Peterloo was an inhibiting factor. A strong tradition of freedom of speech and assembly conflicted with a deep and justified fear of the mob.

Maude asked Wemyss what they should do. Wemyss said he could not give an opinion. At this juncture Sir Charles Shaw rode up. He had already met a large mob, armed with heavy bludgeons, on the Ashton Old Road and he told Maude that they must expect violence. Maude answered that the people he was dealing with had promised to be peaceful and to return home. Shaw reined back his horse. 'Sir,' he said loudly,

I must protest in the strongest manner against these people passing . . . I report to you officially that these men . . . informed me this morning at Ashton that they had turned out all the mills at Stalybridge and were coming to do the same at Manchester and get bread . . .

In fact on their way to Manchester some parties of the Ashton crowd had already turned out mills, and even while this exchange was taking place had entered the town by other roads and started to turn out mills in New Islington and elsewhere. Maude did not know this. The mob that confronted him was unarmed and too numerous to turn back the way it had come. He gave permission for the procession to follow a circular route along Great Ancoats Street, across to Piccadilly and back to the Ashton Old Road.

A frustrated Shaw remarked that he could do no more than 'count the number who are attacking the town'. He did so, and there were between 5,000 and 6,000. It was not to be hoped that the procession would follow Maude's route. Dragoons had been posted already to prevent the entrance to Market Street and the Exchange, although about 500 slipped through. The main body turned to the poorest part of Manchester, Little Ireland, and to the Oxford Road twist mills. Eventually they were persuaded to go home quietly. It seems that the Manchester operatives themselves, naturally taking advantage of the situation, now started to turn out mills round the Oldham Road and Great Ancoats Street. Absalom, on the other hand, implies that on the first day the damage was done by the outsiders.

August 9th, 1842. A mob of about five thousand persons came from Hyde and Ashton to Manchester and turned out the people of several mills and workshops. The police and military were rather observers than anything else. The Borough Magistrates were not assembled. The Mayor is in London. The boldness of the mob was increased by their apparent impunity. They attacked Birley's, and the Oxford Road Mills, and Stirling and Beckton's. Birley and Stirling and Beckton resisted. Windows were broken and the doors injured and it was not until the soldiers appeared and cleared the streets that the mob ceased their violence. I saw Mr Kershaw, who at first was disinclined to act. Then I sent to Mr Higson to say that I thought the Magistrates ought to be called together. He answered that it should be done in the morning.

The night was quiet, but next day the situation deteriorated fast. Absalom says he arrived at the Town Hall at ten o'clock, so despite valiant efforts by the police and Wemyss's Dragoons, the town had been more or less at the mercy of the mob for four hours before the authorities even started to take action.

August 10th, 1842. Met the Mayor and magistrates at the Town Hall at ten. The Mayor had only arrived from London at six and was evidently fatigued. The outrages of the mob continue. Those who have been turned out joined with them and shops have been plundered and are being plundered in the town and money extorted. Message after message arrives for assistance.

I am sent with Mr Stuart and Mr Higson to confer with Sir Charles Shaw. We found him at Kennedy's Mill (which is at work) with about a hundred or two hundred policemen and nearly as many soldiers, taking, as he says, a military view of the matter, and concentrating his force to be ready to move where it may be urgently wanted; the usual patrols withdrawn from the streets and all left exposed. He objects to scattering his force. We return. Colonel Wemyss objects to scatter the military and refuses to supply us with Dragoons for patrol.

In the meantime the gasworks are attacked and the police stationed there are beaten. A police station in the neighbourhood is pulled down. Mr

Callender goes with some Dragoons and Rifles, disperses the mob and occupies the gasworks in force. While this is going on, the mob proceeded in different parts of the town to turn out the hands at mills and workshops and in some cases to help themselves to bread etc. from the shops. In Salford they did the same. They attempted to stop Wilson's Print Works, but were fired at, and three persons were wounded. If, however, the soldiers had not fortunately arrived, the consequences would have been disastrous. As it was, the hands left work.

At one o'clock I drew up a notice in the name of the Mayor and magistrates warning the people of the illegality of their proceedings and threatening punishment. It was printed and posted throughout the town, as were notices that the Riot Act had been read. A requisition was sent to some of the respectable inhabitants calling upon them to attend at the Town Hall to be sworn in as special constables, as the police force is altogether insufficient.

At four in the afternoon I was sent to the gasworks to relieve Mr Callender. I sat in Mr Hampshire's parlour, the windows of which had been beaten in with stones and even the looking glass over the chimney-piece was broken. The floor was littered with stones, some of them very large. However, as the shutters were put up and as they brought some wine and biscuits, the officers of the Rifles and the Dragoons who were there with Edward and myself had no reason to complain of their quarters. I stayed till ten o'clock when I was relieved.

The next day was Thursday. Early in the morning between 10,000 and 15,000 people met in Granby Row Fields not far from the Oxford Road Mills. Here the crowd was exhorted by the local Chartists to stay out until their demands were met. The mayor, William Neild, read the Riot Act, and immediately some ninety Dragoons, a company of Rifles and fifty artillerymen with two six-pounders and all the available police and specials appeared on the ground. The crowd dispersed rapidly.

Later in the morning it was reported that coal miners from Oldham were marching towards Manchester. Troops were posted at New Cross where the Riot Act was read once again and the colliers turned towards Middleton. Absalom spent the entire night at the Town Hall.

August 11th, 1842. The disturbances continue and have spread further into the country. We continue to swear in special constables and mobs are dispersed as far as possible, but all is unquiet and unsafe. John, who is acting as a special constable, has received some bruises from stones and some of the police have been seriously injured.

At the end of the day 122 people had been arrested and 23 treated at the infirmary for wounds.

Manchester began to pull itself together. The mayor presided over a board of magistrates at the Town Hall who were now in constant touch with both the police and the army. Absalom was a member of a committee of six formed to organize the best disposition of the special constables; 2,500 were enrolled. It was decided that a band of twelve specials should guard each of the turnpikes into Manchester, with one mounted man in command.

August 12th, 1842. The disturbances extend in every direction and become very alarming. With our very inadequate force we keep the town tolerably quiet and go on swearing in and organizing special constables, who are immediately sent on duty and are very useful. The heat and confinement and close application make it very hard work for the magistrates and the soldiers, police and specials are much harassed.

The truth was that despite the most energetic local measures, under the conditions of the time there were simply not enough troops to maintain order.

August 13th, 1842. The disturbances continue to extend over the northern and midland counties and are now assuming a more determined political character. 'The Charter or no return to labour' is now the general cry, although to this there are some objectors. They now stop all trades except farmers and millers, and bands of people are wandering about the country demanding charity and ordering all trades to turn out. The explosion has been so sudden that there has been no force adequate to the occasion with which to meet the mob, and there is an increasing fear and timidity on the part of the well disposed.

In our quiet village this is strikingly apparent. Tradesmen have taken down their signs fearing that their shops would be plundered, and no idea seems to be entertained in Northen and the neighbourhood that any resistance can be offered. Indeed, many of the workers appear to think that a revolution accompanied by the putting down of the rich would not be at all an evil. The man who delivered our coal today told Elizabeth that they should bring no more, and that they would now have the Charter, that the soldiers dare not fire and that we should see what they would do at Manchester next Tuesday, August 16th, as they meant to attack it from all quarters. I really believe the fools think that they are now undisputed masters, and this belief may lead to great excesses. No troops have yet reached Manchester and our situation is by no means agreeable. The deputation of the magistrates who were sent last night to London will, we hope, induce the Government to take immediate steps to send forward the military. The news from all parts of the country tonight is bad.

The new commander of the Northern District, Major General Sir William Warre, who had arrived in Manchester on 10 August, advised the magistrates to temporize with the mob when they found themselves unable to enforce the law. This was too much like capitulation, and the three Manchester magistrates Absalom refers to had left for London to ask for reinforcements. The Cabinet agreed, the Queen signed a proclamation and 500 Grenadier Guards, 36 Royal Horse Artillerymen and 2 six-pounder guns arrived in Manchester by train at five o'clock on the morning of Sunday 14 August.

> **August 14th, 1842.** At Manchester till one o'clock. The Grenadier Guards and some artillery came into Manchester this morning. I was very glad to see this fine body of men march down King Street as I stood with the Mayor at the windows of the Town Hall. The Borough and County magistrates had a conference this morning. A proclamation was drawn up by a committee of six – Foster, the Mayor, G.W. Wood, Wanklyn, James Burt, Maude and myself. It was adopted by the whole company of the Borough and County magistrates and ordered to be printed and posted in all directions. It declared all meetings illegal <u>under present circumstances,</u> and that we will disperse all meetings or processions and '<u>if need be, forcibly put down the same</u>'. It is accompanied by a Proclamation from the Queen, denouncing those who have taken part in the late proceedings and offering a reward of £50 for the conviction of any of the principal offenders. These proclamations and the measures consequent upon them – now that we can enforce them – will, I hope, arrest the progress of this dangerous outbreak.

The headquarters of the military were at the York Hotel, King Street, next door to the Town Hall. The committee now set up an additional ring of thirteen stations each one manned by a hundred special constables and a mounted officer. More than forty mounted men were employed to communicate between the stations and the Town Hall, while others patrolled the main roads outside Manchester to give warning of any large body approaching the town. A Lieutenant-Colonel Angelo, specially sent from London for the purpose, organized the Chelsea Pensioners into an effective force. These were the 'out-pensioners', retired or invalid soldiers sent to different places to relieve pressure on the Royal Hospital itself. Absalom spent 15 August in the Town Hall. He was too tired to write much in his diary.

> **August 15th, 1842.** The people show no disposition to return to work, and there is much excitement. We go on swearing in special constables and preparing for the worst.

'The worst' referred to the Peterloo anniversary and the presence of Feargus O'Connor. Manchester was already full of trade unionists who had gathered there for a convention. According to information received by Jonathan Mellor, an Oldham Magistrate, the majority of the delegates at this conference had voted for the operatives to stay out on strike until the Charter was granted. This may have been unrealistic, it was certainly dangerous.

In July O'Connor had laid the foundation stone of a memorial to Orator Hunt at the Revd J. Scholefield's chapel in Every Street. It had been decided then that he would unveil the monument on the next anniversary of Peterloo, and that on the same date a conference of Chartist leaders should be held at the chapel. As Absalom's brief entry shows, the authorities in Manchester were fully expecting further violence and had made preparations accordingly. The military were waiting, all the watch stations were manned, at the Town Hall 100 regular policemen together with as many as 165 special constables were in readiness. After all that, what happened turned out to be a typically English anticlimax.

August 16th, 1842. Today we expected an outbreak owing to Feargus O'Connor being here, a procession to Hunt's monument being intended. However, the procession was abandoned, but a tea party was held! We had excellent arrangements and the knowledge of our force and the declared determination to use it, seems to have kept all tolerably quiet, any little manifestation being immediately put down. I was busy all day at the Town Hall, in Hulme, in Quay Street and in Chorlton, administering the oath to special constables, of whom we have now several thousand.

The next day the Chartist delegates met at the chapel and discussed the strike at length. For all his inflammatory language, O'Connor was not a 'physical force' man. Encouragement of the strike inevitably would mean further violence. Yet to draw back now would weaken his leadership. Counsels were divided. Eventually the meeting agreed with the trade union delegates. It was decided that the strikers should be urged to include the Charter in their demands and to stay out until it became law.

Absalom was exhausted. For the time being he gave up writing a daily entry and merely summarized the events of the last two weeks of August.

August 16th–August 31st, 1842. From this day to the end of the month most of the hands (spinners, power loom weavers etc.) in Manchester have remained out of work and here and elsewhere there has been more or less of apprehension and disturbance. In some places the soldiers have fired, and some lives have been lost and in the Potteries some houses have been burnt, but in Manchester there has been no firing by the soldiers, nobody has been killed, no house burnt and no damage done to property since the first day or two, except the breaking of some windows in factories.

In September the strike petered out. Absalom made a single entry for the entire month.

September 1st–September 30th, 1842. We have continued during most of this month in an uneasy condition both in Manchester and in most of the districts in which the disturbances have taken place. However, the people have gradually and some reluctantly, returned to work both here and elsewhere. The imminent peril has passed, and it now remains to prepare for the future, of which the prospect is gloomy and uncertain.

CHAPTER TWENTY-SIX

'A youth in livery informed us that Mr Dickens was in the drawing-room'

Life became ordinary again. The attempt to save the Zoological Gardens failed and in November 1842 the animals were sold at auction. Some of them were bought by the proprietor of Belle Vue Gardens and were to form the nucleus of a more successful venture. The same month the Bank of Manchester stopped payment and Burdekin, its manager, fled to America leaving its shareholders liable for the sum of £713,082. The Literary Society debated if the working of the American constitution had justified the expectations of its founders; news came of the success of our arms in Afganistan and of a favourable peace concluded with China. Absalom read some Aristophanes, which he thought indelicate, and attended the magistrate's court.

> **December 5th, 1842.** I sent five persons to prison for being drunk and disorderly and felt sad when I had done so. Alas! Human justice is very imperfect.

So were human philosophical systems and confident predictions about the future state of society. On his way to England that November the twenty-two-year-old Friedrich Engels introduced himself to Karl Marx. They met in Cologne where Marx was then editing a radical newspaper. Engels was going to Manchester to complete his business training by working in the offices of Ermen and Engels, a prosperous cotton firm of which his father was a partner and from which he was to do very well. Like Absalom, Engels disliked the work and hated touting for customers on the Exchange.

He was already convinced that the impoverishment of the proletariat would lead very shortly to a social revolution which would be 'the bloodiest ever waged' and before long he would accuse 'the English bourgeoisie before the entire world of murder, robbery and all sorts of other crimes on a mass scale'.

The winter so far had been so mild that on New Year's Day 1843 Absalom listed the flowers in leaf in his garden.

> Periwinkle, Polyanthus, Stock, Wallflower, Daisy, Pansy, Flos Adonis, Iberis,

Christmas Rose, Alpine Strawberry, Pyrus Japonica, Marigold, Virginian Stock, lilac and purple Primrose, Mezereon, Rosemary, the male and female blossoms of the Filbert, the Laurel, White Violet, the Fuchsia, the St John's Wort, Honeysuckle and the Ribes Speciossissima are fully in leaf. The catkins and the female blossoms of the filbert are quite as much out as they usually are at the end of March. The throstle, blackbirds, finches and some other birds have been trying their spring notes.

The troubles of the previous year were swiftly becoming more remote.

February 8th, 1843. In the evening I presided at the Soirée of the Essay and Discussion Society at the Athenaeum. It was attended by a numerous assemblage of both sexes, elegantly dressed and disposed to be pleased. The arrangements were very good. My daughter was particularly struck by the circumstance that every official personage was distinguished, not as is common, by a rosette or ribbon, but by a beautiful white camellia tied with silver thread. After coffee a paper read by Mr Berlyn on the question 'Is an advocate morally justified in defending a criminal whom he knows to be guilty?'

In March the zoo was finally wound up. It had been run as a joint stock company and Absalom lost money in it.

March 15th, 1843. Attended the final meeting of the Zoological Garden Company and moved the resolution of dissolution. All the money is lost, and we are glad to get rid of the excessive chief-rent by giving up all fixed property.

In early May Absalom took his wife and his son John on a jaunt to London. They went by train, arriving in London a little before six in the evening, having left Rose Hill at twenty minutes to eight. They spent a hectic fortnight sightseeing and enjoying themselves.

May 5th, 1843. In the evening to Drury Lane Theatre where we saw Acis and Galatea and Comus. Miss Clara Novello was Galatea. A bad actress, but a very good singer. Macready was 'Comus'. I was astonished to hear an Irish accent in a performer so celebrated.

A few days later they went farther afield.

May 11th, 1843. Went to Windsor by the ten o'clock train. Saw the Castle, walked in the Park, looked once more at Herne's Oak. Looked over Eton. The boys had a half holiday and the Thames was alive with their beautiful light boats and the grounds were filled with groups playing at cricket etc. I observed one angling in a secluded nook. We walked to Slough and went thence to London by the train. John and my wife spent the evening at Mme Tussaud's Exhibition. I went with Mr Brigham to the lobby of the House of Commons.

He was interested in the East India Company's Museum.

May 13th, 1843. The autograph answer of Oliver Cromwell to the petition of the then East India Company is really curious. After leaving the museum we went and had a 'snack' and then proceeded to Chiswick to the Garden of the Horticultural Society. It was the first exhibition of the year. About five thousand persons were present and I never saw finer men or women or more splendid and elegant dresses, and never at a time so many of both. The weather was very fine and azaleas and geraniums superb. I saw a plant of the very rare blue nasturtium. It had been in flower since the previous September and was still full of blooms. Against the wall was a wisteria, the stem as thick as a man's thigh and the branches covered with flowers extending more than thirty yards each way.

For once he was glad to get home. The expedition had tired him. That June he was fifty-six. He spent most of his birthday in court, sitting from half-past ten to half-past five. Trade remained slack and he could not stop tormenting himself with fears that his business would fail and that he would have to leave Rose Hill. John had left home and was now living in lodgings at Strangeways. Absalom enjoyed the resulting peace, it would be painful to be obliged to go now.

August 15th, 1843. Pleased with the deep quiet of my home at night. We are almost buried in wood. I like the place on account of its apparent loneliness – the depth of the wood in front which shuts out all view of road or dwelling, gives our house and garden the appearance of having been formed by clearing a little bit out of the forest.

The weather continued fine.

August 18th, 1843. The corn ripens astonishingly and is everywhere in the course of a few days most remarkably altered in colour and appearance. People are busy – mowing, reaping, carrying, stacking. All is bustle and cheerfulness and a man can hardly be got in 'Our Village'. We shall apparently have a good harvest and cheap food.

It seemed a far cry from Engels and *The Condition of the Working Class*, yet perhaps not so very distant. A few days later he went with some friends by coach to Cheadle.

August 30th, 1843. The day was fine but no weather could make the Potteries or their population look well. A sort of <u>beggarliness</u>, an untidiness, a neglect is stamped upon everything. The ground is broken up, the trees are sickly and every object is smoked.

He determined to find out where he stood financially and what progress he had made. What fixed property had he twenty-five years ago and what had he now? He took a separate piece of paper and worked it out.

December 1818 = £220. October 1820 = £952. August 1821 = £1373. May 1825 = £2254. 1827 = £2381. 1832 = £4176. February 1835 = £4180. February 1836 = £4151. April 1838 = £4352. January 1840 = £4155. February 1842 = £4100. April 1843 = £4100. August 1843 = £4005.

We do not know what he thought of the results of his calculations.

The evenings were still light and Absalom often stayed up reading until he heard 'the thin scattered bird song of early morning.' Bayle's *Dictionary* had always both attracted and repelled him.

August 23rd, 1843. I am almost tired of this book. There is much curious learning in it, and much critical sagacity and great mental power. But he was indeed 'the cloud compelling' – i.e. gathering – Jove of literature. <u>Doubts</u> are the objects of his especial liking and obscenities his delight. In these he revels and I almost always rise from his volumes informed indeed, but uneasy and dissatisfied.

On the other hand he was reassured by the perusal of the *Annual Registers* for 1767, 1768 and 1770.

September 28th, 1843. I have been struck in reading these volumes with the evidently gross state of society, the defective police and the sanguinary justice. We have certainly improved more in knowledge and the mass of the people are more thought of and more cared for.

Edward too was now one of the directors of the Athenaeum. The beautiful white camellias tied with silver thread were expensive. So were the grand new buildings in Princess Street. The institution was heavily in debt and Edward was just the person to help to restore its fortunes. He got himself appointed honorary secretary for the great bazaar held to raise funds and also suggested and organized a series of grand literary soirées for the same purpose. It was probably his idea to ask Charles Dickens to preside at the first soirée in early October.

For some weeks now at Rose Hill they had been reading the instalments of

Martin Chuzzlewit as they came out. At that time Dickens's sister Fanny and her husband Henry Burnett lived in Manchester. Fanny was to die young of tuberculosis. Edward referred to her as a 'self-denying saint if ever one existed'. Dickens stayed with the Burnetts for the occasion and asked for a meeting on the evening before the soirée so as to make the final arrangements.

In his book on Cobden, Edward later published a detailed account of what happened. He and his fellow promoter, Mr Berlyn, first had tea with Samuel Giles, the brother of the Revd William Giles, a Baptist minister and Dickens's old schoolmaster. They then walked to Fanny's house: 3 Elm Terrace, Higher Ardwick.

> Ringing the bell, the door was opened by a youth in livery, who informed us that Mr Dickens was in the drawing-room, obtained our names, and running briskly up two or three steps, looked round, and desired us to 'Please walk up'. Throwing open a door opposite the landing, our guide announced us and we entered. Shaking hands with Mr and Mrs Burnett, we were at once introduced by Mrs Burnett to her brother, standing with one hand on the chimney-piece. He cordially welcomed us and asked us to take some wine, and in passing the decanter upset his own glass and deluged a very pretty book lying on the table.

> Dickens removed the book and asked about the programme for the meeting.

> This I briefly gave him. We then spoke of the speakers and talked of their several qualities in a free and laughing manner – Dickens elevating his eyebrows and nodding his head forward as the remarks struck him. An interjection as to the doubt he had in Pickwick cast upon 'swarries' provoked a quick, funny glance, which preluded an immediate turn of the talk to something else.

> Dickens inquired whom they intended to place beside him. They answered that they had thought of Mr and Mrs Burnett. It would make the occasion less stiff and be more enjoyable for him.

> 'No, I should not wish that,' he rejoined, 'by any means. I am obliged, but I could not allow that. You must look at the result upon your object in choosing my supporters.' 'Then,' we replied, 'we might place Mr Cobden on one side and the Mayor on the other.'

> Dickens said that the success of the Manchester Athenaeum would help to establish others elsewhere, it was the principle of Athenaeums that they were really struggling for.

Mr Giles happened to hint about the utility of appealing to the audience from
the Chair for money. To this I objected that it would be unfair to Dickens
and too much like making a marketable commodity of him. He said, 'Yes, I
should not like to do that, but I will try to excite their liberality in another
and equally useful way.' We arranged that he should come into the Hall
immediately after tea. He talked of the <u>effect</u>. 'Get the tea over – I must
confess to a sort of horror of tea-things (or tea on a grand scale) and I think
the best way to excite and keep up the interest would be to appear
immediately after tea, <u>and go to work at once</u>.'

He admired the ticket that Edward and Berlyn had designed and which had his
portrait on it. But when Berlyn mentioned Pickwick in connection with the
Grand Bazaar, he again turned the conversation away from his own works.

Next morning he was shown over the Free Trade Hall by Cobden, the mayor
and others and in the evening Edward and Berlyn went to fetch him from his
sister's. Dickens was ready and waiting but they had arrived rather early so had to
sit down and talk. Dickens said that he thought Cobden older than he actually was
and spoke of the 'manufacturing district face' and the prematurely aged appearance
of the Manchester people.

On the way to the Hall we talked of Hood and Jerrold. Dickens lamented
Hood's ill-health and poverty and much praised his writings, admired Jerrold
and lauded Punch, which he said, he generally 'saw before it was in print'.

Dickens had recently returned from America and had described his experiences
in *American Notes for General Circulation*. Edward tactfully brought up the subject.

I tried to turn the talk upon America. Heywood asked about the society of
the American universities. Dickens praised it highly – said it was a little world
within itself – that its members banded themselves together in order to
protect themselves from the system of evils of which they were surrounded.
He said he had formed friendships amongst them which would last his life.
He praised the society of Boston and I think of New York and Philadelphia
and said the feeling against slavery was stronger than people imagined and was
growing. I noticed that Dickens occasionally said, when interrupted in
conversation, 'Oh, lord (or law) yes!' 'Oh, law, no!' – a cockneyism.

Edward observed him carefully, but the inhabitants of Manchester were not the
only people to look old beyond their years. Dickens was actually only thirty-one at
this time.

Dickens is in appearance about thirty-five or thirty-six years of age, five feet
eight inches high, elegantly, compactly, but slightly made; his face is not,

strictly speaking, <u>handsome</u>, the features are not <u>very</u> good, as some people say they are. His eyes are very dark and full of fire and when turned upon you, give light to his rather dark countenance, such as I have seldom before seen beaming upon any face. He has a good deal of the eyebrow-elevating, shoulder-shrugging and head-nodding peculiar to people who have travelled a great deal. His voice is well regulated and strong but there is the occasional slight peculiarity, of which the defect of 'maw-mouthed' people would be the extreme caricature. He can look very expressively. When he looks 'droll', he looks <u>very</u> droll, when interested, deeply so. His hair is dark brown and abundant.

Dickens was not the only lion in Manchester. On that very morning Edward had received a hurried note from Cobden informing him that Mr Benjamin Disraeli, the author of *Vivian Grey*, was staying at the Mosley Arms Hotel with his wife. Cobden wished Edward would call and invite them to the soirée. Edward hurried round to the hotel only to find that Disraeli had gone out. He was however kindly received by Mrs Disraeli who assured him that they would both come. Edward added that they would like her husband to say a few words. 'Benjamin will speak,' Mrs Disraeli replied. 'He can always speak at ten minutes notice.'
Absalom saw it all from the outside and from a different perspective.

October 5th, 1843. Went at night with my wife and daughter, Miss Wilson, John and Alfred to the Soirée of the members of the Athenaeum and their friends. It was held in the Free Trade Hall. There were at least one thousand six hundred persons present, half of whom, or more, were ladies. Charles Dickens, the author of Nicholas Nickleby was in the Chair and the younger D'Israeli, Milner-Gibson, etc. were present.

Dickens was to make a sad mess of his private life but other Victorians managed things better. Milner-Gibson had succeeded Poulett Thomson as MP for Manchester. This year a girl had given birth to his illegitimate child, a boy destined to found *The Lady* and to become the maternal grandfather of Nancy Mitford and her sisters.
In his speech Dickens referred with feeling to the education of the poor. It was inspiring to know that amid clanking engines and whirling machinery the mind was not forgotten. He had no patience with the maxim 'a little knowledge is a dangerous thing'. A little hanging was once considered a dangerous thing, with this difference 'because a little hanging was dangerous, we had a great deal of it and because a little knowledge was dangerous, we were to have none at all'. He had recently taken Longfellow to see the night refuges in London. 'Thousands of immortal creatures condemned without alternative or choice to tread not what our great poet called "the primrose path to the everlasting bonfire" but one of jagged flints and stones laid down by brutal ignorance.'

It was on this visit that the idea of *A Christmas Carol* was conceived. The combination of the 'bright eyes and beaming faces' on which he had looked down at the Athenaeum soirée and the crowded, grasping atmosphere of commercial Manchester inspired Dickens. Some time during the three days he spent there the complete story flashed into his mind in a great gust of creative imagination. He finished the tale in six weeks and next spring Absalom was enjoying a dramatic adaptation at the Adelphi Theatre in London.

CHAPTER TWENTY-SEVEN

'Miss Mary Mellor came to our house with Edward to stay a few days'

New Year 1844 opened with some surprising family news.

> **January 18th, 1844.** John, who had been to see Mr Barlow, unexpectedly asked my consent to his leaving the business and giving himself up to study, in order to go to College and to become a minister!!

Mr Barlow had succeeded Mr Hornby. Absalom's astonishment is evident. It must not be assumed that John's behaviour had been any worse than most young men, but his father's surprise may have been prompted by the memory of his son's sexual lapses, which had resulted in the venereal infection when he was eighteen, perhaps because his present way of life exhibited no obvious signs of piety. By 'minister' Absalom meant a Church of England clergyman, not a dissenting pastor.

He himself worshipped where he pleased. He did not by any means always go to church on Sunday at Northenden, but when he did, he attended the parish church, not the Methodist chapel in the village. It would be unfair to attribute this to social climbing, although that may have had a conscious or unconscious part to play. If Absalom had come to appreciate the Book of Common Prayer and a fixed form of service, nevertheless his debt to the Protestant Revival of his youthful years was deep and abiding and the greatest influence for good upon his life. Narrow the chapel may have been, but it nourished his natural reverence and love of God and in so doing unintentionally freed him from the necessity of believing in any single human expression of it. As he grew older, Butler's *Lives of the Saints* came to be among his favourite reading.

The surface of his mind, however, was far from Catholic. He adhered to his own tradition and entertained no high-flown notion that clergymen of the Church of England were priests. They had retained the word it was true, but that was a mere echo from the past, a consequence of the failure of the Established Church to distance itself sufficiently from its Catholic origins.

While Manchester was being rent by the Chartists and the League, the Church of England was being torn apart by the Tractarians. The Oxford Movement had laid bare the essential ambivalence of Anglicanism. It was precisely its Catholic aspect, now so provokingly revealed and insisted upon in certain quarters, that disquieted Absalom. In May 1843 he had read a notice in the *Edinburgh Review* of a book by the High Churchman William Sewell and it had alarmed him.

> **May 23rd, 1843.** Several pages Edinburgh Review, especially the review of Sewell's Christian Morals which sets forth on behalf of 'the Church' such claims as in the darkest ages were made by the Popish Church. God help the people of England if such absurdities are to be maintained by Protestants!

John had no intention of maintaining such absurdities. Absalom consulted Mr Barlow about him and was advised that he should be sent to Oxford. That would be an expense and a totally unexpected one. As for Edward, Absalom had always thought that the boy would gain distinction in one way or another but he was too energetic, too involved in public affairs to the detriment of the warehouse and his very keenness made him insolent and impatient. He and some of his friends from the Athenaeum had agitated for a Saturday half-holiday for shops and businesses in Manchester and actually obtained general consent to the idea. The previous November some 500 warehouses including Absalom's closed at one o'clock. It was strange after all these years of having only Sunday to treasure.

The very half-holiday that Edward himself had helped to introduce meant that it was hardly worth while to go all the way into Manchester on a Saturday morning. Yet Edward seemed to think he was not energetic enough. Absalom made up his mind that he would stay in bed as long as he pleased and one Saturday in early February he did not get up until one o'clock in the afternoon.

> **February 10th, 1844.** When the boys returned from town they brought a letter from Greenwoods stating that they had sold several thousand bundles of their twist at tenpence for thirty shillings while we cannot get more than ninepence halfpenny. This made me sad, especially as Edward was as usual insolent, and altogether unable to meet this proof of his inattention.

As a magistrate, Absalom had a particular interest in the New Bailey Prison and in early March he, Mr Adshead, Edward and a friend were shown round by the governor, the appropriately named Mr Bolt.

> **March 8th, 1844.** We saw everything from the receiving-room to the solitary cells. There is evidence of good management, but from want of sufficient superintendence, after the hours of labour in the yards and day-rooms, all the evils of intercourse, of forming acquaintances and of after recognition and association must infallibly ensue. To my great surprise, Mr Adshead, from his having some time ago noticed and pointed out these evils, was considered as in some measure an objectionable person and it was stipulated by the Governor, at the instance of Lomax and H.H. Birley, the

visiting Justices, whom we happened to meet on entering, that Mr Adshead should ask no questions. Mr Bolt told me that the New Bailey was one of the healthiest gaols in the kingdom. From a remark he made, that he had just ordered two thousand pairs of stockings, I found that hitherto stockings had either been dispensed with or supplied by the friends of the prisoners. I came away <u>sad</u>, reflecting painfully on the imperfections of human justice.

Evidently criticism was not welcome. H.H. Birley had been the notorious Captain of Yeomanry at the time of Peterloo.

Northenden church, it seems, was not unaffected by the Oxford Movement.

March 24th, 1844. At church in the afternoon. I do not like the chanting which Mr Johnson has introduced. He has also put some stained glass into some of the windows and I felt pleased with this, especially when a gleam of sunshine sent the coloured lights into the church.

Edward remained insolent and the family were tormenting Absalom to add an extension to the house when he did not think the state of his business justified the expense, but one piece of luck cheered him. He bought a copy of *Statutes of the Realm* in ten volumes from Petherham's catalogue and found it was Southey's copy, complete with his notes. When the summer came the heat bothered him and sometimes he had to drag himself into Manchester.

July 26th, 1844. Extremely feeble and much depressed at the warehouse. Went at six o'clock to a meeting of the Club at Greaves'. We had at length a full meeting, Jervis coming in last. He has been to the Lakes and visited Wordsworth. Our meeting was pleasant and I returned home in good spirits and with my head full of a new set of ideas. How much have I owed during my life to the influence of the Club!

Thirty-three years had passed since its first meeting. His association with it had added blessings more continuously and with less alloy, than anything else in his life. Yet the sad question remained – what had he done more than other people? What had he achieved? If from his first starting out he had chosen a subject and stuck to it, he might have produced a learned work, become famous or done some great service to mankind.

This reflection is to me always painful and sometimes acutely painful. I am ashamed to confess, even to myself, that I have trifled with that which was no doubt given for other and higher purposes and have reached the evening of life without having accomplished even the work of the morning.

John returned from Oxford where he had been entered at St Edmund Hall.

Absalom was now one of the Auditors of Manchester Assurance Company. He had diversified his business interests for the sake of security. They were now spread between the cotton warehouse, the Commercial Bank of England and the Assurance Company, his working capital divided between property, the firm, and various investments.

At the end of July Edward and he attended a wedding that was to have momentous consequences for the family.

July 31st, 1844. Went to Failsworth to breakfast with relations and friends of Miss Mellor, who was this day married to William Dean of Haslingden. A large party, a handsome breakfast. Edward and I left about half-past twelve and went to Manchester. We returned at four and dined at Mr Mellor's. A sumptuous dinner. Mr Thomas Mellor read very well some humorous pieces.

Hannah Mellor, now Mrs Dean, was one of the daughters of Jonathan Mellor, a prosperous cotton manufacturer of Hope House, Oldham. The family was a large one. Hannah had five brothers and four sisters. From now onwards they were frequently at Rose Hill. Jonathan Mellor was a Justice of the Peace and had served as high constable in 1819, the troubled year of Peterloo. Given blank warrants by the Home Office so that he could arrest any suspected person, he had refused to use them on the ground that they were a dangerous legal weapon. A streak of obstinate integrity ran through the family. Jonathan's nephew, in after years Sir John Mellor and a distinguished judge, had refused to go to Oxford because his Unitarian convictions made him scruple to subscribe to the Thirty-Nine Articles.

That kind of fastidiousness was never in Edward's line. As secretary of the committee which eventually raised enough money to obtain Queen's, Peel's and Philip's Park for Manchester and Salford, he had been busy writing a most cogent pamphlet called *A Plea for Public Parks*, its title obviously derived from Lord John Manners's *A Plea for National Holy Days*.

Absalom thoroughly approved. However, as so often, a small matter unconnected with parks but close to his inner life, spoilt what should have been a pleasant occasion.

August 8th, 1844. Attended the public meeting on the subject of Public Walks and Gardens in Manchester. I was introduced by the Mayor to Lord Francis Egerton. I omitted to thank him for the pleasure, a great and enduring pleasure, which I have derived from his translation of Schiller's Sound of the Bell. I recollected this just after I left him and am still vexed. Lord Francis, Canon Clifton and Mark Philips were the leading speakers. There was no eloquence, but £7,000 was nevertheless subscribed in the room.

This would be about £350,000 in our terms and that such a large sum was subscribed is a tribute to the generosity of the affluent classes in Manchester.

Either the good weather or increasing prosperity had made Northenden a popular place for some of the working classes from the city to spend the day. There were limits to good will.

August 4th, 1844. Some of our apples were stolen in the afternoon and the trees broken. We have had this summer a much greater influx of rude people into the village on Sundays. The neighbourhood is much more noisy and we are much less secluded.

A few days later he had a violent gastric attack, went to bed and after a short sleep finished the life of Beau Brummel. It was a mistake to read it just then. Beau Brummel's end was too close to his own private fears and added to his basic insecurity.

August 9th, 1844. Alas! what a picture of the old age of a clever fool! The companion and almost the leader of the highest circles dying in a hospital, after enduring filth, rags, neglect and all the worst ills of poverty!

Edward was behaving with such unpardonable insolence that Absalom was thankful to see him leave for a holiday in Ireland with one of the Mellor boys. On his return Edward's friend George Wall married one of William Makinson's daughters, Edward's cousin Alice, who used to play the piano so spiritedly at their Christmas parties. The wedding breakfast was given at Rose Hill. It went off well and was hardly over before it was time for the annual soirée organized by Edward and his friends to get funds for the Athenaeum.

Edward thought that Disraeli, Lord John Manners and George Smythe would be a draw. 'Young England' in fact. But what had a Tory reform movement like Young England to do with Manchester? At first Cobden was disconcerted by Edward's suggestion and told him so. 'These Young Englanders are sad political humbugs,' he wrote to Edward, 'but nevertheless, if you think an importation of them will help the Athenaeum, I can't quarrel with your tactics.'

Cobden was unfair. His dislike of the landed aristocracy blinded him to their merits. It is true that a large number were reactionary fools, but Ashley, Russell and Althorp were aristocrats, and William Wilberforce a country gentleman. Cobden deeply resented their continued power and the fact that despite the Reform Bill the most important offices of state remained in their hands.

Young England preached a benevolent feudalism, a union of the upper and lower classes to resist the manufacturers and the radicals – that is to say, Cobden himself. It was not a political party so much as a way of looking at things, a deeply felt and sincere protest against the ugliness of contemporary England, its centralizing tendencies, its vulgar utilitarianism and its meritocracy. 'We have virtually pledged ourselves to restore what?' Lord John Manners wrote in his journal. 'I hardly know – but it is a glorious attempt.'

An air of unreality hung over the whole enterprise, unreality both in its objectives and its sweeping judgements. It was a fact that the industrial towns were hideous, a fact that they were polluted, insanitary and the focus of child labour and wage slavery. But not all manufacturers, merchants and free traders were greasy scoundrels, narrow-minded philistines, out to squeeze the last ounce from their workforce. Absalom was not, many of his friends were not. The very existence of the Athenaeum testified to the contrary.

In the event, the Manchester meeting went off very well, some consider it to have been the high-water mark of Young England's brief success. Absalom was impressed by Disraeli's speech and soon afterwards the Literary Society held a prolonged debate on 'Young England – a progress or retrogression?' Whatever the verdict arrived at in Manchester, the movement broke up the following year over the Maynooth question.

Maynooth was a Catholic college in Ireland. It was in a state of disrepair and Peel proposed to increase its meagre government grant. The idea that Englishmen should spend their money on teaching priests to say Mass and indulge in other superstitious practices outraged Protestant consciences. Over two thousand Petitions against the grant were received at Westminster and the parliamentary debates were lengthy. From the opposition benches Macaulay made a remarkable speech attacking those who opposed the grant.

When I remember what was the faith of Edward III and Henry VI, of Margaret of Anjou and Margaret of Richmond, of William of Waynefleet, of Archbishop Chicheley and Cardinal Wolsey; when I remember what we have taken from the Roman Catholics – King's College, New College, Christ Church and my own Trinity; and I look at the miserable Dotheboys Hall which we have given them in exchange, I feel, I must own, less proud than I could wish of being a Protestant and a Cambridge man.

The dream dissolved in the face of political reality. Manners supported Maynooth, Smythe took a middle line, Disraeli opposed it. A few months later Smythe supported Peel over the repeal of the Corn Laws, Manners remained with Disraeli. The glorious attempt had failed.

Local prominence had not made Edward any easier to live with. Absalom spent an entire day at Rose Hill helping to get the house ready for a dinner party his son was giving for his Athenaeum friends but the boy did not seem to be particularly grateful. However, one reason at least for Edward's extremely tiresome conduct gradually became clear. He had been courting Mary Briggs Mellor.

November 8th, 1844. Miss Mary Mellor came to our house with Edward to stay a few days, it being understood that in due time they will marry.

In due time; that was the trouble. Absalom's firm did not make sufficient profit to support both Rose Hill and the kind of establishment Mary Mellor expected and Edward hoped to be able to provide. It was frustrating for everybody, and with frustration came a sense of guilt. Absalom went to see his friends the Parkinsons, who owned a small factory near Haslingden. After going round the factory and hearing about their life, he felt acutely his own want of industry. In their early days it had been the custom of both Mr and Mrs Parkinson to work in their own factory in the dinner hour until the hands returned. By that means they made an extra £1 a day between them. Mr Parkinson now had an income of £40 a week.

Nothing can save a man from his inheritance. As the days shortened and a clammy drizzle settled on Manchester, John sent up an agonized cry from Oxford. Everything there was too much for him. He was labouring under a dark depression of spirits and one of his brothers must come at once. Edward responded immediately, setting out for Oxford as soon as the letter was received and returning two days later bringing John with him. Temperament and lack of proper grounding in the classics had caused a near breakdown.

Miss Mary Mellor came to spend Christmas with them but it was not a success. Edward was on edge. Indeed he felt so ill that he was unable to go to work. He treated Absalom with 'surpassing insolence' and once grossly insulted him in Mary's presence. John was demented with anxiety and too much study and Elizabeth began to suffer from the tic douloureux. Alfred kept them all calm by reading aloud one of Bishop Horne's sermons followed by *L'Allegro* and *Il Penseroso* but the effect did not last.

January 13th, 1845. Elizabeth is still suffering from the Tic, Mrs Watkin brawling, untidy and slatternly – the house not clean – yet a considerable expense. Edward grossly insolent.

Things were no better the next day.

January 14th, 1845. Elizabeth worse. Edward's insolent madness has caused a relapse.

Absalom thought it better not to go into Manchester.

January 15th, 1845. At home all day. Much occupied by Elizabeth. Stayed up till five in the morning to prepare the Bank accounts for the Inspectors. I have got all ready and am satisfied. Several pages Curse of Kehama aloud to Elizabeth. The measure induced sleep which she wants so very much.

He read the history of the Jesuits and John returned to Oxford. Miss Mary Mellor came again to stay but her presence once more had a bad effect upon Edward. He stayed away from work, remaining at home careless and 'brutally insolent'. It was the same all through February and Absalom felt too dispirited to attend even the Welsh dinner. The spring was dreadfully cold with a persistent east wind.

March 15th, 1845. The fields are quite brown. No corn can be sown and the laurustinuses and other tender evergreens are very much injured. I can never remember such a season.

The river froze over and the ice was nearly half an inch thick. No wonder Sir Thomas Potter died.

March 27th, 1845. Attended the funeral of Sir Thomas Potter in the Ardwick Cemetery. Nearly eighty carriages. A great concourse of people attended in spite of the rain. Poor Sir Thomas! He was in his seventy-first year and died in harness, literally worn out.

It was time for a change. In early May Absalom took his daughter to London. She needed a change too and besides he had some business to do for the bank. As always away from work, his wife and Manchester, his spirits rose and he started to enjoy himself at once.

On the day after they arrived they visited the New Royal Exchange and, of course, St Paul's and went to the Haymarket in the evening where they saw Douglas Jerrold's latest comedy followed by a burlesque of *The Golden Fleece*. Absalom learnt later that Strickland, who played the part of Professor Truffles and appeared to be in such excellent health, had died suddenly some days later. It was another jolt. 'What shadows we are,' he wrote sadly when he was back at Rose Hill.

John wanted to show them his college but made a muddle about the time of their arrival.

May 13th, 1845. We went to Oxford by the Great Western in one hour and twenty-two minutes and were kept waiting for about three hours in John's room at St Edmund Hall, the fool being out. We saw the chapel of Magdalen College, Addison's Walk, the garden of St John's, the quadrangle of Jesus, and Brazen Nose, and the interior of St Mary's church.

The long wait meant that they did not leave Oxford until eight o'clock in the evening and reached their London lodgings after midnight. What in Manchester would have prostrated Absalom he now took in his stride. They went to the play once more and to the opera, where the Queen was present, to the Coliseum, the National Gallery, the Pantheon, the Soho Square Bazaar and Hampton Court. They returned home reluctantly.

May 17th, 1845. Left London, with regret, at four in the afternoon and came in the Express Train in five hours and forty minutes to Manchester. We had in the same carriage Mr Smith, of the Bank of Manchester. He told me he was going to Jamaica to reside on his estates, to prove that free labour was cheaper than slave cultivation. He said that this was quite clear to him and that it had been proved on the Jamaica Railway, of which he is the largest shareholder. He said he could get ten cubic yards of earth removed in a day by a negro for $2. We reached Rose Hill by eleven o'clock.

In June John returned from Oxford late at night. He had passed his preliminary exam. All three of Absalom's sons were now under his roof and for a short while he felt at peace.

June 15th, 1845. It is evening as I write this, a fine evening, the birds are singing and the sweet bells are ringing. I feel all the value of such a peaceful home to an <u>old</u> man. I have thanked God for it, if such industry as I can exercise will enable me to keep it. Miss Mellor has been with us since Saturday week. James Whitelegg here at night. He and Alfred drink too much.

The future throws its own shadows. Alfred was almost twenty and had been working for some time in the firm. He had grown up to be a sociable young man with a sarcastic wit. He loved shooting, boxing, and entertaining his friends to convivial and alcoholic evenings. Absalom worked all day on his birthday but the day after did not get to Manchester until noon.

June 28th, 1845. Edward outrageously insolent. The base wretch! Employed all afternoon at the Bank. John and Alfred with me. They like wine too well. Tired and rather sad at night. Again I stayed up late.

On Sunday Mr Barlow was taken ill in the middle of the service and the congregation had to be dismissed. Fortunately John was at hand.

July 6th, 1845. John read the service at the school, and a sermon of Atterbury's, Felix Trembled. He read the sermon badly, with no expressiveness. It will be hard work to make him a good speaker.

Hannah Makinson got married.

August 12th, 1845. Went early in the morning with my wife, daughter and John to St John's church where H.M. Makinson and Mr Davies of Chester became man and wife. We went after the service to breakfast at

Joseph Makinson's. Captain and Mrs Richardson and Miss Clarke returned
with Mrs Watkin, John and William Makinson to Rose Hill and <u>spent</u> the
day with us . . .

The entry is broken off in the middle and continued in shorthand, a sure sign of
an expression of feelings, not necessarily shameful but too private to risk exposure.

Edward's outrageous insolence was easily explained and soon would be ended
for good. He was unable to marry Mary until he had found another and better-
paid position. The uncertainty of job-hunting together with the tensions of an
engagement had made him extremely difficult to live with. But his fortunes were
to improve. At the end of August he consulted Absalom about an offer he had of a
post as secretary to the newly formed Trent Valley Railway Company. His salary
would be £500 a year and he would have other advantages. Absalom advised him
to take it. He did so and was just in time to push the wheelbarrow for Sir Robert
Peel at the cutting of the first sod. It would prove to be the beginning of the line
for Edward too, the first step on the road to riches, power, a baronetage and a flag
flying proudly over Rose Hill. Now he could get married.

CHAPTER TWENTY-EIGHT

'An air of grave solemnity spread over the meeting as it drew to its close'

On 1 September 1845 Alfred went out as usual with his gun and Edward was absorbed with his wedding preparations. Absalom worked at the warehouse without them and was unexpectedly successful. The ceremony took place two days later in the church at Oldham and the breakfast was given at the bride's home at Failsworth. That meant a very early start indeed.

> **September 3rd, 1845.** Rose at four o'clock and set off at half-past five with my wife and daughter and Alfred to Failsworth. Got there at half-past seven. Soon after eight we and the other wedding people proceeded in four carriages, with postilions in red jackets and on grey horses, to Oldham, a continuous ascent of nearly four miles. There Edward and Mary Mellor were married, Mr Mellor giving her away. After breakfast, Edward and Mary left for Chester.

The festivities were not yet over. It was the custom then for the family and their guests to have a wedding dinner after the departure of the bride and groom for their honeymoon. Those who could do so remained in the house to await the meal but those who had business to attend to left and returned at the appropriate time. Either way, the arrangements do not seem to have been very convenient. Leaving his wife and daughter at Failsworth, Absalom returned to Manchester with Alfred and some other male guests. No wonder Absalom was tired. Edward and Mary had rented a house in the neighbourhood.

> I was quite unwell but got some coffee and made myself up so as to be able to go to Failsworth with Alfred by three o'clock to partake of the wedding dinner. We dined pleasantly and I enjoyed it, although Mr Mellor was in pain and there was an air of abstraction in the countenances of all the young men. After dinner we went to look at Edward's house, which is spacious and well furnished. We then went into the garden of Mr H . . . , his landlord, who lives in a very large house nearby. I never saw a large and well arranged garden in such a state of neglect. The whole is overrun with weeds, the

growth of years. The fruit trees are quite wild, the glass has been sold from one of the grapehouses and all is shattered in the other. Both are falling to pieces from neglect; the vines hang as they may. The old man, with two sons and an old woman servant, live in one or two rooms of the large house, in the style of Jacques Ferrard, spending about twenty shillings a week. Here is a character for romance!

Edward and Mary had a week's honeymoon and the day after their return Edward started work in the office of the Trent Valley Railway. However, that did not mean the end of the festivities even now. The Sunday after they got back a party of Mellors descended on Rose Hill to continue the celebrations. Edward and Mary came, and three of Mary's brothers together with two of her sisters. By this time Absalom had at last increased his permanent domestic staff and was employing two Welsh and one English girl to help in the house. Nevertheless, the Mellors had high standards and more assistance was needed to do the thing properly.

September 14th, 1845. Edward, Thomas and Jonathan Mellor, Hester and Harriet Mellor, with Edward and Mary, spent the day with us, all going to church in the forenoon in wedding costume. James Whitelegg also dined with us. We had a cook and a waiter besides Martha, Jane and Catherine, with some help from the Battersbys and so contrived to present a good dinner in the correct style.

Edward and Mary returned to their own home on Monday morning and on that day Absalom began to reap the benefits of his new railway connections. It was a jungle that Absalom would have been most unwise to have entered without Edward's advice, but on his recommendation he had accepted an offer to become a director of the Oxford, Newbury, Andover, Manchester and Southampton Railway.

The railway boom was at its chaotic height. Speculators were pouring in money, companies springing up everywhere, and lines being constructed so fast that the map of England was being covered with little black threads. Central planning was as yet an alien concept and government control minimal. What a company had to do was to attract investors, then submit a claim to the Board of Trade arguing the case for the construction of the proposed line. Each claim was examined by a parliamentary committee to which MPs were appointed. At first there were literally hundreds of such claims and this year there might be as many as twenty or thirty separate Commons railway committees sitting at the same time in London. The legal costs were enormous, the competition sharp and merciless.

As far as can be gathered, none of the Makinsons had been at Edward's wedding, so Absalom may have wished to make it up to them. William Makinson lived at Lime Place, Broughton, and he visited him there and saw William's daughter, Alice, now Mrs Wall, and her new baby. He then invited Joseph and one of his daughters to Rose Hill.

September 26th, 1845. Assiduous till noon at the warehouse. Returned home at half-past one, taking with me Joseph Makinson and his daughter Elizabeth. At Rose Hill we found Mr and Mrs Hedley, Mrs Makinson and her daughters, Hannah and Mary, and Mr and Mrs Shuttleworth. They dined with us and in order to give them a dinner had besides our two Welsh helps and Martha, a hired cook and a waiter!!! Five helps because nine persons pay us a visit! After all this the house was dirty and all in a state of Irish untidiness except the rooms we occupied.

On Sunday he went to church.

September 27th, 1845. Received the Sacrament and prayed that health and energy might be given to me, to enable me to perform my duty and to endure the labour to which I am doomed. William Henry Mellor and James Whitelegg got tea with us.

This is the first mention of another of Mary's brothers, William Henry, who under the brief designation 'W.H. Mellor' was to play such an equivocal part in the life of Absalom's daughter. She and her mother were planning a large evening party.

October 15th, 1845. Assiduous at the warehouse. Our 'great' evening party. It began at five. We had music and dancing, supper and a good deal of chat and so 'th' night drew an wi sangs and clatter' and it was troublesome and I was glad when this was at an end. Jonathan and W.H. Mellor left us soon after four in the morning and I went to bed and got up about seven and was in town by about nine.

It was now time for the annual soirée at the Athenaeum, which this year was held at the Free Trade Hall. This was the second Free Trade Hall, a brick building with three galleries whose fronts were draped with crimson velvet embossed with a design in gold representing a wheatsheaf inscribed with the word 'free'. The hall was lit by immense gas jets underneath which grids had been built in the floor so as to admit cold air and to carry off any unpleasant affluvia. Behind the chairman's seat an enormous transparency had been erected bearing a single word – Justice.

A few days after the soirée, the League assembled in the hall for a mass protest rally. That year an exceptionally fine June had been followed by a sunny July. Prentice and others of the League who slept with one eye on the barometer were disappointed. There would be an ample harvest for the third year running and once more Peel would not be forced to act. Then in August the rains came and in September the dreaded potato blight. The tubers rotted in the ground and four million Irish peasants faced starvation.

It was not for nothing that Daniel O'Connell had given the Prime Minister the nickname 'Orange Peel'. As Chief Secretary for Ireland Peel had displayed a narrow Protestant provincialism. He had no liking for the Irish – no understanding of their religion, temperament or way of life, least of all their national aspirations.

Yet he was a man who loved justice and hated iniquity. As Prime Minister he had been conciliatory towards Ireland and taken the trouble to use government funds to set up a Royal Commission on the land question and to encourage education, both Catholic and non-sectarian. Now, with starvation staring millions in the face, he said he could not in conscience continue to impose duties on imported foodstuffs. In fact, the failure of the potato crop with its consequent starvation had little in itself to do with free trade or the repeal of the Corn Laws. Most of the Irish peasantry lived on potatoes because their small holdings were not suitable for producing corn. The repeal of the Corn Laws was an irrelevance to those who had no money to buy bread whatever its price and no means of milling cereals had they been offered free. Peel had been moving against protection for British agriculture for some time, the famine gave him the opportunity he needed.

On 3 December, a few days after the Manchester rally, Lord Aberdeen leaked some Cabinet discussions to *The Times*, which duly reported that the Government definitely intended to repeal the Corn Laws. This was not quite correct. Peel had failed to gain the support of all his Cabinet colleagues for repeal, and two days later he resigned. For ten days Lord John Russell struggled to form an alternative administration but failed in the attempt. 'I am going to see the Queen,' Peel wrote in agitation to Wellington. 'I shall return from Windsor as her Minister.' So was the Conservative party split.

It is impossible to understand the deep feelings the Corn Laws aroused or the bitterness provoked by their repeal if they are thought of as a measure undertaken solely to safeguard the pockets of farmers and landowners. The truth was very much more complex. Good and sincere people really believed that the social and constitutional stability of England depended upon the land, and if the status and prosperity of the landowning classes were undermined the country would fall into ruin and anarchy. This was the reason why the issue was debated with such passionate zeal and why Peel's tactics occasioned the same kind of anger and shame that some people felt after Chamberlain's agreement with Hitler at Munich.

That Christmas only W.H. Mellor spent the day at Rose Hill with the family. It becomes plain that Elizabeth was in love with Mellor and that rightly or wrongly she believed he had given her grounds for thinking he would marry her. However, he left Rose Hill without coming up to scratch and the poor girl became so unwell that it was thought she might benefit from the cold-water treatment. Under Alfred's protection she started out for Dr McLeod's fashionable hydropathic establishment at Ben Rhydding, near Otley in Yorkshire.

Edward had left Failsworth and was now living at Woodlands Cottage, Upper Broughton, undoubtedly one of his father's houses and perhaps even his old home. There Absalom dined with Edward and Mary for the first time since their marriage

and the party was joined by Mary's parents. The entry was concluded in
shorthand. Probably he was told that Mary was expecting a child.

Absalom felt pressed. Elizabeth returned home only a little better for the cure
and W.H. Mellor started to visit them again. So did Edward and Mary, her sister
Hester, and Mr and Mrs Dean, and all the time he wanted to get on with an article
for the *Manchester Examiner* on the battles of Moodki and Ferozepore. John arrived
home for the Easter vacation and Absalom had to speak to him about his
expenditure. The interview did not go well. 'He is a selfish, insolent, and
ungrateful boy.'

It was now six months since the effects of the potato blight had been revealed.
Peel had imported maize from the United States and set up a Relief Commission.
A special Scientific Inquiry had printed elaborate instructions explaining how
starch could be extracted from diseased potatoes and the Duke of Norfolk
suggested that the peasantry should follow the example of the Indians and live on
curry powder mixed with water. On 1 April 1846 Absalom attended a committee
to relieve distress and hoped he 'had done something to lessen the sufferings of
those poor people'. Unfortunately, those poor people were the victims of a
multiplicity of forces quite beyond the financial and imaginative capacity of the
British Government to cope with.

Absalom's railway venture was causing him unexpected anxiety.

April 3rd, 1846. Richard Birley asked me for £210 as my share of the
expenses of the projected Oxford, Andover etc. Railway of which I
consented in September to become a Director, being assured by Mr Atherton
that there were 'no duties, and would be no responsibilities.'

Night after night he sat up reading until the small hours then fell asleep and after
a while stumbled up to bed or was found by the servants asleep in his chair when
they came to open the shutters. No wonder he felt irritable and unwell, harassed
and anxious. 'What a fool I am. How dangerous are bad habits.' Good Friday was
spent on his accounts. His property was diminishing. His wife was foolish, his
daughter was foolish and W.H. Mellor seemed never to leave them. Some
Northenden vagabond shot a corncrake and Alfred drank too much. But the
swallows arrived, the cuckoo called and towards the end of May he dined with
Edward at Broughton.

May 22nd, 1846. After dinner walked with him and S.P. Robinson. We
went over Kersal Moor to Agecroft Bridge into Drinkwater's Grounds and
returned through Whit Lane and over the Suspension Bridge. To my great
surprise, I found the house in which my uncle lived in Whit Lane had been
pulled down, all the trees removed and the garden so completely destroyed
that I could with difficulty identify the spot. I was told that a coal pit had
been sunk on the site of the house and filled up again because it did not

answer. When we got over the Suspension Bridge and began to go up the road to Camp Street I met with a surprise of another kind. What I had left a scarcely passable road had become an excellently kept street with elegantly built, tasteful houses and suitable gardens on each side. It looked like a London suburb.

The coal pit had been sunk by John Purcell FitzGerald, the father of the translator of Omar Khayyám, who lost a considerable sum of money in the venture.

On 25 June the third reading of Peel's Bill for the reduction of all duties on cereals to a nominal sum was carried after five months' debate. That same evening a combination of Protectionists and dissident Tories led by Bentinck and Disraeli defeated the Government over an Irish Coercion Bill. Peel resigned and the Conservative party was broken. A general election did not follow. For the remainder of the life of that Parliament, Lord John Russell headed a Whig government.

While Peel's administration was still hanging on its slender thread at Westminster, John returned home for the long vacation. Some Mellors were still at Rose Hill and the pressure of people combined with the unusually hot weather caused Absalom to feel hurried and full of 'nervous imbecility'. 'Alas,' he wrote three days before his birthday, 'I am old and <u>poor</u>.' His spirits had not improved when the day came.

June 27th, 1846. My birthday, fifty-nine. At home all day. Mr Grime's accounts. Spent about an hour clearing the Sherston field of thistles. Better for the exercise. Went with my wife and Hester Mellor to the top of Northen church tower. The view is very pretty; Macclesfield to the south and the vale of Cheshire westward. There is a great deal of wood everywhere. I am <u>old</u>.

In July he went to the last meeting of the Council of the Anti-Corn Law League in Manchester Town Hall. Prentice felt the occasion deeply and wrote

An air of grave solemnity had spread over the meeting as it drew to its close. There were five hundred gentlemen who had often met together during the great contest, and notwithstanding their exultation over a victory achieved, the feeling stole over their minds that they were never to meet again.

Absalom was particularly pleased with Cobden's speech. If Peel had lost office, Cobden said, he had gained a country. 'For my part I would rather descend into private life with that last measure of his . . . than mount to the highest pinnacle of human power.' Cobden was seconded by Bright and the active operation of the League was halted.

They had not achieved precisely the 'total and immediate' repeal the League had always demanded, so it was not altogether dissolved. The fear remained that the protectionist party might yet prevent the final extinction of the Corn Laws at the end of the three years Peel proposed, so a contingency fund was set aside. Vast sums had been given to the League and the name, place and business of each donor was carefully listed by Prentice.

It was then decided to give a silver tea and coffee service of some 240 ounces to certain very active members of the executive council and to open a subscription for both Cobden and Bright to be contributed to by free traders throughout the Kingdom. Because he had devoted all his time to the League, Cobden's business was almost bankrupt. Eventually he received the then enormous sum of £75,000 and Bright was presented with £5,000 which he spent on a splendid library. Cobden now reminded them that they were under obligations to the Queen, who was said to have favoured their cause, and the meeting ended with three hearty cheers in Her Majesty's honour. They should in fact have cheered Prince Albert.

Whatever Absalom said about his health, when he was doing what he liked his energy was still extraordinary. The proceedings in the Town Hall over, he left with Edward.

July 2nd, 1846. Dined at Edward's to met Elihu Burritt, the American blacksmith who is said to know fifty languages. A queer looking, cheerful, not assuming man. Sat up till four writing an article on the month of June for the Examiner.

The bank still absorbed a great deal of his time. The directors took to drinking champagne and judging from the frequency of the shorthand entries, sometimes imbibed too much. One Saturday Absalom took the chair at a meeting to establish ragged schools in Manchester, then came home to find that W.H. Mellor had arrived uninvited. On Sunday, his great day of rest, they had more visitors. George Wall had decided to become a tea planter.

July 18th, 1846. At home all day. George Wall, Alice, their child and its nurse came in the forenoon and stayed till eight. A farewell visit previous to his going to Ceylon. Much tired.

He needed a rest and poured his heart out into his diary.

July 31st, 1846. I close this month with much depression. Business is precarious. Dean is sending part of his cloth to J.B. Lee. I have so much lessened my property that I am not now worth more than £3,000, if so much. This is in part occasioned by my expenditure upon John, and the ungrateful wretch thinks every trifling help that I ask from him too much. Had I foreseen, or could I have imagined, such selfish ingratitude, he should never have gone to Oxford at my expense. I must toil and I will bear up as well as I can till my sixtieth year is completed. Then, I think, I shall give it up and living upon as little as possible, endeavour to make my property last at least as long as my life and that of my wife, with some provision for Elizabeth.

Next Monday he could not bring himself to go to work.

August 3rd, 1846. A close, wet August day, such as that I so well remember in August 1821, on which I went with Grime and Philip Wood to look at the land on which we afterwards built in Broughton. A few pages Life of Frederick – nicknamed 'the great'. He ended as he deserved to end, miserably. I rode a little further than Mr Sumner's on Elizabeth's pony 'Nut'. To my surprise I was quite timid and could not canter. My nerves are obviously out of order. I read too much and sleep too little.

August 14th, 1846. Consulted Mr Smith, the surgeon, at the desire of Edward. He tells me what I know, that I want rest, and advises relaxation and sea air.

No wonder Edward recommended the celebrated Mr Smith; he had just consulted him himself. Edward was paying the price for his unusual energy, drive and determination to succeed. In the spring of that year the Trent Valley Railway was sold for the very large sum of £438,000 to the London, Birmingham and Grand Junction Companies then about to amalgamate under the name of the London and North Western. As secretary, Edward was entrusted with the winding up of the company and he had to balance the books and pay off shareholders. The task was onerous and he was foolish enough to work for days on end without sufficient sleep or regular meals. One afternoon a shareholder called for his cheque. Still chatting to him, Edward started to make it out. What happened next he described later: 'As I was making the upstroke of the letter H in "Houldsworth", I felt as if my whole body was forced into my head and that it was ready to burst. I thought, how strange! I tried again, the same feeling came again and again, till, with a face as white as paper, that alarmed those about me, I fell forward on the desk. Water was given me, but I could not swallow it, I never lost entire consciousness but I thought I was going to die.'

He was put into a carriage and taken at once to the consulting rooms of Mr Smith in Mosley Street. Rest was prescribed, but rest was utterly alien to Edward's temperament. For the moment all he could do was to try to cut down his work and take the opportunity of Absalom's own exhaustion to enjoy two days away together.

Their relationship had altered. They were neither the father and son who together had picked anemones at Prestwich Clough nor the acrimonious business rivals of Manchester High Street. Time and Edward's particular gifts meant that it was now he who guided Absalom.

August 15th, 1846. Left with Edward by rail for Fleetwood. A pleasant journey of three hours and a half. The walk along the shore is pleasant and the sea breeze dry and agreeable. We walked a good deal, read Boswell's Johnson and were in bed by eleven.

He slept well and got up at eight next morning.

August 16th, 1846. After breakfast we walked to Rossall Point and back, being out nearly three hours. After dinner we crossed the Wyre and rambled a mile or two in the opposite side inland. As we returned we met numbers of the country people, not dirty, but with coarse features 'with foreheads villainous low!' Many of the men were drunk and two or three accosted us rudely. These people will be improved by the growth of Fleetwood. We recrossed the river on our return, and as the boat tilted a little from the state of the tide Edward, who is far from well, could not keep down an involuntary agitation of his nerves. After tea, which was very pleasant, we had another stroll. Then we smoked a cigar on the leads in front of our room and read several pages of Boswell and retired to rest about eleven. I slept very well. Edward did not.

They returned next morning and two days later, close to the anniversary of Peterloo, Edward's son was born.

Hester Mellor came again to stay at Rose Hill and as usual on 1 September, Alfred spent the day shooting partridge for the table.

September 4th, 1846. Dinner party. At dinner at five we had Kershaw, Spencer, Greaves, William Makinson and Miss H.A. Mellor. [Hester] We had a nondescript soup, turbot, roast beef, stewed veal, plum pudding, partridges, jellies and custards, with a tolerable dessert. Ann waited badly and spilled the gravy and threw down the forks and the tout ensemble was unsatisfactory, but we got through it with not more than the usual amount of blundering. They left at half-past ten.

Entertaining spoilt him for work.

September 5th, 1846. Rose late, did not go to town till half-past twelve. Several pages Soyer's Gastronomic Regenerator. The book of a most self-satisfied Frenchman. No Englishman could have written it. Fell asleep in the kitchen and did not go to bed till five.

An awkwardness arose at a meeting of the Manchester Assurance Company when the chairman accused Absalom of neglecting his duty as auditor. He defended himself and spent the afternoon at the Bank where he drank four glasses of wine, ostensibly to prevent a cold he felt coming, but more likely to rally his spirits. A few days later he had to be up early in order to join Mr Fildes and others on an expedition to inspect some mills at Stalybridge.

September 10th, 1846. I was struck by the number of factories, the increase of such erections, the evident enterprise shown in the buildings, roads, and railways finished and in progress, and as much as anything with the volume of smoke which obscured the whole country. I should not like to live in such a place, or with such people. I found Mary, the nurse and the baby at our house when I got home.

They were there because the next day was the one appointed for the child's christening.

CHAPTER TWENTY-NINE

'There is no greater honour a man can desire than that of being the unbought representative of such a constituency as Manchester'

Swarms of Mellors arrived and Absalom looked upon the party with mixed feelings.

September 11th, 1846. At three we went to the church and the little boy was christened by Mr Barlow. Alfred and Jonathan Mellor and my daughter being godfathers and godmother. He was named Alfred Mellor. At half-past five eighteen of us sat down to dinner. We had a waiter, a cook, Mrs Battersby, Margaret, Hannah, besides Ann, and so at enormous expense we had a good and profuse dinner, tolerably well served and very prettily put on the table. Our guests did justice to the viands and to the wine, taking champagne freely, but there was no conversation such as I like. They left about eleven and I got to bed about three.

He was quite knocked up next morning, did not get to the warehouse until late and then had to go on to a committee meeting about the Juvenile Refuge and the School of Industry. After all that he stayed up again almost to sunrise savouring the *Antiquities of Syon Abbey*.

Edward and Mary and the baby came to stay for a fortnight. So many in the house got on Absalom's nerves and he was tired of begging subscriptions in Manchester for the Juvenile Refuge, although people gave willingly enough. He found himself getting unexpectedly fond of his grandson.

October 13th, 1846. At home all day. W.H. Mellor here. Edward and Mary and their son who have been here for a fortnight, left this morning. It is surprising how fond of the child his grandmother has become. Even I feel attached to him and felt some pain when he was taken away. The dawn of intelligence in this child of seven weeks old has interested me.

It would soon be six years since the election that resulted in Peel's taking office.

The life of that Parliament, led by the Whigs after Peel's defeat, was coming to an end. A General Election would take place next year and Absalom began to think about a speech he had been asked to deliver in support of John Bright's selection as MP for Manchester in place of the retiring Mark Philips.

Despite their difference of opinion over factory legislation, in some ways Bright was more to Absalom's mind than Cobden. A Quaker, he was a religious man in the sense understood by Absalom, Gladstone and Newman, but not by those who give mere conventional assent to the life of the spirit. It was this that made him unusual, not his constant harping on the moral basis for political action, commonplace enough and the stock in trade of every political leader.

The victory of the League had not been enough for Bright. A single, important battle had been won, the balance of political power, it was hoped, had shifted irreversibly to the middle classes, but other battles remained to be fought before the existing social structures were sufficiently modified. It remained to make effective the doctrines of the so-called Manchester School, to press forward with free trade, reduced taxation, the extension of the franchise, a cheaper, non-expansionist foreign policy and the rejection of legislative interference with labour in favour of self-regulating employers.

Yet the Manchester School was more of an attitude than a programme. Some took up one reforming cause, some another. Bright was now less interested in free trade than in extending the suffrage. He felt even more deeply antagonistic towards the aristocracy than Cobden. Throughout the Corn Law struggle he accepted class strife as inevitable; the aristocracy had to be overthrown if the manufacturing interest was to remain secure. But in 1848 he deplored the revival of Chartism and the class violence it engendered. The only way the workers could improve their condition was by industry, frugality and temperance.

By no means all the liberal manufacturing party in Manchester trusted him. He was forthright, unpredictable and not altogether safe. Represented now by the next generation, the Potters had contributed to Bright's election expenses when he had stood successfully for Durham. Now they withdrew their support. Bright was in any case not a Manchester man and they considered he had become obsessive in his support for the League by insisting upon the total abolition of the Corn Laws instead of accepting a small fixed duty.

Gradualism had become the creed of the *Manchester Guardian*, now bereft of Absalom's friend, J.E. Taylor, and Bright labelled his opponents the 'Guardian Party'. They proposed to put up another candidate, the aristocratic, highly respected Lord Lincoln, son of the Duke of Newcastle. So were the liberals split. Bright's representation of Manchester started with controversy, it would end in his rejection.

Absalom started to write his speech in the middle of November.

November 17th, 1846. This evening there was a beautiful manifestation of the Aurora Borealis, but without any streaming, ascending rays. It was so light that I could discern the hour by my watch. I wrote, after I came home, part of a speech to be delivered tomorrow at the Free Trade Hall, when I am desired to second the nomination of John Bright as representative of Manchester in Parliament. I stayed up very late and was tired and troubled by pain in my teeth and the bones of my face.

The next day plans were altered.

November 18th, 1846. At noon the committee sent word that I should have to propose John Bright, instead of seconding the nomination. I sat down to add to what I had written and brought it to a close at six in the evening. I then went to the Free Trade Hall. There I delivered, with tolerable assurance, as much as I could remember of what I had written and nominated Mr Bright. Alderman Baird seconded the nomination. The meeting unanimously concurred. We were sent to bring him upon the platform.

What happened next was typical of the rough and tumble of public life, but it was just the sort of thing to cause a man of Absalom's temperament the utmost disquiet. When he first came to Manchester his uncle had told him that he needed his face 'rubbing with a brick'. The boy was the man. He had come forward to support Bright and should have expected to have been set upon by the opposing party.

November 21st, 1846. The warehouse till near three. My teeth and face painful. The Guardian has attacked my speech, accusing me of mocking and insulting Lord Ebrington.

Viscount Ebrington, son of Earl Fortescue and the MP for Plymouth, had been one of the guests at the Athenaeum's October soirée. He had been unexpectedly called upon to speak, and surprised and embarrassed apparently made rather a fool of himself. Absalom had started his speech proposing Bright by saying that he himself was no leveller, that he knew how many reforming measures had originated in the Upper House. Having made that observation, he went on to enjoy himself by jeering at the supposed advantages that would accrue to Manchester by having a member of the aristocracy to represent it. This of course, was a reference to the candidature of Lord Lincoln, but Absalom seems to have seized upon Lord Ebrington's unfortunate performance at the Athenaeum to illustrate his point. 'Great is the advantage of a title,' he had said, 'like charity it covers a multitude of sins.'

Its possessor is gratuitously supposed to possess education, hereditary legislative ability, and above all, a courtly grace, manner and style of speaking which no ordinary man could ever hope to obtain. (Laughter). If a scion of the aristocracy or nobility appears among us and speaks for half an hour on some public occasion, uttering but the merest commonplaces and speaking in such a manner that at every sentence you are in fear lest he should not find words to construct another . . .

Here the speech was interrupted by roars of laughter and cheers, caused, according to reporters, by Absalom mimicking the tones and hesitating manner of the noble lord who had spoken recently at the Athenaeum soirée.

then some newspaper editors, or some gentlemen to whose lady the nobleman has addressed a compliment, conceives a most exaggerated idea of his magnificent ability and publishes it as a certain and most undoubted truth that he is the very man to represent this borough. How should a man rocked and dandled into a legislator be competent to understand the feelings, wants, and wishes of a community – struggling, endeavouring, labouring and rising – such as ours?

The *Guardian*'s editorial rebuke was severe. How could the proposer of Mr Bright, a gentleman whose years should have taught him a little courtesy and discretion, have made the noble lord's very natural and excusable hesitation a subject of mockery and insult in a most palpable and unmistakable manner?

Absalom should have congratulated himself. He had drawn blood. His style as a speaker plainly was not that of the diarist. But the sensitivity of the diarist prevailed. He was very upset.

November 24th, 1846. Much talk on Change today about the Guardian's attack on me. I heard myself warmly assailed and as warmly defended.

November 25th, 1846. Urged to reply to the Guardian. Wrote with difficulty. Pain in the bones of the face.

It would have been wiser to have left the matter alone but next day he made another attempt at reply and neglected his business. It may be that he found his task difficult because he had a bad conscience. His was a mocking spirit and he had a sharp eye for absurdities as long as they were not his own. One of his sons was a clever mimic. Lord Ebrington must have been a tempting target.

November 26th, 1846. Too much occupied by the preparation and correction of my reply to the Guardian. I wish I had never meddled with the election of Mr Bright.

He could have put his time to better use. The business community in Manchester was in a nervous state. That year's cereal harvest had failed throughout

Western Europe. American and Russian wheat had to be imported and as a consequence the price rose considerably and was still rising. Just at this moment the American cotton crop failed, the price of raw cotton rose and an industry which accounted for half of Britain's exports found itself in difficulties. On Change that December Absalom found an uncertainty in the market that fuelled his ever-present forebodings.

However much he may have regretted involving himself in Bright's election as their parliamentary candidate, Absalom had started and had to go on. A week before Christmas he attended a meeting of Bright's Committee at Hayward's Hotel and made a speech which was almost immediately attacked by the *Courier*. Absalom was sick of it. He wrote a short, *sharp* letter to the editor and left it at that. His family were closing in, putting pressure upon him to celebrate Christmas more lavishly than he felt inclined. Still a free man, the first to arrive was W.H. Mellor who tactfully kept Absalom quiet by reading aloud two parts of Dicken's *Battle of Life*. On Christmas Eve Edward came to stay with his family and Absalom grumbled because the child slept in their bedroom and gave him a disturbed night. Rose Hill was still far from being the large, ostentatious house Edward was one day to make it. But crowded as they must have been, it is strange that the baby had to sleep with his grandparents and not with his nurse.

On New Year's Day 1847 Absalom wrote a letter to his daughter. Possibly Elizabeth was away, but since Mellor arrived to stay on 2 January, it is more likely that Absalom wished to give her some advice that he felt was too delicate to give to her face. Whatever the truth, W.H. Mellor stayed for four days and escaped unscathed yet again. Absalom wound himself up to take stock. The result was bad. *He must retrench or be ruined.* However, the Commercial Bank of England's affairs seemed at last to be coming to an end.

> **February 10th, 1847.** The Annual Meeting of the shareholders of the Commercial Bank of England held at the Queen's Hotel. We passed all our resolutions and were praised. After discussion the sum of £2,000 was voted to the Directors – £750 to Mr Fildes and £750 to myself, the remaining £500 to the others. As wages this is very inadequate, as an <u>acknowledgement</u> it is gratifying. It comes also just when I want it to make up my losses, and <u>now, I must now, be careful</u>.

Absalom seems to have been disappointed, yet his 'wages' represent something like £37,500 in today's values.

As the spring advanced, Absalom became active in the garden, sowing sweet peas at the roots of the plum trees, nasturtiums, then blue currant and yellow holly by the steps on the terrace.

> **March 10th, 1847.** At home all day. We shall be more forward with our work in the garden this year than I ever remember to have been. Mary and

the nurse and baby still here. I don't know why but they hinder me. In part I believe because they give Mrs Watkin a sort of apology for neglecting other things that she may play the fool with her grandson.

The house was swamped by Mellors.

March 11th, 1847. Late and imbecile. Mrs Dean and Miss Mellor dined with us, Mary being still here. I did not get home till they had left, with the exception of Miss Mellor who stayed all night, much to my annoyance as I wished to be alone, and yet she is so ladylike that I was vexed with myself.

He was so interested in Cellini's *Autobiography* that he stayed up 'like an ass' reading until daylight. On 24 March the nation held a Day of Fasting to atone for the sins which had caused the Irish famine and to pray for its relief. Absalom recorded the fact without comment. Not so Queen Victoria, who considered the practice out of date and superstitious. We were no more sinful now than we were when the potato plant flourished. Easter was early that year.

April 2nd, 1847. Good Friday. In bed till near one. Not well and much depressed fearing the loss of our business and frightened by our profuse expenditure. Edward and Mary and the child here. In my present state of irritation they trouble me. Stayed up very late and slept badly, little Alfred being in our bed. The ground covered with snow.

In May John wrote to say that he had passed his final exams at Oxford. A few days later Absalom and his wife left Rose Hill at five in the morning to go to London. They were joined there by Edward and Mary. Hester Mellor was in London too, staying with her first cousin, John Mellor, who was a successful barrister, soon to be appointed a Queen's Counsel and Recorder of Warwick.

The London Absalom was quite a different person from the Manchester man. He and his wife called for Hester and took her to the theatre and to see the sights, including St Paul's where Absalom was again disgusted by the naked figures. He was full of energy.

May 10th, 1847. In the morning I went to the Pantheon and the Soho Bazaar, thence with my wife and Mary to the National Gallery where we met Edward and went with him to the House of Lords but unable from the crowd to get into any but the unfinished Committee rooms in which the Railway Committees were sitting. After dinner Mrs Watkin and Mary and I went by the railway to Greenwich. In the evening to the Coliseum where we met Edward, Mrs J. Mellor, Thomas, Jonathan and Hester Mellor. We saw all that is to be seen, had some champagne and indulged in a Sherry Cobbler.

They went to the Flower Show, the Opera and Hampton Court, Absalom's wife walked in the Park 'to hunt the Queen' and succeeded in getting a sight of her; they visited Greenwich again and saw the coat and waistcoat in which Nelson was killed at Trafalgar, and paid a last visit to Sadler's Wells. Absalom was happy and in good health but it was all coming to an end.

May 15th, 1847. Went in the forenoon to Regent Street with my wife and Mary. We had some coffee, ice and liqueurs at Verry's, the confectioner in Regent Street and made some purchase of various things. At half-past four we left London by the Express Train and reached Stockport at half-past ten.

He woke up next morning with a headache. He had no appetite and was irritable and 'quite the reverse of the state in which I was while in London'. John returned from Oxford and poor Mr Grime troubled Absalom even from the grave. His will was complicated, his affairs involved, the accounting most tedious. The day before Absalom's sixtieth birthday the Trent Valley Railway Line was opened by Sir Robert Peel.

June 26th, 1847. Left Rose Hill early in the morning for Stockport and thence by rail to Tamworth, along the Trent Valley Line, to be present at the celebration of the opening. About five hundred persons sat down at two o'clock to a splendid déjeuner in a large building run up for the purpose and hung with pink and white calico and ornamented with evergreens and flags. We also had a military band.

The great attraction was Sir Robert Peel and his speech was, of course, the speech of the day and I was much pleased. He has a gentle, manly bearing and carried his head well; his features are good, the mouth being well-formed and the eye not bright, yet not dull. He seems to smile habitually, but the lines of care, and as I thought of cunning, are very visible in his countenance. His voice is good, his utterance extremely distinct and his sentences well formed. I was told by Mr Tootal that he (Sir Robert Peel) had had some days' notice and that he made a few notes, so that his speech could not be called unpremeditated. The allusions he made to the ancient state of Tamworth and to Ethelfreda, the sister of Alfred, as well as his closing eulogy of the Queen, all seemed to have been pre-arranged.

Hudson, a greasy-butcher-looking fellow, with a tremendous bump of self-esteem, made an attempt at a speech and behaved very badly, talking frequently while others were speaking. I enjoyed this day very much.

Three weeks later Absalom had to entertain the Board of the Commercial Bank of England at Rose Hill.

July 15th, 1847. The warehouse till noon and then returned to Rose Hill with H.M. [Mrs Davies]. <u>Board Dinner</u>. Fildes, Johnson, Dr Ogden and Robinson dined with us. At the cost of two bottles of excellent champagne, one of Lacrima Christi, some port and sherry and a good dinner, I kept them all in good humour and old Johnson became quite juvenile. I got a headache and put my stomach somewhat out of order.

The truth was that he was worried. The General Election was now at hand and he was expected to second Bright's nomination. He prepared his speech carefully. It took him two evenings and in view of what was to happen later, some of it reads a little ironically.

In electing Mr Bright you will return a Member peculiarly fitted for the work he has to do. In electing him you will confer upon him the highest honour the people can bestow upon one of themselves, for there is no greater honour a man can desire than that of being the unbought representative of such a constituency as Manchester. You will elevate him to a degree of importance and influence in the House of Commons proportionate to the wealth and independence of this great constituency; you will give him a distinguished place among the representatives of the people, and he will enter the House of Commons unfettered by any pledges, but guided by known principles and strict integrity, prepared to battle with the enemies of the people and anxious to effect social and political improvements.

The excitement of composition again quite knocked him up.

July 29th, 1847. Rose in good time and went to Manchester to second the nomination of John Bright, who was proposed by George Wilson on the hustings in St Ann's Square. There was a very large assemblage and some of the people were very noisy. I delivered what I had written, but very little of it could be heard except by those immediately near me. Also I spoke too fast, and when I had finished I began as usual to doubt the fitness and propriety of what I had written and wish it unsaid. Instead of the well-considered speech of a man, it appeared to me to be the declamation of a schoolboy. I wait to learn what will be thought of it when it is printed.

Despite the noise, the seat was not contested. Milner-Gibson and Bright were the only candidates after all, so the Mayor declared them duly elected. Bright was true to form. His views about factory legislation were not to the taste of a band of operatives, who created a disturbance in front of the hustings. 'I am not afraid,' he shouted above the uproar

to meet any portion of the inhabitants of this town; I have never deceived you, I have never flattered you, I owe you nothing but for the good opinion of me which you have manifested. You owe me nothing, but that I have endeavoured to do something in your service. I should be ashamed to stand here if I did not believe that I am the representative, not only of the electors of Manchester, but of the interests of the vast majority of the working population of this town.

Undeterred by the noise of the crowd, whose surge forward had broken a barrier, Bright went on to defend his action in refusing to support the Ten Hours Bill, and then attacked the recent creation of the Bishopric of Manchester in words which, however true, few candidates today would dare to employ.

I never yet saw any good that the bishops did; I have seen the multitudinous mischiefs that the bishops have done. I believe that hierarchies, state-manufactured clergies, are in themselves evils, and that the time will come when they will be no more known on the face of the earth than some of those great creatures of which we have remnants left, which lived before the Flood.

Absalom's relations with Edward may have been transformed for the better, but things were far otherwise with John. Soon the age-long complaints and the stored-up resentments of a child against his parents exploded in an unpleasant letter which annoyed Absalom considerably.

July 31st, 1847. Worked hard till near four. Returned home and attended to some notices which I had to prepare as Overseer of the Poor, relating to the registration of voters. Walked with Mrs Davies. Concluded A Whim and its Consequences but stayed up very late like a fool. Today I got an impudent letter from John, accusing me of bad conduct in my expenses and bidding me retrench, as if he were master. The blockhead.

Like Edward before him, John had touched a sensitive nerve. Only too frequently Absalom's enjoyment of Rose Hill was clouded by an obsessive fear that financial difficulties would force him to leave it. One summer's day in the middle of August, however, he decided not to go into Manchester but to stay at home and to be at peace.

August 9th, 1847. Made a long breakfast sitting in the parlour with the two east windows open, a pleasant air flowing in, all still, except now and then the note of a robin, or the scream of the jay, or the twitter of some other bird. The hollyhocks gay in the sunbeams and the grass glittering with dew. I felt all the beauty of the place and the season and with a thankful heart I sat till I had looked over the two volumes of Shaw's Lectures on Zoology. In the afternoon and evening I attended to my accounts. I closed this very pleasant day as I had begun it – with thankfulness. When I awoke in the morning, and was repeating slowly the Lord's Prayer, I was struck, as I have often been, with its great comprehensiveness. It is full of <u>mighty</u> truths.

Alfred was continually bringing his friends home and champagne, nearly always noticed by Absalom with an exclamation mark, regularly appeared on the Rose Hill table. Nothing would persuade Alfred to go into Manchester with Absalom on 1 September.

September 1st, 1847. Very assiduous at the warehouse. Alfred at home with Smith and Midgeley, shooting. Dinner and champagne at six: cards and drinking and smoking. What folly!

All that entertaining and drinking and not going into work and yet the boy wished to extend the business. Absalom's warehouse had been in the High Street since 1835 when he moved from Cannon Street. Now Alfred was pressing him to go to a better site in Nicholas Street. But the rent was higher and times were bad; Absalom had just heard of two more failures. He feared that the extent of his business would not justify the outlay of an extra £150 a year. Alfred prevailed but the decision brought about a fit of acute anxiety.

October 23rd, 1847. Hurried and sad at the warehouse. The times are dangerous and I am very apprehensive. All the week I stayed up late and bled a good deal.

No wonder Absalom was worried. Mills were closing, thousands in Manchester were unemployed or on short time. The financial market was in a state of uncertainty. In August the price of wheat had fallen, causing ruin to speculators in corn who involved other firms in their crash. Railway speculators could find no one to buy their shares, there was pressure on the Bank of England and in October the Royal Bank of Liverpool stopped payment.

Alfred went off for a week's shooting with his friends the Smiths of Hill End and from there proved that he too was a blockhead.

November 1st, 1847. The Bank. Really assiduous at the warehouse. Got a saucy and foolish letter from Alfred who is at Hill End. He is 'victimised'!!!

On 3 November Absalom and his wife celebrated the thirty-third anniversary of their wedding. The occasion was not a success. Absalom did not get up until noon, which was not surprising since he had stayed up the night before reading George Sand's *Consuelo* till five in the morning. Mary and little Alfred, Hester and W.H. Mellor came to dinner.

November 3rd, 1847. After dinner Jonathan Mellor [the younger] and his cashier Mr Broome came and stayed to tea. I was tired with the company, disgusted by the state of the house and sick of an expense which I cannot afford. A thoroughly useless day.

He returned from Manchester the following evening to find both Hester and W.H. Mellor still at Rose Hill. Hester left but her brother stayed on and Absalom discovered to his disquiet that Mellor suffered severely from hypochondria and *took opium*. When Absalom refers to hypochondria, he is evidently using the word as Boswell did, to mean someone who suffers from periodic deep depression.

November 14th, 1847. He will take laudanum and of course cannot get better. It is troublesome to have a moody hypochondriac in the house. [Read] the notes of my Conversations with Carlile in 1827. I wrote then in a much better hand and had more full possession of my faculties. In the evening I went over to Edward's and sat some time with him, Mary and Edward Mellor.

Edward now lived at Cheadle and according to his own account of the nervous strain he was enduring at this time, could not have been an easy man to live with. The domestic tension was having an effect upon Mary, as events were to show. The Commercial Bank of England, whose business still concerned Absalom, had rooms for entertaining, washing and changing convenient for those who lived outside Manchester.

November 18th, 1847. Assiduous at the warehouse till four. Then went to the Bank to prepare for the Soirée at the Athenaeum. Mrs Watkin, Mary and Elizabeth did not come till six, an hour behind the appointed time. Then Mary was very ill, sick and hysterical. Alfred and I had to dress. It was past seven before we left the Bank and we were about the latest of those who were on the platform. Mary we had left at the Bank in the care of Jonathan Mellor. The Free Trade Hall was very cold and the speaking was by no means animated. It terminated about ten and then we got some wine which, being cold, we all drank too much. At eleven we went into the Directors' Room and got supper and more wine. Then we went to the Bank and found Mary still unwell and Jonathan with her. Another coach was procured about one and we got off. We left Mary and Jonathan at Cheadle and took W.H. Mellor and [Hester] Mellor to our house. It was near five when I got to bed.

Absalom plainly did not consider W.H. Mellor a suitable husband for his daughter. What Elizabeth thought is another matter. Mellor was still haunting Rose Hill but there was no mention of an engagement. Elizabeth's mother probably hoped for a match. Her daughter was thirty, old for marriage in those days. In early December Mellor was with them again.

December 4th, 1847. W.H. Mellor, who has been here some days, took offence at something I had said and went away to Edward's. My daughter was in a flood of tears and my wife as ill-tempered as the devil. Both united in exclamations against me and finally Elizabeth, with all the energy of the Intense School, accused me of having insulted both her and William. But I will take my own course, the more determinedly for all this opposition.

Mellor was not long gone. The next day was Sunday.

December 5th, 1847. In bed till twelve. W.H. Mellor here. I gave him my hand but took no notice of his folly.

As the days inched their way towards Christmas, business deteriorated still further. Like Edward before him, Alfred began to get downhearted.

December 15th and 17th, 1847. Alfred despairing. Alas! our expenses are too great. Alfred insolent because unsuccessful. Accuses me of selfishness because I refuse to let him lodge in Manchester during the winter. Thieves are abroad, our neighbours have been robbed and he would leave me and his sister and mother to ourselves! And I am selfish!

Neither illness, domestic strife nor business troubles could entirely absorb Absalom. However agitated the surface of his mind, ideas were more important.

December 21st, 1847. At the Literary Society at night. Mr Cobden unexpectedly present. A very full meeting. I had to open the question 'Which has the better title to the admiration of mankind, the Great Frederick of Prussia, or Peter the Hermit, author of the First Crusade?' The influenza had rendered it impossible for me to prepare as I intended, and I had not written anything, not even the slightest outline. Dependent therefore entirely on my recollection and my deep conviction of the merits of Peter, I rose to speak, and to my own surprise, in a fluent address of an hour conveyed my opinion and its reasons so clearly as to secure a unanimous vote. Cobden praised my 'acute knowledge of facts' and my 'beautiful vocabulary' and others 'the interesting manner in which I had brought the subject before the meeting.' All were pleased and even Alfred thought I had done well.

Even Alfred. Yet Alfred had a private reason for his impatient desire for business success. He wished to get married like his brother Edward.

Despite his small triumph, Absalom spent the following day at home, overwhelmed with fears for the future. He could not have been aware of it but he had good cause to be fearful. The year 1848 was barely a fortnight away and the conservative system imposed in Europe after Napoleon's defeat in 1815 was about to fall apart.

CHAPTER THIRTY

'To your tents, Chartists – we are becoming stronger and more united every day'

The move to Nicholas Street was announced in January 1848 and notices sent to all customers. Absalom went over to spend an hour with Edward and Mary at Cheadle. Edward showed his father a 'very panegyrical' vote of thanks from the Directors of the London and North Western Railway Company for his help in the negotiations which had led to the profitable takeover of the Trent Valley Line. Edward was paying a different kind of price. Like many gifted and ambitious people he was entangled in a net of his own making. He had not yet acquired the toughness and confidence of his later years. To succeed in the cut-throat world of the early railway boom he might ruin his health; to ruin his health would shatter his career. The rewards of business promotion were great but the competition was fierce. If he could not work he could not win.

The day after seeing Edward Absalom summoned sufficient resolution to take stock. The result confirmed his fears. He was worth only £2,802 and ten shillings. On Sunday Edward and Mary and W.H. Mellor came over to Rose Hill to hear John preach at Northenden church.

> **January 5th, 1848.** John left us to return to his curacy at Long Benton. Several pages Luther's Table Talk. What a strange exhibition of strength and weakness! God help poor human nature.

> **January 9th, 1848.** Annual meeting of the shareholders of the Bank, all passed off well, although Turner showed his teeth. I dined at the Bank with Robinson and Young. We had two <u>pints</u> of champagne and although Greaves had some of it, I was quite affected by it I suppose from my extreme weakness and the fatigue and excitement of the meeting.

That was one kind of excitement. Towards the last day of February news reached them of another.

> **February 28th, 1848.** The papers confirm the astounding fact that Louis Philippe, who this day week was King of France and apparently secure upon

his throne, has been in three days, by a tumultuous rising in Paris, compelled to abdicate, and is now, with his family, a fugitive. The monarchy is abolished and France is a Republic!!! Can this last?

Louis Philippe had been King of the French since 1830. Son of the notorious 'Philippe Egalité' who had voted for the death of his first cousin, Louis XVI, he was now an old man and the victim of forces he had once harnessed to his own cause. Almost eighteen years earlier he had overthrown Charles X. Charles, however, had made a dignified exit from his kingdom after abdicating, riding to the coast surrounded by the Royal Guard. The experiences of the Citizen King were rather different. He escaped from a back entrance of the Tuileries with the Queen only an hour before the mob broke in and ransacked the palace. From Paris the royal couple made their way in disguise to Le Havre where the British Consul enjoyed himself enormously devising a plan for their escape to England.

Absalom heard the news of the abdication on 28 February. On 3 March the King and Queen were at Newhaven, smuggled across the Channel as 'Mr and Mrs Smith', the King shorn of his whiskers and wearing a cap and immense goggles. The shocked and appalled Queen Victoria thought they had fled too quickly.

It was a leap year. On 29 February the 'French Revolution', as Absalom called it, affected the Manchester market so badly that no business at all was done. At Rose Hill, W.H. Mellor came to say goodbye. He was going to Oxford, for what purpose is unknown, since he was well past the usual age for an undergraduate.

Absalom had been two years old in 1789. His formative years had been spent during the Napoleonic Wars, he had seen many French regimes come and go while the British monarchy remained stable despite revolutionary pressures and the personal unpopularity of George III's sons. He had no high opinion of the French, yet they fascinated him.

March 4th, 1848. Continued St Pierre's Wishes of a Recluse. Much pretty and taking writing, but as politics the most childish nonsense. It is clear that the French are far behind us in political science. I do not think so merely from the silliness of much of this book, but from what the papers state of the conduct of the Provisional Government. They have already abolished all titular distinctions, extinguished both the Chambers and the regal office, and promised to find work and living wages for all the operatives!! They cannot do this, and they will fall or a new Reign or Terror must ensue.

A Republic founded upon semi-socialist principles and universal male suffrage could not fail to influence a neighbouring country which was only just emerging from a commercial depression.

March 10th, 1848. No business, and disturbances in Manchester effectually put down by the police. Attended a meeting of the Magistrates. Special constables sworn in. A conference with Sir Thomas Arbuthnot, the General of the district. We have troops enough and need not fear.

Yet fear there was.

March 14th, 1848. The French Revolution is producing its effects: bankruptcies, disappearance of specie, absurd claims of the rabble, and fears of those who have something to lose. God help us. At home, too, there is excitement and a foolish sympathy with the French. In London, Glasgow, etc. there have been disturbances.

It seemed that the whole of Europe was in a ferment. The South German states were meeting to set up a parliament based on universal male suffrage and on 15 March, the day Absalom went to call upon the erstwhile revolutionary Joseph Johnson to talk over events, Metternich was forced to fly from Vienna. This was just the sort of stimulus the apparently moribund Chartists needed. Despite the depression and the fact that O'Connor was now in the House of Commons, an appeal the previous year for a new National Petition had fallen on deaf ears. But as the revolutionary ball bounced back from the walls of Paris, Heidelberg, Naples, Palermo, Vienna and Berlin, meetings were held up and down the country and people flocked to sign the Charter.

'To your tents, Chartists,' O'Connor was declaring. 'We are becoming stronger and more united every day.' That was a half-truth. Certainly events on the Continent had given revolutionary impetus to people already weakened by economic instability. It was also true that the Chartist leaders were out of prison and that the movement had been momentarily strengthened by its alliance with the Irish.

Inexplicably, the Irish did not appear to be grateful to the English for the efforts made by both Government and voluntary organizations to relieve their sufferings. They were proving more difficult than ever. O'Connell had died in Italy the previous year, a broken man. 'Ireland is in your power,' were his last, barely audible words in the House of Commons. 'If you do not save her, she cannot save herself.' Everything he had fought for seemed to be in ruins. His country was prostrated by famine and fever, the Repeal movement taken over by men with very different ideas from his own. The truce with England was over, gone was moral force, peaceful persuasion and constitutional means.

Absalom attended a meeting of magistrates.

March 16th, 1848. It is apprehended that we may have a row, as tomorrow is St Patrick's Day and the Repealers and the Chartists (whom God confound!) are to hold a great meeting in the Free Trade Hall. From Dublin we had a letter informing us that Liverpool, Manchester, Birmingham and Glasgow would be set on fire tomorrow by these gentry. Captain Willis says that he has no reason to fear any such thing. However, more constables are to be sworn in, and we are well prepared.

Once more the Chelsea Pensioners were drilled and it was reported that at reviews their 'volley firing was much steadier and more simultaneous than that of younger and better practised troops'. Meanwhile all remained quiet and life went on; pleasure, business and apprehension mingling.

March 20th, 1848. The Bank. We had a bottle of champagne and joked Johnson about getting married, much to his satisfaction. At the Town Hall two hours with the Mayor etc. Mark Philips came in, said the French were unprincipled, offered his young men and himself as special constables and hoped we should have no disturbances. We are very quiet and apparently shall be so – and we are well prepared.

Alfred had been saying goodbye to his friends the Whiteleggs, off to visit Madeira.

March 21st, 1848. One of the worst markets we have yet had. Assiduous but quite unsuccessful. Alfred returned from London having, as he says, spent £5 in three days; he is travelling free thanks to Edward. This expense is wrong.

Absalom's daughter engaged another servant 'athough our expenses are already too great and our prospects discouraging'. Everything remained uncertain.

March 31st, 1848. At the Court all the forenoon at the meeting of the magistrates to appoint two Inspectors of Weights and Measures. There were a hundred and fifty-seven candidates. Mrs Mordacque, who has just returned from France, here at night. She says that in the neighbourhood of Dieppe, where she has been, a factory was burnt down by the operatives of another town, but the people generally in France, meaning those who have something to lose, do not approve of the measures of the Provisional Government.

In London, where the Queen had just given birth to a daughter who was to live to see Hitler's invasion of Poland, the Chartist leaders announced their plans. On 11 April they intended to hold a monster meeting on Kennington Common from where they would go in procession to Westminster and present the Charter, now, so they claimed, signed by almost six million people. So far, so good, but what was going to happen after the Charter had been rejected, as surely it would be? Were the Chartists either willing or able to set up an alternative government composed of Delegates to their National Convention? Any attempt to do so would mean either immediate and humiliating arrest from a well-prepared Government or at best a civil war, a civil war they had little rational hope of winning. The choices were stark and the Chartist leaders vacillated, agreeing among themselves neither about practical steps nor political theory.

The Duke of Wellington was in command of the defences of the capital. The Yeomanry were called up, troops from the provinces drafted into London and people urged to defend themselves by enlisting as special constables, which they did in great number. Among them was Prince Louis Napoleon, soon to play a very different role on the European stage, and Sir Robert Peel, a sure sign, remarked Jerrold's *Weekly Newspaper*, that he was planning to carry the People's Charter through Parliament before many years had passed.

It was important for the police presence to be seen, but troops were provocative. Four batteries of artillery commanded bridges over the Thames and 9,000 troops were concealed at strategic points like the Tower, the Bank, and Millbank prison.

A difficult birth together with reflection upon the sufferings and indignities endured by the French royal family with whom she had close personal ties, had made the Queen exceedingly nervous. She wept uncontrollably and shivered to think what would happen if a Republic were to be proclaimed and her little family with the two-week-old Princess Louise were forced to flee they knew not where in the clothes on their backs. It was a temporary weakness. The Government advised the royal family to seek the safety of Osborne House and two days before the Chartist meeting a platform at Waterloo station was cleared for their departure. Protected by several hundred special constables, the Queen, the Prince, and the royal children boarded an express for the Isle of Wight.

Manchester's plans were along familiar lines.

April 6th, 1848. At the Town Hall in the forenoon. We are swearing in special constables and preparing for the threatened outbreak of the Chartists next Monday.

In the event, the Kennington Common meeting and the subsequent presentation of the Petition to Parliament turned out to be a fiasco. O'Connor, who was in bad health, had already lost his nerve. Before the Queen left London a Proclamation had been issued forbidding the procession on the grounds that it was an attempt to intimidate the House. On the day itself the numbers attending the meeting were far below the half a million the Chartists had boasted.

The bales of the National Petition were taken from the wagon so gaily decorated with the Irish and Chartist colours and put into three cabs which made their sombre way through rain-soaked streets to Westminster. Queen Victoria wrote to her Uncle Leopold, King of the Belgians:

Thank God the Chartist meeting and Procession has turned out a complete failure; the loyalty of the people at large has been very striking and their indignation at their peace being interfered with by such wanton and worthless men – immense.

Yet the future lay with the wanton and worthless. The years would grant the Chartists all their demands save annual parliaments. The letter of Chartism was destined to be fulfilled while its spirit remains with us, uneasy and unpropitiated because its real hopes are unattainable in a fallen world.

Manchester's troubles were yet to come. There, 10 April turned out to be as great an anti-climax as it had been in London.

April 10th, 1848. At the Town Hall and the Bank. All passed off quietly. I began to write an Address to be issued by the Mayor.

If the *Manchester Guardian*'s conclusion that the workforce in the town had begun to see that their interests and those of their employers were identical was far too sanguine, nevertheless it contained some truth. The League had brought the social classes together, a common cause had dissolved some of the hostility between masters and men upon which Chartism fed. Moreover, it is plain from Absalom's diary that the social conscience in Manchester, although almost incredibly sluggish and hard by modern Western standards, was active and sensitive according to the perceptions of the time. The liberal reformers had done something to ameliorate the harsh conditions brought about by too concentrated and rapid industrialization.

The day after the Kennington débâcle was also quiet.

April 11th, 1848. At the Town Hall twice. I concluded the Address for the Mayor, which was approved by the Justices and ordered to be printed.

Absalom was gratified by the reception given to his address. He did not put his name to it. Why a man who deeply desired public recognition should so frequently have worked secretly and behind the scenes remains curious.

April 15th, 1848. I see by the Guardian that my Address for the Mayor is generally approved. Alfred tells me the same and that people ask, "Who wrote it?"

Good Friday was spent at Rose Hill with the usual crowd of Mellors. Edward remained unwell and depressed. W.H. Mellor had returned from his mysterious sojourn in Oxford.

April 21st, 1848. At home all day. Edward, Mary, Miss Mellor and Hester Anne here in the afternoon. Today I have been forty-one years in business. To how little purpose!

This reflection drove him to take stock yet again and his fears were confirmed. Alas! his property amounted only to £2,687. Mrs Butler, the former Miss Fanny Kemble, read aloud from *Much Ado About Nothing* at the Athenaeum but Absalom's spirits were soothed only to be agitated once more by Alfred.

May 10th, 1848. Did not rise till ten. Idled about in the garden till four – then accounts. Alfred came home depressed and desponding. His feelings affected mine and when I walked into the kitchen garden, in one of the most lovely evenings I ever saw, and looked upon the place which is now very straight and free from weeds and mostly sown and gay with young leaves, and the lilac flowers and the blossoms of the fruit trees – all enriched, goldened, by the gleaming sunshine – I stood and looked and feared the future and doubted if I could remain here or if I might not even want food and raiment.

The very beauty of Rose Hill saddened him. It was not securely his and even while possession hung in the balance his family continued to throw away money in extravagant entertaining. There could be no question now of retirement.

May 13th, 1848. Assiduous at the warehouse till three. Gardened a little at home. Irritated by the state of my home and the foolish and wasteful expenditure. Again we have W.H. and Hester Mellor here and yesterday we had Mrs and Mary Makinson.

Next day was Sunday and he stayed in bed until eleven o'clock. Then he re-read his diary for 1827. It was over twenty years ago and they had still been at Broughton.

May 14th, 1848. Always I have been hindered by my fool of a wife. Edward and Mary dined and got tea with us. Edward was harassed by the uncertainty of his position. Depressed after they left by considering my situation and our heavy and absurd expenditure. W.H. and Hester Mellor still here.

As far as Manchester was concerned the peace of the previous month proved to be the calm before the storm. Towards the end of May Absalom's old friend Joseph Johnson visited Rose Hill and once more they sat together 'to talk about the times and the danger of disturbance'.
The Kennington Common fiasco had irreparably damaged the Chartist movement and left it in the hands of the physical-force rump. Its Irish connection was now the occasion for one final splutter. On 27 May the revolutionary agitator John Mitchel was condemned in Ireland to fourteen years' deportation; that was the reason for Johnson's call at Rose Hill and his gloomy forecasts, which turned out to be only too true. Lancashire teemed with Irish immigrants and Manchester was full of them. With the physical-force men in command of the Chartists and

the Chartists allied with the Irish Repealers, the situation looked critical and Absalom was back again at the Town Hall.

May 30th, 1848. Disturbances are probable. Attended two meetings of the magistrates on the state of affairs. It was determined not to permit a meeting of Chartists and Repealers advertised to be held tomorrow in Stevenson Square for the purpose of 'sympathizing' with the Irish demagogue John Mitchel, who has been sentenced to fourteen years transportation for his infamous incentives to sedition and rebellion.

It seemed to be 1842 all over again. Only this time they were prepared.

May 31st, 1848. At the Town Hall from nine in the morning and mostly there till nine at night. A deputation of Finnigan, Donovan, Hoyle and Cropper Clarke came to expostulate with the magistrates about the stoppage of their 'legal and peaceable meeting'. They were told that it was illegal and would be stopped and that if they attended it, they must take the consequences. Between ten and eleven we had information that the people about Oldham were turning out the mills and were advancing upon Manchester. Thereupon the military and police were ordered to their several pre-arranged stations and Stevenson Square was occupied by a strong force of police and specials. In this way the Oldham people were kept out, or at least could only enter the town in small numbers and nobody was allowed to remain in the Square.

The town mob was a little troublesome and one of the mounted specials, the son of Mr A. Henry, was cut in the face with a stone and his horse stabbed with a pike. Some others had blows from stones, but the scamps had the worst of it, and some were apprehended with their weapons. The Oldhamites, as they could not meet in Manchester, declared that they would hold a meeting in Failsworth and went off there with some of the Manchester people. General Arbuthnot, hearing this, went after them with the Hussars and two county magistrates, but the rain had damped their zeal and no meeting was held. The General, his aide-de-camp and the magistrates returned to the Town Hall drenched with rain which the old soldier treated lightly, but his attendants were glad of some wine. A little before five o'clock all was reported quiet, and the troops, police and specials, all miserably wet, were mostly recalled or relieved and the troops sent to barracks.

I left to meet the Literary Society at Mr Pollock's but while I was there, the people began to crowd round Stevenson Square. A mounted policeman galloped off for reinforcements. A strong body of police with cutlasses and a company of the Town Hall Guard came in quick time up the street and there was a clearing of all the streets up to Ancoats Lane.

I went back to the Town Hall and found that new commotions had arisen near New Cross and that part of the pavement had been pulled up. The harassed troops were recalled. Maude, Trafford, John Potter and afterwards Watkins, went on with successive bodies, and a company was placed in the Town Hall, as nearly all the police and specials had been sent to the scene of commotion. There the streets were cleared and the pullers-up of pavements well beaten and a few apprehended. Then the military and civil force confronted the mob, keeping the streets open and the mob, mostly I suppose, idle and curious spectators, stood looking at the authorities and doing no serious mischief, till they were tired. Then a shower coming on, all was quiet about ten o'clock.

Absalom went home and dipped into Wilkinson's *Ancient Egyptians* and *The Anglo-Saxon Chronicle*. There was some trouble in the night, easily put down by the police.

The town was at peace but the market remained bad.

June 7th, 1848. At home all day. Accounts. [Poor Law] assessment book and papers. Just as I was going to bed Alfred gave me a letter asking for £30. I was extremely depressed by this unreflecting folly. My property is melting away and I shall be beggared unless I retrench.

It was decided at the magistrate's meeting to forbid and prevent another gathering the Chartists had advertised to be held in Stevenson Square on 12 June. Absalom took some blue pills and prepared for yet another vigil.

June 12th, 1848. At the Town Hall at intervals till half-past eight at night. The town is unusually quiet. The Chartists made no attempt to meet in Stevenson Square, but issued an abusive placard adjourning the meeting to the Hall of Science at seven o'clock and calling on the people to attend 'in their thousands'. The call was ineffectual, the hall only about two-thirds full and the speaking, except for abuse of the magistrates and the middle classes, very tame. There was not even the usual amount of noise in the streets.

That year there was no haymaking party. Absalom stayed at home to see it stacked, took another blue pill and attended to his accounts.

June 15th, 1848. To my surprise and consternation my property is reduced to £2,620. I felt extremely sad, the more so as it is, even yet, inexplicable to me, how can I have lost, since January 1844, £1,400 exclusive of John's college expenses which would be covered by the sum of £750 which was given to me by the Bank. It is quite inexplicable.

In view of his recent stocktaking, it is puzzling that Absalom should have been so upset at the figure he arrived at. He must have known then what he had lost since 1844.

Mrs Davies, her little boy and his nurse arrived to stay at Rose Hill. Absalom took yet another blue pill and stayed up sleeping in his chair until six in the morning. He felt harassed, tired and on edge and then Alfred threw some light on his mysterious request for £30. He had written to Mr Mellor to propose marriage to his daughter Hester. He may have wanted the money for an engagement ring. It was not a propitious moment. We must never forget that Absalom was a child of the first French Revolution and that it had left an indelible stain upon his mind.

June 26th, 1848. News of direful tumults in Paris and great slaughter. Alas! the madness of human beings!

Elizabeth fell ill. Perhaps she was upset by the news of her brother's engagement when she had failed to secure W.H. Mellor. Mr Jordan was called in to attend to her and stayed to dinner. Edward and Mary were about to leave the district to live in London and came to Rose Hill, bringing little Alfred to stay with his grandparents during the move. Two days after his sixty-first birthday Absalom spent a weary time in Liverpool on business.

June 29th, 1848. I was knocked up for want of rest and our meeting was disagreeable, and protracted till half-past five. It was half-past nine when I got home. I found Edward and Mary at Rose Hill. They had quarrelled and Edward was, like myself, worn out and dejected. I stayed up late and slept uncomfortably, little Alfred being in our bed.

Edward and Mary had hardly left before W.H. Mellor arrived to stay, much against Absalom's will. Marriage was in the air, yet for Elizabeth just out of reach. There was a further piece of bad news.

July 8th, 1848. Attended the funeral at St Stephen's church, of my cousin John Watkin who was found dead in his bed on Tuesday morning. A post mortem ascertained the cause to have been apoplexy. When I got home at half-past four, I found W.H. and Hester Mellor still here and the house in a bustle and the servants overworked. John came with us, [to the funeral] having taken priest's orders.

Apparently none of the family was present at John's ordination. The death of Absalom's cousin John must have come as a shock. Another link between Absalom and his boyhood in Whit Lane was severed. It was an unfortunate family and was to be still more so. John had seen his sister Mary die of consumption when she was little more than a child and now the poetic, impulsive boy who had played the clarinet and kissed Anne Stoneley under the oak tree was the victim of a stroke at Salford.

Yet he left some tincture of himself behind. His son, John Thompson Watkin, was to grow up to be a distinguished archaeologist and as such to merit the kind of immortality Absalom so ardently desired, a place in the *Dictionary of National Biography*.

CHAPTER THIRTY-ONE

'Old Trafford sentenced him to two months imprisonment and a severe whipping'

After John Mitchel's conviction preparations for an armed uprising were made openly in Ireland. At the end of July 1848 Lord John Russell brought in a bill to suspend habeas corpus. In Manchester the market was almost dead.

> **July 24th, 1848.** There was no business to be done and the state of Ireland, which is on the verge of rebellion, has thrown a gloom over the markets and after a fortnight of apparent revival, we are again in a state of doubt as to the future. Edward returned to London this morning, taking with him little Alfred, much to the sorrow of his grandmother.

The situation did not improve.

> **July 26th, 1848.** Attended the meeting of the magistrates at the Town Hall on the state of the town. We agreed to recommend an addition of two hundred men to the police and to issue an Address to the people. I spent some time after the meeting in preparing the Address.

Next day *The Times* informed its readers that the entire south of Ireland was in the hands of the rebels, but the report turned out to be a hoax. In Manchester, Absalom's proclamation was shortened, agreed upon and ordered to be printed. The next day it was posted up all over the city. The Irish, however, were too cowed, poor and hungry to rise in any significant numbers, nor were the disturbances in Manchester anything like so extensive or violent as they had been in 1842.

The European revolutions together with the Great Famine hastened the change in the direction of Irish politics. Just as the Corn Laws were far more than a fiscal measure, so Irish land reform, revealed now in all its urgency, transcended economics and was bound up with political and national aspirations. From now on the repeal of the Union for some patriots increasingly became an outdated, half-hearted, mean sort of ambition. The Irish were starving because strangers had appropriated the land. The owners of the soil must be the Irish themselves, free to organize their own lives and to govern their own country as they thought fit.

But who were the strangers and who the natives? The complicated pattern history had woven in Ireland, the intermingled threads of race and religion and divided loyalties, would render a solution to the problem as remote as the struggle to resolve it would be bitter. 'unmuzzle the wolf dog,' the revolutionary James Fintan Laylor was writing. 'There is one at this moment in every cabin throughout the land, nearly fit to be untied – and he will be savager by and by.'

So it would prove, but not yet. That autumn the blight reappeared and the potato crop, which had been awaited with such ardent hopes, was dug out of the ground a black mess of stinking rottenness. It was better to flee than to fight, for the huddled masses to seek refuge across the Atlantic or over the Channel to the western coasts of the British Isles.

In Manchester the market improved and life returned to normal. When September came Alfred as usual shot for the pot and preparations for a grand dinner party went ahead. Absalom spent an entire morning putting away his books to make room for card tables and on the day itself did not go into Manchester at all.

September 7th, 1848. Occupied till noon in arranging and preparing for the dinner. We have had a cook two days, and today a waiter, and Margaret Battersby besides our two helps and old Nathan who has been here a month. Then my daughter has been about and exerting herself in spite of Mr Jordan's express command that she should be still. With all this help, and W.H. Mellor assisting Elizabeth, I was the only person who was ready when our guests arrived at one for a dinner at three. We had to dinner old Mr John Mellor of Leicester, Mr John Mellor of London, his wife and their eldest son and daughter, Mr Mellor of Oldham and Mrs Mellor, Miss Mellor, Hester Mellor and W.H. Mellor. With some trouble from our confined space, we wore away the two hours between the arrival and the dinner. After dinner we removed into the garden and while we were away the dining room was cleared and converted under Elizabeth's direction into a drawing-room. We had coffee and tea, some music and dancing and soon after eight they left us.

All in all it had been an anxious year and Absalom was thankful to get away. He and Edward made arrangements to go on a tour together, first to London via Leamington and then to the West Country to seek out the Devonshire village where his mother had spent her childhood. Absalom had never yet been so far afield. After visiting Leamington they went to Kenilworth before taking the train to London and Edward's house in Guildford Street.

September 15th, 1848. Went in the morning to the British Museum and saw the Lycian sculptures and those from Nineveh and Babylon. Struck with the strong <u>individuality</u> in the countenances of the latter. After dinner I went with Mary and little Alfred to the Pantheon. There are some good paintings and I was struck and amused by the delight and wonder of Alfred among the paintings and the toys. I bought him a jack ass on wheels and a sixpenny watch and these with a cake made him quite happy. I had afterwards a walk by myself and then tea and then I fell asleep.

The plan was to go to the West Country and take in Bath by the way.

September 16th, 1848. Spent the forenoon in walking about and made some small purchases. I dined with Edward and Mary at the Victoria Hotel and at half-past four Edward and I left London by the Great Western Railway for Bath. We got to Bath at seven, having stopped fifteen minutes at Swindon station, at which there is a very elegant refreshment room. At Bath we put up at the Greyhound, a good and cheap commercial inn. We got tea and afterwards walked out by moonlight to see the city. We went up to Walcot church where my parents were married and then down the whole length of the noble street called after the Earl of Bath, Pulteney Street. We were in bed soon after eleven but people were in the streets and noisy, men and women, until one.

September 17th, 1848. I rose about six and was out soon after seven. Took a walk to King's Mead and about the Abbey. Returned and found Edward still in bed. We breakfasted and looked at the market. I bought some bunches of sweet violets and some peaches and Edward a lobster. Then we set off by rail to Wellington. We got to Wellington and took a chaise to Ashbrittle, a ride of seven miles constantly up and down on roads scarcely wide enough for carriages to pass abreast, and enclosed between hedges so high that we could only see the country when we came to a gate. The country fine, well wooded, well cultivated, exceedingly varied. Many apple orchards. The soil generally a reddish loam.

Ashbrittle, my mother's native place, is a small village on the top of a hill commanding an extensive prospect. The name is evidently derived from three fine old ash trees which stood conspicuously on the green not far from the church. The church is a very plain whitewashed structure, fitted with homely pews and the Royal Arms temp. George II and discovering, as did nearly all the houses, gates etc., a remarkable absence of paint. The churchyard is large and has a fine old yew tree with four or five stems, of which I brought away a slip. We found the wife of the parish clerk and we got access to the registers, but I could find no record of my mother's baptism or the baptism of any of her brothers and sisters. There were no entries relating to the Sayers until long after. The family, however, was known but only one young woman who had borne that name remained in the village. Her father and mother were dead. She had married a shoemaker named Culverwell and kept a school.

We went to see her. A low, long cottage, with a peculiar earthen floor of the country and having a pretty flower garden in front and standing opposite the church is her residence. We found her, a young woman, perhaps twenty-three, with a pleasing countenance, a sweet voice and neatly dressed. The room was plainly furnished. In a cradle before her was fine boy of about six months old, with a noble forehead.

I introduced myself as a descendant of the Sayers and we got into talk about our common ancestors. But I fell into the error of forgetting our relative ages, twenty-three and sixty-two and so I spoke of her father as having been my mother's brother instead of her nephew and so we blundered and I did not discover my error until we had parted. We left after a short conversation which interested me as being probably our first and last meeting – my first and last visit to the birthplace of my mother. A healthy and well situated but out of the way place even now, and which must have been much more so about a hundred years ago. Returning to Wellington we dined and I ate for the first time some clouted cream, a Devonshire luxury of which my mother used frequently to speak. After dinner we went to the railway and proceeded to London. It was eleven at night before we got to Guildford Street. I was tired and slept well with my grandson.

Edward had been very fond of his grandmother and later, when he became rich, he had an elaborate stained-glass window put into Ashbrittle church to honour both her memory and that of his father.

The next day was a Sunday.

September 18th, 1848. Rose late. After breakfast walked with Edward to Regent's Park. Very hot, tired. Dined and fell asleep. Got tea and then went with Edward, Mary and little Alfred and the servant, Esther, to Hyde Park. As we walked at the higher end, the statue of the Duke of Wellington on the triumphal arch stood out clear against the sky and caught the attention of Alfred who exclaimed 'dat a donkey up dere'. We had a pleasant walk and were early in bed.

September 19th, 1848. After breakfast I once more looked into the British Museum and then walked very slowly along Oxford Street, Holborn and Ludgate Hill to St Paul's, very much amused by examining the shop windows. At a confectioner's close to the Mansion House I got for the first time in my life some Mulligatawny soup. It is eaten with rice and as there was the leg of a fowl and a mutton chop in it, I made a very good dinner. I returned as slowly as I had progressed. Looking into St Paul's, the cross of which is surmounted by a little wooden room, occupied by the persons employed in the trigonometrical survey. In Fleet Street I stopped to look at Bolt Court and then went to Lynn's and ate half a score of oysters. In

Chancery Lane I bought two books and reached Guildford Street tired and quite ready for tea. After tea Edward and I left by railway. In five hours we reached Stockport and by eleven, that is in six hours, we were at Rose Hill.

That memorable journey to London with Grime and Andrew in 1818 had taken them twenty-eight and a half hours.

Pressure built up again. The market was bad, W.H. Mellor spent the whole of Sunday with them and Mrs Thomas Watkin came round to Absalom's warehouse and asked for money. Not many of us have to undergo the scrutiny of our thoughts and actions to which the keeping of a diary exposed Absalom. The facts are too scanty to make any informed judgement but it does seem that his treatment of Mrs Thomas Watkin was less than generous.

Her husband was dead, her son John was dead, so was her daughter Mary, and although Absalom did not record it, so now was her remaining daughter, Frances. Thomas had not been a success in business nor had John. In 1841 he got into financial difficulties and in exchange for his help mortgaged half his Audlem property in Absalom's favour. He described himself as 'gentleman' on the indenture and was probably no businessman but the kind of literary dilettante Absalom might have been had his character been different.

However, Absalom's debt to John's grandfather was very great. John Watkin the elder had taken pity on his nephew when he was a boy, had given him a home, a place in his warehouse and the chance to make his way in the world. Something unexplained hangs over Absalom's relationship with his uncle's family, some long ago, deep-seated resentment lay twitching beneath the accumulated sediment of almost half a century. In response to the cry for help, Absalom allowed Mrs Thomas Watkin £5 a year, not a princely sum even when the value of money in those days is taken into account. Yet he does not appear to have felt he ought to have done more.

October 21st, 1848. Mrs Thomas Watkin came home with me. She has no income, all her children are dead. She is in her seventieth year. I told her I would allow her £5 a year and give her the first £5 on January 1st, 1849. I have already given her £2. I look back forty-four years to the period she and Thomas Watkin were keeping company at Whit Lane. Now she has been twenty years a widow, she is childless and destitute.

Absalom spent Sunday reading the *Life and Letters of John Keats*. His books were his solace.

October 25th, 1848. Going to look for a volume I wanted, I was confronted by the sight of all my books. What an endless store of enjoyment and pleasure! While I keep them I cannot be long unhappy.

He read *Jane Eyre* with much pleasure and had to go in the dark and damp to Liverpool only to be met on his return by another of Alfred's demands.

December 13th, 1848. As we came home at night Alfred asked me for £50!!! which he says he owes!!!

Edward, Mary and little Aflred were to come from London to spend Christmas with them and the day itself was almost unbearable.

December 25th, 1848. Walked in the forenoon with Edward. Mr and Mrs Sumner and Jonathan Mellor dined and got tea with us. It was a terrible task to entertain them for seven long hours. W.H. Mellor came as soon as they were gone, much to my discomfort.

He sat up late to see the New Year in and went out into his garden to listen to the bells and a band of music playing at Didsbury.

Peel's measure had provided that the duty on corn should be totally abolished at the end of three years. Those three years were up on 1 February and on 31 January Absalom attended the celebration banquet. The proceedings went on until midnight and as the clock struck twelve and the Corn Laws expired, the whole company broke into long and sustained cheers. For Absalom the occasion fell flat.

January 31st, 1849. Went at five o'clock to Manchester and attended the Banquet in honour of the final abolition of the Corn Laws, which expire tomorrow. It began at seven and was kept up till half-past twelve. The speaking by Villiers, Bright, Cobden, Colonel Thompson, Milner-Gibson etc. was mediocre but the Free Trade Hall was filled and all were unanimous in applause.

He read the *Itinerary of Benjamin of Tudela* and Lingard on that 'infernal wretch' Henry VIII. At the Literary Society Alfred's question: 'Would an equally efficient reformation of the church have taken place in Europe in the sixteenth century independent of the exertions of Luther?' was warmly debated. Absalom now began regularly to read *The Dublin Review*. He had picked up a number before Christmas and thought it 'a feeble, Papistical' publication. He still thought it papistical, but it was nevertheless interesting.

John came on a visit and Edward joined them so that in March once again all his children slept under his roof. John took the whole service at Northenden church and preached twice to an attentive congregation. Absalom did not go. It was sufficient to have to deal with W.H. Mellor, who was haunting Rose Hill yet again. Nothing was said about marriage. The disappointed Elizabeth fell ill with the tic and could not attend church the following Sunday. To restore her Absalom read the Liturgy, the Epistle and Gospel and the Book of Ruth, followed by the first two books of the *Iliad* in Cowper's translation.

The trouble with Absalom was that once he had started a book in the evening he could not bring himself to stop. He found himself stupidly sleepy and to Alfred's irritation frequently stayed in bed until past twelve in the morning in the middle of the week. Later that spring Edward came again to stay and suggested that he and his father should go and see William Makinson at his house, Lime Place, Broughton. It was an opportunity for Absalom to visit the places he had known since he was a boy and which had been so familiar when the family lived at Woodlands Terrace. Everything was the same, yet it was not the same. He himself had aged.

April 16th, 1849. In the afternoon I went up to Broughton with Edward. We smoked a pipe with William Makinson and then set off to Prestwich with Hannah and Sarah Makinson. We rode to the entrance of Prestwich Clough, descended into it and rambled on to the steps ascending to the churchyard. Then we took the footpath towards the moor, ascended two hills and returned over the moor and across what was the black field, between two lines of back doors to the high road. I was astonished to find that this walk was too much for me. My breath failed in ascending the hills, or if I walked otherwise than slowly, my legs ached. I was glad that an omnibus was passing as we reached the road at the exit of the black field and I rode to Lime Place. Evidently I am extremely weak, both in my lungs and in my limbs. We got tea and sat a couple of hours very pleasantly at William Makinson's.

Two days later Absalom started to read *Wuthering Heights* at the warehouse. 'A foolish book.' He was able to get through a business journey to Liverpool only by taking brandy. 'Continued Wuthering Heights. I blame myself for reading such rubbish.'

April 21st was an anniversary he always recorded.

April 21st, 1849. Today I have been forty-two years in business. I have thrown away my opportunities and must work when I ought to rest. Still I have great reason to be thankful, none to complain except of my own folly.

Old Mr Jonathan Mellor had been ill for some months. On 1 June Absalom went to see him at Oldham and found him 'much reduced'. Back at home he read the second installment of *David Copperfield* and found it painful.

While Jonathan Mellor moved slowly and alone towards death, Absalom lived to another timetable. He had undertaken to wind up the affairs of the Liverpool Company, Watson Brothers, which involved constant journeys back and forth.

June 9th, 1849. To Liverpool on Watson's affairs. Dined on lamb and green peas, an octave of port, and cream cheese – all for two and a penny, including

the waiter's fee of a penny. Sat up till four, like a fool. My hay was stacked, a
tolerable crop of rough stuff – well gotten.

The condition of Mr Mellor worsened. On 12 June Absalom went over to see
him and heard next day that he had died at ten in the morning. Edward, Mary and
little Alfred arrived at Rose Hill and the funeral was held at Oldham.
'Methodism, that is the religion of the heart . . .', Wesley wrote when he was
eighty-four. Like Absalom and his mother, the Mellors had been strongly
influenced by the Protestant revival. Jonathan Mellor used often to tell how when
he was a boy of six in 1789, his parents left him at home while they went to the
opening of the Methodist chapel in Oldham where Wesley was to preach. It
happened that the Revd Mr Grimshaw called in at the house and finding
Jonathan's parents already left, thought it a shame that the boy should miss the
opportunity of meeting such a holy man and took him along to the chapel. Wesley
was then nearly at the end of his life. As he was coming down from the pulpit he
caught sight of Jonathan, put his hand on his head, and blessed him. Whether the
Mellors remained in the Methodist communion for long after its gradual separation
from the Church of England is doubtful; its influence however remained deep and
abiding. Rose Hill became grand and worldly but when the time came for
Edward's wife Mary to die, she asked her daughter to recite the Wesleyan hymns
she had known since her childhood.
Absalom spent his sixty-second birthday on an expedition with friends.

June 27th, 1849. I went to Booth Hall with F. Robinson, Dr Ogden and
W.F. Johnson. At Cheadle I saw the Catholic church, lately erected by the
Earl of Shrewsbury. It is small, but the most gorgeous place of worship I ever
saw. The Temple Church in London is nothing to it.

Absalom never went anywhere without taking reading matter and this habit was
to prove a trap for a child thief and an opportunity for the exercise of
contemporary legal brutality.

August 3rd, 1849. The Dublin Review and one of my neck handkerchiefs
were stolen from the sociable after I left it in Northen in broad daylight.

The thief turned out to be a boy of twelve who appeared before the magistrates
a week later.

August 8th, 1849. Went to Stockport to appear against the lad who stole
my book and handkerchief from the sociable. Poor creature! No father. His
mother is an abandoned woman who has deserted him. I was prevailed upon
by Mr Newton to send him to Knutsford in the hope that he might be
admitted into the Government Penitentiary. I returned home from Stockport

to receive the members of the Literary Society who were to spend the evening with us. Thirteen of them came and all passed off pleasantly.

It was not so pleasant for the little boy. In five days time his case came up at Knutsford.

August 13th, 1849. I went to Knutsford to appear against the boy who stole The Dublin Review and a neckcloth from the sociable on the third. I was induced to go in consequence of the hope, held out by Mr Newton, the magistrate, that this poor deserted child of twelve years old would be admitted to the Government Penitentiary. We were, however, disappointed, and old Trafford sentenced him to two months imprisonment and a severe whipping!!! Of course, only to be turned out to do worse. I left the court sad.

He had arranged with Edward to make another visit to Ashbrittle. They spent the first night at Cheltenham.

September 20th, 1849. Rose in good time, breakfasted in haste and set off by rail through Gloucester and Bristol to Wellington. From Wellington we set off in a chaise to Ashbrittle. We had a pleasant up and down ride and went direct to Culverwell's. We saw him and a younger sister of my cousin, (his wife) and his little son, John Sayer Culverwell, whom we saw last year in his cradle but was now running about, a fat blue-eyed boy. I left for him an illustrated New Testament which I had brought for the purpose and after a little chat we bade them goodbye, passed through the churchyard to get a few sprigs from the yew tree and set off on our return to Wellington. We found a good dinner, including some 'clouted cream' quite ready, and then once more on the railway we proceeded to Bath. We went into the Abbey Church about seven o'clock. There was a good congregation, and we heard a well delivered sermon about Jonah. The walls are literally covered with marble tablets. There are about five hundred, and as I looked around upon these records of mortality, I thought of Sir Lucius O'Trigger's consolatory remark to Bob Acres. 'There's snug lying in the Abbey.'

Before breakfast next morning Absalom walked round the abbey again and through the market. It was the prelude to a literary pilgrimage.

September 21st, 1849. After [breakfast] we took a coach and rode up to the top of Lansdowne to look at the cemetery where Beckford, the author of Vathek, is buried, and the tower he erected on the ground near his tomb. We ascended the tower, the lower part of which is the chapel of the cemetery. From the summit there is a most extensive panoramic view. We looked at the granite tomb and then descended to the Crescent to see the house in which he had lived. It is now empty and looked cheerless but the windows must command pleasing and extensive views. We descended by a succession of terraces but observed many good houses to let.

On his return from the West Country Absalom wrote nothing in his diary until late October. Then he recorded his first visit out of England, to Belfast, probably on Watson's business.

October 19th, 1849. Assiduous all day at the warehouse. Went by rail at six in the evening to Fleetwood and at ten left in the steamboat for Belfast. At first the weather was fine and the sea calm, but when we were rounding the Isle of Man the wind freshened and at length we had a stiff gale. There was much sickness but I was not sick and although I was startled at first by the novelty of my situation, I soon got over it and bore the tumbling etc. very well. I did not undress.

He was silent again until the very last day of 1849 when he wrote that he was at the warehouse, 'busy, unwell, irritable and pinched by the cold.'

Elizabeth was pining for W.H. Mellor. The previous August he had stayed at Rose Hill for several days. 'He and Elizabeth play the fool,' Absalom had commented. The situation worried him. At the end of January he wrote to ask Edward's advice.

January 17th, 1850. Edward came at tea time. Both he and I were tormented all the evening by Elizabeth's nonsense about W.H. Mellor.

It was a wasted visit. Edward could no more help his sister than Absalom could. Perhaps Mellor failed to send Elizabeth a valentine; she became very ill on the night of 14 February and a week later Absalom summoned medical help.

February 20th, 1850. At home all day. Mr Jordan dined with us, he and Occleston meeting to consult about Elizabeth's case. She has jaundice and is very ill.

Elizabeth took some months to recover from jaundice but she was never to recover from her obsession with William Henry.

CHAPTER THIRTY-TWO

'I know not of a Unitarian nation, or a Methodist nation, or a Catholic nation, or a Protestant nation, I know only of a British nation'

More than a dozen years had passed since a meeting at the Theatre Royal had agreed to form the Manchester Society for Promoting National Education. The proposal had borne little practical fruit. The times were against it. The energies of many of its supporters were taken up with the agitation for the repeal of the Corn Laws. Moreover, the Chartist disturbances had put some of the middle classes against the whole idea of a national system of elementary education. 'How,' the Chartist leader William Lovett asked, 'can a corrupt government withstand an enlightened people?' The answer might be to keep them in the dark.

This was decidedly not the opinion of Lord Ashley, who went on protesting that despite increased government grants, the manufacturing districts were a great and terrible wilderness and that scarcely more than half the children in England and Wales were receiving any education at all. Should nothing be done, he predicted, we would be overrun by a 'multitude of untutored savages'.

However, the voluntary schools had not laboured altogether in vain. If literacy is understood in its narrow sense as the ability to read, it was a far more widespread skill than is commonly supposed. The Report of the Committee of the Manchester Statistical Society in the 1830s concluded that about two-thirds of the adults in the district were literate. Modern scholarship has calculated that roughly speaking, throughout the country as a whole, in the following decade as many as two-thirds or even three- quarters of the working population could read, probably twice as many as those who could write. So some degree of literacy was universal among the working classes but as we well know, the ability to read does not necessarily include its exercise.

In 1843, as part of his famous Factory Act, the Home Secretary, Sir James Graham, had attempted to establish compulsory education for children aged eight to thirteen who were living in workhouses or employed in the textile industry. He had distrubed a hornets' nest. The proposal that these schools should be supervised by the Church of England caused nearly two million Nonconformists to sign a petition against the measure and furious meetings against it were held up and down the country.

'I know not of a Unitarian nation,' Thomas Wyse had said at the Manchester meeting in 1837, 'or a Methodist nation, or a Catholic nation, or a Protestant nation, I know only of a British nation.' Wyse had been the spokesman of a more enlightened tradition, one shattered by the French Revolution, Papal intransigence, Irish immigration and Protestant prejudice.

In 1784, when Manchester was expanding rapidly and the problem of child illiteracy was becoming evident, a meeting of Catholics and Protestants held at the Bull's Head had formed a committee to organize Sunday Schools on non-denominational lines, and an appropriate catechism had been drawn up. 'We have different creeds and modes of faith,' Rowland Broomhead, the Catholic parish priest of St Chad's remarked, 'but we are all of the religion which makes us wish to do good.' Neither party had intended to dilute its own particular tenets. They wanted to isolate fundamental Christian doctrines and form a common foundation for children's education. But the attempt to formulate a basic Christianity was wrecked on the rocks of deeply held sectarian convictions. Not until the breakdown of traditional Roman Catholicism brought about by the forces released by the Second Vatican Council and the consequent regrouping and dismantling of historic barriers could such an approach be considered.

In Absalom's time the Roman Catholic Church still held fast to its ancient liturgy and distinctive doctrines and was developing its own schools. Protestants were divided in faith and worship. On one side was the Church of England, on the other Dissenters who hated state interference and accused the Church of England of believing whatever Parliament told it. There was enough truth in this to hurt. All groups wanted their own schools and most resented paying any contribution to maintain what they considered to be error or to have their children educated in establishments run by managers not of their own persuasion.

To whom, then, was education to be entrusted? How were government funds to be allocated? Were the children to remain a barbarous, beggarly, street-roaming mass of ignorance because no one could agree upon what variety of Christianity they should be taught?

Absalom had long grown away from the culture of the Methodist chapel, but he was staunchly opposed to enlightened materialism or faith in self-sufficient human progress. Nor did he come into the category of Matthew Arnold's 'light half-believer in our casual creeds'. What he believed, he believed deeply. In his shrubbery, where he so often walked alone at Rose Hill, he had had some stones erected inscribed with various texts from the Bible. Some are still there today. It was the Protestant equivalent to the Catholic Calvary or statue of Our Lady and served the same purpose.

It seemed to him and to many others that the time had come to cut the Gordian knot. Any attempt to have elementary schools managed by denominational bodies should be abandoned. The schools should be secular in the sense that no particular religious group was placed in control of them, no creeds or catechism taught, only selections from the Bible. In place of formal religious instruction, the schools were to be closed at special times to allow for the teaching of doctrinal religion given by each denomination to its own adherents. It was further proposed that a county board of education should be elected with the power to control both schools and teacher training and that a local rate should be levied for this purpose.

This valiant attempt to make a fresh start was called at first The Lancashire Public School Association. It ran into difficulties almost at once. In Manchester one of its most bitter opponents was Canon Stowell, Vicar of Christ Church, Salford. Stowell came from the evangelical wing of the Church of England and was a popular pastor and gifted speaker. He hated Catholicism and disliked the Dissenters. In his eyes education without formal religious teaching was worse than no education. The proposed scheme would be only 'elevating man from the brute to approximate him to the fiend'.

At the end of March 1849, Absalom had helped to organize a meeting at the Town Hall to get support for the association. That meeting has been described as one of the most extraordinary ever held in Manchester and 'possibly one of the most remarkable educational gatherings anywhere on record'. Such was the interest aroused and the passions provoked that after hours of discussion the vote was not taken until four in the morning and even then there was no decisive majority.

Almost the entire argument had centred upon the religious question. Canon Stowell and a Wesleyan minister, the Revd George Osborn, moved an amendment begging Parliament 'not to sanction any system of general education of which the Christian religion was not the basis'. That was the nub of the matter and an exchange took place between the Revd William McKerrow, a Presbyterian minister, and Mr Osborn that illuminates both the complexity and profundity of a problem that still troubles us.

McKerrow: What is Christianity? Every man must judge for himself. We must not introduce the religious element therefore into our system of education. They had been asked what they would teach. They would teach truthfulness, honesty, sobriety, and brotherly kindness.
Osborn: On what grounds?

When at last it was time for the vote the mayor could not tell by a show of hands which side actually had the majority, so he asked the meeting to divide on opposite sides of the hall. Absalom's account had been as short as the meeting was long.

March 29th, 1849. Went to Manchester and attended the Meeting in the Town Hall to petition for the establishment of Secular Education in the county of Lancaster. I seconded the first resolution and reproved Mr Stowell for his attack on the Requisitionists. He moved an amendment which after a discussion of nearly five hours, was carried by a bare majority.

It was a temporary reverse. Now, a year later almost to the day, the argument continued, Stowell still making common cause with the Methodists.

April 1st, 1850. Nearly all day at the Town Hall at the meeting on the Lancashire Public School Association. Stowell and Hayden, the Methodist preacher, were beaten after a contest of five hours and a half. Our Petition was triumphantly carried.

So far, so good. It was agreed to hold another conference in October. Absalom felt tired and began to suffer again from an intense nervous irritation on his skin. He held a meeting of the Club at the Commercial Bank of England but only Greaves turned up. Back at Rose Hill he took calomel and senna, then John returned and caused more trouble. He had not yet found a living and took his disappointment out on his father.

April 14th, 1850. Unwell and in bed till noon. John abused me for not having given him a better education and for my extravagant expenditure.

The last accusation was one which either Alfred or John would make until almost the end of their father's life. Whether it was justified or not is hard to say. Earlier on it had been the children who had asked for Rose Hill to be extended and Absalom had given his consent only reluctantly. Now that he was a partner in the business and wished to get married, Alfred evidently thought that his father should put capital back into the firm and not spend it on improvements at Rose Hill. Since Absalom's own accounts suggest that the business was underfunded, John and Alfred may well have been right.

The justice of the other complaint is more difficult to decide. At first sight it is one of the curiosities of Absalom's life that a man who felt so deeply about education did not give his children a better one. Almost nothing is said in the diary about the schools his children attended or what they were learning. The name of no school is given; there are direct references only to a school in Nantwich, doubtless recommended by the Stoneley's or Absalom's aunt at Audlem, to which John and Alfred were sent for a year or two. For the rest of the time they must have gone to one of the numerous small private establishments run by people like Mrs Soulby and the Makinsons. Their educational standards were not likely to have been high and the boys left when they were thirteen or fourteen. Such indeed had been the extent of Absalom's own formal education. For the most part he taught himself.

It is true that Edward's friend, Herbert Ingram, who came from the same social background as Absalom, sent his sons to Eton and Winchester. But Ingram was far richer than Absalom and moreoever belonged to a different generation. In Absalom's time it was customary for the sons of moderately well-off merchants to attend local day schools and to leave young in order to go into their fathers' businesses. Absalom's grandson, not his son, went to Harrow. Nor should it be forgotten that Absalom had sacrificed a large proportion of what he earned from his work at the Commercial Bank of England to pay for John's fees at Oxford.

The next day Absalom had another blow.

April 15th, 1850. My old friend and member of the Club, John Davies, died today, the victim, I fear, of intemperance. Alas! a life thrown away – and a warning. The Bank in the forenoon. A really industrious day both there and at the warehouse. Sat up very late.

Davies had been a member of the Club since February, 1818, thirty-two years, before any of the boys had been born. They had met for the first time at old Makinson's and Davies had agreed to read a paper on hydrostatics.

In the middle of May news was sent from Guildford Street that Edward's wife, Mary, had given birth to a daughter. Hester wished to go to her sister and so Alfred accompanied her to London, returning later to Rose Hill with little Alfred. Absalom's wife insisted on taking the child to the warehouse, causing a troublesome interruption of business. Perhaps Absalom had been stung by John's complaint about his education, for he sat down and wrote a letter to Lord Carlisle soliciting his influence to obtain a living for his son. He was kept up late 'by the folly' of W.H. Mellor and Elizabeth, who was still weak from her attack of jaundice. Absalom thought it a good idea to take her to London when he went to stay with Edward so in the middle of June they set out together. They went to the theatre and saw *The Cat's Paw* and *None but the Brave Deserve the Fair*, and Absalom accompanied Edward to the function he had come to London to attend.

Mr Glyn was the banker George Glyn, later Lord Wolverton, Chairman of the Railway Clearing House. Captain Huish was the General Manager of the London and North Western Railway, and notorious for his unscrupulous business dealings. Edward was then his assistant and learnt a great deal from him.

June 18th, 1850. In the evening I went with Edward to Blackwall, to the dinner given by the railway staff to Mr Glyn. The Lord Mayor of London, the Mayors of Dublin and Manchester etc., Lords Lonsdale and Powis, etc., Sir James Graham and other notabilities were present. The dinner, including whitebait, was good, the speaking but so-so, the speeches of Glyn and Sir James Graham being the best. We left at ten o'clock after a pleasant evening. Captain Huish who was in the chair, showed his knowledge of Greek by saying Kyropedia instead of Cyclopaedia.

It was not the ancient but the modern Greeks who were troubling the government at that moment. While Absalom was in London, Parliament was debating the affair of Don Pacifico. Don Pacifico was a Spanish Jew born in Malta and therefore a British subject. He lived in Athens and after civil commotion there claimed an enormous sum in compensation for damages from the Greek government. When this was refused, he appealed to Great Britain. Lord Palmerston, who disliked the Greek administration, without consultation ordered the Fleet to enter the Piraeus and seize shipping to the amount of the claim. From the Tory benches Sir Robert Peel challenged the Foreign Secretary to justify his preposterous action which he did, speaking throughout the short summer night from brief notes and not touching the two oranges or glass of water placed beside him. His famous peroration he had learnt by heart:

> as the Roman in days of old held himself free from indignity when he could say <u>Civis Romanus Sum</u>, so a British subject, in whatever land he may be, shall feel confident that the watchful eye and the strong arm of England will protect him against injustice and wrong.

Palmerston won his vote of confidence but it was the triumph of a particularly vulgar kind of nationalism over justice and common sense, insidious because it roused emotions so nearly akin to patriotism and pride in one's country's achievements. It was to have a bad influence upon others besides Absalom.

Peel's challenge to Palmerston was the last time he spoke in the House. The very day after the debate he fell from his horse on Constitution Hill and got entangled in the bridle. According to Palmerston, Peel's horse stepped on him and a rib pierced his lung. He lingered in agony for almost four days and died on 2 July. Manchester was not slow to honour the man who had repealed the Corn Laws. A public subscription was quickly got up for the purpose of erecting a statue to the great man and Absalom was appointed to serve on the committee.

Alfred had waited to marry Hester until it was felt that the firm's finances were in a sufficiently healthy state to support her. Whether they were or not, the marriage took place in the second week of September.

September 11th, 1850. A little frost in the morning. The day beautiful. At six in the morning my wife, Mr and Mrs Smith, Miss Walker and I set out for Oldham. We called to meet Alexander Makinson and went on with him and little Alfred in the four wedding chaises to Oldham. All along the roads the grey horses and scarlet jackets of the postilions stopped work and caused smiles. We stopped at Failsworth for Thomas Mellor, and the gathering of smiling faces increased as we went on. Alexander said a benevolent man would wish to get married, as the thing produced so much general good humour. At Oldham we found the people in an agony of preparation. At last Mrs Smith, Alfred, Alexander and I walked to the church and in due time the others followed in chaises. John performed the ceremony, but not so impressively as Mr Lowe, who married Edward and Mary. Hester was given away by her uncle, John Mellor of Leicester. We returned to a profuse wedding breakfast, after which Alfred and his bride set out on their wedding trip.

Alexander Makinson was one of Joseph's sons. There is no mention of Elizabeth being present. Perhaps she could not face another Mellor wedding in which she was not taking the principal part. The honeymoon lasted a little under a fortnight and does not seem to have been altogether a success.

September 24th, 1850. Active and assiduous. Alfred and his wife returned from their wedding tour. He is jaded and depressed.

That October the Lancashire Public School Association held its promised conference and someone Absalom had not seen for many years briefly re-entered his life. They had disagreed in the past; they were to do so now.

After he had recovered from his first breakdown in health, Dr Kay had left Manchester to join the Civil Service as Assistant Poor Law Commissioner. He was then appointed the first Secretary to the embryonic Ministry of Education: a Committee of the Privy Council formed to administer the government grant. He was no longer the plain 'Dr Kay' of his Manchester days but Sir James Kay-Shuttleworth. Eight years earlier he had married Janet Shuttleworth, only child and heiress of Robert Shuttleworth of Gawthorpe Hall, Lancashire, and added her name to his. After ten years of marriage she left him and their five children to go and live abroad with a woman who had once been the family governess.

Kay-Shuttleworth had always felt very deeply about education. He saw as clearly as Disraeli and indeed Engels, for a time his fellow townsman in Manchester, the evil effects of the alienation of the poor from the classes above them. He realized that if the rootless products of industrialism could not be integrated willingly into society, then force alone could keep them in subjection.

He had spent the middle years of his life attempting to organize and to fund an effectual system of schools and teacher training only to be convinced that his efforts had been rendered almost useless by sectarian religious rivalry. In this he was wrong. There is a difference between educational standards and religious instruction. He had accomplished much. Owing to his work and that of his colleagues, the control of educational standards, (not religious teaching), was transferred from the churches to the state by means of licensed training colleges and government-appointed inspectors. Kay-Shuttleworth was not a man to withstand continuous strain. The tensions within his marriage can only be guessed at, but they must have added to the constant grind, the pressures and disappointments of his work. In 1848 he had a second nervous breakdown, resigned his office and was created a baronet.

Absalom put forward the first resolution at the conference, a proposal to change the name of the Association to the National Secular School Association. This was a mistake. The word 'secular' was a sensitive one. It suggested that the supporters of non-religious education held no religious convictions and therefore did not think it desirable for children to be taught any. Conscious of their vulnerability, Cobden was for dropping the word as misleading. W.E. Forster, who was to be responsible for the first Education Act of 1870, went so far as to threaten resignation from the committee were it used. After lengthy discussion the title of National Public School Association was fixed upon.

As luck would have it, events outside the conference hall were providing a farcical commentary on the arguments within. The country was going through the most extraordinary outburst of religious hysteria since Titus Oates had informed Charles II that 3,000 ruffians under the direction of the Pope, the General of the Jesuits and the Archbishop of Dublin were plotting to massacre the sleeping citizens of London.

With more truth than tact, Augustine Birrell used to refer to the Church of England as 'the cuckoo church'. At the Reformation the Catholic bishoprics had been taken over by the Protestants, and the Catholic remnant was governed from then on not by bishops but vicars apostolic. Now that the laws against them had been abolished, the poor birds asked, not to be given back their nests, but for permission to build new ones. Consent was obtained and Pope Pius IX re-established the Catholic hierarchy in England, replacing the vicars apostolic with bishops who, however, did not take the names of those sees now in Protestant hands. The matter was delicate but if carefully handled all might have gone off smoothly. Unfortunately, Dr Wiseman, appointed Cardinal Archbishop of Westminster, issued a foolish, flamboyant pastoral letter from Rome entitled 'From out the Flaminian Gate', which included the words, 'Catholic England has been restored to its orbit in the ecclesiastical firmament from which its light had long vanished'.

It was enough. All the smouldering prejudices against Papists that lay beneath the surface of Protestant England burst into flame. Newspapers shrieked warnings against 'papal aggression', protest meetings were held up and down the country, the Duke of Norfolk apostatized, the Duke of Devonshire pondered the propriety of keeping a bust of the Pope in the gallery at Chatsworth and Queen Victoria momentarily concluded that for Catholic congregations to pray for the Pope before the Royal Family infringed her prerogative. Just when the Educational Conference started in Manchester, Lord John Russell fed the national neurosis by addressing an open letter to the Bishop of Durham in which he attacked the Catholic party within the Church of England. Their innovations, he declared, which included honour paid to the saints, the use of the Sign of the Cross, and auricular confession, had been 'the most forward in leading their flocks step by step to the very verge of the precipice'.

It was not a precipice Kay-Shuttleworth was in any danger of falling over. Like

Absalom he had been brought up a Dissenter, like Absalom he now worshipped in
the Church of England. But the outcry highlighted just those difficulties he had
spent his life trying to overcome. It emphasized the gulf between the Catholic and
the Protestant parties within the Reformed Churches and the unlikelihood of any
successful attempt to secure an agreed Christian syllabus. He had met it all before
and the strain had contributed to his breakdown. The attempt to establish a system
of nationwide, undenominational schools was doomed to failure. He was
convinced that any national system would have to work through denominational
bodies. The so-called Secular Solution was not worth pursuing. He refused even
to attend the conference and made his opposition plain through the pages of the
Manchester Guardian. The scheme was neither practicable nor desirable.

Absalom thought otherwise. So long as light was preferable to darkness, he told
the conference, and knowledge to ignorance, charity to bigotry, every man 'who
was desirous of promoting the glory of God by doing good to his fellow creatures,
would be a friend to the plan which the Association had propounded'. Speaking
tired him. He was thankful to get home and to be left in peace to finish the final
number of *David Copperfield*.

The festive net was closing in. A large meeting to denounce Papal Aggression
was held in the Free Trade Hall, Absalom went to London again and a few days
before Christmas Elizabeth fell ill but recovered sufficiently soon to sit in the
company of W.H. Mellor from noon until six in the evening. Nothing was settled
between them and she could not bear to let him go.

December 31st, 1850. Assiduous at the warehouse which I reached about
noon, having been detained by my own weakness and the unreasonable folly
of my daughter, who wished still to detain William Henry. The Literary
Society. I heard Alfred's paper on Chivalry. The debate was very poor. I
came home and heard the bells ring out the Old Year. Went to bed and slept
well.

The century was half over.

CHAPTER THIRTY-THREE

'I went to the Exhibition of the Industry of all the Nations at the Crystal Palace'

At that time New Year's Day was not a holiday, nor was Boxing Day, but Absalom was his own master and could stay at home when he wished.

> **January 1st, 1851.** The birds were singing as if it was February and I gathered several sweet violets under the window of the sitting room. Hester and Miss Wilson here at dinner and all night – a sad bore. I stayed up late like a fool.

Two days later little Alfred came to stay with them and Absalom's wife as usual hindered his work by bringing the child into the warehouse. The Peel statue had been thrown open to competition.

> **January 11th, 1851.** I attended the meeting of the Peel Statue Committee in the Royal Institution. We sat for an hour and a half in the room in which were the seventeen models and arranged the manner of deciding upon the best. Hester had come before. At half-past one in the morning Edward came, having been detained a long time on the rail. Continued Lamartine's French Revolution of 1848. It was four when I got to bed.

The next day was a Sunday.

> **January 12th, 1851.** We gathered sweet violets in the garden, <u>very fragrant</u>. The winter aconite is in flower. All is too forward. Edward, Alfred, and Hester here all day and all night. Unwell and much tired.

That Monday, for the first time, Absalom recorded without comment that his wife drank.

> **January 13th, 1851.** Assiduous at the warehouse till half-past three. Returned to Rose Hill and found my wife intoxicated. The Spectator Newspaper. Stayed up very late.

It was a significant entry.

Absalom's marriage was a failure but not a tragic failure in the same way as Kay-Shuttleworth's or Richard Potter's, whose wife had left the house after the birth of their fourth child and could never be induced to come home. Absalom had found Elizabeth incompatible fairly soon after marriage, but the violent, bitter outbursts were a thing of the past. No longer did he walk full of pent-up rage for miles in the country, or sit grieving alone in his warehouse among the shadows of the passing year. He was resigned to her ignorance, bustle and untidiness, nothing he could do or say could alter her now. He records her increasing drunkenness with a mixture of disgust and pity. If he made no comment in his diary when he first found her intoxicated, he felt it the next day.

> **January 14th, 1851.** A very bad market. Depressed by the state of my affairs and the beastliness of my wife. The Literary Society. Stayed up absurdly till six in the morning.

So absorbed is Absalom in his own feelings that he does not seem to have asked himself from what unhappiness his wife was seeking to escape. She may well have been just as disappointed in her marriage as he was. Her daughter was a semi-invalid and unlikely now to fulfil even modest maternal ambitions. Most probably she would never have a respectable establishment of her own where her mother could visit and enjoy her grandchildren. She herself was bound to a man of a nervous, irritable temperament, who was frequently ill and often felt tired, who disliked his work, refused to go to bed and expected, not indeed domestic luxury, but a high standard of cleanliness and order. Absalom's diary contains thousands of words, yet the reality of his marriage, perhaps his whole life, eludes us.

The matter of the Peel statue was still undecided.

> **January 17th, 1851.** Attended the meeting of the Committee for the Peel statue. We reduced the seventeen models to eight, the work of five artists. The meeting of the Club at William Makinson's. I was the only member present except Makinson and suffered badly from the toothache. All my useful teeth are giving way. I stayed up very late and read several pages Pausanias's Description of Greece.

The old church in Manchester had gone up in the world. Not without some hurt pride and general obstruction, the Dean and Fellows had been substituted for the Warden and Fellows of the Collegiate Church, which was now the Cathedral, and Dr Prince Lee became Manchester's first bishop. A brilliant headmaster, Prince Lee was not so successful in charge of a diocese. He was low church, as befitted one of Russell's appointments. He rejoiced that the Church of England had rejected the word 'altar' in favour of 'holy table', complained of a representation of the Virgin Mary in stained glass in the church of Absalom's former parish of Broughton, and even looked upon such a simple aid to devotion as a wooden cross as a detestable novelty. He knew Absalom in connection with the education question. He was in sympathy with the aims of the Association, but he would not consent to the exclusion of doctrinal teaching in schools. He now made his presence felt.

January 24th, 1851. I spent three hours at the meeting of the Committee of the Peel statue, which was held at the Royal Institution. Our final decision was made contrary to my opinion, but in deference to that of the Bishop. We divided eleven to nine. Mr W. Calder Marshall is the successful artist. Much tired when I came home. I sat up late.

The bishop may have been in favour of Calder Marshall because his version was an emasculated Peel that Absalom found amusing. Tired or not, he sat up 'like a fool' the following night until six in the morning re- reading *Tristram Shandy*, and to four o'clock the day after. Lack of rest made him incapable of going into work so he spent time at home peacefully doing his accounts until a letter arrived from Manchester announcing that one of his customers had withdrawn his consignments, which threw him into the deepest gloom. That would deduct £120 a year from his already insufficient income. But spring was round the corner and on the first day of February he felt energetic enough to walk the eight miles into Manchester.

February 1st, 1851. I walked to town. The walk pleasant. Returned by the three o'clock omnibus, washed by seven, took tea, fell asleep in my chair and was not in bed till three.

The Catholic question had occasioned a great deal of commotion and anguish but the truth was that large numbers of the people of Great Britain held no strong religious convictions whatsoever. A census is a blunt instrument when it comes to establishing what human beings really think, but it can give some indication of how many people attend church services and where. With unexpected imagination, unfortunately for the first and only time in our history, a government decided to attach questions about religion to the ordinary ten-yearly census. Ministers of religion were asked about the number of buildings used for public worship, the seating accommodation and the numbers present on Sunday 30 March.

The accuracy and interpretation of the figures obtained are debated, but certain trends are sufficiently plain for the census to be called a landmark in the history of England. Roughly half the adult population who were presumed free to attend church went to no place of worship at all. Of those who did attend, half were Dissenters. As far as numbers went the Church of England had no right to be called the church of the nation. But neither had the Dissenters. There was no church of the nation. Canon Stowell was quite wrong to claim that 'two thirds of the population, urban or agricultural, belong to the Church of England and did not object to its teaching'. They did not object to its teachings because they knew nothing about it. Whatever effect the influence of squire and parson had upon country churchgoing, Christianity had lost the mass of the urban population.

Diminishing numbers of churchgoers did not, however, result in more tolerance among the faithful. In the month before the census was taken Absalom continued to agitate on behalf of elementary education and to encounter the same difficulties as before.

February 10th, 1851. In the evening I took the chair at a meeting of the National Public School Association in the Corn Exchange. Rylands, W.J. Fox, Walker of Oldham and McKerrow were the speakers. The meeting lasted till eleven o'clock and it was one in the morning before I got home. I felt better for the excitement.

Alfred and Hester lived at Sale, which was about four miles from Rose Hill and had a railway station.

February 22nd, 1851. Went to and returned from Manchester by the railway at Sale. The walk in the morning to Sale was very pleasant. I returned by the second class for fourpence. William Makinson here in the evening. He told us that Joseph was ill-treated and that an attempt had been made to rob him at the bottom of Fairy Hill Lane at half-past eleven last night. Continued Macaulay's History of England from the Succession of James II.

On a Sunday in the first week of March Edward came to stay. It was not a successful visit.

March 2nd, 1851. In bed till one. Edward came in the afternoon. A very unpleasant night, Elizabeth being strangely unwell. Edward enraged and everyone uncomfortable.

For Edward, his sister's behaviour must have been just one further anxiety added to the pressures of his business life, to the strain of for ever clawing upwards. It has been suggested that of all decades of our history, the 1850s is the one in which a wise man would choose to be young. Few wise men would choose to be young, but for the intelligent and tough it was most certainly an age of opportunity, as the career of Edward's friend Herbert Ingram showed.

Ingram was the son of a butcher and grazier at Boston, Lincolnshire, who had died when the boy was a child. From this apparently unpromising background he was to bring about a revolution in journalism. Educated at a charity school and

apprenticed at fourteen to a printer in the Market Place in Boston, where he now
has a statue, he joined his brother-in-law's printing and bookselling business in
Nottingham. There he noticed two things: papers sold more copies when they
were illustrated and people were for ever inquiring what the news from London
was. He concluded that what was needed was an illustrated weekly paper
containing news of topical interest and edited from London.

The idea was derided, but he felt that he had the ability to produce such a paper
and, making use of capital obtained from the marketing of an aperient pill whose
secret recipe he had learnt from a druggist in Manchester, succeeded brilliantly.
Ingram was a stocky, well-built man with protruding teeth who was said to
resemble Napoleon. Napoleon or not, the *Illustrated London News* became one of
the most celebrated papers in the world.

Ingram declared in his address to his readers in the very first issue:

> Here we make our bow, determined to pursue our great experiment with
> boldness; to associate its principles with purity of thought that may secure and
> hold fast for our journal the fearless patronage of families, to seek in all things
> to uphold the great cause of public morality, to keep continually before the
> eyes of the world a living and moving panorama of all its actions and
> influences.

Middle-class respectability with vicarious enjoyment; pursue his great
experiment with boldness, Ingram did. It is not known when they first met or
became friends, but Ingram was a man after Edward's own heart: energetic,
pushing and tenacious. Like Edward, he had a flair for publicity. Before the first
number of the *Illustrated London News* came out in 1842, he employed 200 men to
march up and down the Strand bearing placards announcing 'Thirty Engravings!
Price 6d!' To attract readers he timed the launch of his paper to coincide with a
fancy-dress ball at Buckingham Palace.

This was a magnificent occasion attended by 2,000 people, with the Queen and
Prince Albert taking the leading parts. All the costumes were carefully researched,
some of the men wore real armour. The *Illustrated London News* not only described
the whole scene in words and pictures but gave a list of some of those present
under the heading 'Court and Haut Ton'. Papers thrive on disasters even more
than on the extravagances of the rich and Ingram had a stroke of luck just before
his first number came out. There was a terrible fire in Hamburg and with the help
of a print from the British Museum he quickly had an engraving made which
showed the scene of the conflagration and was able to print it on his front page.
The first issue sold 26,000 copies and by the end of the year the circulation had
reached 60,000.

'Haut ton' Edward and Herbert Ingram certainly were not. They lived
dangerously. The economic freedom which gave talent and hard work its chance
meant that there was no safety net to catch the unfortunate venturers. Should

illness strike, bad markets intervene, or for whatever reason their touch falter before they had accumulated sufficient capital, they were ruined.

Absalom never thought of himself as safe. Edward was the family high-flyer but the effort to keep aloft continued to be too much for him. He had successfully completed the sale of the Trent Valley Railway, now amalgamated with the London and North Western Company where he was assistant manager, but his constitution could not stand the strain of constant stress. It was a vicious circle. He was rich enough to consult the Queen's physician, Sir James Clark, but it was the gaining of enough money to pay Sir James that had made him ill in the first place. He was able to analyse his state of mind quite objectively.

I felt the price I was paying for the privilege of labour and for its remuneration. But I thought of my wife and little babies and the thought roused me to a kind of desperation and made me feel for the time as if I could trample weakness under foot and tear out and break in pieces and cast away those miserable, over-sensitive organs which chained, cramped and hindered me.

The race was to the swift. If he fell the other jockeys would soon see to it that he was trampled underfoot. It was useless for Sir James Clark to prescribe rest. Captain Huish would have no pity on him.

By resting, I was restless. Unfit to work, I was tormented by an unnatural desire for action. Thus I rushed on with the day's duties as if all the work of the world had to be done in that one day and that day was the last. But an hour or two usually settled the contest. Head swam, heart beat, fluttered, stopped, struggled – knees knocked together – and out oozed the cold clammy sweat which reminds one of weakness and the grave.

Naturally he was impatient of Elizabeth but his father had asked for his help and he gave it, evidently arranging for her to go to London either for a change, or for treatment, or perhaps simply to get her out of the way of his brother-in-law, W.H. Mellor.

April 30th, 1851. Edward brought his two children and a nurse to our house. He is not well. I wrote at his suggestion, a soothing letter to Elizabeth. She is at last at Mr Robinson's.

Robinson was probably the physician and family friend of that name.

It was fortunate that Elizabeth was away from home, for a fortnight later Absalom went over to Oldham for yet another Mellor wedding. A sister of Mary and Hester, the now-widowed Mrs Dean of Haslingden, had decided to marry a Mr Worsley, a widower with a son. Hannah's first marriage had been the occasion for bringing the Watkin and Mellor families together. Her second was to have as far-reaching consequences, since her stepson eventually married Edward's only daughter, Harriette.

Absalom's spirits were lowered by too many visitors and attention to his accounts.

May 31st, 1851. Mrs Sewell, Hannah and Elizabeth Makinson came in the morning and stayed all day. Sewell came to tea. I returned from Manchester by the two o'clock omnibus and was sadly bored by their presence, my wife's stupidity and little Alfred's rudeness. After they left I completed the stock taking. The result is terrifying. At this rate my property will be gone in four or six years. I must set seriously to work to prevent it. Mrs Watkin, who appeared to have drunk too much, was quite furious after they had gone. I did not get to bed till five. Extremely depressed.

Absalom seems now to have had only £1,911 (about £95,500 in 1990 values) left in his business. Edward came up from London to talk things over. He stayed for one night and his father saw that he was unwell and overworked but did not yet realize the extent of his fatigue. We do not know what advice Edward gave, but whatever it was it did not prevent Absalom's projected visit to London. He wished to see Elizabeth, but perhaps still more to see the Great Exhibition, housed at Hyde Park in that marvellous building of light, air and iron designed by Joseph Paxton and so aptly called by Douglas Jerrold, the Crystal Palace.

Paxton belonged to the same vigorous Victorian subculture, that network of enterprise and blatant opportunism, which included Edward Watkin and Herbert Ingram. The families were to be connected by marriage as well as mutual interests. The seventh son of a tenant farmer, Paxton was the nineteenth-century version of the Renaissance Man, an astonishingly talented amateur, combining in himself imagination, botanical knowledge and technical skill. He also enjoyed the patronage, indeed the friendship, of the very rich Duke of Devonshire.

He had an excellent head for business and made a fortune from speculation on the railways. At Chatsworth he had designed the Arboretum, the Great Conservatory, the Emperor Fountain, the Great Rockery and last of all a structure of glass and iron, 'the lightest, the strongest, the most economical thing you can imagine' to house the giant water lily from British Guiana, *Victoria regia*. The Crystal Palace was a conservatory on a colossal scale, four times the area of St Peter's in Rome.

Paxton had newspaper as well as railway interests. He sent his plans to Herbert Ingram, who published them in the *Illustrated London News*. It was a scoop for Ingram and the publicity Paxton was given ensured the success of his revolutionary design.

Absalom was fascinated by the Crystal Palace and what it contained. It was almost as if it had replaced St Paul's Cathedral in his estimation. Indeed the motto of the Exhibition, printed at the top of every catalogue, was 'The earth is the Lord's and all that therein is.' At the opening, the united choirs of the Chapel Royal, St Paul's, Westminster Abbey and St George's, Windsor, sang the Hallelujah Chorus. The Queen confessed that the ceremony filled her with more devotion than any church service she had ever heard.

The Exhibition was intended not merely to be a huge shop window but to promote international peace, to exalt the gospel of work, encourage free trade and to give thanks for progress and the British constitution. There were over 100,000 exhibits from all over the world, divided by the organizing zeal of Prince Albert and his Committee into six main parts: raw materials; machinery; textiles; metallic, vitreous and ceramic manufactures and; last but not least, the fine arts. It was a glorious extravaganza, a combination of inventive ingenuity, respect for the past and artistic corruption.

Spanish mantillas, Crown Derby, Irish lace, French weaving machinery, Venetian glass, American grand pianos, Indian silks; kettles, steam engines, chandeliers, japanned trays, agricultural implements, font covers, minerals, lamps, grates, sentimental statuary, Buhl sideboards from Bond Street, rococo cats, marble nymphs, bronze lilies, classical gas jets and the Koh-i-noor diamond – all under one iron-girdered transparent roof. No alcoholic beverages were permitted and Lord John Russell complained about the number of crucifixes exhibited.

John Watkin, still seeking a living, met his father in London. Hoping to attract visitors to the Exhibition, the famous French cook Alexis Soyer had just opened Lady Blessington's former home as a restaurant.

June 16th, 1851. I went with John and Elizabeth to the Exhibition of the Industry of all the Nations at the Crystal Palace. Afterwards we dined in the Baronial Hall at Soyer's Symposium at Gore House.

Next day Absalom saw Elizabeth at Mr Robinson's before going again to spend 'four admiring hours' at the Exhibition. He took Elizabeth yet again a few days later. 'We stayed a long time and I was much tired.' He was greeted by a violent thunderstorm on his arrival back in Manchester.

June 21st, 1851. I left London at ten a.m. and reached Stockport at six, getting home in time to comfort my wife who as usual had gone into the cellar during the storm.

Almost immediately he was involved in another public duty. In the eyes of liberal England the Hungarian patriot Louis Kossuth was a national hero. After the failure to free Hungary from Austrian domination and Kossuth's flight to Turkey with other political refugees, Austria and Russia had demanded his extradition. Palmerston's response was robust. He not only encouraged the Sultan to refuse this request but sent gunboats to the Dardanelles in the belief that a British presence would be useful in the event of trouble. Now Kossuth was planning to visit the land of free speech and institutions, and Manchester was not slow to welcome him. Absalom went through the familiar routine of committee meetings and resolutions and then sat up until morning trying to write a speech.

July 16th, 1851. Attended the meeting at the Town Hall in favour of Kossuth and his companions. I moved the first resolution badly. Dr Vaughan, J.J. Taylor and Mr Beard spoke well. Mesuros, the Hungarian ex-minister of War was present and spoke well in imperfect English.

Tired as he was, Absalom stayed up until four in the morning reading Goldsmith and on Saturday night did the same with Tacitus. No wonder he could not summon enough energy to go to church, besides he was suffering badly from toothache. The next day was a sad one.

July 28th, 1851. Between two and three p.m. there was a solar eclipse, but no unusual diminution of light. In the forenoon I was at the Court and the Bank. In the afternoon I went with Mr Adshead to the Borough Gaol. It is now very full. There are several very young boys and girls, some of the latter pretty, with a <u>look</u> of such <u>innocence</u>. One not more than fourteen had been imprisoned before. I asked what had brought her there. 'Bad company. Her father had left her mother who lived with another man.' She was neglected by both.

One of Absalom's front teeth fell out as he was 'mumbling' some sopped bun and to the great alarm of Alfred and Hester, W.H. Mellor was threatened with legal proceedings for pulling the nose of Mr Marsland, churchwarden of Ashton-upon-Mersey.

CHAPTER THIRTY-FOUR

'So ended the most brilliant day that Manchester ever beheld'

It seems that Mr Marsland had offended Hester and W.H. Mellor had sprung a little too vigorously to his sister's defence. Edward had more serious things on his mind. He had gone to the country on business and while there was seized in the street with faintness and violent palpitations.

> I had to take refuge in a shop; to resort to brandy, physic, and a doctor; and, at the close of a day's confinement to my room, to sneak back to London, as miserable as any poor dog, who having run about all day with a tin kettle on his tail, is at last released to go limping and exhausted home.

He became convinced that some functional derangement had become organic disease and that his days were numbered. Sir James Clark, Dr Quinn the homoeopathist, the water cure, all had been tried and none had done him any good. He decided to have a complete change and to visit the United States and Canada. Absalom went to Liverpool to see him off.

Ten days after Edward's departure John married Priscilla Walker, a girl from Romansby in Yorkshire, eight years older than himself. Absalom makes no mention whatsoever of the wedding. It seems that neither he nor his wife were present. Perhaps they did not approve of Miss Walker, why we do not know. In September John brought his bride to Rose Hill. A dinner party was given in their honour but it was not altogether a success.

> **September 11th, 1851.** Very late at the warehouse. Returned at two. We sat down at six. John and Priscilla, Alfred and Hester Anne, Mary, little Alfred and ourselves. The dinner was good but we did not get on very well. While we were at table Mrs Sumner, Mrs Muter and Miss Sumner came – all stayed to tea and supper. With some music and singing we got through the evening but when they were about to go John and Alfred had a foolish unseemly quarrel and I went to bed late, depressed and sad.

Absalom's wife was anxious to visit the Great Exhibition before it closed in

October. Absalom had to see a dentist about getting false teeth. Cheap and usually crowded 'trip' tickets to London for the Exhibition were issued in Manchester costing fourteen shillings and twopence return. Absalom and his wife caught the train at Stockport and it took them nine and a half hours to reach London. Mary had taken lodgings for them at a Miss Smith's in Guildford Street where they found Elizabeth waiting for them. Her condition seems to have remained unchanged. Next day Absalom bought some books and took his wife to the Pantheon and then to the Crystal Palace. He was energetic enough when he was doing what pleased him.

September 24th, 1851. In the forenoon I went to the British Museum, saw once more the Assyrian sculptures, looked at the autographs, charters, missals, mss, early printed and curiously bound books which are now shown to the public and which gave me great pleasure. I walked slowly into the City, bought a volume or two, dined with Mrs Watkin and my daughter at Miss Surr's, and then left them and went up to the Mansion House. In Cheapside a paper was put into my hand announcing that newspapers might be seen, and materials for writing found for a penny. Wishing to write to Alfred, I went in, found a good collection of London and provincial papers and two comfortable rooms. I wrote my letter and then walked back.

Once more they visited the Pantheon and the Exhibition, where Absalom particularly admired the Gobelin tapestries, but his wife felt unwell. She was probably exhausted. However, she recovered sufficiently to visit the Pantheon again next day.

September 26th, 1851. I went in the morning with Mrs Watkin to the Pantheon. We looked at the collection of paintings. In the afternoon I walked up to Oakley Square and sat an hour or two with Elizabeth who was in bed. I spent the evening at Miss Smith's reading the Essays of Montaigne.

Saturday had been fixed for his dental appointment.

September 27th, 1851. I went in the morning to Mr Barrett's the dentist in Finsbury Square and had some five stumps pulled out preparatory to the insertion of some artificial teeth. The pain was momentary – the crush severe. I am to go again in a month.

Absalom did not often go to church when he was at Northenden. London was different and the choice had to be made as carefully as the buying of a theatre ticket.

September 28th, 1851. We attended the morning service at the Foundling Hospital. The children and the choir sang Addison's beautiful version of the twenty-fourth psalm very pleasingly and the anthem from Job was finely sung by the choir. The organ extremely well played. The sermon, semi-extempore, was well delivered, but poor as to composition and poorer as a sermon. After dinner I walked to Hungerford Market and over the Suspension Bridge in order to have a view of the City and the new Houses of Parliament from the bridge. I was rather too late but the sun setting behind Trafalgar Square threw out very finely the Nelson and York columns and the higher buildings. The front of the Parliament House was somewhat in the shade and the smoke from the river steamers obscured the view. At several places in the market I read the notice that ginger beer or <u>ice</u> might be had for a penny!

It was their last day.

September 29th, 1851. We left London at seven in the morning, got to Stockport at half-past four, and were home at a quarter-past five. On the way I concluded Wilson's Account of the Pellew Islands. It was late when I got to bed.

Early in October Edward returned from North America in improved health and settled down at once to put together an account of his trip. He had travelled both in the United States and Canada and kept his eyes open. With Edward no experience was wasted. His visit was but the overture to what later he would look back upon as one of his greatest achievements, the work he did to unite the provinces of Canada by an arterial railroad, in pursuance, in his own words, of 'the great idea – to be realized some day, distant though that day might be – of a great British nation, planted, for ever under the Crown, and extending from the Atlantic to the Pacific'. He brought back with him the American edition of Macaulay's *History*, which Absalom devoured eagerly and might have reminded them both of the vanity of human wishes.

Kossuth was not the only visitor expected in Manchester that year. The Queen herself was to make her first visit ever to the city.

Edward's life spanned exactly the same years as that of the Queen, but Absalom was not a Victorian. He had been born in 1787, on the very summer's day that Gibbon had written the last page of the *Decline and Fall*. He was fifty when Victoria came to the throne, he remembered the death of George III, had heard the proclamations in Manchester of George IV and his brother William. In Absalom's youth and middle age the general feeling towards the monarchy was tepid. That had changed, but even now there were those in Manchester who were prepared to give a warmer welcome to an Hungarian freedom fighter than to their Sovereign.

Nevertheless, official preparations for the event were elaborate and carefully planned. Three fountains had been designed to throw up jets of water as high as 30 feet and special platforms built in Peel Park to bear the weight of over 80,000 schoolchildren. The natural delight human nature takes in dressing up had overcome reforming priggishness. To Cobden's disgust those very 'corporation baubles such as maces, cloaks and chains' he supposed a high-minded city like Manchester would never tolerate had been introduced the year before.

The Queen and Prince Albert were staying with Lord Ellesmere at Worsley Hall. Prince Albert was extremely tired. The preparations for the Great Exhibition had absolutely exhausted him. The sheer donkey-work involved had been enormous and he had had to face constant criticism of all kinds and lack of any consistent funding. Queen Victoria, who was expecting her eighth child, described the day in her journal. It started badly. At one o'clock in the morning Prince Albert felt so sick and wretched that the Queen was terrified for the visit. 'Thank God,' she wrote in her diary, 'by eight o'clock he felt much better and was able to get up.' They left for Manchester at ten, the Queen continued:

October 10th, 1851. The day was fine and mild and everything to a wish. Manchester is called seven miles from Worsley, but I cannot think it is so much. We first came to Pendleton, where as everywhere else, there are factories and great preparations were made. School children were there in profusion. We next came to Salford, where the crowd became very dense. It joins Manchester and is to it, in fact, as Westminster is to London . . .

The mechanics and workpeople, dressed in their best, were ranged along the streets, with white rosettes in their buttonholes; both in Salford and Manchester a very intelligent painfully unhealthy-looking population they all were, men as well as women. We went into Peel Park before leaving Salford, the Mayor having got out and received us at the entrance, where was indeed a most extraordinary and, I suppose, totally unprecedented sight – 82,000 school children, Episcopalians, Presbyterians, Catholics (these children having a small crucifix suspended round their necks), Baptists, and Jews (whose faces told their descent), with their teachers. In the middle of the Park was erected a pavilion, under which we drove, but did not get out, and where the address was read.

All the children sang 'God Save the Queen' extremely well together, the director being placed on a very high stand, from which he could command the whole park. We passed out at the same gate we went in by, and through the principal street of Salford, on to Manchester, at the entrance of which was a magnificent arch. The Mayor, Mr Potter, who went through the proceedings with great composure and self-possession, beautifully dressed (the mayor and Corporation till now have been too Radical to have robes) received us there and presented me with a beautiful bouquet.

We drove through the principal streets, in which there are no very fine buildings – the principal large houses being warehouses – and stopped at the Exchange, where we got out and received the address, again on a throne, to which I read an answer. The streets were immensely full and the cheering and enthusiasm most gratifying. The order and good behaviour of the people, who were not placed behind any barriers, were the most complete we have seen in our many progresses through capitals and cities, London, Glasgow, Dublin, Edinbro' etc. – for there never was a running crowd. Nobody moved, and therefore everybody saw well, and there was no squeezing. We returned as we came, the sun shining brightly, and were at Worsley by two.

Absalom's experiences were rather different. The tickets for admission to the Exchange cost £1 each and before the Queen arrived, Mr Heron, the town clerk, gave them all a lecture on royal etiquette. The Shuttleworth Absalom mentions is none other than his old friend the once-fiery reformer, John Shuttleworth, with Absalom's help now transformed into a distributor of stamps and a city alderman.

October 10th, 1851. Left home a little before seven in the morning and went with Mrs Watkin to the Bank. We were joined there by Alfred and Hester Anne. Having breakfasted, we all went to the Exchange having tickets of admission. We waited about two hours, and then the Queen, Prince Albert, the Prince of Wales etc. etc. entered the room which had been prepared to receive Her Majesty. The National Anthem was sung. The Corporation in their new robes, the Mayor in his jewelled collar, the Recorder in his wig, all looked very hot. The Recorder read the Address, not well. The Queen replied in a clear, distinct and sweet voice. The Mayor, Neild and Shuttleworth, the mover and seconder of the Address, kneeled on the throne and kissed Her Majesty's hand. Then the Mayor was knighted by two slight blows with the sword, one on each shoulder, and then the royal party retired amid the loud cheers of all present, and the clang of martial music. The Queen was in mourning and dressed very plainly, as were the children. They all appeared to take the affair as so much <u>work</u>, discovering no emotion.

At seven o'clock in the evening Absalom's party walked to see the illuminations. All coaches were at a standstill because of the pressure of people.

James Whitelegg and Alfred took Hester between them, and I followed with my wife. We went down Piccadilly, down Portland Street, and by York Street into Mosley Street. The crowd was great and the pressure severe, but people were very good-humoured, and we got on tolerably well as far as the Portico. The Infirmary with its three fountains, Westhead's warehouse, Houldsworth's, Thornton and Co.'s with the American stars and the motto 'E Pluribus Unam' in gaslight, Fletcher's and Potter's warehouses, were most to be admired, and the wide space and the reflection of the scene in the Infirmary pond made a beautiful and dazzling <u>tout ensemble</u>.

Afterwards they all went down King Street to look at the decorations, just as Absalom and William Makinson had done all those years ago when the Bourbons were restored in 1814 and Absalom was in love with Elizabeth. Then thousands of lamps had been arranged in the shape of a rainbow outside Mr Greg's house; there were no private houses now, only shops and offices.

We went down into King Street, and here the Club House, the Bank of England and the Town Hall and John Hall's shop were splendid. We went into St Ann's Square, observing the Triumphal Arch and the Exchange. At the entrance of Exchange Street from the Square the crowd was great. We forced our way about half-way up to look at Agnew's and Ollivant's shops, but then were jammed in between two streams of people, one from the market-place and the other from the Square, and were excessively squeezed and should hardly have got out but for the strength and stature of James Whitelegg. We found that Hester's pocket had been cut and her purse stolen. We succeeded in reaching home by midnight. It was a beautiful night, and the returning groups in all sorts of conveyances and on foot amused us by their loyalty, good-humour and hilarity. And so ended the most brilliant day that Manchester ever beheld, and no doubt a day of the greatest and purest happiness to the numbers of people who were congregated in this one place. 'God Save the Queen!'

At eight o'clock next morning a deputation of the Workmen's Singing Classes arrived at Worsley Hall from Manchester to sing under the Queen's window. She was already up and the choir were invited to come inside when they sang 'Lo! the early beams of morning.' This was followed by a spirited rendering of 'Now Pray We for Our Country.'

> Now pray we for our country,
> That England long may be,
> The holy and the happy,
> And the gloriously free.
> Who blesseth her is blessed!
> So peace be in her walls,
> And joy in all her palaces,
> Her cottages and halls!

Later that day the Queen added a postscript to the account in her diary of the Manchester visit.

October 11th, 1851. The Mayor told me last night that he thinks we saw a million of people between Manchester and Salford. There are four hundred thousand inhabitants in Manchester, and everyone says that in no other town could one depend so entirely upon the quiet and orderly behaviour of the people as in Manchester. You had only to tell them what ought to be done, and it was sure to be carried out.

This judgement was perhaps a little too sanguine.

The following week Mary and Hester's first cousin, the barrister John Mellor, came to visit Absalom. Mellor had just been appointed a Queen's Counsel and was leader of the Midland Circuit. As a judge he was to try the Tichborne Claimant for perjury and to be a member of the commission which tried and condemned to death the 'Manchester Martyrs'. They were men executed outside Salford Gaol in 1867 for attempting to rescue Fenian prisoners from a police van in the course of which the officer in charge was killed. Engel's second wife, the Irish Lizzie Burns, helped one of those involved to escape. Mellor talked at length about his recent tour in Germany and Switzerland. Absalom had ceased to wish to go abroad. Despite the ambitious plans of his youth, he had never in his life left the British Isles.

Dislike of Russia was widespread among liberals in the latter half of the nineteenth century and Absalom shared it. To a mind like his, tyranny was as wicked as it was incomprehensible. His very love of freedom stultified his imagination. Living in a country that with all its faults was a bastion of liberty, he was too provincial, too inexperienced, to understand how human beings slide into slavery and gradual acquiescence in the suffering of others, which is the price of survival.

He would have been unable to imagine how the German people came to accept the dictatorship of Hitler, occupied countries to hand over Jews to certain death and Eastern Europe to knuckle under the successors of Stalin. But there was another, less admirable, aspect of his thought. A robust defence of liberal institutions against the absolutist powers could turn into an aggressive nationalism, a popularist notion that Great Britain was the world's policeman, that the Royal Navy existed to protect liberal movements abroad and to enforce the balance of power in favour of enlightenment.

The Literary Society had arranged to hold a debate about Russia. Absalom agreed to speak and spent some anxious nights reading.

October 28th, 1851. The Court in the forenoon. The Literary Society. I opened the question 'Are the liberty and civilization of Europe endangered by the power and policy of Russia?' I was not well prepared, but I had thought a great deal on the subject and arranged my materials in my head. I spoke with tolerable fluency for thirty-five minutes, was heard with attention and applauded at the end. The debate was lively and adjourned for a fortnight. Sat up till five.

Edward came up from London to see his old friend George Wall, returned from Ceylon, whom Absalom and his wife intended to entertain at Rose Hill.

November 5th, 1851. At home all day, preparing for our dinner. We had Skinner, his wife and Margaret Battersby in addition to our two helps. Our guests were Mr and Mrs Jervis, Mrs Spencer, Mr and Mrs Edwards, Edward, George Wall, Alfred and Hester Anne. Our dinner was good, well cooked and ready at the time. Edward's American stories, George Wall's details of Ceylon and Alfred's sallies made the time pass pleasantly, and sitting down to dinner at five, they did not leave till eleven. I sat up late.

In the adjourned debate Absalom's question about Russia was decided in the affirmative by twenty-one votes to five, and at last Kossuth arrived in Manchester. He was given a tremendous welcome.

November 11th, 1851. Attended the meeting in the Free Trade Hall to present an Address to Louis Kossuth. The Hall was filled, the speaking good and the enthusiasm great. I seconded a resolution, but made no speech. I slept at the Bank.

The following day they met.

November 12th, 1851. I went to Alexander Henry's at the Woodlands, Crumpsall, to see Kossuth. There were about a hundred and fifty persons to breakfast. Kossuth made an excellent speech and then left for Birmingham.

Prince Louis Napoleon had been elected President of the French Republic soon after King Louis Philippe's exile in 1848. Now, on 2 December, the anniversary of his uncle's victory at Austerlitz, the Prince dissolved the Assembly and made himself Emperor of France. Without consulting his colleagues, Lord Palmerston told the French Ambassador in London, himself a natural son of Napoleon I, that he approved of the *coup d'état*. This action gave the Court and Lord John Russell at last the excuse to dismiss Palmerston as Foreign Secretary and the crowned heads of Europe rejoiced at his downfall.

Another Emperor of the French however was not a pleasant prospect. The Channel seemed to have contracted, the outlook was stormy and others besides Absalom were alarmed. Prince Albert informed Russell

It is quite clear to the Queen that we were entering upon most dangerous times in which Military Despotism and Red Republicanism will for some time be the only Powers on the Continent, to both of which the Constitutional Monarchy of England will be equally hateful. That the calm influence of our institutions, however, should succeed in assuaging the contest abroad must be the anxious wish of every Englishman.

Altogether it had been an eventful year and if Absalom had hoped for a long sleep on 1 January 1852 he was disappointed.

January 1st, 1852. The Gatley band roused us almost as soon as it was light and played 'Hail, smiling morn', 'Auld Lang Syne', 'God Save the Queen', and 'Rule Britannia' in capital style. I went to Manchester about the [publication of] Edward's book and returned by train to Sale.

Edward's book about his visit to Canada and the United States cost half-a-crown. It was published by W.H. Smith and the entire edition sold out.

After the first week in January Absalom makes no further entries in his diary until the end of April. He starts abruptly with a description of a dinner party at Rose Hill.

April 21st, 1852. At home all day. Messrs Fildes, Ogden, Higson and Robinson, Mrs Higson, Mrs Robinson, Mary Watkin and Hester Anne dined with us at three. We had a good dinner, well cooked and well served and all went off tolerably well, except that Mr Fildes who is becoming very deaf, groaned every now and then as he ate, and could hardly take a fair share in the talk, and except that I carved awkwardly and did not talk as sensibly as I might have done. Alfred came about five and they were all away by half-past ten. The enjoyment is not worth the cost.

Business was slack, he tired himself arranging his books and sitting up until morning 'with strange, habitual folly'. Whether the case of W.H. Mellor and the churchwarden's nose ever came to court is not recorded, but Mellor himself had by no means ceased to hover over Rose Hill and the affections of Elizabeth. Absalom had never lost touch with him and on 1 May the whole sad cycle of encouragement and rejection began to revolve again. Elizabeth was thirty-five. She had been a year away from Rose Hill and may have thought that only there had she a chance to secure a home and happiness.

May 1st, 1852. In bed till one. Wrote to Edward, Elizabeth and W.H. Mellor. Just as we were about to get tea Edward and Elizabeth came up the garden. She had suddenly challenged Edward to bring her down, and although his eyes are still inflamed, he accepted the challenge and brought her. She bore the journey better than she expected.

Next day his wife continued to read aloud the third number of *Bleak House*, but the excitement of the return over, Elizabeth was unwell. Absalom decided that something would have to be done.

May 7th, 1852. Tolerably assiduous at the warehouse but out of order.

Bowels confined. I <u>troubled</u> myself to write a smart letter to W.H. Mellor and after all did it badly. Very sleepy at night.

We do not know what answer he received.

Manchester was preparing for another General Election. The Government had not long survived Palmerston's dismissal. In February Russell had lost a vote of confidence and resigned. After almost six years of undistinguished government the Whigs were out. Lord Derby formed a Tory administration with Disraeli as Chancellor of the Exchequer. Parliament was due to be dissolved in July in any case. Absalom spoke at a public meeting in the Town Hall and attended committee meetings. His birthday was coming round again, the accusing finger on the dial of a clock. The day before he went on an expedition with his wife to Ashbourne. It brought back memories. He had last been there as a young man, thirty-five years ago, on that famous excursion to Derbyshire with Grime and Andrew.

> **June 26th, 1852.** We intended to have seen Dovedale, but had not the time. We arrived at Ashbourne at about one o'clock. We called upon T.J. Mountford, looked at his garden, tasted his rhubarb wine and then left him and his family to look at the church, with the monuments of the Cockaynes and the Boothbys, and at a tablet to the memory of Melville Horne, who died here at the age of eighty. Then we walked about in the walk in the churchyard, shaded on each side by lime trees, which I saw once before in 1817, in company with Grime and Andrew, both of whom have been dead many years.

Absalom's birthday was on Sunday.

> **June 27th, 1852.** In bed till noon. I am today sixty-five. In tolerable health. My blessings are many and great. My life has been on the whole so happy that I would gladly live it over again. I might have done more had I been true to myself. I have had no steady industry except that which has been forced upon me. It was necessary to <u>work</u> or <u>starve</u>, so I <u>worked</u>, and Providence opened a way for me, while many abler and better men have failed. It only remains to make the best use I can of the few remaining years. May God assist me.

This summary of his life is entirely in character and as far as can be judged, true. He had not directed his undoubted intellectual gifts to any single end. Knowing as we do the anguished passages of his early life and middle years, it is surprising and a little touching that he looked back upon his life as such a happy one.

CHAPTER THIRTY-FIVE

'Free trade, peace, freedom. Oh happy England'

The General Election took place in the middle of a heat wave. It was a fudged election, with the Government shuffling miserably over free trade. The furore over Papal aggression had left its mark and Disraeli had to tread delicately. It would not have done for the Whigs to have appeared as the sole champions of the pure milk of the Gospel and his election manifesto carefully asserted that the 'crown of England shall still be a Protestant crown'. That was not the question the electors of Manchester were concerned about at the moment. They feared not the Pope but Protection.

> **July 7th, 1852.** Another hot day. The nomination of members for Manchester took place in St Ann's Square, which was filled with people. Gibson and Bright, our Members in the late Parliament, were opposed by Captain Denman, the son of the late Chief Justice, and Mr Loch, the agent of the Earl of Ellesmere. The show of hands were decidedly in favour of Gibson and Bright. There was much noise but no tumult.

The Conservatives increased their vote in the country at large but still did not command a majority in the House. The electorate, however, did not decide the nature of the government and Derby and Disraeli were back for as long as they could scrape together enough parliamentary votes to keep them in office.

Not long after the election John and Priscilla came to stay at Rose Hill and hardly had they left before W.H. Mellor arrived to speak to Elizabeth. 'Uselessly,' Absalom wrote in his diary.

If his sister's life had turned out to be a bitter disappointment, Edward was pressing forward resolutely and now earned £1,000 a year. Promoting railways could be remunerative but the trains themselves were not always safe.

> **August 7th, 1852.** Edward informs me that the train in which Mary went to London on Thursday sustained a collision between Madeley and Stafford. Two persons were killed and several hurt. Mary escaped with a severe shake.

She came to Rose Hill to recuperate, bringing with her the nurse and the two-year-old Harriette. Little Alfred was already with his grandparents. The house was full and Absalom was considering a speech he was to deliver later in the month at the Athenaeum.

The previous February Dickens had visited Manchester together with a troupe of amateur actors who were performing plays throughout England for the benefit of the Guild of Literature and Art. Their appearance had been enormously successful. Four thousand people had stood up in the Free Trade Hall and cheered the performers. A delighted Dickens was told by a stage-carpenter: 'It's a universal observation in the profession, Sir, that it was a great loss to the public when you took to writing books.' The company's tour was now almost at an end but Manchester was being complimented by a return visit.

The Guild of Literature and Art was Bulwer Lytton's idea. Both he and Dickens had long felt that there was a pressing need to help struggling writers. The beginners, the unappreciated, the unfortunate, should not have to depend for their bread upon the caprice of private patrons or the occasional meagre government pension. Writers and painters should band together and by various means accumulate a fund to enable the distressed among their number to pursue their art.

The imagination of Lytton and Dickens soared. Lytton would give land from his Knebworth estate, an artist's colony would be established with a warden, neat cottages and an assured £170 a year. No future Johnson would ever again have to sell his rights in a masterpiece to pay for his mother's funeral. 'I do devoutly believe,' Dickens announced, 'that this plan carried, will entirely change the status of the literary man in England and make a revolution in his position which no government, no power on earth but his own, could ever effect.'

Such a scheme needed funds. What better way to obtain them than by amateur theatricals, presenting plays performed by Dickens and his friends, productions that had proved so successful in the past. Lytton set to work to write a comedy, *Not so Bad as We Seem*, and Dickens and the editor of *Punch*, Mark Lemon, contributed the farce, *Mr Nightingale's Diary*. The Duke of Devonshire lent Devonshire House for the first performance, the Queen consented to attend, and Paxton built a special box for her, set in a bower of magnolias, jasmine and roses. The tickets cost £5 each. The Queen, so the actors were told, 'got restless after midnight', so the farce which usually followed the main play was not performed on the first night. She missed an experience she would have enjoyed. Dickens excelled in the farce, it suited his receptive nature perfectly. He had to impersonate six characters and his success was great.

He had left Liverpool that spring almost 'blinded by excitement, gas, and waving hats and handkerchiefs'. Now he and Lytton were back again at Manchester to be entertained with a banquet at the Athenaeum which had honoured him with life membership after the soirée Edward had helped to promote in 1843. Dickens was to explain the objectives of the Guild, Absalom to reply.

August 31st, 1852. Dined at the banquet given to the Members of the Guild of Literature at the Athenaeum. I responded to the toast 'The Manchester Athenaeum', which was proposed by Dickens. Bulwer-Lytton and Dickens were the principal speakers. Dickens spoke tolerably.

Absalom's speech was brief. If Dickens was the godfather of the Athenaeum, he himself could claim to have been present at its birth. He ended by thanking Dickens 'on behalf of the happy of our land whose happiness he has increased, and he thanked him still more on behalf of the miserable, whose misery he had always sought to alleviate'.

Dickens was able to announce that £4,000 (about £200,000 in 1990 values) had been made from the performance of the plays, and Bulwer-Lytton, who had just been returned as MP for Hertford, informed the audience that he intended to introduce a bill to incorporate the Guild. He kept his word. The cottages too were eventually built at Stevenage on land given by Lytton, but no writers or painters lived in them. They were not wisely situated nor are creative minds the easiest in the world to help. At the end of the century the Guild was dissolved and its funds were taken over by the Royal Literary Society.

The next day Absalom, Hester and one of her brothers went to the Free Trade Hall to see Dickens and his 'Splendid Strollers' in the comedy *Used Up*, Planché's *Charles XII*, and *Mr Nightingale's Diary*. The hall was too hot, but they enjoyed every moment of it.

Local excitement was by no means at an end. The Public Libraries Act had been passed that year and Manchester became the first municipality to have both a free reference library and one for home reading. The library, which was in Deansgate, was opened the very day after the play and the unfortunate Dickens had to speak yet again.

September 2nd, 1852. I went with Hester to the opening of the Manchester Free Library. The room was filled, and there were many ladies. Bulwer-Lytton, Dickens, Lord Shaftesbury, Sir James Stephen, the Bishop of Manchester and W.M. Thackeray (Vanity Fair), all spoke and most of them well, but the best speech was that of Sir James Stephen. Thackeray broke down.

Whether through Lord Carlisle's exertions or not, John had at last procured a living and, unless he disgraced himself, was set up for life. His parish was Stixwould, a remote and sparsely populated village in Lincolnshire. The living unfortunately was not a rich one but it was respectable and a very pleasant Georgian house went with it. The church was for the most part modern, but an ancient font with curious carvings had been salvaged from the medieval building. Even more curious was a stone slab near the chancel arch placed in memory of a local man who early in the eighteenth century had stabbed his mother to death in a little chapel by the old Priory. For this he had been hanged at Lincoln Gaol but his body had been taken home and lay in the churchyard as one day would John and Priscilla's.

Absalom would have appreciated the font and he would have certainly pondered the fate of the murderer, but it was not he but his wife who went into Lincolnshire to inspect their son's new home. He never made the journey. She was away for almost a month and Fanny Smith, the daughter of their old friends at Hill End, came to Rose Hill to keep house. Elizabeth was evidently incapable of doing so. His wife had scarcely left when Absalom had a slight accident.

October 7th, 1852. In getting out of the sociable at the top of Carr Lane on Tuesday night, I struck the back of the right leg just above the ankle against the edge of the step in consequence of the horse moving on. There was a momentary sharp pain, but I walked home without difficulty, felt nothing of it all day yesterday but this afternoon my boot appeared to pain the right instep so I took it off and put on a shoe. The pain increased till I could hardly bear to put my foot to the floor or to move about and I had to use a stick to get to the lecture. Miss Smith and my daughter came with me and when we got home, my legs were put into hot water and I took a pill.

He spent the following day at home.

October 8th, 1852. My foot better. Physicked by my daughter with a pill and black draught which worked violently – perhaps beneficially. Elizabeth and Miss Smith and I read aloud in turn about a hundred pages of Uncle Tom's Cabin. It is wonderfully clever. We laughed and shed tears.

Parliament reassembled and Manchester feared that under a Tory Government there might be a return to Protection.

November 2nd, 1852. Attended the Free Trade Banquet in the Free Trade Hall. Bright spoke well. The meeting was large and unanimous in denouncing a Protectionist Ministry.

They need not have worried. Disraeli had hounded Peel from office over that very question but he could smell a lost cause from a long way off and was the last person in the world to pursue it.

In December W.H. Mellor came to Rose Hill, much to Absalom's vexation. He stayed the night and started once more on 'the old business of explanation'. There was nothing now to explain. He had come, he had raised Elizabeth's hopes, he had not fulfilled them. His sister Mary had not yet fully recovered from her unfortunate accident of the summer and she came once more to Rose Hill with her little daughter and her nurse. Elizabeth, like her mother, was now drinking too much. Apparently she persuaded her sister-in-law to follow her example.

December 11th, 1852. Rose late, having been disturbed by the illness of Mary, occasioned by the folly of my daughter who had given her too much wine and spirits. Dr Occleston was sent for. [An erasure].

This is the first but by no means the last time that a passage in the diary has been erased. We cannot be certain who was responsible. It is unlikely to have been Absalom himself and was most probably done by Edward after his father's death.

A few days before Christmas a combination of Peelites, Radicals and Irish defeated the Government in the vote on Disraeli's budget. Although their politics were so different, Disraeli had a curious rapport with John Bright, perhaps because they were both outsiders. On the night before his defeat in the House, Disraeli invited Bright to come and see him at Grosvenor Gate. Bright went and arrayed in his morning gown, surrounded by his books, pictures and mirrors, Disraeli spoke with extraordinary frankness about his almost certain defeat on the morrow.

His own party had swallowed so much already, he said, if he modified his budget in the direction Bright and his friends wished, surely they could stay neutral? The old guard could be got rid of, there was no reason why Bright, Cobden and Milner-Gibson should not serve with him in a Cabinet one day. Shocked, Bright answered that putting aside the immorality of such a suggestion, Manchester would never permit it. 'Oh,' Disraeli very truly replied, 'a man of genius and power may do anything with a large constituency; I think I could represent Manchester and be a very popular Member.' Bright rather smugly assured him that the people of Manchester could not be trifled with. But whatever gods Disraeli worshipped, Man was not among them. He knew perfectly well that the people of Manchester could be as easily trifled with as the rest of the world. Before long Bright would find this out for himself.

Next day Derby and Disraeli had to resign and the Whigs and the Peelites combined to form the first coalition government for nearly fifty years. Lord Aberdeen was Prime Minister. Russell's No-popery campaign had seriously damaged his position and he was passed over largely because of Irish opposition. He became Foreign Secretary and Gladstone took Disraeli's place as Chancellor of the Exchequer.

On Christmas Day at Rose Hill Elizabeth drank too much and there is an extensive erasure. Boxing Day was Sunday.

December 26th, 1852. I wrote for an hour or two. Again my daughter drank too much. At night we had some music. The wind very high at night, many trees broke down, two of my poplars broken.

Edward was under strain, so much so that his two children were being looked after by their aunt, Miss Mellor, for some of the time and were often at Rose Hill. He was deciding whether or not to leave Captain Huish and the London and North Western Railway and to offer his services to another company.

When the spring of 1853 came, Absalom had two trees planted, one over the grave of his daughter's pony, Nut, and another over the grave of their cat, Kitty. He made arrangements to go to London in March to have his false teeth fitted and decided to take with him both his daughter and the maidservant, Mary Anne together with his niece, Hannah Davies. He determined to give them all a good time.

March 17th, 1853. Went to London by the express train from Stockport with my daughter and Mary Anne. At Stockport we were joined by Mrs Davies. We had a very cold ride to London which we reached at five p.m. We went to Miss Surr's, at her new house, 44, Skinner Street, Snow Hill. We went to the Prince's Theatre in the evening and saw The Corsican Brothers.

March 18th, 1853. In the afternoon we went to St Paul's and descended into the crypt, where we saw not the tomb of Nelson and the coffin of Wellington, but the wooden case in which they were concealed. We ascended to the Golden Gallery, saw the library, and the clock, I bought a few books. In the evening I dined with Edward.

Absalom went to the dentist and later determined to show Mrs Davies and Mary Anne the sights of London.

March 22nd, 1853. Went with Elizabeth and Mrs Davies in the morning to the National Gallery. Then I went to the British Museum. In the afternoon I went with Mary to look at the house, 18, Tavistock Square, which Edward has bought, and to which they are about to remove. In the evening I went with Mary Anne to the Coliseum. We saw the Sculpture Gallery in which there are many fine pieces and after that the view of London by night, the sky, with the moon and stars, the coming on and passing off of a thunder storm. All is so perfectly represented that it was scarcely possible to think it otherwise than real. I was much pleased.

He was as usual indefatigable. The National Gallery, the British Museum, the Tower, Covent Garden, the Guildhall, the Houses of Parliament, the Abbey, St Paul's – his companions should miss nothing. Edward had given him a free railway pass to visit some friends at Dover.

March 24th, 1853. In the morning Mrs Davies, Mary Anne and I went to Guildhall and saw the Hall, Gog and Magog and the pictures in the Council

Chamber . . . Passing Sydenham [on the railway], I saw at a distance the new Crystal Palace. We had a cold ride to Dover. When we got to Tunbridge we found the ground covered to some depth with snow. I reached Dover at about half-past one, paddled through the wet snow, and ordered some dinner, which I greatly enjoyed. Mulligatawny soup, a veal cutlet, half a pint of sherry, a cup of coffee and a liquor glass of pale brandy and [the tip for] the chambermaid and waiter cost me seven shillings and sixpence. I was the only person in the coffee room. All the articles were good, the linen beautifully white, the knives and forks [extremely] clean and the silver, it <u>was</u> silver, clean and bright.

On the first of May, back again at Rose Hill, he heard the cuckoo and a few days later the corncrake. He planted the copper beeches that still thrive in front of the house and a week later it snowed, giving the hills round Northenden a strange, alpine look. But Absalom felt content.

May 21st, 1853. This is the last day of the Whitsun Week and the people of Manchester have never enjoyed it more, nor have I ever seen clearer evidences of general well-being. Our country is, no doubt, in a most happy and prosperous state. Free trade, peace, freedom. Oh happy England! Mayest thou know and deserve thy happiness!

His tranquil mood continued.

May 29th, 1853. The late rain has made the country and the garden very beautiful, although the poplars, ashes, acacias and oaks are not yet fully in leaf. There is a profusion of blossom on the fruit trees and bloom on the flowering shrubs. The Persian lilac is one mass of bloom. Lilacs, red, white and purple, laburnums, double blossomed cherry, double blossom gorse, hawthorn, a few rhododendrons, azaleas, these and others with varied tints of the young foliage render the scene before me as I sit at the east-end of the window exceedingly beautiful. I look out upon it and up to the glowing evening sky with delight and I hope with thankfulness to Him who has given me all, and with all, the power to enjoy it by better health and spirits.

Yet even as Absalom was writing, the great powers were wrangling in Constantinople. Before the cuckoo flew again over the woods or the corncrake was heard in the meadows, that happy England was at war.

CHAPTER THIRTY-SIX

'Seems to me privately I have hardly seen a madder business'

France was England's traditional enemy. Yet in the conflict to come Napoleon III was her ally. By force and guile Napoleon had transformed his Presidency into a hereditary Empire. His position depended upon popular support, support which included an army longing to avenge the defeat at Waterloo. Snubbed by the Tsar as a parvenu, he had in addition a personal motive to act as an international statesman and to embroil France in a war which was fought to prevent an expansionist Russia profiting from the imminent collapse of the Ottoman Empire.

In May Russia threatened to occupy the Danubian Principalities of Moldavia and Walachia (Romania) unless Turkey accepted her right to protect the ten million Greek Orthodox Christians in the Sultan's Empire. These provinces were under nominal Turkish rule.

Palmerston was Home Secretary. He proposed decisive action in response and was supported in Cabinet by Russell. Russian troops should not be allowed to occupy the Principalities; the Fleet should be sent to the Black Sea and the Tsar warned that Britain would go to war if the invasion took place. Aberdeen dithered and took half measures. No ultimatum was sent to Russia and the Mediterranean Fleet was ordered, not actually to join the Turkish in the Black Sea, but to leave Malta for Besika Bay, ten miles south of the Dardanelles.

The situation was grave but war not yet certain. For Britain, even if it did come, there would be no conscription, no possibility of invasion, no risk of terrible weapons devastating the lives and property of civilians at home. What was done or what might be done would happen offstage. Nowhere was there any sense of urgency. A few days after the Fleet left for the Dardanelles, Absalom, Dr McKerrow and Mr Smiles went to London as members of a deputation on behalf of the Public Schools Association. They had an appointment to see Lord John Russell at Chesham Place.

Russell was much more interested in parliamentary reform than in foreign affairs. Education was closely linked with any plans for the extension of the franchise. Russell was as anxious as anyone for the establishment of a system of national elementary education but, like Kay-Shuttleworth, did not think the idea of secular schools along American lines was practicable. He thought pupils would have to get their basic religious instruction at schools run by the various denominations.

If it had been left to Russell, that instruction would have been very basic indeed. He deplored the trappings of religion, repudiated the Church of England's assumption of sanctity and her claim to be the special depository of truth together with a narrowness of spirit that, in his opinion, made her the enemy of free thought and progress. He considered the English Catechism wholly unfit for children and himself refused to be cramped or controlled by any man-made sect. His wife wrote

> He looked forward to the day when there would be no priests or rather when every man should be a priest and all superstitious notions – such as implied in the notion that only a clergyman ought to perform certain offices of religion – should be cast aside by Christian men for ever.

Absalom was staying at Miss Surr's, where his daughter had been left after their visit in the spring.

June 3rd, 1853. I went first to Morley's Hotel to meet the deputation. We arranged the order of our proceedings, and drove in four or five cabs to the residence of Lord John Russell in Chesham Place. As we arrived at his door, he returned from a ride. Milner-Gibson was the introducer of the deputation and we had the countenance of James Heywood, Cobden, Gardner, Brown, Sir Joshua Walmsley and Ricardo, M.P.s. In the absence of Mr Bazley, I had to begin the statement, and was desired to state the objects of the Association, and to defend it against the charge of irreligion; also to claim the right of independent administration of the money to be raised by local rates. This I did with some trepidation. I was followed by McKerrow, Swaine, Lucas, Tucker, Baynes of Leeds and at last by Dr Watts. They all spoke to the purpose and Watts remarkably well. Lord John was evidently perplexed and found he could not answer. He praised us, and in a good many words, delivered hesitatingly, said as little as possible and requested that a summary of what we had said should be sent to him. He looks ill and in some of his postures reminded me of Mr Grime.

Perhaps Grime had been small too; some people considered Russell to be hardly more than a dwarf.

Edward's wife, Mary, became ill that summer and took the waters at Malvern, leaving the children sometimes with Miss Mellor and sometimes at Rose Hill. James Battersby, the son of Absalom's gardener, drove the sociable.

July 7th, 1853. Edward's children came from London. James got drunk before I left town and was stupid and unmanageable all the way home and sick and incapable when we reached home. Happily we had no accident.

Rose Hill was crowded with children, parents and aunts all coming and going. Mrs Wall, formerly Alice Makinson, had returned to Ceylon leaving her two daughters with her parents, the William Makinsons of Lime Place, Broughton.

The Makinson family were obsessed with the name Hannah. Joseph's daughter, now Mrs Davies, was a Hannah Maria, another brother's daughter was Hannah Maude, and William's daughter was just plain Hannah. The charms of Mrs Stoneley and Mrs Shuttleworth had long faded but Absalom remained attracted to a pretty woman and his wife knew it. The exaggeration and coarsening of this awareness in her mind had led to the unpleasant scenes which had so often spoilt Hannah Davies's visits to Rose Hill when she was a girl. Towards the end of July Mrs William Makinson and her daughter Hannah came to dinner, bringing with them Mrs Wall's two children.

July 21st, 1853. The Court till noon and the Assurance Board. I returned at one to meet Mrs Makinson, Hannah and the children of Mrs Wall. We had dinner mostly of fragments. Hannah played some tunes very prettily and they left at half-past six. At night after they were all gone to bed, and I was sitting half asleep over a book, my wife came into the room in her night clothes and after demanding if I would answer a question and my replying that I would, proceeded to ask, 'Have you <u>kissed</u> Hannah Makinson?' I replied very truly that I had not and she withdrew.

Absalom was in court for most of that week.

July 22nd, 1853. At night reminding my wife that I had answered all her questions about Hannah and others, I asked her if she would answer in the same way questions about her conduct. She shuffled exceedingly and endeavoured to get to know to what the questions would refer – to what persons – what times – what places? I did not satisfy and at last loudly professing her faithfulness to her marriage vows she 'preferred not to answer'. I urged her to do as I had done, but conscious of guilty improprieties, she was resolute.

Absalom was deeply upset. He spent the morning in court and the afternoon at the warehouse. On his return home he found his wife still determined not to answer his questions. He felt too unhappy to go to work. He took out his old diaries and searched their pages for clues, looking for the people, places and times she refused to talk about.

July 24th, 1853. At home all day. Unwell and depressed. For <u>what</u> have I lived and laboured? Alas. Several volumes of my diary for 1824, 5, 6, 1829, 1831, etc. Alas! I will <u>try</u> to do my duty, but it is hard, very hard.

The next day his wife gave in. Most of the entry is in shorthand.

July 25th, 1853. Mrs Watkin confessed [shorthand]. Many years ago [shorthand] impropriety.

That is all we shall ever know about the matter. Absalom makes no further direct reference to what plainly distressed him considerably. For her part, his wife remained vigilant and kept a close eye on him when they went to have tea at Lime Place a few days later.

His daughter returned from London and continued the reading aloud of the painter Benjamin Haydon's *Memoirs*. Haydon had committed suicide in 1846.

August 7th, 1853. Rose late. At home all day. Looked at my notes for 1831. Began the third volume of Haydon's Memoirs. Poor fellow! Harassed as he was by continual pecuniary difficulties I wonder he was able to effect what he did or that he bore up so long. I should have died under it or have shot myself some years earlier. But then he had had an affectionate wife who was worthy of him. And in the midst of his desperate necessities he had days and weeks now and then, of great success and high enjoyment.

On 3 July Russian troops had crossed the River Pruth and occupied Moldavia. They now controlled the mouth of the Danube. The Great Powers conferred in Vienna and war crept closer.

Absalom had always loathed the absolute government of the Tsar and abhorred Russia's treatment of the Poles and the Hungarian patriots. Step by step he was allowing himself to be drawn into the war party, and step by step Aberdeen's Cabinet committed itself to the support of Turkey.

August 9th, 1853. There is a mad market, owing to the dispute between Russia and Turkey. I think <u>we</u> shall have to fight those barbarians, the Russians. Really assiduous at the warehouse. Continued Haydon and sat up till not two, but five. Very absurd and destruction to my health.

Lack of sleep sapped his energy. He went with Alfred to dine with some Mellors, Thomas Fielden and J.R. Kay, probably Sir James's brother, the economist and lawyer.

August 19th, 1853. We had a good, not a <u>very</u> good dinner, and <u>two</u> waiters who looked more like gentlemen than nearly any one of us. I proposed the health of Mr Mellor and afterwards that of Mrs Mellor and afterwards that of Jonathan, in doing which I <u>forgot it was his birthday</u>. J.R. Kay proposed my health and praised me extravagantly, being well steeped in champagne. I replied <u>weakly</u>. It is difficult to speak of ourselves with propriety. We left at nine, when having drunk not largely, but rather freely, all were becoming <u>very</u> good humoured and <u>rather affectionate</u>. I did not get to bed till nearly three.

Alfred complained of piles and for the hundredth time Absalom regretted his own late hours.

August 21st, 1853. Very sleepy all day and really sad at the thought of my own imbecility. I must <u>prepare</u> more, and think <u>more</u>, and <u>read less variously</u>.

The 3 September was Edward and Mary's wedding anniversary. Mary was staying at Rose Hill.

September 3rd, 1853. Assiduous at the warehouse till three. This being Edward and Mary's wedding day we had Alfred and his wife to dine with Mary. Edward was unable to come. We had a good dinner, two bottles of champagne and all would have gone off well, but Alfred and Hester Anne became sulky and all was spoiled. I have often resolved, and I again resolve, to have no visitors on Saturdays.

Next Monday was his wife's sixty-third birthday.

September 5th, 1853. At the warehouse early. Assiduous there till three. Returned with Alfred to Rose Hill to dinner in honour of the day. We had a decent dinner and two bottles of champagne but Mrs Watkin had taken too much ale while hot with cooking and she betrayed it by talking absurdly.

A week later Absalom and his wife went to London together. From there they went by train to Winchester, had a meal and then walked to see the Hospital of the Holy Cross. When they reached it Absalom realized to his embarrassment that they had only one shilling and tenpence left between them.

September 20th, 1853. We durst not ask to see the interior of the Hospital having no money to pay for the sight. We passed the outer court and entered the inner and there, at the porter's lodge, required the horn of ale and the slice of bread to which every visitor is entitled by the will of the founder. It was given to us and we drank to the health of William of Wykeham. Then we walked round the inner court, which is surrounded by the lodgings of the Brethren, having flower gardens in front. One of the Brethren sat at his door. He was a hale-looking old man, wearing a blue cloth gown having a silver cross on his breast.

They returned to Winchester intending to visit the Cathedral but found to their dismay that a service had just finished and that the doors were about to be shut. They had no money to pay any official who might allow them to enter.

In this dilemma I made an appeal to the Verger and he consented to show us the Cathedral on my <u>promise</u> to remunerate him by a remittance from London.

After seeing the Cathedral they went to the Bell and Crown for a small strengthener before leaving for the station but again found their lack of funds troublesome.

After indulging in another pint of ale, I asked the landlord to give us credit for a cup of tea. He assented. We had it in the parlour – hitherto we had sat in the taproom – when it was finished we took a walk round the Cathedral Close and I got some roots of the ivy-leaved snapdragon from the wall near the King's Gate. Once more we went to the Bell and Crown, had a bottle of soda water and a glass of brandy and then walked to the station.

The next day Absalom paid what was to prove to be his last visit to his beloved Bromley.

September 21st, 1853. Went by steam boat to Greenwich, thence in an open carriage to Bromley. Dined there and walked about. Could not find the cottage in which I used to live when at school there – or rather the site of it – nor yet the Green, or the public house which was formerly near it. I suspect the ground has been laid out in plots for building, but I was annoyed at being unable to make out the locality and intend to go again and try to make it out. I got some roots of the ivy-leaved saxifrage from the wall of a garden on the road to Chislehurst and one or two other plants from hedges.

Back at Rose Hill they found all much as usual.

September 24th, 1853. Hannah Makinson and Fanny Smith having been the assistant housekeepers while we have been away, Mrs Watkin began to pout before we reached home and was quite rude to the poor girls.

On 23 September the Mediterranean Fleet under Admiral Dundas was ordered to leave Besika Bay and sail through the Dardanelles to the Golden Horn to be ready to defend Constantinople. The Foreign Secretary, Lord Clarendon, wrote to a friend

I see little chance of averting war, which even in the most sacred cause is a horrible calamity; but for such a cause as two sets of Barbarians quarrelling over a form of words, is not only shocking but incredible.

Turkey declared war on Russia on 5 October on the ground that the Tsar had refused to withdraw his armies from Moldavia and Walachia. With the majority of the press, Absalom cheered on the Turks.

War fever mounted. Christians of a kind the Russians might be, but many thought their avowed concern for the Holy Places in Turkish hands was humbug, a device to conceal territorial ambitions. Their empire was already the largest the world had yet seen, their Tsar a despot, a supporter of hangmen and floggers, a crusher of liberal ideals and legitimate national aspirations. Charles Kingsley announced that the Turks were fighting on God's side and Karl Marx that the forces of history were inexorably driving the British and French to fight the Tsar.

Lord John Russell thought that British troops should be employed 'at every point where Russia can be resisted or attacked'. The Queen and Prince Albert were more circumspect, and Sir James Graham, the First Lord of the Admiralty, shared their doubts. If Great Britain encouraged the Turks to act rashly, were we in that case bound 'to be dragged into hostilities by a Barbarian whom we are unable to control?'

Absalom was an ardent free trader but he does not seem to have felt there was any conflict between his views on that subject and his zeal to go to war. Yet there was a contradiction. The movement for free trade extended far beyond commercial considerations. It had developed a philosophy and become a moral crusade. Free trade was imagined to be the instrument for ensuring worldwide and permanent peace since governments would no longer be able to declare war when the peoples of the world knew each other through their commercial dealings and were dependent upon each other's prosperity. 'I believe,' Cobden told a meeting in Manchester in 1846, 'that the desire and motive for large and mighty empires, for gigantic armies and great navies, will die away when man becomes one family and freely exchanges the fruits of his labour with his brother man.'

Both Cobden and Bright supported the Peace Society, which held conferences up and down the country and had a significant following in Manchester. At the beginning of the year Bright had spoken on 'Arbitration in Place of War' at the Corn Exchange and had been heard with satisfaction. But that was months ago. Our fleet was now in sight of Constantinople and feelings were very different.

In the palmy days of the League, Tennyson had subscribed to the dream of universal peace:

Till the war drum throbbed no longer, and the battle flags were furled,
In the parliament of man, the Federation of the world.

Now he too succumbed to war fever and in the spring of 1855 would include foolish and unjust lines against Bright in *Maud* which he later suppressed:

This broad-brimmed hawker of holy things,
Whose ear is cramm'd with cotton, and rings
Even in dreams to the chink of his pence . . .

As war came closer popular attitudes coarsened and feeling about the Peace Society was expressed in the lines of a less subtle poet than the Laureate.

Go home, you idle teachers! You miserable creatures!
The cannons are God's preachers when the time is ripe for war.

Absalom had come to think so too and in the middle of November a month after the British and French fleets had passed the Straits, he made his first public declaration of where he stood in the approaching conflict.

November 16th, 1853. I presided at a meeting to express sympathy with Turkey, which was held at the Corn Exchange, and at which Sir Charles Napier and Mr David Urquhart attended and took part. The meeting was noisy but unanimous.

Sir Charles Napier was not the general who had commanded the Northern District in 1839, but his cousin, the controversial Admiral Napier, later to command the Baltic Fleet. Urquhart was a most extraordinary man. To him we owe the introduction into Great Britain of a modified form of Turkish baths; the well-known establishment in Jermyn Street was built under his direction. That was not the reason he was in Manchester.

A diplomatist, secret agent, author and controversialist, Urquhart had fought for the Greeks in the War of Independence and been badly wounded. His intimate knowledge of the Levant led to his appointment as attaché to Stratford Canning, British Ambassador to Turkey. He was later recalled by Palmerston whom he denounced as a Russian agent and declared to be guilty of high treason and worthy of impeachment. Palmerston thought him 'more than half mad, and wholly bad'. Urquhart's views were peculiar and added another dimension to the debate into which Absalom had now most foolishly got embroiled.

Urquhart hated Russia but repudiated the idea of a European protectorate over the Christian subjects of Turkey being substituted for the Russian. This he considered to be interference with the internal affairs of Turkey. The Turks, he maintained, were perfectly well able to cope with Russia without outside help.

The whole matter was perplexing and just as Absalom was trying to thread his way through a maze of differing opinions, one more Hannah came to stay at Rose Hill. She was Hannah Maude, the daughter of yet another of his wife's brothers and the one of Absalom's nieces to cause him the most trouble.

December 8th, 1853. We have had Hannah [Maude] Makinson here. She plays and sings and is willing to do her best, but she is rude and rather vulgar. Still, her liveliness has agreeably varied our daily course of life.

On Sunday his wife read aloud Blair's sermon *On the Duties of the Young* to her

niece and on Monday morning Absalom drove her back to Manchester in the
sociable.

December 12th, 1853. As we drove to Manchester together, I spoke to her
freely of her character, and situation, and of her danger. Poor girl, she has an
unhappy home and inherits from her mother a violent temper and much
obstinacy.

On that very day, 12 December, the news reached London that the Russian
fleet had attacked and annihilated a Turkish squadron at anchor in the harbour of
Sinope in the Black Sea. It was the last occasion wooden vessels were in conflict
and 4,000 Turkish sailors were said to have perished. The action was hardly
surprising since the two nations were at war, but the attack caused an outcry in
England. It was felt to be a humiliation, the British Fleet, after all, was anchored by
the Golden Horn, supposedly protecting the Turks. Lord Aberdeen, still valiantly
negotiating, was accused of cowardice and even of betraying his country to Russia.

It was a bitter winter. Absalom caught cold because snow soaked through the
leather soles of his boots. As a matter of course some of the family spent Christmas
at Rose Hill.

December 25th, 1853. Little Alfred attacked by the measles. Edward and
Mary here. Edward very figetty. Our Christmas dinner came off at four. We
had Mr and Mrs Worsley, Edward, Mary, Alfred and Hester Anne. Our
dinner was good and well dressed but Edward was out of humour and the
time dragged on unpleasantly. They all left early, except Edward and Mary,
who remained.

Things were not very much better on New Year's Day.

January 1st, 1854. We had a tolerable dinner cooked with the help of Mrs
Battersby, Sarah Hough and two of Mary Anne's sisters. But in spite of my
champagne it went off rather heavily, Edward being busy and out of humour
and some of the others indisposed to be pleased.

Absalom's views about the Russian–Turkish conflict had not endeared him to
many of his former free trade colleagues. Despite the ever- increasing war fever in
the country at large, a number of the reforming group in Manchester belonged to
what today would be called the appeasement party. When Absalom went into the
city to chair a meeting on the education question he was not sure how he would
be received.

January 18th, 1854. The meeting was crowded. Peter Rylands, T. Milner-
Gibson, John Bright, D.C. Gilman of Connecticut, Cobden, McKerrow, Dr

Watts were the chief speakers, and all spoke well. At the end Bazley took the chair and Alexander Henry moved, and Gibson seconded, a vote of thanks to me as chairman. I said little but to have been placed in the chair on this occasion, after my appearance as chairman of the Turkish meeting, at which I had condemned the lukewarmness of all the persons who were actively present this evening, was to me an unexpected personal triumph and I do really believe that my decided and independent course in the Turkish matter has brought me consideration, even with my opponents. I left the meeting but after starting home the horse cast a shoe in St Peter's Street. We could get no blacksmith and I was forced to leave the sociable and horse in Manchester, to take a cab to the fifth milestone, and to walk thence home over the meadows. We did not get home till half-past twelve.

At the end of January the Liberal MPs held a soirée at the Albion Hotel. Absalom attended it and heard Gibson, Cobden and Bright make long speeches about parliamentary reform and the Eastern Question. They were strong for peace and non-intervention and listened to with approval. However, it would not be many months before Bright would be burnt in effigy.

Hannah Maude came to stay at Rose Hill again, sulky and difficult to deal with. On Sunday they did not go to church but read aloud Blair's sermon *On the Weariness of Life*. It was decided to give a dinner party and old Battersby's son, James, was asked to act as an extra waiter for the occasion. His lapse had been forgiven and now it was his turn to watch the intemperance of his betters.

February 22nd, 1854. By a quarter past two we sat down to a good dinner, which with the help of two bottles of champagne, passed off tolerably well. At tea we had Alfred and Mr Sumner and after tea music and singing enabled us to get along till it was time to separate. [Long erasure] Mrs Watkin gave evidence of having taken too much – and so the day closed unpleasantly and I went to bed sadly but slept well.

In February the Tsar withdrew his ambassadors from both London and Paris. In response Great Britain and France withdrew theirs from St Petersburg. The *Illustrated London News*, whose circulation had risen to 100,000 copies a week, anticipated a three-month campaign, conquest of the Crimea, gains in the Caucasus and victories in the Baltic. The First Battalion the Coldstream Guards left their London barracks for Malta accompanied by cheers, but next morning *The Times* struck a sombre note. Medical supplies had been moved from the Apothecaries Hall and Savory and Son of New Bond Street, and taken to the Tower. A Danubian campaign, the paper calculated, would require a thousand yards of adhesive plaster and a thousand pounds of lint.

Still war had not been declared and Lord Aberdeen went on refusing to accept that it was inevitable. He told the Queen that he had a terrible repugnance for war in all its forms. He was all for patching it up. The Queen was not. A woman of great common sense, at first she had been very lukewarm about the whole Eastern imbroglio. She did not consider that there was any threat to the British route to India and judged the differences between Russia and Turkey not to be of great importance. Besides, the detested Palmerston was behind the anti-Russian party. Even after Sinope in December she distrusted 'the absurd and mischievous blusterings of newspapers and popular meetings'. Yet gradually she too caught war fever and decided that patching up was dangerous.

At the end of February Britain and France sent an ultimatum to the Tsar telling him that he must withdraw his forces from the Principalities within a month. The days passed. No reply was received and at last, on 28 March, war was declared against Russia in support of Turkey. Lord Aberdeen told Bright that 'his grief was such that he felt as if every drop of blood that would be shed would rest upon his head'.

Walter Savage Landor felt very differently. 'At last we are on the field of battle, no more flirting with Bellona, no more pouring rose-water on the mustache of Mars.' The Queen rose early to watch a battalion of Guards, drummer boys at their head, march off for embarkation and at Spithead she waved goodbye to her Fleet. Thomas Carlyle was finishing the first volume of *Frederick the Great*. He too heard the tread of marching men. 'Never such enthusiasm among the population. Cold, I, as a very stone to all that; seems to me privately I have hardly seen a madder business.'

'You must excuse me if I cannot go with you. I will have no part in this terrible crime'

Because of its faltering beginnings and persistent mismanagement, the Crimean War is often dismissed as a slightly absurd Continental adventure undertaken after forty years of peace by a group of incompetent veterans. Yet not all the commanders in the field were incompetent or even veterans; a despotic regime sustained a temporary defeat, men and women showed they were capable of most remarkable bravery, valuable experience of combined operations was obtained and hospitals learnt a great deal from the conditions which prevailed at Scutari.

Nevertheless, battles should not be fought in order to demonstrate the courage of the human race nor legs amputated to facilitate advances in medical science; neither should men perish with cold and horses starve to death to benefit knowledge of logistics. 'Never was so great an effort made for so worthless an object,' *The Times* wrote five years after the end of the war. With that verdict most people today would agree.

Casualty figures are notoriously difficult to establish with any certainty but it has been estimated that over the eighteen months of war half a million British, French and Russians lost their lives. This does not include those who fell as a consequence of the Baltic engagements or those who died of fever at Varna. The Turkish figures are not available. The majority died of disease; on the British side fewer than one in ten deaths occurred in battle. The gains, immediate or in the long term, from all this horror and misery were paltry. Russia got back full sovereign rights in the Black Sea only fifteen years after the peace was signed. It has been suggested that the real beneficiary of the conflict, ironically enough, was Prussia, since Bismarck was able to unify Germany without Russian interference.

On the British side much of the responsibility for the war must lie with Lord Aberdeen, too good a man to make a successful politician. While it would be absurd to equate the Russian threat in 1853 with the ambitions of Germany some eighty years later, it may not be altogether wide of the mark to think of Aberdeen as playing the part of Neville Chamberlain to Palmerston's Churchill. Unlike Churchill, Palmerston was in the Cabinet and if Britain had followed the resolute line urged by him and supported by Russell, war might have been avoided because Palmerston's bellicosity would have left Russia in no doubt where Great Britain stood.

In the pause that followed the declaration of war and before engagement with
the enemy, Absalom and his wife went up to London to visit Edward, who had
been moody and on edge for months. The reason was indecision about his career.

He had determined to leave the London and North Western Railway and had
been weighing up the prospects of the various companies eager to employ him.
Eventually he resolved to accept the post of General Manager of the Manchester,
Sheffield and Lincolnshire Company at a salary of £1,200 a year (about £60,000
in 1990 terms) plus, and this was important, a percentage of the profits. In
gratitude for his past services the London and North Western Railway had got up
a subscription and intended to present him with plate worth £750 (about
£37,500). This was to be presented at a dinner held in his honour at the London
Tavern. John had come up from Stixwould for the occasion accompanied by
Priscilla, who was to be privileged, like the other ladies, to watch the spectacle
from a gallery. Absalom and his wife took the express train from Manchester the
day before and as usual stayed at Miss Surr's.

April 4th, 1854. In the morning I went with my wife and called upon Mary
at the Euston Hotel. She was 'Not at Home'. We proceeded to Alexander
Makinson's and then returned to Miss Surr. In the afternoon I had my hair
cut and dressed and at six I went with John to attend the dinner. Sir Cussac
Roney was in the chair, supported by Mr Geach, M.P., Mr Peto, M.P., Mr
John Mellor, Mr Alderman and Sheriff Wise and a large party. The chairman
was able and ready and presentation was made very neatly. Mary, my wife,
Lady Roney, Hester, Mrs Walrond and others were in a gallery. The dinner
was good. Edward did not speak very well.

Edward was almost thirty-five and on the threshold of his greatest achievements.
Under his leadership the Manchester, Sheffield and Lincolnshire Railway was to
construct the last main line into London and transform the company into the
Great Central Railway, with its sights on Paris, Pekin and St Petersburg.

Just then people in England were not thinking about St Petersburg in that
connection. In his address at the opening of the Great Exhibition in 1851, Dr
Sumner, the Archbishop of Canterbury, had been both pious and optimistic. 'It is
of Thee, Oh Lord,' he had said, 'that nations do not lift up the sword against each
other nor learn war any more; it is of Thee that peace is within our walls and
plenteousness within our palaces.' That was three years ago. The joke then had
been 'Paxton vobiscum'. It sounded a little hollow now.

The Crystal Palace was no longer in Hyde Park. Paxton had wanted it to
remain there as a permanent giant conservatory to house tropical birds and plants.
The House of Commons, however, voted for its removal. Paxton therefore
formed a new company, bought the Palace from the exhibition commissioners and
had it re-erected at Penge Park, on a hill overlooking Sydenham with fine views
over Kent and Surrey.

The new building was far larger than its predecessor. The original Crystal Palace was a celebration of peace and free trade and the brotherhood of man; the intention of the second was not simply to amuse but to educate. It was laid out in a series of great courts, each illustrating the art and architecture of various historical periods. The Assyrians, the Egyptians, the Greeks, the Romans, medieval Christendom and Renaissance man all had their own exhibition displayed with appropriate statuary and works of art. There was, too, a Hall of Science, and great conservatories for tropical plants and fruits. The pomegranates had formerly been the property of the unfortunate King Louis Philippe. The lower parts of the grounds were devoted to geology and prehistoric animals. Plaster casts of iguanodons, plesiosaurus and pterodactyls were placed on islands specially built for them. It was just the sort of thing to please Absalom immensely but it took a long time to prepare and when he made his first visit it was not quite finished.

April 6th, 1854. At two o'clock we left London by the Brighton Railway to go to Sydenham to see the Crystal Palace. At Sydenham station we discovered that we were a mile and a quarter from the Palace, and we had a toilsome, dusty march uphill to the entrance. My wife, Hester Anne and Miss Mellor were all hot and Mrs Watkin was not by any means in an amiable temper. At the Palace we were joined by John, and we spent about three hours in a very imperfect examination of this wonderful building. When finished, the beauty of the site and the assemblage of rare objects within and without must render it particularly attractive. We returned by railway and got back about eight.

Lord Clarendon was now proclaiming sentiments very different from those he expressed in private a year earlier. Then the Turks were barbarians, now they were Britain's partners in the battle against barbarism for the independence of Europe. Indeed, in the country as a whole the war was proving even more popular than the Great Exhibition. The Poet Laureate was in the van. Tennyson declared,

> Though the niggered throats of Manchester may bawl,
> What England was, shall her true sons forget?
> We are not cotton spinners all,
> But some love England and her honour yet.

The niggered throats of Manchester, however, were not all saying the same thing. A great number, like Absalom, agreed wholeheartedly with Lord Clarendon and the Laureate. Others held more moderate views. One of the more convincing and sober statements of British war aims came from the pen of a writer in the *Manchester Guardian*. No well-informed or candid person, he said, pretended that we were taking up arms out of regard for the Sultan or preference for the internal economy of his dominions over that of the Tsar's. 'We are going to war to avert the dangers to ourselves which are obviously involved in the transference of Constantinople to a great power which already possesses an excess of the resources and opportunities for conquest.' There were others who yet hoped that the conflict could be avoided. A few were still on the side of the peace party led by Cobden and Bright.

At the end of April David Urquhart came again to Manchester to propagate his peculiar views. Eccentric, knowledgeable, vehement and unbalanced, Urquhart, whose son 'Sligger' was to captivate generations of Balliol undergraduates, remained passionately pro-Turkey yet anti-war. He still maintained that the Turks were capable of fighting their own battles and brought with him a number of supporters, nearly all of whom, according to a reporter, 'were distinguished by tremendous mustaches'.

April 19th, 1854. Went to Manchester to attend the meeting in the Corn Exchange called by David Urquhart to condemn the Ministers and to pray for the recall of our Fleet and army from Constantinople. I got there at half-past seven and stayed till half-past ten. It was dreadfully hot, crammed with people and very noisy. Abel Heywood took the chair and filled it very well. The tail of Mr Urquhart consisted of an Irish attorney, Conyngham, who libelled Prince Albert, a dissipated-looking, bearded stout man who was called Captain Roland, another Irishman called Pare or Pares, and a Mr Hart. Some of these people had been hired, perhaps all. Colonel Chesney, of the Euphrates Expedition, was also present, and spoke, but disclaimed any participation in the resolutions proposed by Urquhart. About ten o'clock I moved an amendment to the second resolution: 'That this meeting, concurring in the opinion with the great majority of the British people that the war with Russia in defence of Turkey is just and necessary (applause) desires to express its earnest wish that the war may be carried on with the utmost vigour and continued until the dangerous power of Russia shall be reduced within such limits as will be consistent with the peace and safety of the world. That in furtherance of this view, the restoration of Poland, Hungary and Italy to the state of independent nations having free institutions is greatly to be desired.' I spoke only a few sentences which were scarcely audible and left at half-past ten, but my amendment, put as a resolution, was carried. I was in a state of profuse perspiration, but I drank a glass of brandy and water, smoked all the way to the station, and so escaped a cold. It was very late when I got to bed.

Much to the Queen's disgust, a national Day of Humiliation had been decided upon. She thought that there was not the least necessity for any humiliation. The war, she told Lord Aberdeen, was all the fault of the Tsar, our conduct had been unselfish and honest throughout. It would be more appropriate for her subjects to recite the petition enjoined in the Prayer Book, 'To be Used before a Fight at Sea against any Enemy.' Her advice was not taken and on 26 April Absalom did not go into Manchester. Unlike his Sovereign, Days of Humiliation suited his cast of mind.

April 26th, 1854. <u>Day of Humiliation</u>. To church in the forenoon. At Northen £4 two shillings and a penny were collected for the wives and children of the soldiers who are going to Turkey. In Manchester about £1,700. John came at night. He is to marry Mr Hamilton and Fanny Sumner.

Mr Bright, the MP for Manchester, felt very differently from both Queen Victoria and Absalom. 'Prayers for success,' he wrote in his diary, 'seem much like a gang of burglars seeking Divine blessing upon their guilty enterprises.'

Fanny Sumner's wedding may have upset Elizabeth for Absalom wrote to W.H. Mellor and made an arrangement to meet him at Rose Hill in the afternoon. He returned early from the warehouse with that intention but 'the scamp did not come'. Mellor arrived a few days later.

May 3rd, 1854. W.H. Mellor at last came to our house to meet Elizabeth. They had a long recriminatory dialogue which lasted all day and till late at night which irritated me and which ended in his staying all night, contrary to my wish and will.

It was all to no purpose. W.H. Mellor left the following day and Elizabeth fell ill as a consequence.

The annual dinner of the Literary Society was held at the Palatine Hotel and Absalom proposed 'Our Native Land'. His speech suited the mood of his listeners. England was on the march. Lord Raglan had been appointed commander-in-chief of the British troops. A brave man and able soldier, he had lost an arm at Waterloo. But he was sixty-five and had not seen active service for nearly forty years. In May, under Austrian pressure, Russia started to withdraw from the Principalities. The actual *casus belli* had evaporated.

Absalom entertained the reunited Wall family to dinner together with their ayah, then stayed up until morning reading the *Letters of Lady Mary Wortley Montagu* and Disraeli's *Tancred*. He could no more break himself of this habit than poor Lord Raglan could stop himself referring to the enemy as the French.

June 3rd, 1854. Assiduous at the warehouse. Surprisingly better for my washing at night. I was tired, dirty and dejected. As I scrubbed myself all this crept away and I had the feeling of comfort and good health. Mrs Watkin continued Tancred. Much pleased with my little place and I hope grateful for my many mercies, but strongly self-condemned for my continued indolence.

Nevertheless, after staying up one night until five in the morning reading *Ordericus Vitalis*, he began to feel his lack of rest and as so often, it took the form of intense nervous anxiety. He was seized by the old familiar fear of bankruptcy.

June 20th, 1854. A dull market with us. I came home unusually depressed. I could think only of ill success and decline. I even thought that I was greatly in debt. This feeling came over me after I had slept and I was not easy till I had looked over the ledger. I stayed up till five.

On Midsummer Day a Cabinet meeting was held at Lord John Russell's house and the question of where and how the war should be fought was finally decided. The main Anglo-French force would sail to the Crimea and invest Sebastopol, the base from where the Russian fleet had sailed to sink the Turkish ships at Sinope. The task was a formidable one. The intention was to assemble the British, French and Turkish troops at Varna, a port on the Black Sea in Bulgaria, and from there make a combined assault upon the Crimea. Some 60,000 men were to be landed to the north of Sebastopol while the navy attacked it from the sea. That was not to be the only theatre of war.

Admiral Napier, in command of the Baltic Fleet stationed at Kiel, was expected to attack the Russian naval base of Kronstadt. He was a sailor of the old school and when he hoisted his flag, signalled to his ships

Lads, war is declared with a numerous and bold enemy. Should they remain in port, we must try and get at them. Success depends upon the quickness and precision of your firing. Also, lads, sharpen your cutlasses, and the day is your own.

At Rose Hill patriotic hopes could not subdue domestic anxieties.

June 28th, 1854. Mr Burnett, his son and Alfred and Hester Anne dined with us. With the aid of Mrs Ratcliffe, the cook, we had a good dinner, which all appeared to enjoy. At dinner I began to suffer from a cold in my head which almost took away my voice. Mr Burnett became unwell after dinner and my daughter was sick.

Mr Greaves had to be called in to attend her and Absalom again began to get into a nervous state about his expenditure. The uncertainties of war had not improved his business.

July 4th, 1854. A dull market. Somewhat dejected by the state of my affairs. Mrs Watkin severely affected by erysipelas. I found to my great disgust, W.H. Mellor when I got home. [Erasure] He stayed all night to my great dislike.

Absalom's wife and daughter were becoming increasingly unmanageable. Only too often he came back from Manchester to find them 'muddled with ale'. Edward had now bought a house at Timperley. He invited his father over to meet the Paxtons but when Absalom returned to Rose Hill he was 'disgusted by the state in which I found my daughter by the imbecile folly of my wife'. He was beginning to dread leaving them alone. Edward gave a second, grander dinner party and the presentation plate was displayed in the dining room but Mary was unwell. Perhaps, after all, the plate was not worth the effort of obtaining it.

Absalom's reputation as a man willing to help every good cause was widespread.

July 31st, 1854. Two ladies found their way to Rose Hill at night to ask me to preside at the Anti-Slavery Conference tomorrow. I consented.

He attended and was elected president. So the summer passed and while the allied troops, many of them sick and dying of cholera, dysentery and colic were waiting at the port of Varna to embark for the Crimea, at Rose Hill a second crop of hay was being got in safely.

September 2nd, 1854. At home all day, employed in observing and directing the men. Much pleased with the place and the progress of the operations. At night I gave them a supper of roast beef, apple pies, cheese and ale. I believe all were pleased, and none were intoxicated.

That was more than could be said of his wife and some of his children. Absalom was irritated to hear from Manchester that Alfred had spent the day shooting and had not put in even an appearance at the warehouse.

It was reported that Admiral Napier had promised to be either at Kronstadt or in heaven within a month of entering the Baltic. He was at neither. The Russian fleet had refused to come out and Napier would not risk his ships in the shallow waters; they might run aground within range of the fortresses. Thomas Cochrane, tenth Earl of Dundonald, proposed that 'sulphurous craft' should be sent to overwhelm Kronstadt's defenders with poisonous fumes. The plan was considered and finally rejected as neither morally right nor practicable. All Napier could do was to blockade the Russian ports and, with the help of French troops, capture the fortress of Bomarsund in the Aland Islands. By September he had decided that Kronstadt was impregnable with the forces at his disposal and, disobeying orders, brought the fleet home. 'The Baltic Fleet, with fifty thousand men, sailed up the seas – and then sailed home again,' the *Illustrated London News* jeered.

Uncertain news from both theatres of war continued to affect the market.

September 5th, 1854. Not a good market. I sold very little. I went home by Sale and got late to Rose Hill. I fell asleep in my chair and did not get to bed till five.

He took his wife into Manchester and on their return they found that Elizabeth, no doubt drunk, had fallen off the sofa and hurt her shoulder. Alfred and Hester were away on holiday and Absalom lamented the state of his home and grieved even more when Elizabeth came into Manchester and spent far too lavishly on provisions for a dinner party.

She came in again the following day.

September 26th, 1854. Late in Manchester. My daughter again there. She fainted repeatedly at the warehouse and I had great trouble in getting her home. Much hindered by her at the warehouse. Plagued by the absence of Alfred and depressed by the extreme dullness of the market. The London Printing Company has stopped payment. They owe £2,000. Went to bed sad, very sad.

Even on the day of the party preparations were not quite complete and Absalom had to bring some things back with him from Manchester.

September 27th, 1854. We had Mr and Mrs Spencer, Dr Fraser, Mary, George and Alice Wall, Miss Mellor and Mr Greaves. The dinner was good, we had a waiter and a cook, Margaret and Harriet and our two helps and so got through pretty well. In the evening we had some music but my daughter repeatedly fainted and of course made all unpleasant. Mr and Mrs Spencer stayed all night. Some pages Xenophon's Anabasis.

Next day he found on his return from Manchester that some of the servants had helped themselves to what was left of the food and wine. The consequences of this indulgence have been erased.

Five weeks on the Bulgarian coast had cost the British and French 10,000 deaths from disease. Now the expeditionary force left Varna taking cholera with them. They crossed the Black Sea and landed unopposed at the Crimea on the morning of 14 September. Not enough ships had been provided. Thousands of soldiers were crammed into transports and so small was the space available that medical supplies, tents, and some of the men's packs had to be left behind. In any case, no winter equipment had been provided as Raglan had been informed that Sebastopol could not be defended from the north and the campaign, therefore, would be a short one. It might have been, were it not that the town was attacked from the opposite direction.

The beach was a scene of confusion. There was a shortage of transport, of tents, and of water. Cecil Woodham-Smith has described it.

The British Army had alighted on the shore of the Crimea like a flock of birds, but without wings to fly away. They had no transport, no ambulances, no litters, no food; they knew nothing whatever of the country ahead of them; they had no base. Within an easy march must be a Russian army, equipped with artillery and accompanied by Cossacks, but of the size and whereabouts of that army no one had any idea.

Yet on 2 October news reached Manchester of an allied victory on the River Alma.

In spite of sickness, thirst, miserable rations and insufficient transport, at the cost of over 3,000 lives, the army successfully stormed the heights above the Alma where the Russians had established themselves in order to block the road to Sebastopol. The enemy retreated. Hardly had the news been received than wildly optimistic rumours swept the country. Lord Clarendon told the Queen that he had had a dispatch from Constantinople reporting the fall of Sebastopol with enormous Russian casualties. The Royal Family were at Balmoral and a joyous Queen and her three excited daughters ran up the cairn to inspect the preparations for a victory bonfire. Manchester got ready to celebrate.

October 3rd, 1854. News of our success in the Crimea, and the reported fall of Sebastopol. Manchester is all in a flutter with exultation at the news from the Crimea. Flags hoisted, and congratulations on all hands. Read some pages Clarke's Travels Relating to the Crimea.

Four days later Absalom's diary was bleak and to the point.

October 7th, 1854. Sebastopol has not fallen.

It had not indeed. If the army had moved immediately against Sebastopol it would have fallen and there would have been an end to the war. But the Allies lingered, burying their dead, caring for the wounded and the sick, while their commanders discussed what to do next. In the end it was decided to outflank Sebastopol and attack it from the south. Accordingly the army turned its back upon the town and marched south to form a base at Balaclava. There was a three-week pause. The first attack on Sebastopol took place on 17 October and the hard-won battle of Balaclava a week later. The mad, valiant, useless Charge of the Light Brigade was a military disaster. Nature had made the harbour at Balaclava beautiful, man turned it into a squalid mass of amputated arms and legs, dead horses, sheep's carcasses and excreta so it stank like a cesspit. It was a pity Absalom could not have smelt it.

Human beings have little enough control over the direction of their lives, horses none at all. Thousands of them endured an appalling journey by ship, at the end of it only to die of heat, starvation and thirst or to have their guts blown out on the battlefield. Some slight notion of the horror of war came home to Queen Victoria when she inspected some wounded men from the Grenadier and Coldstream Guards. The sight of legless and armless soldiers, some with faces shattered and their eyes blinded, affected the Queen so much that words of condolence stuck in her throat.

It was now the middle of October. Absalom's 'poor silly wife' became fuddled with ale; Joseph Johnson came to Rose Hill and they drank champagne together and talked things over. Frost gave the dahlias in Absalom's garden their *coup de grâce* and just before the Battle of Inkerman he met Bright in the street in Manchester.

Bright never spoke against the war in the House of Commons before it was declared, but he did so four days afterwards because he wished to clear his conscience. 'I despise from the bottom of my heart,' he declared, 'the man who speaks in favour of this war, or of any war which he believes might have been avoided, merely because the press or a portion of the people urge the Government to enter into it.' Like many Quakers, Bright was not a complete pacifist. He justified the military action of the North in the American Civil War and the suppression of the Indian Mutiny. He objected to this particular war because he thought it was unnecessary. We had no just cause. Its consequence would be needless misery, vast expense and ruin to our trade.

Absalom was shocked by the despotism of the Tsar and amazed that any man could subject himself to such tyranny. But he himself had fallen victim to the subtler tyranny of public opinion. If only he had stuck to his analysis of the human scene made on the eve of the riots in 1842. 'Man,' he wrote then, 'has always been "the animal man" – credulous, impetuous, quarrelsome, and occasionally insane.' But for the moment wisdom deserted him. As a consequence of meeting Bright in the street that day he is remembered by specialists of the period as the man who provoked Bright into making an extensive, closely argued statement against the war which has been called an epoch-making point in the entire controversy.

Naturally enough, when they met, the two men talked about the war and Bright declared it to be one of the wickedest things this country had ever engaged in. His words stung Absalom. He had a certain respect for Bright's opinions. Besides, they were such old friends and colleagues. In that long ago October of 1838 they had served together on the very first committee of the Manchester Anti-Corn Law Association and he had twice proposed Bright as MP for Manchester.

It may be that Bright's words touched some instinct overlaid by the more superficial emotions of the time. As much, perhaps, to justify his own position as to convince Bright, Absalom returned to Rose Hill and pondered the matter afresh, referring to his library and in particular to a book by Emerich de Vattel called *The Law of Nations* published in the previous century. He had used Vattel extensively when he was writing about the First Crusade. Peter the Hermit now entered his life again, this time apparelled in the scarlet uniform of the British soldier. Absalom wrote to Bright confirming his own attitude. He had already helped to organize a public meeting to raise money for a Patriotic Fund for the relief of war victims. That would be a good opportunity for Bright to explain himself:

As Manchester will meet next Thursday to commence a subscription for the
widows and orphans of those who fall in the contest, and as the Members for
Manchester ought to be there, I shall be exceedingly pleased if you will then
state the conclusive reasons for your condemnation of the war, and enable us
to determine either to give it our hearty support, or then and there to
petition for peace.

Bright replied with an open letter on 29 October, two days later. His letter was
afterwards printed in the *Examiner* and in *The* (London) *Times* on 3 November.
On further consideration, Bright wrote, Absalom would surely see that the
Patriotic Fund meeting would be a most improper occasion to discuss the justice
of the war.

Just or unjust, the war is a fact, and the men whose lives are miserably thrown
away in it have clearly a claim upon the country, and especially upon those
who, by the expression of opinions favourable to the war, have made
themselves responsible for it.

He then turned to the point at issue.
Vattel, the First Crusade and even poor Peter the Hermit got short shrift. Bright
attacked the warmongering of Stratford de Redcliffe and the absurdity of military
interference in a dispute between two independent states 3,000 miles away. It was
wrong of Russia to invade the Principalities, but was it any more wrong than
Palmerston sending ships to the Piraeus to menace Athens on behalf of the
dishonest claims of Don Pacifico?
If we had to involve ourselves in a quarrel between Russia and Turkey, we
should and could have settled the matter by diplomatic means. Bright spent a long
time on a careful analysis of the negotiations between the four powers at Vienna.
There was no material difference, he maintained, between the Russian note drawn
up by Prince Menschikoff and the Vienna note drawn up by England, France,
Austria and Prussia. It was our government that would not allow the dispute to be
settled, our government whose policy was marked by unexampled imbecility.
We were building our Eastern policy on a false foundation.

Namely, on the perpetual maintenance of the most immoral and filthy of all
despotisms over one of the fairest portions of the earth which it has desolated,
and over a population it has degraded but has not been able to destroy.

It was a wretched delusion to imagine that we were fighting for civilization and
our sacrifices for freedom were a pretence. Was not our greatest ally Napoleon III,
the monarch who struck down a free constitution and dispersed the
Representative Assembly by violence? We should never have intervened. 'The
danger of Russian power was but a phantom; the necessity of permanently

upholding the Mahometan rule in Europe an absurdity.'

Bright devoted the last and most eloquent pages of his *Apologia* to the human suffering endured by the participants in the war. Absalom must have read the tidings from the Crimea and shuddered at the slaughter. The final paragraph was written with intense feeling.

> This is war – every crime which human nature can commit or imagine, every horror it can perpetuate or suffer; and this it is which our Christian government recklessly plunges into, and which so many of our countrymen at this moment think it patriotic to applaud! You must excuse me if I cannot go with you. I will have no part in this terrible crime. My hands shall be unstained with the blood which is being shed. The necessity of maintaining themselves in office may influence an administration; delusions may mislead a people. Vattel may afford you a law and a defence; but no respect for men who form a government, no regard I have for 'going with the stream', and no fear of being deemed wanting in patriotism, shall influence me in favour of a policy which, in my conscience, I believe to be as criminal before God as it is destructive of the true interests of my country.

Absalom was flustered. His opinion was unshaken, he could and would reply to Bright but the task daunted him. As he sat down to compose his reply the Battle of Inkerman was being fought. It was a confused and doubtful struggle but after many hours of desperate fighting in a thick mist the Russians retreated, leaving the British base secure and nearly 12,000 dead or wounded to 3,500 British and French.

The consequence was a stalemate. The Allies could not be driven from their position above Sebastopol but neither had they sufficient troops or ammunition to capture the city before the winter. However, Lord Raglan was promoted to field marshal and Herbert Ingram informed the readers of the *Illustrated London News* that 'the field of Inkerman and the fifth of November will henceforth be linked in glory on the page of European history'.

On the day before the battle Florence Nightingale had arrived at Scutari. The day after it found Absalom still writing.

November 6th, 1854. Perplexed after I got home by considering my reply to Mr Bright, fearing to do it badly. Looked over Mackintosh's Discourse on the Study of the Law of Nature and Nations.

He got on so slowly that he was obliged to write to the *Examiner* and announce the letter's postponement. He read books by David Urquhart, consulted Mackintosh and Vattel yet again, took his papers to the warehouse and sat up very late at night. The act of composition as usual excited him. He felt weary, but at last the task was done.

November 17th, 1854. I finished my letter and had it copied at the warehouse. By an accident the copy got mixed, and I had to go to the <u>Examiner</u> office to put it right and afterwards to correct the press.

The letter appeared next day, prefaced by two long quotations from Vattel. Absalom began his argument by saying that he would overlook Bright's rhetoric and the epithets with which he had heightened his picture.

To these I say nothing; but to the charge of complicity in the bloodguiltiness of an unjust war, I indignantly reply, for my country, not less than for myself – NOT GUILTY.

It was a spirited beginning but it must be admitted that the letter contained no convincing answer to Bright's case. Absalom made no real attempt to meet the accusation that Britain was responsible for the breakdown of diplomatic negotiations but contented himself for the most part with denouncing the Tsar and all his works. He was the aggressor, and it was the obvious duty of all civilized nations to repress his further advances. Why had Russia been allowed to act as it had done? Because of the influence of the Peace Society and a government which cut back on defence. Bright had made great play with the fact that the seat of war was 3,000 miles away, but 3,000 miles or not, Russia had stopped and visited our merchant vessels by force, interfered with the navigation of the Danube and, to make it supreme in the Black Sea, compelled the Sultan to forbid the entrance of warships.

As he continued his letter, Absalom's feelings and the expression of them became warmer and warmer. The guilt of bloodshed lay with the Tsar but yet more heavily upon those unprincipled sophists who had supplied him with lying pretexts for aggression. Absalom did not actually name Bright, but as his letter drew to a close his meaning was clear enough. Most guilty of all was the man:

who, being the citizen of a free country, and a member of her legislature, claiming to be an ardent lover of liberty, of knowledge, of progress, and the general welfare of mankind, from some unaccountable wrong-headedness prostitutes the ability which was given him for the noblest purposes, to become the apologist of one of the most flagitious despots whose existence ever cursed the earth.

When he thought of those brave and devoted men who had fallen so heroically at the bidding of their country, his eyes filled with tears. He mourned their loss but did not pity them the manner of their death.

Impartial history will testify to their unrivalled valour, and account them worthy of their ancestors by whom our liberties were won in many a bloody field.

There was little more Absalom could say, yet Bright's remark about the immoral and filthy despotism of the Sultan evidently rankled.

Probably there never existed upon earth a despotism more emphatically immoral, cruel and filthy than that of Russia. It is a libel on the Sultan and his subjects to compare his government with that of the House of Romanoff . . . If that domineering and insolent Power were seated at Constantinople and had possession of the seaports and islands now belonging to Turkey, instant alarm would seize all Christendom and instant and immense preparations would have to be made and kept up to meet an expected irruption of barbarians into the heart of Europe.

Absalom's peroration is strongly reminiscent of the arguments used between the wars by those who urged rearmament against the growing power of Nazi Germany.

The termination of this state of things would be war, at such time as suited the convenience of Russia – and war not 'three thousand miles away' but on our own shores, or in the adjacent seas. Probably single handed, but certainly under all the disadvantages to which the immensely increased power of Russia, arising out of our fatal supineness, would have subjected us.

Absalom's letter was a lively and intelligent defence of the war and as such was an immediate success. The *Manchester Guardian* printed it, and he was congratulated on all sides.

November 25th, 1854. This morning I had a letter from Mr Fort, the High Sheriff, inviting me to be on the Grand Jury at the next Assizes and congratulating me on my letter. All the week I have been 'famous'! The editor of the Durham Advertiser sends me a paper containing a laudatory leading article, and Mr Thomas Atkinson tells me that the Hereford paper, mistaking me for W.B. Watkins, will have it that I am their 'respected fellow citizen'. Very much tired when I got home and fell asleep in my chair and did not wake till four.

Ten days after the Battle of Inkerman, Balaclava was devastated by a storm which blew down the tents, destroyed the field hospital and wrecked more than twenty ships laden with winter supplies in the harbour. There could be no hope now of taking Sebastopol before the spring and the marooned army had to face the worst winter within living memory.

CHAPTER THIRTY-EIGHT

'You might have – had you been honest'

Until recently, in time of war nearly all bishops, whether Catholic or Protestant, slavishly followed the lead of the state. The Bishop of Manchester, Prince Lee, does not seem to have been an exception. Absalom had a great many further compliments on his 'glorious' letter and at a meeting in the Town Hall the Bishop came up and publicly offered his hand.

Some clergymen thought that the war might turn out to be that final struggle foretold in Scripture which presaged the Second Coming. The Revd Archibald Boyd predicted that Turkey might be destined to be the last great convert to Christ before the final catastrophe, and the Vicar of Kenilworth that since this country had been appointed as the instrument to prepare people for that unspeakably glorious event, the last trump would surely follow a British victory.

Charles Kingsley was more down-to-earth. The fact that most Turks were Mahommedans was awkward, but it was his duty to make British soldiers realize that despite this drawback they were fighting on God's side. He therefore wrote an encouraging pamphlet called *Brave Words to Brave Soldiers*. The troops needed to have a corporate and national religion. 'That is what Cromwell's Ironsides had and by it they conquered. That is what the Elizabethans had up to the Armada and by it they conquered.' Absalom was of the same mind.

The indignation of the war party against Bright intensified when his letter to Absalom was published in the *St Petersburg Journal* and other foreign papers. The world must be shown that Manchester repudiated the views of its MP. Absalom drew up a requisition to the mayor asking him to call a public meeting 'to declare the dissent of the citizens from the opinions of Mr Bright and our approval of the war'. He collected signatures in support of a meeting which was held on Monday 18 December in the Town Hall.

Absalom was invited to second the resolution:

This meeting, having learned that the letter of Mr John Bright on the war has been translated and circulated in Russia, desires to declare that the citizens of Manchester do not concur in the opinions expressed by Mr Bright, but, on the contrary, they are convinced that the war is just and necessary, and do earnestly desire that it may be carried on with the utmost vigour until it shall be terminated by an honourable peace.

If Absalom had hoped for almost unanimous support he was to be disappointed. The peace party was stronger than he seems to have anticipated. With its cadre of independent, Dissenting, non-territorial, sometimes obstinate liberal reformers, Manchester was by no means typical of the country as a whole. The controversy split the Manchester liberals and former comrades in arms found themselves on different sides. Some of Absalom's old friends now disagreed with him. William Shuttleworth, the Methodist minister whose wife's charms had once so captivated Absalom, had played a prominent part in the struggle for the abolition of the Corn Laws. Like his brother John, he was an effective speaker and had often shared the platform with the other Leaguers. Now he and Absalom found themselves in profound disagreement.

Feelings ran too high for reasoned arguments on either side to be listened to calmly. National pride was at stake. Husbands, sons and brothers were being killed or wounded. Few wished to be told that those they loved had given their lives for nothing. It is a tribute to English tolerance and a reflection upon the remoter quality of war in those days that opposition to it could be stated publicly at all. In a later, more heavily manipulated society, such a wartime meeting would be unthinkable. In 1917 *The Times* refused to print Lord Lansdowne's letter advocating a compromise peace with Germany and some British Roman Catholic bishops of the time even attempted to suppress the appeals of the Pope for a just settlement of the conflict. However, it had not been wise for Absalom to press for a public meeting at that juncture. Common sense should have told him that nothing could be expected but turbulence and ill-feeling.

December 18th, 1854. I attended the meeting in the Town Hall to approve of the war. The League had mustered all their forces – all the blackguards whom they have in their pay – and on the other side Dr Hudson had intimated to the Protestant Association that their presence was desirable. The consequence was that the Town Hall was filled long before the hour of the meeting and the people were most uncomfortably hot. At eleven o'clock the Mayor, Mr Nicholls, took the chair amidst great noise. On his right were the principal friends of Mr Bright, including Dr Halley, Dr McKerrow, Davidson, W. Shuttleworth, A. Henry, James Watts, W.B. Watkins. On his left were the originators of the requisition, Entwistle, Ross, Dorrington, Harter, Neild, J.A. Turner, W.R. Wood, myself, etc. etc. We were all comfortably seated on the platform with the reporters at our feet and a row of policemen seated behind them, keeping the space immediately in front of the platform clear. The crowd in the body of the Hall being closely packed and thrust upon from behind, were in a state of deliquescence and very noisy. At last the requisition was read and W. Raynor Wood rose to move the first resolution. Immediately cheers, groans, hisses, plaudits and all sorts of noises drowned his voice, and although the reporters came just under him, he was heard by them only partially, by the meeting not at all. I seconded the resolution with little more success.

Then W.B. Watkins moved a resolution approving of Bright's conduct as to the war and condemning the requisitionists. Alexander Henry seconded the amendment. Both were inaudible except to the reporters. Entwistle rose to reply, spoke well, and having a powerful voice, was better heard than any other speaker. Bright, being called for by his friends, rose, but the noise was so deafening, the mingled storm of applause and reprobation was so great, that he stood for more than ten minutes before he even attempted to speak. At last he uttered a few sentences, only audible to the reporters who were close to him, and then sat down. With much difficulty and amidst great clamour, the amendment and the original motion were put. The numbers were so nearly equal that after five several attempts, the Mayor declared 'on his conscience' that he could not decide which had the majority, and he therefore dissolved the meeting. Both sides claimed the majority and the Mayor was told by Alexander Henry that the next time they, the Bright party, would provide him with a pair of spectacles. I shook hands with Mr Bright before he left the meeting. There was a large concourse outside, and he was cheered and hooted all the way to the League Room. There the mob tried to ascend the stairs and being resisted and some stones being thrown upon them, a sort of battle ensued in which S.P. Robinson had his spectacles broken.

The House of Commons gave Bright a fairer hearing than the audience in Manchester Town Hall. After midnight on 21 December he made the first of his two great speeches against the war and was listened to in silence. His conclusion struck home and no one followed him.

I am a plain and simple citizen, sent here by one of the foremost constituencies of the Empire, representing feebly, perhaps, but honestly, I dare aver, the opinions of the very many and true interests of all those who have sent me here. Let it not be said that I am alone in my condemnation of this war and of this incapable and guilty Administration. And even if I were alone, if mine were a solitary voice, raised amid the din of arms and the clamours of a venal press, I should have the consolation I have tonight – and which I trust will be mine to the last moment of my existence – the priceless consolation that no word of mine has tended to promote the squandering of my country's treasure or the spilling of one single drop of my country's blood.

Absalom had a pleasant surprise on Christmas Eve.

December 24th, 1854. I received a letter from my old friend Thomas Hallworth, from Rivershead, Long Island. I thought he had been dead. He is in his seventy-sixth year. I owe his renewed correspondence to my letters to

Mr Bright, which have, he says, appeared in the New York Times.

Christmas Day was subdued. The unpleasantness Absalom refers to most probably meant that his wife and daughter took too much to drink.

December 25th, 1854. Mr Smith came about eleven. We had our Christmas dinner party. An expensive, well prepared dinner, but rendered uncomfortable by several unpleasant occurrences. Only Mr and Mrs Smith, Alfred and Hester Anne and Edward's two children were present. We had prepared for fourteen or sixteen and had, including the children, only six!! They left early and I was glad. I wrote to Hallworth.

On the last day of 1854 Absalom heard the robins singing and wrote 'Try Again – And Again' on the fresh volume of his diary. He could not leave the war question alone. He was determined not only to justify his own position, but to make others agree with him. The matter must be considered by the Literary Society.
    Cobbett was one of the sons of William Cobbett; to him his father had entrusted the care of Tom Paine's bones. Jacob Bright was John Bright's brother.

January 2nd, 1855. The question which I had to open, 'Is the war of the Allied Powers against Russia a just war?' was discussed in a very full meeting in a very lively manner. Jacob Bright, Simpson, a visitor, W. Evans and E. Shawcross maintained the negative. I, Cobbett, Saunders, who spoke with unusual ability, the affirmative. The question was adjourned for a month.

Two days later Absalom attended the Annual Meeting of his Library Committee. 'I returned home late and tired and found . . .' What he found we shall never know. Someone had torn an entire page out of the diary. Very likely his wife and daughter were more than usually inebriated; they may have been violent and damaged either themselves or the house. It seems that Edward was consulted and true to form, quickly obtained the services of a companion-housekeeper named Miss Thompson. Absalom went over to Timperley to inspect her and a few days later she was installed at Rose Hill. The whole matter evidently shocked Absalom considerably and it seems he had a slight stroke.

January 12th, 1855. All day chilled, having a heavy pain at the top and on the left side of my face. I do not seem able to move readily or to turn my attention easily from one subject to another. At night I perceived that my fingers had not, on the left hand, the power of contracting readily or forcibly. I could not grasp anything with the fingers of the hand, so as to hold it firmly.

Hester was staying with them and the next day Elizabeth was violent and kept her up all night. They must have been grateful for Miss Thompson's presence.

Absalom recovered the grasp of his fingers but remained very tired. In a day or two, however, he was able to attend a very convivial dinner given by one of Edward's railway colleagues, a Mr Edmund Buckley. Buckley was fond of dirty stories and Absalom recounted one which the transcriber of the diary considered too nasty to write down. It was the only indecent tale he found in Absalom's entire journal.

January 15th, 1855. I went to the Clarence Hotel to dine with Mr Edmund Buckley. We had an excellent dinner, beginning with turtle soup and carried on as to eatables, wine etc. regardless of expense . . . Buckley told several other stories, all droll, some witty, but mostly indecent and dirty. And oddly enough he now and then turned to me and said, 'You must excuse us, Mr Watkin. We're all lads you know.' He is seventy-five, Watkins near seventy.

Times were difficult and prompted perhaps by his father's recent illness, perhaps by the knowledge that Hester was expecting a baby, Alfred was anxious to have his partnership in the firm legally established. Absalom evidently agreed because he attended a lavish dinner party at Alfred's house to celebrate the event.

Poor Hallworth could not have been a great success in America because Absalom wrote a letter to Kershaw soliciting help for his old friend. The adjourned debate at the Literary Society on the justice of the war was decided in the affirmative by twenty votes to three. The soundness of the British cause, however, was one thing, the actual conduct of the war another and news from the front tended to confirm the general uneasiness.

William Howard Russell had been sent to the Crimea by *The Times* as a war correspondent. This was the first time a journalist had reported regularly from any battle front and Russell's dispatches had the same kind of impact on the British public as the television pictures of the Vietnam War had on the American people. Russell benefited from the newly invented electric telegraph and was not hampered by censorship. He described the slaughter, courage and confusion of the battles as they were actually fought, exposed the incompetence of the commanders in the field and told readers at home about the appalling mismanagement of those in charge of supplies and transport.

Russell was by no means the sole correspondent in the Crimea, but he was the most outspoken. The majority of the leading London papers had by now also sent war correspondents and the *Illustrated London News* led the field as the only picture paper to cover the entire conflict both in the Crimea and the Baltic. It made use of the sketches of William Simpson and itself sent out a team of six war artists, among them Joseph Archer Crowe and Constantin Guys. Guys had been with Byron in Greece and his sketches of the fighting in Paris in 1848 had helped to double the circulation of Ingram's paper. The drawings that accompanied the text were sent from the front to skilled wood-engravers in London who worked on small blocks later carefully bolted together to form a single picture.

In the spring of 1855 the pioneer photographer Roger Fenton arrived in the Crimea, sent out by Thomas Agnew of Manchester to produce a series of pictures for subsequent sale. He had ingeniously converted a wine merchant's van into a mobile home and darkroom. He could not take photographs of the actual battles because of the time needed for an exposure, in any case his employers had forbidden him to photograph dead bodies.

The war was reported from so many angles and with such a mixture of truth, evasion, attempts to glorify the conflict and play down the grim and squalid reality, that those at home must have been confused about what was actually happening. In a cruel winter, the army lacked proper clothes and tents, cooking equipment, fuel and even food itself. The bland lack of understanding of local conditions is shown by the reply given by the commissary-general's office when complaints about consignments of green coffee reached it. 'The soldiers will no doubt find some means of overcoming any difficulties that may arise from the lack of mills and coffee roasters.' The military hospitals were short of drugs, splints and bandages; cholera, dysentery and acute diarrhoea were rampant. If the official figures given later for British casualties were correct, then out of some 19,300 men who died in the Crimea, over 15,700 died of disease. Only sixty-one of these were officers.

Public indignation grew. Some watchful old Chartists came out of hiding and spoke about a Charter for the private soldier. Palmerston wished to appoint Edward as head of the commissariat but he evidently refused. Much as Prince Albert detested the majority of war correspondents, he was himself far more intelligent than most of his wife's generals or heads of civilian departments. He had made a meticulous diagnosis of the trouble. No wonder he was disliked. He wrote

We have no generals trained and practised in the duties of that rank; no general staff or corps; no field commissariat; no field army department; no ambulance corps; no baggage train; no corps of drivers; no corps of artisans; no practice, or possibility of acquiring it, in the combined use of the three arms – cavalry, infantry, and artillery; no general qualified to handle more than one of these arms; and the artillery kept as distinct from the army as if it were a separate profession.

It was a bitter winter for others besides those in the Crimea. In London the Serpentine froze over and thousands strolled about on the ice. At Rose Hill Absalom saw to it that the birds did not starve.

February 21st, 1855. The birds now depend upon us for most of their food. The robins, the sparrows, the blackbirds and the little buff breasted titmouse come to the parlour window to receive it. The robins become daily more tame and would, I believe, be completely so, were it not for our three cats. I have not lately seen a throstle. The robins appear to have a low, peculiar, sweet note of recognition and appeal when I am near them, the very reverse of the sharp, quick note of alarm with which they proclaim the approach of the cats.

At the end of January the government had been defeated in the House by as much as 157 votes. Much to Disraeli's disgust, Lord Derby soon gave up the attempt to form an administration. There was nothing for it but to invite the man the country was clamouring for, the Churchill of his time, the truculent John Bull, Henry Temple, Viscount Palmerston in the peerage of Ireland. The furiously disappointed Disraeli told Lady Londonderry:

An imposter utterly exhausted, and at the best only ginger beer and not champagne, and now an old painted Pantaloon, very deaf, very blind and with false teeth, which would fall out of his mouth when speaking, if he did not hesitate and halt so in his talk . . .

Bright's reaction was the same. 'What a hoax,' he wrote in his diary. 'The aged charlatan has at length attained the great object of his long and unscrupulous ambition.' Lord Aberdeen had had no faith in public opinion, especially in matters relating to foreign affairs. In the July before the outbreak of war he wrote to Palmerston and reminded him that when Alcibiades found himself loudly applauded by the crowd he inquired what particularly foolish thing he had just said. But Palmerston owed his position to the crowd, he was the very articulation of its sentiments and to that gift he owed his position.

The spring came and Sebastopol was not taken. Instead Lord John Russell went to Vienna to take part in Austrian-inspired peace negotiations. Bright seized his opportunity and delivered one of the most impressive speeches in the House he had ever made. He spoke for half an hour only. Why carry on the war? Why not an armistice now? Let Lord Palmerston crown his career by returning the sword to its scabbard.

The Angel of Death has been abroad throughout the land; you may almost hear the beating of his wings. There is no one, as when the first-born were slain of old, to sprinkle with blood the lintel and the sideposts of our doors, that he may spare and pass on; he takes his victims from the castle of the noble, the mansion of the wealthy and the cottage of the poor and lowly, and it is on behalf of all these classes that I make this solemn appeal.

Disraeli told Bright afterwards that he would have given all he had to have made the speech. 'You might have,' Bright answered, 'had you been honest.'

Palmerston had no wish to make peace until Sebastopol had fallen and then only if the Tsar relaxed his efforts to turn the Black Sea into a Russian lake. Nor had he any intention of overthrowing the Tsar or getting involved in active campaigns for the independence of Hungary or Poland. But Absalom and some of his friends still imagined that the war would benefit small nations struggling to be free. 'You failed to aid Hungary,' Kossuth was telling the English audiences, 'when the Tsar first struck down her young republic and now you will have to pay for it with your blood in streams and your money in millions.' Absalom believed him.

March 5th, 1855. I attended a meeting in the Town Hall, to advocate the reconstitution of Poland as an independent nation, and seconded the first resolution, which was proposed by James Aspinal Turner. The meeting was crowded. All the resolutions were passed unanimously.

Absalom's wife left to visit the Stixwould family and Miss Thompson kept house.

March 9th, 1855. Mrs Watkin left at half-past nine to go to see John and his wife and family. Assiduous at the warehouse. At half-past five I took the chair at the dinner of the Literary Society to celebrate the four hundredth meeting. About twenty persons sat down to a capital dinner at the Palatine Hotel. The evening was pleasant and we left a little before eleven. Two or three had drunk freely. We finished with coffee and Anchovy Toast. The latter for the first time. It was after twelve when I got home. I fell asleep in my chair and did not get to bed till after three in the morning.

The next day he heard that Joseph Makinson was extremely ill. Joseph was his eldest brother-in-law and the years had attached him closely to Absalom.

March 10th, 1855. Went to Broughton to see Joseph Makinson. Found him incapable of seeing and apparently unconscious. Breathing laboriously and incapable of swallowing, indeed manifesting an aversion to let a little liquid to be put into his mouth.

Joseph died next day and Absalom felt the blow. He spent the evening looking over old volumes of his diary, living again the expeditions to High Legh, the nutting, the mushroom gathering, the days spent exploring London and listening to sermons, the return to Manchester and the nightingale's song on the stopping of the coach. But the Makinsons' acted true to form, awkward even in death. Absalom went to Manchester expecting to attend the funeral but received no invitation. Perverse in his turn, he remained in the warehouse and Joseph was buried at St John's without him.

Edward was deeply involved in the affairs of the Manchester, Sheffield and Lincolnshire Railway and was in the course of presenting the case for one of its extensions before the parliamentary committee acting for the Board of Trade. Absalom decided to visit him and in the first week of May left for London in the snow.

Public disquiet had forced Palmerston to accept an inquiry into the condition of the army in the Crimea. The committee was still sitting and members of the public who were able to get seats were allowed to attend the hearings. Absalom was lucky. Albert Smith, the novelist and entertainer, had climbed Mont Blanc and his show at the Egyptian Hall was one of the most popular in London.

May 9th, 1855. Went into the Committee Room of the Committee for Inquiring into the State etc of the Army before Sebastopol. I heard part of the examination of Admiral Dundas, who appeared to give his evidence in a straightforward, sailorlike manner. I stayed till the room was cleared. In the afternoon I went with Mary, the children, Mrs Chapman and Mrs Cuthbert to see Albert Smith's 'Ascent of Mont Blanc'. The views are pretty. As a mimic he is clever. His volubility is remarkable, but he did not move me to much laughter. I came away convinced that to risk one's life merely to get to the top of a very high mountain and this with no scientific object in view – indeed, merely to say you have done it – was a very silly affair, and one that, as it imperilled the lives of the guides also, could be justified neither prudently nor morally.

The following day he visited the Exhibition at the Royal Academy, thought none of the pictures remarkable and went again to the House of Commons to the hearings of the Sebastopol Committee.

May 10th, 1855. I heard for two hours the examination of Lord Hardinge, the Commander-in-Chief, which he gave with much clearness and ability. Then I lunched in the Lobby and as I went back a thunderstorm broke over the building and rain and hail rattled against the windows and lightning flashed across the Lobby and the thunder pealed magnificently.

St Paul's seems to have taken second place to the Crystal Palace. On Sunday Absalom went to Sydenham for the third time. It was to be his last visit.

May 11th, 1855. This time I got as far as the island in the lake which is peopled with extinct animals and to the Geological Cliff. All is deserving of much more attention than I could give to it. I stayed till the last and then returned to London dissatisfied.

It may have been morally wrong to risk the lives of others indulging in mountain-climbing but nothing Absalom heard at the Sebastopol Committee diminished his zeal for the justice of the war. Back at Rose Hill he spent Whit Sunday writing in defence of it. The season was the latest he ever remembered. On 1 June the elder trees were not yet in flower.

June 1st, 1855. The Italian poplars are only coming into leaf and the hawthorns not yet in blossom. We have had such a continuance of east winds as I do not remember. The grass is short and although I have for more than twenty years always begun to mow about the end of May, and once or twice have had my crop on the stack by the twenty-ninth of May, the growth is so short that I do not expect to mow in less than ten days. One fact is curious. We have a colony of martins in the Hay Shade; they usually arrive about April the twenty-fourth. This year they were first seen on the twenty-fourth of May and began to repair their nests on the twenty-fifth. The ash and the hickory have only a few leaves at the extremity of the spray.

Hester came to stay, Absalom's wife and daughter drank too much, and on 18 June, the anniversary of Waterloo, a combined English and French attack on Sebastopol failed at the cost of 6,000 French lives and 600 English.

On 27 June, Absalom celebrated his sixty-eighth birthday.

June 27th, 1855. Edward and Mary, Alfred and Hester, Jonathan Mellor and his wife, Fanny Smith, Lucy Paxton and little Alfred dined with us in honour of the day. Towards the close of the day, little Alfred brought out the three cannon which had lain upstairs for many years and which he had spent a day or two in cleaning. Edward, Alfred and Jonathan, at his request, loaded these pieces and discharged them on the terrace, making a great noise and he enjoyed the fun very much. We had a good but expensive dinner. The day passed off tolerably well, except that Alfred was rude to Elizabeth and she furious in consequence. Alas! How silly we all are.

The day after Absalom's birthday Lord Raglan died in the Crimea. Some said of fever, others of a broken heart.

CHAPTER THIRTY-NINE
'Farewell, beloved child'

George and Alice Wall were about to return to Ceylon and Absalom gave them a farewell dinner party at Rose Hill. It was a very modest affair compared with the entertainment Edward and Mary were preparing at Timperley.

> **June 28th, 1855.** At eight I went with my wife to Mary's large party. There were about seventy persons. They danced, played at cards, took wine, supped, had some conjuring, acted charades etc and the whole finished at a quarter to one in the morning. I could not arrange the cards in my hand and play with precision.

It was a warning but not one Absalom heeded. After their return he stayed up reading until four in the morning. The firm had become Absalom Watkin and Son, and Absalom put over £1,000 of extra capital into it. They had been renting the warehouse in Nicholas Street. Alfred now wanted to buy it.

> **July 6th, 1855.** I was a good deal up and down in Manchester during the day and perspired much. From four to six I was at the Town Hall swearing in Militia Men and found the heat and the ill odour of nineteen dirty fellows very disagreeable. We bought the warehouse at 9, Nicholas Street for £3,250. I was much tired at night and fell asleep. It was near two when I went upstairs. I continued Withering's Botany and was in bed by three.

The warehouse was expensive, about £162,500 in our values. Absalom does not say how he found so much capital. Perhaps Edward had given him sound advice about railway shares.

His old friend and comrade-in-arms Archibald Prentice came to Rose Hill and enjoyed a strawberry tea. On Sunday Absalom went to church, 'made some good resolutions and prayed earnestly and with hope'. For the moment Alfred was hopeful too. He was now a partner, they had put more money into the business and secured the premises, he had bought a new house and Hester would very soon be having her baby.

Absalom read some pages of Mary Wollstonecraft's *Vindication of the Rights of Women* and approved of it. 'This is an outspoken book, telling some plain truths.'

He and his wife spent a night at Accrington with Hester's sister, Hannah, now Mrs Worsley. Mr Worsley's son, Henry, would one day marry Edward's daughter.

July 26th, 1855. I went with my wife, Alfred and Hester by the East Lancashire Railway to Accrington, to dine with Mr Worsley of 'The Laund'. There was a party of twenty. A good dinner and a hearty welcome from Mr and Mrs Worsley. I had to make two little speeches and I did it badly — moreoever my want of ability in carving put me to the blush. We stayed all night and the house, which has been recently almost rebuilt, has the walls by no means dry. I took cold, although everything had been done to make us comfortable.

Still Sebastopol had not fallen. Palmerston was quite prepared to use Dundonald's 'sulphurous craft' to smoke its defenders out with poisonous fumes, but once again the idea was dismissed and such barbarities reserved for the exercise of a later generation. On 17 August, the day Hester gave birth to a son, the conventional bombardment of the city began. It continued for three weeks, at the cost of a thousand Russian casualties a day. On 7 September the French made a final thrust and the Russian general withdrew the survivors of the garrison over a pontoon bridge to the northern shore. When that was done, he destroyed the bridge and set the city on fire. Not until 10 September was it possible for the Allies to enter the smoking ruins.

It was sad that in the end Sebastopol fell to French troops but nevertheless captured it was, and at Balmoral the Queen lit the bonfire so hopefully prepared the year before. At Northenden a photographer took a room at the Church Inn and made a good likeness of little Anne Battersby for a shilling and at Rose Hill preparations were being made for the christening of Alfred and Hester's baby.

September 13th, 1855. The ceremony was performed at Northen church by Mr Woolnough. Edward and James Whitelegg were the godfathers and Mrs Worsley was the godmother. The boy was called Edward William. My wife and I and Miss Thompson went later to Alfred's, where we dined. In all we were nineteen. We had a good dinner, good wishes, some jokes and some speeches. I got to bed about four.

None of the Makinsons were present. Perhaps this was the reason for their failure to turn up at Rose Hill the following day. 'Cannel' is a kind of bituminous coal which burns brightly.

September 14th, 1855. The Makinsons of Lime Place should have dined with us but sent excuses. I went to Manchester, was sent for by the Court and spent two hours and a half settling assaults, by women chiefly, and much dirty abuse. I got extremely cold and came home in that state. I roused up the fire, added some cannel and after washing sat down by the fire to get tea. The warmth was so genial and soothing that I fell asleep, in spite of my wife's calling and teasing me, till five in the morning when I awoke, washed my face, ate an egg, drank a cup of tea, took a basin of gruel and went to bed.

The Smiths of Hill End invited Absalom and his wife to stay in order to meet the Assemblage of the Book Society.

September 20th, 1855. The party comprised Mr Hoole, the clergyman and his lady, Captain Harrison, Mr and Mrs Ecroyd, Mr John Massey and Miss Stickney. We had a pleasant time and some agreeable talk about books. Also a little discussion about the war, Mr Ecroyd being a semi-Quaker and a believer in John Bright.

The next morning they went in the phaeton to call upon the Ecroyds and when they returned were weighed in the Smith's weaving shed. Absalom was slight and spare. He weighed a hundred and twenty-one pounds – eight stone, nine pounds. His wife was almost nine stone. On the following afternoon the Smiths took them on an expedition which Absalom greatly enjoyed.

September 22nd, 1855. After dinner Mr Smith drove my wife, myself and Mrs Smith to Marsden Hall, the ancient seat of the Waltons' but which since the death of the late Miss Walton has come into the possession, in the right of his wife, of an illiterate and drunken man of the name of Hallam. The house is situated so as to command a view of the Marsden valley and of the whole extent of Pendle Hill. It is surrounded by woods and gardens, with fountains and ornamental architecture. In the entrance hall are two large bookcases filled with valuable and expensive books, splendidly bound. They have some very fine missals, but these were locked up.

Leaving his wife behind to go on for a holiday at Harrogate, Absalom left with his daughter early on Monday morning.

September 24th, 1855. I rose at six, and at a quarter past eight was taken with my daughter to Nelson station. From quitting Hay Gate till we reached the station all was life and beauty in the landscape. All the country was bright and the sky clear. Pendle Hill cloudless. We reached Manchester about half-past eleven. All the country was gay with tricolour flags in honour of the fall of Sebastopol. The Assurance Committee. We got home about six and I found Rose Hill looking very well. The night was beautifully moonlit. It was midnight before I got to bed.

He had hardly reached home before a family scandal broke out. Scattered but occasionally detailed references to it are made in the diary and from these it is possible to reconstruct something of what occurred, although much must remain conjecture. In December 1853 Absalom had warned his wife's niece, Hannah Maude Makinson, that her conduct and manner might get her into trouble. He had been right. It seems that she had contracted venereal disease. Her parents appear to have been either unable or unwilling to cope with the situation and it was left to Absalom to seek out the unfortunate girl.

September 29th, 1855. This morning I hunted out poor Hannah Maude Makinson. With some difficulty I got to the house of Mrs Douglas in Camden Street, Adelaide Street, Hulme. It was almost eleven when I got to the door. She was in bed but an old woman who was cleaning the lobby desired me to sit down saying Mrs Douglas would see me in a few minutes. I sat in the parlour which was unexpectedly furnished with a piano, sofa, armchair, some coloured engravings of a pretty woman, etc, at which I was looking when Mrs Douglas, a pretty, but prematurely faded young woman, entered the room. I inquired for Hannah and at last got from her that Hannah had been sent, the day before, to Liverpool, to the Lock Hospital there. 'I kept her eight weeks,' said Mrs Douglas, 'and as they do not take them here without pay and she had no means, I sent her there.' She could not, or would not, give me any address saying that she did not know what name Hannah would assume. I stayed a short time, apologised for the trouble I had given her, and left the place.

A 'lock hospital' was a special hospital for the treatment of venereal disease. There were only a few of them in the country and the one at Liverpool was part of the old Liverpool (Royal) Infirmary in Aston Street. Hannah Maude's parents together with the William Makinsons came to Rose Hill, most probably for a family conference but what was decided upon can only be inferred from later events.

Thomas Makinson, the son of Joseph who had married Miss Soulby and gone to Australia, returned to England on a visit. Ordained an Anglican clergyman, Thomas had been received into the Catholic Church in 1848. What Absalom thought about this, we do not know. Thomas and his wife now had eight of their eleven children and the family were staying at a hotel in Liverpool. Absalom invited all of them over to Rose Hill.

October 13th, 1855. Thomas and Sarah Anne Makinson and the children spent the day at Rose Hill. Mary and Edward, little Alfred and Harriette Sayer came in the afternoon. Much eating and drinking and much noise, with much enjoyment to the little folk all day.

Two days later the Makinsons left for Sydney. Nothing is said in the diary but their arrival from Australia probably settled Hannah Maude's fate. James Battersby, the driver of the sociable and the son of Absalom's gardener, was suffering from something worse than the consequence of a drunken bout.

October 27th, 1855. At the warehouse till three. On my return to Northen I went with Mrs Watkin to James Battersby's and with James, his father and his wife, we received the Sacrament, which was administered by Mr Woolnough, James Battersby being apparently not far from his end.

That was on Saturday. The following Monday Absalom went to Liverpool to see Hannah Maude. He had already written telling her he would come.

October 29th, 1855. I drove to the Lock Hospital to see Hannah Maude Makinson but found she had quitted it half an hour before. I was informed that she meant to go to Manchester. I stayed till the last train. She came and I brought her to Manchester and took her to Rose Hill. I sat up late.

So Hannah found refuge at Rose Hill. She stayed there a day or two then left suddenly without telling Absalom where she was going. He wrote to inform her father and coming back to Rose Hill at midnight after a meeting of the Club, found both her parents waiting for him. They stayed the night.

November 3rd, 1855. At home all day. <u>No letter from Hannah Maude.</u> [Mr] and Mrs Makinson left us to go to seek Hannah Maude.

We hear no more about her for another month.

The fall of Sebastopol did not mean the immediate end of the war. The French, however, wanted peace and an exhausted and by now rather peevish John Bright was urging the immediate end to hostilities.

Bright was heading for a nervous breakdown. For two years he had battled against the tide, enduring insults, unpleasant innuendos and widespread disapproval. It was all becoming too much for him. Next winter he was forced to go for rest and recovery to the same hydropathic establishment in Yorkshire that Absalom's daughter had gone to for treatment ten years ago. Now he came to dine at Rose Hill.

November 22nd, 1855. We had two waiters, a cook, and Lizzy, besides our two servants, Battersby cleaning knives, etc. As guests we had John Bright, M.P., Alderman Watkins, William Ecroyd of Spring Cottage, Alexander Ireland, Edward and Alfred, Mary and Hester, and our visitors T.T. Smith, F. Ellis and F. Robinson. We had a good dinner and it passed off tolerably well. Mr Bright and I had agreed not to talk of the war, but somebody started the subject and he went off, maintaining the, as I think, fallacy that the whole expense of the war was borne by the commercial classes. I kept to my engagement. I proposed, and they drank, the health of the Queen, and I gave the health of John Bright. I told them that we differed, and must differ; that we looked at different sides of the shield; that we had been opponents, and might be so again; that we were both pugnacious and both sincere; that I esteemed Mr Bright's sincerity and appreciated his abilities. I reminded them that I had kept my promise not to speak of the war. Then they drank his health.

He did not pointedly reply, but said he could perceive how sincere men might differ and that he had made that remark to Sir Henry Inglis. He spoke of no member of parliament with much respect except Gladstone, of whom he said that he spoke well and reasoned well, but sometimes so refinedly that he, Mr Bright, could not follow him. He declared Palmerston to be a humbug, immoral and insincere, of Clarendon he said that he was grossly immoral, and that Lansdowne, although an old man, was equally so. Indeed, listening to him, I could see that he thought himself superior on the whole to anyone else. I observed also that he was considered an oracle by Pilkington, Ecroyd, Ireland and Watkins. They left at half-past eight.

Mrs Thomas Watkin was still alive but causing Absalom some anxiety. Her daughter-in-law, John Watkin's widow, now lived in Paris with her son. What had become of the Audlem property we do not know. Audlem was a different world. Mrs Thomas Watkin was old and poor and lived by herself at Flixton. She was suffering from influenza when Absalom and his wife visited her.

If the orchards and fields and church bells of Audlem were far away from Mrs Thomas's sad bed, so too was the superficial *bonhomie* of Edward and his glossy colleagues.

November 27th, 1855. I went by special train with Edward, Jonathan Mellor and others to Hill End, near Mottram, to dine with Mr Chapman, the High Sheriff of Cheshire. We had a large party, and a capital dinner served by the Sheriff's men in liveries. Everything was done with quiet exactitude and our reception was hearty. We left early. The larger part of the company remained later and even while we stayed, the Sheriff's turtle, champagne and port of 1841 began to produce their natural effects. Several songs were sung. Mr James Andrew sang two very good, very pleasing and very unexceptionable songs, 'A Thousand a Year' and 'The Pilot'. Mr Bagshaw then sang another of the same kind. Then to my surprise, James Aspinal Turner sang 'James Greenfield' and was followed by Watkins with one dirty and one indecent song. We got to Manchester in time to catch the eleven o'clock train to Bowden. As Able returned to Sale, two men attempted to drag him from the box but he made his horse gallop and he got away. I got home at half-past twelve, not at all the worse for my outing.

Very soon Absalom had another encounter with John Bright and this time got on with him better.

November 28th, 1855. I went to Bowden to dine with Mr Ireland. Quite unexpectedly I found there John Bright and also H. Rawson and H.B. Peacock, Professor Morell and Count ——, one of the Roman triumvirate of 1848. We spent a pleasant evening, Mr Bright being rather less dictatorial and more opposed, especially by Morell and Rawson. He dwelt on what he asserted to be the fact that we were paying in taxes £70,000.000 a year more than the United States, said that we had of necessity to compete with them, and triumphantly asked me if we must not be beaten. He questioned our social improvement as a nation and dwelt upon the immorality of our public men. Mr Bright apologized for having, at my house, talked of the war, and was altogether more fair and friendly than I expected – told me that he believed that I wished the real good of our countrymen as much as he did.

A little over a week later Absalom suffered what was evidently a further slight stroke.

December 6th, 1855. The Assurance Board. The Library Committee. In returning home I fell down at the station at Sale and to my surprise, could not rise without help. Arrived home, I found my speech and motion so altered that I believe I have had an attack of paralysis.

The handwriting in the diary for that day is strange. Absalom however insisted on going into Manchester next day and on returning went to Battersby's funeral where he got thoroughly chilled. He spent Sunday at home.

December 9th, 1855. Mrs Watkin read to me the Litany and other parts of the church service. In the afternoon came Edward and Mary, Alfred and Hester Anne with the children. They all stayed and I was much tired.

Edward insisted that he saw the doctor.

December 10th, 1855. Mr Smith, the surgeon, was brought here by Edward at noon. He examined me carefully and told me what I knew before, that it was a clear case of paralysis and that I must keep warm and be very quiet, etc. etc.

Fanny Smith came to help and after she had gone Absalom's wife and daughter took over some of her tasks. Absalom was able to write one or two letters again and he listened with satisfaction to his wife reading aloud the memoir he had written of his old friend, Mr Grime. Some Makinsons came. They were kind but they tired him. He did not go to church; instead his wife read the Litany and Ogden's sermon *On the Punishment of the Wicked*.

Edward gave them all Christmas Dinner and two days before the end of the year Mr Makinson came to Rose Hill to consult Absalom about his daughter's future. Hannah Maude had been found. She was now back in her father's house and arrangements for her to emigrate to Australia were near completion. Absalom told his brother-in-law that he should go to Liverpool and inspect the vessel in which Hannah intended to sail.

The next Sunday he had a shock.

December 30th, 1855. About noon, Edward and Alfred came unexpectedly. Edward came in first, told me that he had bad news, that Alfred's little boy was very ill, that he was dead! Alfred came in, dreadfully dejected. We were all very much affected. Only on Christmas Day I had seen him full of life, smiling and cooing, and trying to talk. When he went to bed last night he was apparently quite well. This morning at eight he died.

The child was four-and-a-half months old.

December 31st, 1855. I went with my wife and daughter to Alfred's house, 'Holly Bank'. We saw little Edward. He seemed asleep. I kissed him and almost believed he was alive. His fingers were flexible.

The last time Absalom had seen a dead child was in 1828 when he had sat by the bedside of Mary Watkin. By chance on this very day he had arranged to visit Mary's mother.

We took the train to Stretford and a cab thence to Flixton. There I made out Mrs Thomas Watkin's affidavit for the [Commercial] Clerk's Society. Swore her to it and got it certified by three of her neighbours. After that my daughter and I returned to Stretford. We took the train to Manchester and I went to the Clerk's Society, presented the claim and got the money.

That was the last day of 1855. Absalom chose a motto for the fresh volume of his diary and wrote it on the top of the page: 'Work, while it is day, for the night cometh, wherein no man can work.'

January 1st, 1856. The Gatley Band came as usual before we were downstairs and played the usual tunes under the windows very prettily. I wrote to Mrs Thomas Watkin, Edward and Mary, and John and Priscilla. Alfred and Hester spent the day with us. We had a good dinner and but for the sadness we all felt for the death of little Edward William should have spent a pleasant day.

He was buried at the foot of the tower under the window by their old pew.

January 3rd, 1856. John performed the service. Edward, Alfred, Jonathan Mellor, James Whitelegg, my wife and daughter and myself were present. Farewell, beloved child!

On most evenings Absalom's wife read Butler's *Lives of the Saints* aloud to him and he listened with his usual mixture of incredulity and edification. He went occasionally to the warehouse and found the business in a bad state. A firm that owed them some money had failed and Absalom feared that his reputation for prudence would be damaged. A worried and anxious Alfred sent yet another scolding letter. The nightly reading of the *Lives of the Saints* continued and Absalom contributed towards the outfit Hannah Maude needed to take to Australia. W.H. Mellor made his last recorded entry into Absalom's life and they met, not at Rose Hill, but in Alfred's house.

January 17th, 1856. Had tea at Alfred's with W.H. Mellor. He has just returned from Messina. He thinks more highly of England. At Messina he witnessed an execution by the guillotine of an assassin.

In early February Absalom went into Manchester.

February 5th, 1856. In town all day. Alfred depressed, Edward cross. I wrote a short letter to the Editor of the Guardian against war with America. I wrote also to John, urging him to exertion. Mrs Watkin continued as usual, Butler and the Perennial Calendar.

Tension between Britain and the United States had been intensifying for some time. This was due partly to the attempts of the British Minister in Washington to enlist recruits for the Crimea, and partly over the interpretation of a treaty that had defined the attitude of both powers towards Central America in the event of a canal being built between the Atlantic and the Pacific.

Absalom had had enough of war. 'May the good sense of the citizens of Manchester,' he wrote, 'be shown by the public declaration of their confirmed belief that a war with our brothers in the United States is an event not to be contemplated without horror and which it is the duty of the legislator to avoid by all allowable and honourable means.' It might have been Bright speaking.

Two days later he wrote again, despite sustaining a nasty fall in the street.

February 8th, 1856. In town all day. In returning from getting my hair cut I fell over the handle of a small truck which had been improperly left on the flags in Cross Street. Dirtied my clothes a good deal, hurt my knee a little and scraped the skin off the left palm. I was not otherwise hurt although my fall was an ugly one. I sat up too late reading Davies's Account of Nice. A very poor book. I wrote another letter against war with America to the Editor of the Guardian.

The matter was plainly on his mind. The carnage of the Crimea was so recent; perhaps he regretted his former bellicosity. God forbid, he wrote, that devastation and destruction should arise 'out of too great belief in our power to inflict calamities upon our opponents and too light an estimate of the misery which would be returned upon ourselves'.

On 22 February he gathered yellow crocus, pink hepatica, primrose, snowdrops, yellow aconites and sweet violets from his garden. Another firm stopped payment.

February 22nd, 1856. Alfred in despair. He proposes that Hester Anne and he shall come and live with us and that he shall let his house furnished for a year or two. I think he is wrong and that he is not in a state to judge correctly.

Alfred disregarded this advice and advertised his house in the paper. Final arrangements about Hannah Maude still had to be made.

February 27th, 1856. At home all day. Busied in the garden. Mrs Makinson and her daughter Hannah Maude dined with us. We arranged for the passage of Hannah Maude to Australia. Mrs Watkin continued Cowper.

Absalom was clearly not well. He was tormented by boils on his neck, under his arm and in his groin. His wife was of little help, no doubt she was feeling the strain of Absalom's deteriorating health and her niece's disgrace.

March 4th, 1856. At home all day. Mrs Watkin intoxicated and violent. Alfred and Hester disgusted. My daughter strangely excited. Mrs Watkin, while sober, continued Cowper.

Absalom sowed seeds of mignonette and went to dine with the William Makinsons at Lime Place where all the girls were extremely kind. He spent the following day drafting a letter to the Catholic Archbishop of Sydney for Hannah Maude to take with her to Australia. The Archbishop was Dom Bede Polding, a Benedictine monk from Downside. Thomas Makinson acted as his secretary and perhaps the matter had been discussed during the visit to England.

That was the last recorded good deed of Absalom's life. On 19 March, a little over a week before the Peace was signed at Paris, his diary comes to an abrupt end. Probably he had another stroke. He retired altogether from business and lived on an agreed allowance from the profits of the firm which was run by Alfred alone.

With the end of the diary as we have it, our intimate knowledge of Absalom ceases. However, the stroke, if stroke it was, cannot have been severe because we know that he kept another diary, now lost, until he was finally stricken with paralysis three years later when Edward and Mary came to live at Rose Hill and helped to look after him. He died without pain or struggle on 16 December 1861, aged seventy-four.

CHAPTER FORTY
'Tell Uncle I love him just as dearly'

Absalom's wife and daughter did not long survive him. Elizabeth died in 1864 to be followed two years later by her mother.

Edward succeeded far beyond even his father's expectations and became one of the greatest railway promoters of the age. He ended up as an MP, a baronet, Officer of the Order of Leopold of Belgium, Officer of the Order of the Redeemer of Greece, president of the Grand Trunk Railway of Canada, and chairman of the Manchester, Sheffield and Lincolnshire, South Eastern and Metropolitan Railways.

From Absalom Edward had inherited a strong imaginative streak, in his case combined with business acumen, courage and relentless ambition. Three years after his father's death he was elected Liberal MP for Stockport and throughout his life disliked being referred to as a railway king, thinking of himself rather as a politician with railway interests.

Early in his career he was asked by the Duke of Newcastle to sort out the tangled affairs of the Grand Trunk Railway in Canada. He realized that if it were to succeed financially it would have to expand to the Pacific. The Hudson's Bay Company stood in the way, a tract of land equal in area to European Russia. Using his particular skills of persuasion and manoeuvring Edward promoted the sale of the company into hands which made its eventual transference to the Canadian government very much easier. He felt that he had played a significant part in the formation of the Dominion of Canada and when, towards the end of his life, he came to be painted by Herkomer, he asked the artist to depict him holding a map of that country in his hand.

A man of enormous energy, he helped to build the railway between Athens and the Piraeus, advised on the Indian network and organized the rail transport of the Belgian Congo. He proposed a tunnel between Scotland and Ireland and actually began a spectacular pleasure park at Wembley where the main attraction was to be the Watkin Tower, designed to be 160 feet higher than its Paris rival. As chairman of the Metropolitan Line, he secured 280 acres of land for his plan and the tower reached the height of 155 feet before it was blown up by gunpowder in 1907. That was just as well, since it stood in the middle of what is now Wembley Stadium.

His greatest project was his revival of the idea of a Channel Tunnel. He was determined that passengers should be able to travel in the same train from

Manchester to Paris. It was with the intention of forming a through line from the north of England that he got company after company under his control and inaugurated the Grand Central Line. He founded the Channel Tunnel company, of which he was chairman, and until stopped by influential pressure groups, supervised the building of a tunnel which stretches from Shakespeare Cliff for nearly two miles under the sea towards France. Although the work ceased in 1882, the tunnel is still there and watertight, a monument to an obsession of a most extraordinary man.

We know him as Absalom knew him, the affectionate child, the frustrated adolescent, the restless and fiercely ambitious young man. Yet even then he shared some of his father's philanthropic interests. While still working in the family firm he had pioneered the Saturday half-holiday movement in Manchester and was one of the moving spirits behind the establishment there of public parks. As railway manager he saw to it that each stationmaster along his line was given a turkey for Christmas, he initiated savings banks and benevolent funds for the staff and encouraged the setting up of schools for the education of employees.

Ironically, his most lasting memorial has turned out to be neither railways, towers nor tunnels but the Watkin Path up Snowdon. This leads up literally from the front gate of his Welsh retreat, a small house a thousand feet above Llyn Gwynant and Llyn Dinas, to the summit of the mountain. Built by his engineers and workmen with local stone, the path was opened to the public by Mr Gladstone at the beginning of his fourth and final ministry in 1892.

Soon after Mary's death in 1888, Edward married the widow of his old friend, Herbert Ingram, the founder of the *Illustrated London News*, whose business he had for so long helped to manage. He bought hundreds of acres in Northenden and greatly extended and embellished Rose Hill, where he died in 1901. He is buried in the churchyard at Northenden close to his father, his mother, his sister and his first wife.

The life of Edward's only son, the 'little Alfred' of the diary, would have disappointed Absalom. Rose Hill was sold to Manchester Corporation immediately after Sir Edward's death and Absalom's fine library dispersed. Because presumably he did not care for it, Alfred left behind a huge oil painting depicting icebergs, which had belonged to his father. Over eighty years later the painting was noticed by someone from Manchester City Council, discovered to be a masterpiece by Frederic Edwin Church and, to the profit of the Council, was sold in the United States for the equivalent in English currency of £2,750,000.

A civil engineer by profession, Alfred became MP for Great Grimsby for a short while and was director of several railway companies, but he exhibited no marked interest either in religion or literature. Indeed, his greatest pleasure was to drive the locomotives on the South Eastern Line. His father wished him to make a respectable match and he obliged by marrying the eldest daughter of the Dean of Canterbury. It was not a success. When in London Alfred lived at the 'Watkin town house', that is to say, the Charing Cross Hotel. Here he kept two mistresses, each in separate suites, who were known as 'the ladies in waiting'. His wife, however, survived him. They had no children so the baronetcy died out.

Alfred's sister, Harriette Sayer Watkin, married her Aunt Hannah's stepson, Henry, later Sir Henry Worsley Taylor of Moreton Hall, Lancashire.

Oxford gave John a Doctorate of Common Law, but he never got any further preferment and stayed in his pleasant vicarage at Stixwould until he died, comparatively young, in 1870. He had three sons.

The cotton business of Absalom's youngest son, Alfred, prospered despite his anxieties. He ended up as Mayor of Manchester, relishing those baubles 'such as maces, cloaks and chains' which Cobden had once so deplored. Unfortunately Alfred's love of entertaining, so early displayed, led him into self-indulgent habits. He drank too much port and died when he was barely fifty. Moreover, the death of his first child was an intimation of sadness to come. Four of his six children died young; only two sons reached manhood.

W.H. Mellor never married.

A letter, slipped between the pages of the diary, throws a momentary shaft of light on the fate of Hannah Maude Makinson. Addressed to her parents and signed 'Magdalen', it was written in 1858 from Crosswick Creek, near Ballarat, Australia, and must have been brought over to Rose Hill for Absalom to see. Hannah had evidently married a man who abused her and whom she had left. She was working as housekeeper to an Irish doctor but she had to leave him because he had proposed marriage under the impression that she was a widow. She sent Absalom some seeds for his garden. 'Tell Uncle,' she wrote, 'that I love him just as dearly.' She mentioned the possibility of a divorce, let us hope she obtained one and that the rest of her life was happier than its beginning.

The Makinsons held their own. The elder Australian branch prospered, and the good reputation of Makinson's school survived beyond the next generation. Another Joseph Makinson was called to the Bar and appointed stipendiary magistrate for Salford. A Cambridge blue, he was considered the most brilliant all-round cricketer of his day.

Northenden is now in Greater Manchester. Caravans are parked beneath a motorway which runs above the place close to where the Boathouse Inn once stood. For many years Rose Hill was a juvenile's remand home and there is little left now to remind anyone of Absalom and his simple farmhouse, although the conversion of the billiard room into a chapel for the boys would have pleased him. By the copper beeches before the front portico a stone records Absalom's birth, marriage and death. On its sides are barely legible texts, and the careful observer, strolling in the rough grass of the shrubbery, will find there its two companions, each proclaiming in faded letters those truths by which their owner once lived.

If the stranger ventures further and walks past the flagstaff and along the gravelled path towards the kitchen garden, he will find Absalom's sundial. Here the inscription on the base is clearly inscribed: Our Days on Earth are as Shadows.

APPENDIX ONE
The Diaries

According to Absalom's son, Sir Edward Watkin, his father kept a diary from 1803 when he was sixteen, to 1859, two years before his death. Unfortunately the volumes which dealt with the earlier and later years have been lost altogether. After the death of Sir Edward some of Absalom's papers passed to his grandson, Alfred Watkin of Danebank, Lymm, Cheshire. These included the diaries for the years 1811–56. They were written in a clear hand in notebooks with a hard-marbled cover. In 1920 extracts from the diaries were edited by one of Absalom's great grandsons, yet another Alfred, and published by Fisher Unwin.

When he was lent the original diaries in the 1920s my father, E.I. Watkin, transcribed the unprinted passages into four exercise books and one large hardbacked notebook. His writing was very small and the entries compressed. They contain about two-and-a-half times the amount of the printed edition. He was less meticulous in copying out every single word of the earlier part than he was of the later. Occasionally he contented himself, for example, with drawing attention to a long walk, a list of guests, the books Absalom was reading or the flowers in his garden without giving the text in full. However, he always put these summaries in brackets, so that there is no possibility of confusing them with Absalom's own words.

Any gap caused by the use of shorthand was nearly always precisely indicated and he supplied from the manuscript nearly all the omissions in the printed entries. My father also copied out the loose bits of paper he found between the diary pages, which included some of Absalom's expenses, lists of his property and the letter of Hannah Maude Makinson to her parents.

Absalom made far fewer entries in the early years than he did in the later. The years 1811 and 1812, for example, have 8 and 10 entries, respectively; 1825, 148 entries and 1843 over 320.

We know that Absalom had good handwriting since one of his botanical notebooks (together with some shorthand), part of a paper he wrote about 'the Club', probably for the shortlived *Manchester Iris*, and a letter to Alfred have all survived. Judging from E.I. Watkin's transcript, he tended to overpunctuate. Sometimes I have altered the punctuation and occasionally modernized the spelling. A great deal has been omitted, partly because so many entries are routine and repetitive, partly because a book has to be kept within reasonable length. Only a fraction of the text is given and that fraction may not be what everyone would have chosen.

APPENDIX TWO

The Value of Money

Fortunately for us, economists have worked out that between 1790 and 1914 there was little alteration in the general level of prices, although the price of particular items changes. For example, in 1825 a contemporary calculated that on a yearly budget of £250 for a household consisting of 'a gentleman, his lady, three children and a Maid-Servant', the cost of food worked out at 8s. 6d. per head a week. It has been estimated that at the beginning of this century precisely the same amount per person, per week, would suffice for 'plain but sufficient living.'

Things are very different now and it has already been suggested that the reader should multiply the sums given in the diary by approximately fifty. It may be helpful to consider that Gibbon complained of having, as a single man, to live on between £300 or £400 a year. In Jane Austen's *Sense and Sensibility*, Elinor, who was thinking of marriage and therefore of having children, considered £350 a year was not enough to supply a family 'with the comforts of life'. £850 would be sufficient, £1,000 wealth. The income of Jane Austen's mother, known to have been left in reduced circumstances after her husband's death, was increased by her sons to £450 a year. In 1828 Fanny Kemble states that her father's income was barely £800 a year. However, £300 had to go on her brother's Cambridge expenses, leaving them with £500 a year. This meant 'very close and careful work' if the family were to remain solvent.

These people were gentry. Absalom was not and his expectations were different. In 1817 he tells us that he could live comfortably and support a family on an income 'so much less' than Gibbon's. When in 1824 he played with the idea of retiring from business altogether and living on the rents from his houses, he calculated that he and his wife and children could 'live comfortably' on an income of £150 a year. 'I do not mean that I could spend as much money as I do now in books and superfluities, but that everything necessary to my comfort and theirs might be obtained with that income.' His wife and children might not have been so keen.

In 1831 a Mrs Coddington informed a receptive Absalom that her mother never required more than £2 for household expenses for a family of seven. Out of this, Mrs Coddington claimed, her mother paid for everything except rent, taxes, schooling and liquors yet still had something over. Just before Christmas in 1834 Absalom calculated his expenses for the past year and they amounted to £240.

The following spring he added up his assets and they amounted to £4,840. If we accept that his pound was worth £50 at 1990 prices, we find that he was living at the rate of £12,000 a year and that according to the calculations he then made, his capital assets amounted to £242,000.

In 1823 Absalom remarks that a factory in Manchester, seven storeys high and including the land, could be built for £1,930. He bought his own land at Frog Place, Broughton, in 1821 at twopence a yard. In 1823 he sells one of his Broughton houses for £500, plus £10 for fixtures. Rose Hill with its seven acres cost £1,100. On the other hand, in 1832, Cobden had to pay 3,000 guineas for his large house in Manchester and towards the end of his life Absalom bought his warehouse in Nicholas Street, Manchester, for as much as £3,250. He let one of his own houses at Broughton for £40 a year, more than the £35 a year rent which the Carlyles (who lived on £300 a year) paid for the rent of their house in the then unfashionable Cheyne Row.

In 1851 agricultural labourers were still the largest occupational group, followed by domestic servants. The wage for the agricultural labourer varied throughout the country but after the Napoleonic Wars until towards the end of the century he received, on average, about 10s. a week, plus a cottage. Absalom, however, records that Mr Picton, a Broughton farmer, gave 'his men 5/- or 6/- a week and their meat, drink, washing and lodging.' Absalom does not say what he paid his staff, but as a rule indoor servants received about £12 a year together with their keep and some clothes.

Mr Mangnall's 'bowkers' were paid 5s. 4d. for twenty hours work at a stretch, and in 1825 Absalom recorded that a 'navigator' working on a canal was paid 2s. for removing twenty square feet of earth, one foot deep. The surveyor thought that 1s. per square yard a high price for cutting a canal through stone.

Semi-skilled workers received between £40 and £50 a year. Builders were paid about 16s. a week. In 1833 the bricklayer at Rose Hill was paid at the rate of 6d. a yard. Absalom recorded in 1824 that a silk weaver 'working hard' who wove between twelve and eighteen gross of ribbon in a week would receive £1 for the work. Richard Carlile refers to his 25s. a week as a tinplate worker. The master at Chorlton school had a wife and six children and was engaged by the National Society at a salary of £100 a year, which Absalom thought 'a pittance'. Yet the lawyer who drew up the mortgage on Rose Hill received £57, more than half the schoolmaster's amount for the whole year, although most probably a house went with that job. The gap between the skilled, the semi-skilled and the manual worker was enormous.

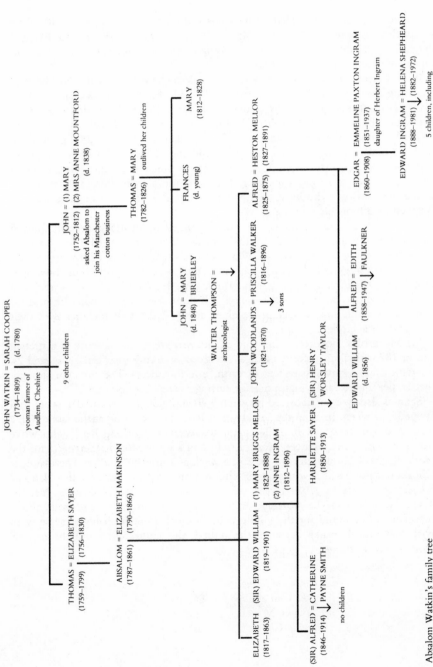

Absalom Watkin's family tree

Select Bibliography

Aston, J., *A Picture of Manchester*. Didsbury, E.J. Morten, 1816 (reprinted 1969).

Axon, W.E.A., *Annals of Manchester*. John Heywood, 1886.

Axon, W.E.A., *Cobden as a Citizen: a Facsimile of Cobden's Pamphlet Incorporate Your Borough: a Letter to the Inhabitants of Manchester,* 1838 (Fisher Unwin, 1907).

Bamford, S., *The Autobiography of Samuel Bamford*, 1844 (reprinted with an introduction by W.H. Chaloner, Cass, 1967).

Bancks, G., *Manchester and Salford Directory*, 1800 (reprinted Swinton, Richardson, 1982).

Banks, L., *The Manchester Man*, 1876 (reprinted Didsbury, E.J. Morten).

Barker, F. and Hyde, R., *London As It Might Have Been*. Murray, 1982.

Bee, M., *Industrial Revolution and Social Reform in the Manchester Region*. Swinton, Richardson, 1984.

Belchem, J., *Orator Hunt*. Oxford University Press, 1985.

Blake, R., *Disraeli*. Eyre and Spottiswoode, 1966.

Briggs, A, *The Age of Improvement*. Longman, 1959.

Briggs, A., 'Background of Parliamentary Reform in Three English Cities', *Historical Journal*, 10, 1952.

Briggs, A., *Victorian Cities*. Odhams, 1963.

Briggs, A., *Victorian People: a Reassessment of Persons and Themes 1851–1867*. Odhams, 1954 (revised Penguin, 1965).

Briggs, A. (ed.), *Chartist Studies*. Macmillan, 1959.

Briggs, A. (ed.), *The Nineteenth Century: the Contradictions of Progress*. Thames and Hudson, 1970.

Bright, J., *The Life and Speeches of the Rt Hon John Bright, M.P* (ed. G.B. Smith). Hodder and Stoughton, 1881.

Bright, J., *The Diaries of John Bright* (ed. P. Bright). Cassell, 1930.

Brill, B., *William Gaskell, 1805–84*. Manchester Literary and Philosophical Society, 1984.

Brown, L., 'Chartists and the Anti-Corn Law League', in Briggs (ed.) *Chartist Studies*. Macmillan, 1959.

Bruton, F.A., *A Short History of Manchester and Salford*. Sherratt and Hughes, 1924.

Burnett, J., *A History of the Cost of Living*. Penguin, 1969.

Burney, G.E., *Linnaeus Banks*. Manchester, 1969.

Chadwick, O., *The Victorian Church* (2 vols). Black, 1966–70.

Chaloner, W.H., *The Hungry Forties:* a *Re-examination.* Historical Association, 1957.

Chaloner, W.H., 'Manchester in the Later Half of the 18th Century', *Bulletin of John Rylands Library,* 1959.

Clapham, J., 'Corn Laws Repeal, Free Trade and History', *Manchester Statistical Society,* October 1945.

Court, W.H.B., *A Concise Economic History of Britain from 1750 to Recent Times.* Cambridge University Press, 1954.

Curtis, S.J., *History of Education in Great Britain.* University Tutorial Press, 1965.

Dean, F.R., 'Dickens in Manchester', *The Dickensian,* 34, 1938.

Dictionary of National Biography. Oxford University Press (1917 onwards).

Dobkin, M., *Broughton and Cheetham Hill in Regency and Victorian Times.* Swinton, Richardson, 1984.

Dow, G., *History of the Grand Central Railway.* Locomotive Publishing, 1959–62.

Ellis, H., *British Railway History, 1830–1876.* Allen and Unwin, 1950.

Engels, F., *The Condition of the Working Class in England,* 1845 (trs. and ed. W.H. Chaloner and W.G. Henderson) (Blackwell, 1971).

Fairlie, S., 'The 19th Century Corn Law Reconsidered', *Economic History Review,* 2nd series XVIII, 1965.

Frangopulo, N.J. (ed.), *Rich Inheritance.* Manchester Education Committee, 1962.

Gaskell, E., *Mary Barton (1848).* Dent, 1967.

Gaskell, E., *North and South,* 1855. Oxford University Press, 1976.

Gay, P., *The Bourgeois Experience* (2 vols). Oxford University Press, 1964.

Gérin, W., *Elizabeth Gaskell.* Oxford University Press, 1976.

Grindon, L.H., *Lancashire: Brief Historical and Descriptive Notes.* Seeley, 1892.

Grisewood, H (ed.) *Ideas and Beliefs of the Victorians: an Historic Revaluation of the Victorian Age.* Sylvan Press, 1949.

Halévy, E., *A History of the English People in the Nineteenth Century* (4 vols) (Trs Watkin, E.I.) (revised edns. 1949–51).

Hammond, J.L. and Hammond, B., *The Age of the Chartists.* London, 1930.

Hannavy, J., *Roger Fenton of Crimble Hall.* Gordon Fraser, 1975.

Hayes, L.M., *Reminiscences of Manchester in the Year 1840.* Sherratt and Hughes, 1905.

Hewitt, E.J., *A History of Policing in Manchester.* Didsbury, E.J. Morten, 1979.

Himmelfarb, G., *The Idea of Poverty: England in the Early Industrial Age.* Faber, 1984.

Himmelfarb, G., *Marriage and Morals among the Victorians.* Faber, 1986.

Hinde, W., *Richard Cobden.* Yale University Press, 1987.

Hinton, J.H., *The Case of the Manchester Educationalists: a Review of the Evidence Taken Before a Committee of the House of Commons 1852* (2 vols) (reprinted Didsbury, E.J. Morten, 1972).

House, H., *The Dickens World.* Cambridge University Press, 1941.

Hovell, M., *The Chartist Movement.* Manchester University Press, 1918.

Jenkins, M., *Friedrich Engels in Manchester*. Manchester, Lancashire and Cheshire Communist Party, 1951.

Jennings, H., *Pandaemonium, 1660–1886*. Deutsch, 1985.

Jerman, B.R., *The Young Disraeli*. Princeton University Press, 1960.

Johnson, E., *Charles Dickens: His Tragedy and Triumph*. Penguin, 1979.

Johnson, P., *Front Line Artists*. Cassell, 1978.

Kay-Shuttleworth, Sir J., *Autobiography* (ed. B.C. Bloomfield). University of London: Institute of Education, 1964.

Kay-Shuttleworth, Sir J., *Four Periods of Public Education as Reviewed in 1832, 1839, 1846 and 1862* (Includes 'The Moral and Physical Condition of the Working Classes in Manchester, 1832'). Harvester Press, 1973.

Kemble, F., *Record of a Girlhood* (2 vols). Bentley, 1879.

Kidd, A. and Roberts, K. (eds.), *City, Class and Culture*. Manchester University Press, 1985.

Kingsley Martin, B, *The Triumph of Lord Palmerston*, 1929 (revised Hutchinson, 1963).

Lawson, P., 'Reassessing Peterloo', *History Today*, March 1988.

Lee, C.H., 'Marketing, Organization and Policy in the Cotton Trade: M'Connel and Kennedy of Manchester, 1795–1835', *Business History*, 10, 1968.

Lloyd-Jones, R. and Lewis, M.J., *Manchester and the Age of the Factory*. Croom Helm, 1988.

Longford, E., *Victoria RI*. Weidenfeld and Nicolson, 1964.

Love, B., *Manchester as it is*, 1839 (reprinted Didsbury, E.J. Morten, 1971).

Macaulay, Lord. *Life and Letters* (ed. G.M. Trevelyan). Longman, 1876.

Maltby, S.E., *Manchester and the Movement for National Elementary Education*. Manchester University Press, 1918.

Manchester Faces and Places, Vol. 2. V. Chambers, October 1890.

Markham, V., *Paxton and the Bachelor Duke*. Hodder and Stoughton, 1935.

Marmion, J., 'Catholic Manchester', *Priests and People*, July–August 1987.

Mather, F.C., 'The Government and the Chartists', in Briggs (ed.) *Chartist Studies*. Macmillan, 1959.

Meinertzhagen, G, *From Ploughshare to Parliament: a Short Memoir of the Potters of Tadcaster*. Murray, 1908.

Messinger, G.S., *Manchester in the Victorian Age*. Manchester University Press, 1985.

Mills, W.H., *The Manchester Guardian: a Century of History*. Chatto and Windus, 1921.

Mitchell, E.A., 'Edward Watkin and the Buying-out of the Hudson's Bay Company', *Canadian Historical Review*, XXXIV (3), 1953.

Moore, D.C., *The Politics of Deference*. Harvester Press, 1976.

Morley, J., *The Life of Richard Cobden* (9th edn.). Fisher Unwin, 1903.

Newsome, D., *Godliness and Good Learning*. Murray, 1961.

Ogden, J., *Manchester 200 Years Ago* (ed. W.E.A. Axon) (based on the 1887 reprint *Manchester 100 Years Ago*). Swinton, Richardson, 1983.

Ormond, R., *Early Victorian Portraits* (2 vols). National Portrait Gallery and HMSO, 1983.

Palmer, A., *The Banner of Battle: the Story of the Crimean War*. Weidenfeld and Nicolson, 1987.

Perkin, H., *The Age of the Railway*. Panther Books, 1970.

Pictorial History of the County of Lancaster. Routledge, 1844.

Piette, M., *John Wesley and the Evolution of Protestantism*, 1925 (English edn., 1938).

Pope-Hennessy, U., *Charles Dickens*. Chatto and Windus, 1945.

Prentice, A., *Historical Sketches and Personal Recollections of Manchester, 1793–1832* (2nd edn.) (ed. Donald Read). Cass, 1970.

Prentice, A., *A History of the Anti-Corn Law League* (2 vols), 1853.

Procter, R.W., *Memorials of Manchester Streets*. Sutcliffe, 1874.

Read, D., 'Chartism in Manchester', in Briggs (ed.) *Chartist Studies*. Macmillan, 1959.

Read, D., *Peterloo*. Manchester University Press, 1958.

Read, D., 'The social and economic background to Peterloo', *Transactions of the Lancashire and Cheshire Antiquarian Society*, LXIV, 1954.

Redford, A., *The History of Local Government in Manchester* (2 vols). Longman, 1939.

Reid, R., *Land of Lost Content: the Luddite Revolt*. Heinemann, 1986.

Ridley, J., *Lord Palmerston*. Constable, 1970.

Robbins, K., *John Bright*. Routledge, 1979.

Rose, A.G., 'The Plug Riots of 1842 in Lancashire and Cheshire', *Transactions of the Lancashire and Cheshire Antiquarian Society*, LXVII, 1958.

Shaw, C., *When I Was a Child*, 1903 (Caliban Books, 1977).

Shercliffe, W.H., *Wythenshawe: a History of the Townships of Northenden, Northen Etchells and Baguley* (Vol. 1 to 1926). Northenden Civic Society, E.J. Morten, 1974.

Slugg, J.T., *Reminiscences of Manchester Fifty Years Ago*. Simpkin Marshall, 1881.

Smith, F., *The Life and Work of Sir J. Kay-Shuttleworth*. 1923.

Stevens, T.H.G., *Manchester of Yesterday*. Sherratt and Hughes, 1958.

Stoker, G.J., 'The Opening of the Liverpool and Manchester Railway', *Railway Magazine*, 10, 1902.

Swindells, T., *Manchester Streets and Manchester Men* (5 vols), 1906 (reprinted Didsbury, E.J. Morten).

Taylor, A.J.P., 'John Bright and the Crimean War', in *Englishmen and Others*. Hamish Hamilton, 1956.

Taylor, A.J.P., 'Manchester', *Encounter*, 42, March 1957.

Taylor, T., *The Life of Benjamin Robert Haydon* (3 vols). Longman, 1853.

Thomson, W.H., *History of Manchester to 1852*. Sherratt, 1967.

Wadsworth, R.P., *The Lancashire Cotton Pageant*. Manchester University Press, 1932.

Wadsworth, R.P. and De Lacy Mann, *The Cotton Trade and Industrial Lancashire, 1600–1780*. Manchester University Press, 1931.

Walmsley, R., *Peterloo: the Case Reopened*. Manchester University Press, 1969.

Watkin, A., *Absalom Watkin: Extracts from His Journals, 1814–1856* (ed. A.E. Watkin). Fisher Unwin, 1920.

Watkin, Sir E.W., *Canada and the States: Recollections 1851–1886*. Ward Lock, 1887.

Watkin, Sir E.W., *Alderman Cobden of Manchester*. Ward Lock, 1891.

Watkin, Sir E.W., Fragment No I. *Manchester* 1874 and Fragment No. 2. Alex Ireland, 1878.

Watkin, Sir E.W., *Memoir of Lady Watkin*. Published privately, 1888.

Webb, R.K., 'Working Class Readers in Early Victorian England', *English Historical Review*, XLV, 1950.

Whiteside, T., *The Tunnel under the Channel*. Simon and Schuster, 1962.

Woodham-Smith, C., *Florence Nightingale, 1820–1910*, Constable, 1951 (revised Penguin, 1955).

Woodham-Smith, C., *The Great Hunger*. Hamish Hamilton, 1962.

Woodham-Smith, C., *Queen Victoria: Her Life and Times* (Vol. 1 1819–1861). Hamish Hamilton, 1972.

Woodham-Smith, C., *The Reason Why*. Constable, 1953.

Woodward, E.L., *The Age of Reform, 1815–1870* (Oxford History of England, Vol. XIII). Oxford University Press, 1936.

Young, G.M. (ed.), *Early Victorian England 1830–1865* (2 vols). Oxford University Press, 1934.

Young, G.M. and Handcock, W.D. (eds.), *English Historical Documents XII, 1833–1874*. London, Eyre and Spottiswoode, 1956.

Contemporary newspapers

Manchester Courier, Manchester Evening News, Manchester Examiner and Times, Manchester Guardian, Manchester Mercury, Manchester Times and Gazette. There is no copy of the *Manchester Iris* in the British Library.

Index